# WASHINGTON HOMES

# WASHINGTON HOMES

## Buying, Selling, and Investing in Seattle and Statewide Real Estate

by Jim Stacey

Sasquatch Books
Seattle

Designed by Jane Jeszeck
Cartoon illustration by Frank Renlie, text by Jim Stacey
Diagrams by Karen Schober
Back cover photo of the author by Mary Wallace
Typesetting by Scribe Typography

Stacey, Jim,   1942–
   Washington homes: buying, selling and investing in Seattle and statewide real
estate / by Jim Stacey.
     p.   cm.
     Includes bibliographical references and index.
     ISBN 0-912365-27-7 : $14.95
     1. House buying—Washington (State)    2. House selling—Washington (State)
3. Real estate investment—Washington (State)    4. Real estate business—
Washington (State)    5. House buying—Washington (State)—Seattle.   6. House
selling—Washington (State)—Seattle.   7. Real estate investment—Washington
(State)—Seattle.   8. Real estate business—Washington (State)—Seattle.   I. Title.
HD266.W2S73   1990
643'.12—DC20                                                                                    90-8568
                                                                                                          CIP

SASQUATCH BOOKS
1931 Second Avenue
Seattle, Washington 98101

*Dedicated to Mamie Spencer*
*A neighbor who made a difference*
*and a great cushaw pie*

COVER PHOTOS

*(front, clockwise)*

1. This 1921 Seattle Craftsman bungalow is an excellent example of "pride of owner-ship" (by a tenant, no less). The Craftsman style originated in southern California, and was the dominant style for smaller houses from around 1905 to the early 1920s. This particular house would be described as "cross-gabled." From 1985 to 1988 the price would have been in the $80,000–$100,000 range. In 1990 the asking price would be closer to $150,000.

2. This ornate Victorian was built in 1889, the year of Seattle's "Great Fire," and had an unobstructed view of that inferno. The house was converted to a duplex in 1914.

3. This Spokane "American Foursquare," a subtype of the "Prairie" style, has a charac-teristic hipped roof. This house was on the market in 1989 in one of Spokane's nicest neighborhoods for $85,000.

4. Seattle has its share of world-famous architects, and one of them is Wendell Lovett who designed this contemporary home which was built in 1983. The proud owner named it "Laurie's House" after a close friend.

*(back, top to bottom)*

1. This empty "octagon" in central Washington may fit the dreams of thousands of buyers who would like to restore an ornate old fixer. But this house also serves to illustrate how reality must sometimes slap us awake. The site is about 20 miles from the nearest tiny town, and two hours from any town large enough to have a movie theater. The buyer would need a small fortune and a desire for more solitude than most people could handle. No, it could not be moved any distance; the cost would be astronomical. The house is owned by the daughter of the builder. She lives in a modern rambler just a few hundred yards away.

2. The author's home, six blocks upwind of the Seattle zoo. This 1920s Craftsman was bought for $94,000 in 1987 and would bring around $170,000 in 1990. The author recently enclosed the porch, making a determined effort to keep the work in tune with the original architecture. This house would be described as a "story-and-a-half."

Please note: The author has promised to keep the addresses of these properties con-fidential.

# CONTENTS

## FOR SALE TO ADULTS ONLY

Due to the sensitive and frank nature of the material, this book is to be sold to adults only—namely those readers who are able to recognize the author's biases, if any, and who have the good and common sense to seek out independent and expert advice to verify or adapt-ify the given information.

The author is a real estate broker, not an attorney, accountant, appraiser, engineer, loan officer, paper hanger, underwriter, interior decorator, or chimney sweep. He does not give legal, structural, or taxation advice herein. He merely reports a few thousand facts and his own observations and conclusions. He has made a diligent effort to ascertain that the information is accurate, but believes that some expert somewhere will eventually find a reason why this is not the first perfect book.

# ACKNOWLEDGMENTS

These are the people I promised to give the credit they deserved if they would just let me keep any royalties: My manager and friend, Mary Wallace, who is made of spring steel, and sugar and spice. My editor, Anne Depue, a real pleasure and a real pro, and her Sasquatch Books team. Mom, just because. Marcia Mellinger, an attorney who brings credit to the law. Michael Somers, an attorney who brings credit to California. Lance Lambert, an appraiser without measure. Connie Zinter and Debbie Steck of Phoenix Mortgage, and Rick L. Peterson of Select Mortgage, my trusty loan officers who called every five minutes with the latest in financing. Gabriella Girvalo, assistant manager at William A. Bain, Seattle condo expert, and wise, wise woman. Doug Hallauer, an example of what a can-do man can do. And may the sun always shine on the two guys who saved my sanity when the computer was trying to demolish it: Paul Calver and Joe Lesser.

Friends and professionals in Seattle: Clem Buckley, Alan Tonnon, Barb Schwarz, Jamie Fisher, Barry Bolduc, George Guttmann, Richard Cohan, Dave Burton, Lex Cooper, Don Wallace, Lisa Ray, Jim Albright, Emily Jones, Pat Leahy, Jeff Shearer, Beth Jensen, Sara Selfe, Ph.D.

In Spokane: Rob Higgins, Ellie Chambers, Lorene Riggs, Frank Bartel. From other corners of the state: Nick Adams (Washington Association of Realtors), Bob Mitchell (Department of Licensing). From Tennessee to the Mile-High City: Albert Santi, Barry Miller.

Thanks to the good-humored agents and brokers who found the time to sit still for interviews and just plain, dumb questions. In Anacortes: Mini Reink; Bellingham: Frank Sova; Cle Elum: Digby Granger, Margo O'Neil; Dayton: Marcene Hendrickson; Everett: Jim Morse; Diamond Lake: Mary Stephens; Lake Cushman: Peggy Mott; Mount Vernon: Ron Gilbertson, Susan Cooper; Newport: Mel and Jo Ann Goldberg; Richland: Louise Olsen; Sequim: Billie Hoaglund, Dick Olson, Gloria Mantle; Spokane: Rita Jensen, Marion Canett, Ron Criscione; Vancouver: John Relyea, Gloria Denney, Jane Moniot; West Seattle: Lori Brankey; Winthrop: Archie Eiffert; Yakima: Rick Lind, Pam Aylmer.

I especially want to single out two pleasant and helpful agents who made efforts above and beyond the call: Jerry Smith (Dayton) and Emily Holman (Bellevue).

# INTRODUCTION:
# THE WASHINGTON RAMBLE

### MISCELLANEOUS OBSERVATIONS AND OPINIONS
### ON THE LAY AND LAW OF THE LAND, PRESENTED FOR
### THE AMUSEMENT AND POSSIBLE ENLIGHTENMENT OF THE READER

This is a fishing manual. Surely you've heard the maxim "If you give a man a fish, you feed him only for a day, but if you teach a man to fish, you won't see him again till Super Bowl Sunday." Helping consumers achieve a high degree of independence is an important goal of this book. When my friends first heard of this effort, they assumed that I would write about which parts of Washington, and even which neighborhoods, offer the best buys in real estate. In other words, they thought I would hand them the fish, not just the bait and rod. But that's unwise and impossible: Washington has over 900 sites that could be called towns, and Seattle alone has over 90 neighborhoods. As my editor keeps reminding me, a good book is smaller than a hangar.

Furthermore, statistics quickly grow old, and laws and towns change, whereas good principles can land fish for a lifetime. The statistics in this introduction will soon be useful only for purposes of comparison, and the individual county and city problems mentioned here will, one hopes, be solved soon. But the value of this data as a reminder of what can go wrong in real estate transactions will remain. My goal is to teach the reader how, what, and where to ask for the latest information on real estate.

How about market predictions? I generally leave those to astrologers, economists, and unbridled egomaniacs. I certainly don't want to make any predictions that might stampede a gullible herd into Bankruptcy Gulch. I've got enough guilt to live with, so I will confine my guessing to which filling station up ahead has the cleanest restroom.

Finally, it is not my intention to convince others to move here. Nor do I intend to discourage them. One thing I like about America is the right to get up and move, without a passport, when the urge hits. Whether you are moving within, into, or out of Washington, my primary goal is simply to assist you in having as safe and pleasant a real estate experience as possible.

## THE RAMBLE

I could have written this book without leaving my office, doing all the research by telephone, but that wouldn't have been much fun. I'm always looking for a reason to explore, especially when I can call it a legitimate business expense. So I visited 35 of our 39 counties and talked to farmers, reporters, waitresses, real estate agents, and lots of motel clerks. I share here only a *fraction* of those conversations and observations as well as a sampling of some characteristics of real estate transactions in Washington. There are two important points I want to get across: (1) we can learn an awful lot just by listening to our neighbors, and (2) we always need to get a second opinion or independent confirmation of their information.

---

### SEEING THE SITES

A drive around Washington's perimeter is not an afternoon's undertaking. We do have a fairly good-sized chunk of real estate: slightly over 68,000 square miles altogether, approximately 360 miles east to west and 240 miles north to south. Washington is so roomy that it could accommodate every human being on earth with almost 350 square feet per person, which is only slightly less crowded than a Mariner baseball game when there's a good movie on TV. With our present population estimated at about 4.7 million, that's about 69 people to the square mile, or 1 for every 418,000 square feet (over 9 acres per person). The state is not crowded when viewed that way, although the residents of Puget Sound, where both the majority of our citizens live and the problems of rapid growth are taking place, would not agree.

---

I remember one 20-minute conversation in Tonasket (Okanogan County) with a rancher who quickly gave me an encyclopedic summary of apple farming: "Apple prices the same as 20 years ago, everybody's moving up on the hills to get away from the frosts like they should have done to start with, the land they're leaving behind is full of lead arsenate....Can't afford to run electricity to the house, costs almost $15,000 per mile, have to use propane refrigerators...." A buyer-dreamer who was also listening got in his car and drove back to Bellingham without further research or confirmation. If I do my job effectively I will convince you never to give up so easily and never to be so accepting.

Most Washington towns are quite small, and may even be wishing for growth. The Seattle area, including Bellevue, has around 1,400,000 residents, but Seattle proper has only half a million people, and our second largest city, Spokane, has about 170,000. Of the remaining 995 spots with names, only 27 have more than 20,000 residents. Approximately 78% of our residents live west of the Cascades in that north-south Interstate 5 strip some call the Can-Am Corridor. On the other side, one 700-square-mile county in Southeast Washington, Garfield, has only 2,500 residents, and its only official town, Pomeroy, contains 1,700 of that total. You *can* get away from it all. I'll always remember Pomeroy because the road southwest of town didn't have a yellow line; gravel's just too hard to paint.

## WEATHER YOU WANT IT OR NOT

Although the eastern half of Washington may be relatively short of people, it has a measurably larger share of the sunshine. For example, Spokane has 30 more days of sunshine each year than Seattle, and a summer day in Yakima is as hot as a jeep seat in July. Don't ever ask if there is a phone booth in the shade, unless you want to be known as new in town. But that old broiler in the sky attracts a lot of real estate purchasers, including serious agriculture interests. Altogether we have 38,000 farms, many of them producing world-famous apples

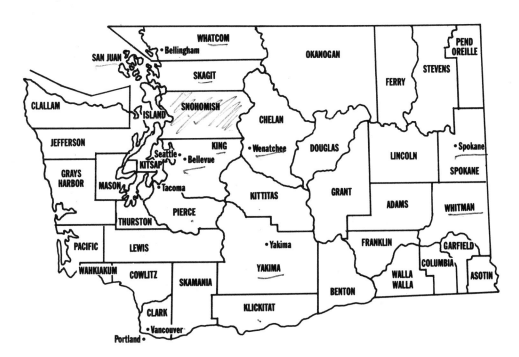

and wheat. But that ain't all. In the Yakima Valley the number of wineries has grown from 6 to over 60 in the last 18 years. I wonder if our own citizens might occasionally forget how important our weather is to our economy: Agriculture *is* our number one industry (Seattleites think it's sailboats).

As for the sun's significance in attracting property buyers other than farmers, a number of real estate agents in the Cle Elum and Wenatchee areas said that the majority of their business is finding cabins and second homes for buyers from the Puget Sound area. This almost included me. As I traveled I kept my eyes open for a fishing cabin. In fact, the first several weeks of writing this book were spent in a friend's primitive cabin just northeast of Cle Elum. One of his main reasons for choosing that pine-studded site was sunshine. But it was there that I got an insight into how to choose the best place for me. A small plane buzzed the cabin one day and got me to thinking about commuting by plane from a cabin to my business in Seattle. When I talked to a pilot he pointed out that if I stayed on the western side of the Cascades the plane itself could be less expensive than one outfitted with the instruments needed to cross the mountains. I think he indicated the difference could be as much as $40,000. That buys a lot of night crawlers.

Another modification to my hopes for a fishing cabin occurred when half-a-dozen Washington rivers flooded in the 1989–90 winter. That prompted me to limit my choices to lakefront property. I also learned that some of the sites I looked at on Kachess Lake could easily receive as much as eight to ten feet of snow in a season, making a cabin unreachable by any method other than one of those rape-and-pillage machines, the snowmobile. No thanks.

But if snow is what you *are* looking for, we can offer plenty of it; you just may have to drive to find it. We have 16 ski resorts with lifts, 12 of those in the Cascade range which divides the state north to south, just slightly west of the center of the state. Construction of a 17th site is expected to start soon in Okanogan County at a place known as Early Winters, near Winthrop. Real estate speculation has been going on there since the first environmental impact studies were started. But those drawn-out studies have meant the earliest buyers might have been as well off with savings bonds. Even as the last studies are completed—and almost everyone concedes that Early Winters will probably become a reality—buying land near the proposed resort is still the type of purchase that I recommend only for those investors who need to diversify and acquire some holdings for the *long* haul. No recreational use before 1993 is anticipated, and no one can be sure that an area as remote as Early Winters will ever catch on with the ski crowd. But if you just want a cabin in a scenic spot, and you don't mind a long, beautiful drive from Seattle or Spokane, then forget the investment viewpoint and check out this tranquil area. Prices are already running anywhere from $10,000–$30,000 an acre, so don't count on finding any bargains.

Another possible investment would be to buy a condo near the existing downhill ski areas. Alpine studios only 50 miles from Seattle on Interstate 90 can be bought for less than $30,000. As with many non-city sites, however, there are little details that city-slickers need to become aware of, such as the fact that the land under some of these condos is leased and will not be included in the sale and may become an additional expense for the owner in the future. I spoke with a very helpful agent with 15 years of experience in selling condos around Alpental, and her conclusions were that these condos should be bought for enjoyment, not for investment. She said that many buyers don't use them year-round as they should, and raved about the sweet huckleberries found

along the trails in August when virtually no one is there to enjoy them. Some people buy one of these studios thinking it will pay for itself if they rent it out for $100 a night. But the ski season is short, and homeowner's dues can be relatively high ($125/month or more). Besides, renters often party vigorously, and the resulting upkeep can devour profits and peace of mind.

It is not unusual for some of our cabins and resorts to be built on leased land, such as around Tacoma's City Light–owned Lake Cushman in Mason County (present lease ends in 2065, with another 99-year option), or on national forest land (one-third of our state consists of national forests or parks). Many people jump to the conclusion that private ownership does not exist in national forests, but twice I bought acreage in national forests, land that had been owned by private parties for many years. Once the U.S. Forest Service acquires a piece of land, the chances of the property reverting to private ownership are practically nil, so buying a piece next to government land *may* mean that some degree of tranquility is ensured (as long as the adjoining timber isn't auctioned off). About another seven percent of our state is also off-limits to the average real estate buyer because it exists as military or Indian reservations, with 19 Indian reservations making up the majority of the restricted areas (11 of those, the smaller ones, are on the coast).

All the same, there is quite a bit of available land and quite a variety of resort and vacation sites, just as we frequently have quite a bit of snowfall in our mountains (as much as 100 inches in one week). Otherwise, you won't find nearly as much of the white stuff as you might expect for a state so far north. Our climate is tempered a great deal by a substantial saltwater shoreline, over 2,400 miles of it altogether. Seattle alone has 172 miles of shoreline, including some freshwater lakes. So much surrounding water means that in some parts of the state it rains frequently, but not always a lot. Our rain forest on the Peninsula is the wettest spot in the Lower 48 (148 inches per year), but Seattle's reputation for rain is somewhere between the truth and a rumor spread by KOBO agents ("Keep Other Bastards Out"). With generally less than 40 inches a year, spread over 160 days, Seattle's precipitation is more of a heavy mist. In fact, one interesting weather phenomenon in Washington is the existence of "rain shadows," areas where very little rainfall occurs because of the mountains blocking it and capturing it as snow, such as happens with the Olympics on the Peninsula. One such shadowed place is that jewel of a town, Sequim, where about 16 inches of rain falls a year, the same amount that Spokane receives 277 miles to the east. Both areas require irrigation for growing anything more serious than mildew. Speaking of irrigation, one project, the Columbia River Basin project centered at Moses Lake, could add half a million acres to its benefitted area in the next four decades. This is the type of proposal that farmers and land speculators always try to know about years before the public even hears of it, but my general investment advice is: Do nothing that depends on the government.

Another shadowed area is the San Juan Islands, where the annual rainfall is often under 20 inches. Indeed, enlightened real estate purchasers in that county always inquire about the water situation before making any offer. The smart Washington real estate buyer is one who assumes nothing and asks lots of dumb questions. For example, an assumption that a town within 15 miles of Sequim, such as Port Angeles, would have approximately the same rainfall would be only half right.

San Juan County is one of 15 counties with marine shoreline and one of 12 counties that include inhabited islands, one of the most popular forms of real estate to be found in this state. But just as we saw with the rainfall complication, there are often many challenges in acquiring and inhabiting land in these islands, not to mention price. In the first place, we have to define "island." Are there 468 or 780 islands in the San Juans? Depends on the tide and who's counting; some writers call a rock at low tide an island. I suppose most of us are smart enough not to buy something that might be underwater late in the day, but are we knowledgeable enough to avoid complications due to the Shoreline Management Act or the State Environmental Protection Act (SEPA)? Most of the terms and concepts unique to island or waterfront property are almost self-explanatory, such as high-bank and low-bank, and most consumers are soon comfortable with them as long as they take a little time to ask a lot of questions and don't rush into anything. But this is the first of many opportunities in this book for me to put in a plug for attorneys; with every complication and new regulation, you are one day closer to being a daredevil if you don't hire an attorney for even the friendliest transaction (no state law requires an attorney's participation).

Speaking of situations that give cause to pause, the timeshare option is one that comes up for discussion with some of my acquaintances. These alternatives to tenting and moteling must meet some people's needs or they wouldn't exist. One of my own agents has a two-week timeshare at Lake Chelan. He says that if he didn't, he might never take a vacation. Send me 10 more workaholics just like him. However, timeshares have proven to be such an unworkable situation for so many buyers that they have spawned a second industry: the timeshare resale business, which has perpetrated some unique fleecings, such as collecting a fee from the seller, then doing nothing to earn the fee, and even renting out the timeshare without the owner's knowledge. My first comment to anyone interested in timeshares is that at any given moment half of them are up for resale, typically for 70% of their original price. If I were going to buy one I would look for an individual seller and avoid any presentations that include free gifts. Somehow I think those gifts from developers are very expensive. Timeshares are also found in abundance at Ocean Shores, as well as many other resort communities (for locations and information, see the Appendix—"Condos").

As for the costs of a timeshare condominium, one observer pointed out that a particular unit cost only $8,000, or a "pro-rated" $400 a year, a "reasonable" fee for a week or so at a hotel. I take issue with the calculation. There is something called the "future value" of money, i.e. the possible value of that money if it were placed in a real estate investment, which a timeshare is not. Even a mediocre real estate investment of $8,000 should provide at least $20,000 in equity in 20 years, and you do not usually build any equity in a timeshare. Even if that $8,000 were put into an ordinary Certificate of Deposit, the annual interest would go far toward a vacation, and the depositor would still control the money. As you may suspect, I think the fishing cabin is a better way to go.

## ENVIRONMENT: SOUND OR JUST NOISY?

Tourism and outdoor recreation are well-known major industries in Washington; in fact, it was the challenge of climbing Mt. Rainier that first brought me to Washington in 1975. At Camp Muir I met a mail carrier from Seattle, originally from Indiana, who shared his reasons for moving here: "I could go sailing in the morning and skiing in the afternoon." A well–thought-out and convincing argument. I already thought of the world-famous REI as the greatest combination of the best of environmentalism, capitalism, and socialism the world had ever seen. I expected the entire state to be as enlightened and progressive in the realm of environmental concerns. If only that were so.

Oh, most of the people here *care* about the environment. Even the ones who shoot up the road signs tell you that they "love the woods." But fewer residents than you might expect can agree on what or how much legislation is needed. "Confrontational democracy" is an advanced art, leaving us with a legislature that frequently does only one thing consistently: disappoints. Great ideas die from exhausting arguments. Good ideas die from lack of funding. We have 550 of the most dangerously polluted sites in America, from Tacoma's Asarco to the Hanford reservation where 22 corroding silos of nuclear waste may someday create an environmental Halloween. Yet we are not making any rapid moves to deal with these problems; Washingtonians as a group don't normally raise hell and demand rapid changes, even when it's imperative. We vote, write an occasional letter, and try to fit in a public hearing between hikes. That's the way polite people do it, even when it's too dangerous for our own good. What do you expect when the state motto is "Alki," an Indian word for "by and by"?

All the same, Washington is rated the nation's number one state in recycling, and we have developed quite a body of environmental regulations that are affecting real estate and which won't get any easier to deal with in this century. SEPA has recently been applied to single-family housing building permits (even for remodeling) in any area that is considered "sensitive." Protection of the flora-and-fauna–rich wetlands is receiving an increasingly greater amount of attention, both by those who sincerely care about the environment and by those who will use any means to slow development in the Puget Sound area.

Skagit County has attempted to control growth by instituting "forestry zoning." If an owner-builder has less than 20 acres, she may have to pay a "penalty" to build on her land. In one instance, an owner faced a $13,500 fee. Her solution was to apply for a rezoning while also looking to see if she could acquire another half acre for a house site. With several counties having their own unique concepts, such as "recreation zoning," a trip to the county assessor and/or building department is always in order. (See Appendix—"Washington State Resources".)

Owners of properties bordering streams in King County recently faced a set of proposals that would have denied them the use of lawn tractors and possibly even the ownership of a dog (the dog would have to be kept leashed 150 feet from the stream at all times). At press time, this proposal had been shot out of the branches, but it or other equally restrictive measures are bound to resurface.

Not all of our environmental concerns are so obvious or headline-grabbing as wetland-destruction, or finding pesticides and nitrates in well water (the result of recent sample testing in Whatcom, Thurston, Yakima, and Franklin counties), or discovering that several areas have radon levels that concern the authorities (Spokane, Black Diamond, and the Columbia Gorge were just three areas where some sample readings exceeded the "action level"). No, a more typical everyday concern for the average Washington countryside buyer would be the failure of the septic tank. As one inspector pointed out, many tanks were built to last only a few years in the belief that sewers would soon be available; we practiced built-in obsolescence on a scale similar to that of the automotive industry. There are somewhere in the neighborhood of 640,000 septic tanks in the state (400,000 in the Puget Sound area), of which it is estimated that at any given moment four percent are in a failure stage. One agent told me she ran across a system built out of a common 55-gallon drum. A recent change in state law will force every rural home builder to own enough land to accommodate two septic systems (in case one should fail and another must be added). A few landowners have discovered that they can no longer build.

All buyers of waterfront property should be especially vigilant in investigating the septic systems. All of Vashon Island may even be designated a "health hazard zone" if the problems there get any worse. The area known as Skyway, in south King County, is miles from any waterfront, yet it too reports that up to one-fourth of its septic systems may be failing. It has been designated a health hazard zone, and supposedly no permits for remodeling or loans are being granted until sewers are installed. If you are looking for a cause and you want to do this state a real favor, take up the promotion of alternative toilet systems; these have proven successful in Europe for decades. They're legal in many counties, but scoffed at. We're still horse-and-buggy when it comes to disposing of home wastes.

## LOOK OUT FOR THAT BOOM

One group that seems to be the most damaged and probably the most embittered by environmental restrictions is the logging industry. Timber cutting in old-growth forests has been somewhat curtailed out of concern for the spotted owl; in response, a few of the residents of logging communities have shot a number of owls, which is a public relations torpedo for their industry—as if they hadn't already made themselves look like the most insensitive group on earth by clear-cutting without consistently leaving buffer zones to soften and veil the hideous patches. Some analysts say that many of the cutbacks and job losses in logging have little to do with environmental restrictions. Although we in the Puget Sound area are experiencing something of a real estate boom, the same is not true for the rest of the nation. With national building permits at a relatively low point, and with other timber states giving Washington a run for its money, the high unemployment figures of small logging towns, like those on the Peninsula, may not improve anytime soon.

While Washington's logging jobs were falling by 27% in the eighties, we saw an offsetting 32% increase in employment at Boeing, the state's second largest employer (the federal government is first). In some ways, the employment at Boeing may be said to be too important to the state. In the first place, it is estimated that, directly or indirectly, from 1 in 6 to 1 in 10 jobs throughout the state are dependent on this company, the nation's 10th largest defense contractor. Second, even though the state has several times seen an upswing in its economy when Boeing was on the downturn, our residents still have a morbid fascination with and fear of every change at the plants. When a partial strike occurred near the end of 1989, my real estate students were asking me if this wouldn't cause a leveling of real estate prices in Seattle, even though there were still ten buyers for every seven houses. Methinks they dost accord too much impact to the big B. But a belief held strongly enough can have greater significance than facts not widely known.

Fortunately, Boeing has enough orders for civilian aircraft to keep it humming for decades to come; otherwise the almost inevitable defense cuts in the near future could hit this peace-loving state awfully hard. This may also be true in Everett, where a naval base has been on the drawing board for some years. People who say the glass is half empty say the port will never be completed; people who say the glass is half full are hoping, but glad they have one last drink if needed to drown any sorrows.

As we enter the nineties, Washington is ranked 18th in per capita income ($16,500), but 21 of our 39 counties have recently been considered "distressed," with unemployment that is 20% or more above the state average of 6.8%. And from 7 to 23 of our counties lost population in the eighties (depending again on which set of statistics one uses), while the state as a whole was seeing an 8.5% increase. Half of the state's new jobs originated in King County, which experienced a population increase of 13% in the eighties. Snohomish County surpassed King with a 27% increase while Kitsap County, something of a bedroom county for Seattle, reportedly saw a 50% increase in population. Its largest island, Bainbridge, reports that over 80% of its 14,000 residents commute by ferry to Seattle (Washington has America's largest ferry system). One real estate broker begged me not to write anything about how popular Kitsap's Bainbridge Island had become. I think her worries are belated. San Juan County saw the second-largest population increase, at 28%, but the vast majority of buyers there bought for retirement or relaxation, not for employment opportunities or to find an affordable home near Seattle, as did Bainbridge and Snohomish folks.

Admittedly, any discouraging employment statistics may sometimes seem at odds with some details about our state. For example, we are a major refinery state, having five refineries on our coast (one at Tacoma and the other four within rock-chucking distance of Bellingham), but this is an industry that for all its visibility actually employs relatively few people. On the other hand, we have a quite new and less conspicuous 800 million dollar industry (some say two billion)—software—that is already employing 10,000 of our residents, or would be if our schools were keeping up with the demand. Just as we have to import workers to pick our bountiful fruit, the software industry estimates that it has had to recruit 95% of its engineers from out of state because our state universities are not meeting the challenge.

This particular deficit in our educational system, along with general turmoil, is the second shocking and unexpected thing the starry-eyed newcomer might encounter (after the environmental problems). Washington ranked next-to-last in the eighties in increases in teachers' salaries. Mortgage companies in Seattle might as well put a sign on the door that reads: "Schoolteachers need not apply." An experienced teacher probably cannot afford an average Seattle condo, much less a house. The school system in Seattle has seen a drop in enrollment in recent years, due in good part to the frustration of busing and a general displeasure with the quality and funding of the schools. From what I could learn, there is no such general displeasure with Spokane's schools. In fact, if I were a family man looking for a moderately progressive community where there are more scout troops than street gangs, I would seriously consider Spokane. But it may not be to everyone's liking. In fact, the following details may reveal more about Spokane's political atmosphere than a week's worth of interviews: Spokane is 95% white and its female employment rate is 9% below the national average. Its symphony is going strong but its ballet recently collapsed after a 10-year struggle (Seattle's ballet is healthy, but the ticket prices require a home equity loan). All the same, neighborhoods don't get any nicer than Spokane's South Hill. Trees. Lots of trees.

Where does the state get its income? We have no state income tax, but we do have a high monkey-on-the-back sales tax that generally ranges from 7.5%–8.1% (variations due to local rates; the state gets 6.5%). Cars are taxed annually according to their estimated value, prompting many a luxury car owner to register in Oregon and risk a fine. We also have a regressive business and occupation (B & O) tax which businesses pay on their gross receipts, prompting many a low-net business to set up shop elsewhere. Spokane has elected not to have a city B & O tax because, as they explained it to me, "No telemarketing business will ever locate in a city with one." And finally, as a state, we have the nation's second-highest real estate excise tax, (1.53% in early 1990), which is usually paid from the seller's net proceeds at closing (a sale of $135,000 results in a tax of $2,065).

On the bright side, our property taxes are limited to an annual increase of 6%. At this time, a Seattle homeowner pays $13.56 for each $1,000 of assessed value; the Spokane homeowner pays approximately 75 cents less for each $1,000. The assessments are supposedly 99% of the value (he said with a wink).

You may have read that Washington was rated a "tax haven" (sixth-best) by *Money* magazine, and Oregon a "tax hell." However, the economists have already started analyzing the figures that led to those conclusions and they found that the prototype family used in the study never bought clothes or went out to eat, so that's one study that may not be too believable. Once again, the wise are skeptical without being cynical.

What can we believe? Perhaps the Commerce Department's conclusions that Washington recently rated third in job growth and eighth in pay increases. A life insurance study concluded that we are the 11th healthiest place to live. The Canadian border crossing at Blaine in Whatcom County is now the third-busiest in the nation (after Buffalo and Detroit), with over 22 million annual crossings. I met one would-be investor who begged me not to talk about how the traffic at Blaine is affecting real estate prices at nearby alternative crossings. I lost those notes anyway. Since Canadian gas and food prices remain relatively high, and since the Canadian dollar has seen a tremendous surge in value in the last couple of years (up 15.3% in five years), a Canadian can save the price of a fishing rod just by dropping down for a bag of groceries and a tank of gas. The new malls at Bellingham are reporting very strong sales, with estimates that up to 90,000 Canadians are dropping in each weekend. With the "free trade agreement" taking hold, these numbers can only increase (Bellingham has begun to worry that it does not have sufficient housing to meet new demands; in addition to the malls, its relatively cheap housing, proximity to outdoor recreation, and increased popularity as a port are making it increasingly attractive, and builders have turned to custom houses, creating a demand for cheaper homes). It may come as a surprise that Canada is our number two foreign employer (as of 1988), employing about 12,000 Washingtonians. European and Japanese investors employ 15,000 and 10,000 Washingtonians, respectively. When you consider that renting a perfectly ordinary apartment in Tokyo can require $12,000 in cash, up front, or that an ordinary condo costs $400,000, it is easy to imagine more and more Japanese businesses looking to relocate their businesses, money, and even their executives to Northwest sites.

## YOU'RE WELCOME?

Washingtonians are at least as territorial as wolves, and only slightly less so than Oregonians. By that I mean we can turn downright mean when we feel invaded. For example, in 1989 King County experienced a net migration of about 32,000 people, 65% of whom make over $30,000 a year. Before long, the demand for housing pushed the prices up and these newcomers *seemed* to be the ones who could best afford to pay. The KOBO agents started frothing, and just like that cry I heard all too often as a teenager in the South, they blamed our troubles on these "outside agitators." Like people everywhere, we usually have only ourselves to blame for our troubles. We place people in elected office and then fail to hold them accountable; we don't participate ourselves in making tough decisions that need to be made. But that's another grim fairy tale, and even with our white-bread, don't-make-waves politics I haven't seen any place I would prefer to live. Ironically, even with recent double-digit appreciation, Seattle enters the nineties only 10% above the national cost-of-living average for comparable cities, and it has been pointed out that our cheaper utilities allow us to make house payments 10% higher and still make the same savings deposits as people do in those average burgs. (The typical two-can garbage/sewer/water cost in Spokane is $37, and $50 in Seattle; a thousand kilowatts of electricity costs about $43 in Spokane and $32 in Seattle.) Another study showed that Seattleites spend 31% of their income on housing, whereas the average for major metropolitan areas is 32%, a fact that might normally be soothing except that many of us suspect that we are still many months, or even years, away from the leveling of the price climb.

Of the 150 major metropolitan areas in America, Seattle ranks 72nd in housing affordability, Tacoma 42nd, and Spokane an inviting 11th. On the cover of this book there is a charming blue and white "four corner" that I photographed in the South Hill area of Spokane. I knew that such a house in Seattle could bring anywhere from $225,000 to $400,000, depending on such factors as its distance from the center of town. Thus I was amazed to learn that its Spokane price was $85,000! May I have six to go, please? Overall, Seattle's cost of living is 8% above the national average, whereas Spokane's is 6% below. Spokane is also very high on itself, and with some justification: Developer/entrepreneur David Sabey is pumping 40 million bucks into a mall, Seafirst has relocated its credit card business there, Boeing has opened a plant employing 350, a major new 23-story building is planned for downtown, and Idaho's tourism is spilling over into the city.

But success has its price: foul air. Spokane's carbon monoxide level is rated the 19th-worst in the country and its airport is the 15th-foggiest. It has taken steps to improve its environment, including banning phosphates, and it may soon ban the farmers' annual rites of burning off their grass fields. A recent mayoral election featured an entrenched battle between those who favored an incinerator and those who would prevent it, even if it cost a fortune to shelve the plans. But even if Spokane's air is as foul as Seattle's during one of its choking inversions, Spokane at least has trees on its streets. That means a lot to an old Boy Scout. Two-thirds of Seattle's streets have *no* trees. I blame it on some of the early settlers who grew up on tundra and thought of trees as just weeds that blocked the smell of reindeer and the fjords. So how can such a treeless city be rated the nation's "Most Livable" by *Places Rated Almanac*? And how could *Money* magazine reach the same conclusion? Why were we rated by *Savvy* magazine as America's second-best city to raise children in? Because we have no trees! Why do CEOs favor us as the second-best place to locate a business, and why were we considered the fifth-favorite spillover city by people leaving more crowded areas? No trees! Just think, we could have been first in every category, and driven the KOBO agents loonier than they are. As it is, we're America's worst city for raising a dog.

Seattle is the Lower 48's coolest large city in July with an average temperature of 59° (Spokane's average is 70°). In December, we drop only 18° to 41°, whereas Spokane drops to 29°. Seattle's mild climate is as good an explanation as any as to why we have such a relatively low murder rate (11 per 100,000)—29th of 34 major cities studied. All the same, we spend around 54% of our county budget on some aspect of crime. Only Yakima is worse, spending as much as 70% of its budget on criminal "justice" (1988 figures). It's nice to know where our taxes are going. (Remember, these statistics do not give a complete picture of a town or area. You must do your homework and research the good and the bad.)

Spokane has cheaper real estate, but Seattle has more variety. We have all the usual choices, plus one that is found in very few cities: houseboats. Seattle has the largest floating-home community this side of the Orient. This is definitely one of the world's most romantic forms of real estate, and most expensive on a square-foot basis (both sides of $200 per). A buyer who makes less than $60,000 may not even get his calls returned. "You want a closet, sir? That will be another $25,000." Actually, there are some houseboats for under $100,000, but they typically have a few complications. You may have to lease the moorage, and homeowner's dues of $150–$180 a month are not unusual. A leased moorage means that in the worst case (eviction), your floating home could become almost worthless overnight (admittedly, not a common problem). Isn't it funny that one of today's most exclusive and desirable homes was once nothing more than the barracks for logging crews on a lake that resembled a cesspool? The more things change, the more expensive they get.

Here's a good reason not to live in Seattle at all: An earthquake will devastate us sometime in the next thousand years. We are on a major fault or sliding plate, and we are generally complacent about it. In other words, we should all be carrying earthquake insurance, but only around 1% of us do (versus 29% in San Francisco). Yes, I have it, even though it has a deductible of $9,000. We former rescue workers may tend to err on the side of caution. One of the things that some of us learned from the San Francisco Shudder is that buildings on fill dirt are more likely to disintegrate. That describes any number of places in Seattle, the town that long ago demonstrated its idea of an efficient landscaping technique—erosion. Even that benign scene around Green Lake has fill sites.

Combine that with an older house not bolted to its foundation, or a foundation of stone or bricks, and...uh, well, I'd be packing.

## THE PRICES

Name a price and you can find something with that pricetag, whether we're talking $10,000 or $10 million. The challenge is to get the desired price in the desired location. Real estate does not come to us; we go to it. The fishing cabin that I would like for $20,000 exists, but it may be more than the two-hour drive from Seattle that is my limit. The large old house that you may want for $75,000 exists, but it may be in a town where there is no demand for your job skills. You can buy a waterfront lot within an hour of Spokane for $10,000, but in Seattle you will pay that much or more for a "front foot" on a lake. It is not a mere coincidence that the words "reality" and "realty" are so much alike.

To gather all of the reality I could, I carried a picture of my Seattle house with me everywhere I went (the blue and white bungalow on the back cover). I then asked agents in each town, "If your high school principal owned this house, in a nice, middle-class neighborhood, what would it sell for?" I never mentioned that it was my own house, or what it would sell for in Seattle (probably around $170,000 in early 1990). I also did my own pricing based on other houses on the market in those towns and, as many consumers have concluded,

I too had to admit that the agents frequently seemed to be a bit—"optimistic," shall we say? In many a town, I thought I saw comparable houses for $50,000, and even less, but the agents, even in the smallest towns with the highest unemployment, usually felt that it would bring at least $60,000. They may be right. The most amazing thing for me was the general consistency: The price was almost always around $65,000, in towns ranging from Anacortes to Spokane to Vancouver. One agent did feel that in Pasco such a house might be found for $50,000, and in Winthrop, with so much speculation due to the possible Early Winters ski resort, a broker offered a price opinion of around $80,000. Only in King and Snohomish counties could I be sure that the price would be substantially higher. However, as we will see, with towns like Bellingham (Whatcom) and Mt. Vernon (Skagit) becoming such beehives, King and Snohomish are probably not going to be the only counties with double-digit appreciation in the decade of the nineties.

Prices and appreciation haven't always been the whole story in evaluating some of the state's real estate possibilities. In Yakima a broker showed me duplexes that could be bought with a $12,000 down payment. Even after paying a management firm, this investment would return a positive cash flow of well over $100 a month. But property moves slowly there, despite the 2% vacancy rate. Is this a contradiction? No, it simply reflects the relatively low incomes of an agriculture-centered community. There are plenty of renters, but not people with sufficient income to qualify for loans.

A friend pointed out that Ellensburg real estate has been increasingly affected by Central Washington University, which has seen an increased enrollment for five years in a row. Juniors are now allowed to live off-campus, creating a greater demand for rentals. These are the kinds of statistics and changes that most of us only learn about after the fact, until we learn what to look for.

Another place that's worth keeping an eye on is our own Vancouver (as well as Canada's). When the bridge improvements over the Columbia are finished, Vancouver is likely to become even more of a bedroom community for Portland than it already is. Those Oregonians may gladly trade a commute for our no-income-tax "haven" and cheaper property taxes, while keeping their cars registered south of the river, for a best-of-both-worlds scenario. An agent there also pointed out how and why the area east of Vancouver has grown so much, while the town core looks so depressed. The town had a *long* battle in the 19th century over some land that did not have clear title. While the battle raged, Portland bustled on, and even dredged its side of the river. Vancouver stagnated, and for all practical purposes the town doesn't seem to have ever recovered. Pay attention when you come to the sections in this book on title and title insurance, you hear?

Everywhere I looked, people were teaching me to see. There is only one observation that I will take sole credit for. I was driving on the interstate when I saw a truck drive under an overpass towing half of a manufactured house. If the roof had been any higher it wouldn't have cleared. Bingo. Those low-pitched roofs, that make a row of those squatty boxes look like Shantyville, must be built to conform to our national highway system. I sure hope I'm remembered for something other than being the first to point this out.

My trips around this state have been delightful as well as educational. I have learned about my own industry from a consumer's point of view. I called agents in many of the towns I visited and observed firsthand a wide range of manners and service, from shocking rudeness to cheerful sacrifice. I even had brokers and agents offer to show me properties (knowing that no sale could possibly come of it), whereas others wouldn't give me the time of day. It's up to you to see that you are well served, consumers: Hang up on the rude ones, and stay loyal to the good ones.

In Anacortes I knew that real estate was a hot topic when I saw eight real estate offices in the first half-mile, but when I could find only one of them with its phone number prominently displayed I knew that we still have a ways to go before we can correctly think of ourselves as professional communicators and marketers. On the other hand, I was very pleased to run across several small-town agencies that offer buyer brokering, a service that I feel is long overdue, and one which is something of a barometer in revealing how responsive my industry is becoming to meeting the public's needs.

In closing, I want to say thanks to the many helpful agents, and the many, many fine and decent people of this state who have made me feel that I don't have to apologize to anyone for adopting this piece of earth as my home. I hope this book makes a down payment on my debt.

Happy hunting,

*Jim*
*April 28, 1990*

# LANGUAGE/SLANGUAGE

### TERMS-THEORIES-LAWS

When I was a teenager in the U.S. of A., I learned "high German." But when I went to Germany I learned *Berliner Dialekt*. Either that or I'd never be able to order anything but wienerschnitzel. This is similar to the way a consumer or beginning agent learns about real estate: First they must learn the definitions and the theory, then they must tackle the applied terms in all their confusing reality. Mastering real estate can be described both as a learning and an un-learning process. But no matter how difficult it is, learning the language gives one power and protection.

---

### THE REFERENCE

My trusty reference for this chapter is an excellent book called *Washington Real Estate Law*, by Alan Tonnon. It should be on every agent's desk as well as the desk of every consumer who thinks a good reference book gives longer, more lasting pleasure than an expensive dinner. See the Appendix for information on how to order this book, and for the names of several other helpful books.

---

Most of the terms used in this book are defined in the chapter in which they are introduced, but others need to be introduced right away. In addition, I will provide a digest of Washington real estate law.

**Real estate** is what personal property is not: immovable. **Realty** is another word for real estate, but since many companies have used the word in their names, such as Shimmering Leaves Realty, it has come to mean "office" in the minds of many of us. I may say, "I own a realty," when actually I mean that I own a company.

Real estate is not just land; it is also (1) things attached to the land in such a way as to make them almost as immovable as the land itself, and/or (2) rights necessary for the use and enjoyment of the land. These could be crops and easements, which are called **appurtenances**, or fences, buildings, signs, etc., which are called **fixtures**.

Fixtures are the source of many an argument; the courts have to settle far too many disputes about whether an item is personal property or realty. A mobile home is personal property as long as it is on its wheels and ready to roll, but if those wheels are removed and the mobile home is permanently attached to a foundation, then it becomes a fixture and realty. If we install kitchen cabinets, they are almost certain to be so permanently attached as to be considered fixtures. However, a portable dishwasher that is not installed in or under a counter, and which could be moved without damage to the property, would almost certainly be considered **personalty**. Not every situation is so clear. What is wall-to-wall carpeting? It has been ruled to be both personal property and a fixture, according to how it was attached and what the intentions or agreements of the parties were. Both buyers and sellers can save themselves a great deal of trouble if they make out detailed lists of what they expect to be included in a real estate sale.

There are many other guidelines that pertain to crops and minerals. For example, a seller will often be able to return to his sold property, under the **doctrine of emblements**, to harvest the first crop that resulted from his efforts. Land may be sold separately from the **mineral rights**. Whoever owns the mineral rights will have the right, under certain guidelines, to enter the land and do whatever is necessary to mine or recover those minerals. Even the airspace above a piece of property may be sold.

A landowner is entitled to the support from adjacent land. This is known as **lateral support**. If I dig a ditch on my land that causes slippage on your land, I may be liable for your damage, and I cannot use as my defense that I am entitled to do whatever I want on my own land.

The use of and access to water is so complicated as to defy summarizing. In our arid West, water is considered a valuable resource, and the disputes and laws that have risen over its use are as complicated as one would expect when stakes are high. The water rights of a new owner who attempts to obtain a water permit from the state will depend on actions by previous owners taken many years before. For those who know a bit about the law in this area, we can say that Washington has moved toward a system of **appropriative rights**. As the kids might say, "first come, first served." Since 1974 the only right that a property owner could be sure of, if there was no prior recorded water permit or right, was the right to use water bordering his property in such a way as not to diminish its quantity. Canoe, yes, but don't water the garden. Well, not much anyway.

If a body of water can be used for commercial navigation, then most likely it will be owned either by the state or the federal government, which means the private owner can only own land to the high-water mark. If the water is non-navigable and bordered by several owners, then they can agree to own to some particular point in the lake or riverbed.

**Easement** is another concept that causes a great deal of confusion and frequent lawsuits. A *positive* easement is simply a right-of-way, but that is where the simplicity ends. A utility company requires easements so that it can reach its wires or pipes for replacement or repair; the owner's rights to build on or over, or to use an easement, can be severely curtailed. Also, if you own 100 acres and you sell 10 acres enclosed within its boundaries, you must provide an easement for the new owner; and, in general, you cannot even try to control or block that easement (with a locked gate, for example). In addition, if that new owner walks across one of your fields to the river to fish, in time (10 years) that path may "ripen" into an easement and you will no longer be able to deny her use of that path. But the law says that for the path to become an easement, her use of it must be continuous and "hostile" (without permission), so some owners will make a point of giving permission or interrupting the use from time to time.

A *negative* easement prohibits an owner from doing something, such as cutting the trees in a **greenbelt**—an area that is to be maintained in its natural state. This restriction is also known as a **covenant**.

An easement may be **recorded** or **unrecorded**. In the farm example above, when we write a contract to sell the 10 acres we normally write in a description of the easement (how wide, where, etc.) and record it in the public records with the other documents of the sale. But the path to the river that may have ripened into an easement will most likely remain unrecorded and will possibly become a point of contention when the owner of the 10 acres sells her piece.

**Covenants, conditions, and restrictions** (or CC&Rs) are pretty much what they sound like: a set of rules that either require actions or restrict actions by the owner. CC&Rs are most common with either condominiums or subdivisions that have hoity-toity aspirations toward grandeur. They may be considered very reasonable or very rigid, depending on the situation and one's point of view. Which would you consider these: "No pets over six pounds," "Pickup trucks may not be parked overnight in the community," and "No trees shall block the view, i.e. the height limit shall be 18 feet"? Now that you know what CC&Rs are, you won't go a year without reading about some "criminal" who owns a fat cat or a pickup truck, or who violates "community standards" in some other way.

Many first-time buyers are shocked when they encounter a deed that contains language along the lines of "colored people will not be eligible for ownership in this area." This is, of course, an illegal and unenforceable covenant, but one that was common until a few decades ago; the language has simply been left in many deeds because of the legal hoops that must be jumped through in order to rewrite them. A skeleton in our real estate closet. It is now illegal for county recorders to record deeds with discriminatory covenants.

One requirement of any real estate contract is that a **legal description** be included that leaves no doubt which property is being sold. Even that easement mentioned above in the 10-acre sale would probably require a detailed description, and typically a survey would be needed, unless some natural or man-made boundaries delineated all or most of that easement.

In the countryside, we would most likely depend on the **government survey** (range and township) method of delineating property. An example of this might be, "The northeast quarter of the northeast quarter of section 6, township 8 south, range 2 west," and so on, until the property is totally described or the reader is asleep. Perhaps you can see how this method is likely to require the skills of a surveyor (to find the lines or write the description).

In cities or subdivisions we generally rely on the **lot and block** (or **recorded plat**) method of description. A detailed description of that lot is on file in the county recorder's office; it incorporates the government survey method, so an abbreviated form of reference is acceptable, such as "Lot 6 of Baker's addition, Seattle, King County, Washington, page 7, volume 12 of King County Records."

Where do condominiums fit into all this? For this unique situation we have created a unique concept—the **air lot**—which requires a measurement of elevation from sea level. Fortunately for the consumer (and the agent), an abbreviated method similar to the city lot description can be used.

Our society is either very trusting or very stingy, if we judge by the frequency with which surveyors are called into transactions, especially in the city. I don't remember ever having a city buyer ask for a survey. The majority of property owners accept the fences and the hedges as their property lines and never give them another thought. However, when I did some research on one buyer's property line I concluded that every lot on that street was 18" off. When I pointed this out to the city engineer, he said, "Yeah, happens all the time, but as long as no one complains, there's no problem."

Our little problem with the location of the lot would come to light if a survey were required, which it frequently is in cases of extensive remodeling, rezoning, or the establishment of a **common easement**, better known as "a driveway between two houses" that is used by both neighbors.

There are also ways in which a property's lines might be changed accidentally or deliberately without involving a surveyor. Let's say that I put a fence on my lot that extends a foot over onto my neighbor's lot. If my neighbor and I agree to call that location the property line, then, providing that zoning allows it, in 10 years it becomes the new line by **agreement and acquiescence**.

If, however, my neighbor and I don't discuss it, but I use and maintain it, that foot of property will most likely become mine, by **adverse possession**, in a period of either 7 or 10 years, depending on several technicalities. If I were to sell this property before seven years had passed, and I knew that the fence was not on my original lot but I did not disclose this to the buyer, I would be guilty of **actual fraud**, i.e. intentional deception. If, however, a misrepresentation occurred through negligence or carelessness, then I'm guilty of **constructive fraud**. Actual fraud may incur criminal charges, whereas constructive fraud is more likely to result in a civil action. So to speak.

Misrepresentations are, and should be, a major concern of agents and brokers. The courts have excused agents and brokers in some **innocent misrepresentations**, while holding the owners (sellers) responsible for them. If a seller stated that a row of trees was a boundary, this might seem so obvious that an agent would pass it on. However, if the agent either knew, or should have known by reading the legal description, that the creek beside the trees was the boundary, then the agent is more likely to be held responsible for any damages for the buyer.

One common misunderstanding is that agents and sellers can escape culpability just by saying that the property is sold "as is." This is patent nonsense. Both parties must practice **full disclosure** of any **hidden defects**. Basically, any material fact that affects the value, use, or habitability of the property must be disclosed, even if the buyer doesn't ask. There are numerous gray areas, however. Does the projected building of an apartment house a block away affect the value? Does a suicide that occurred in the house a month before? Five years before?

The buyer also has responsibility in the disclosure arena. The seller and agent do not have any duty to point out the obvious. If the chimney has collapsed onto the driveway, even if the seller never mentions it the buyer is not likely to collect any damages for this. The buyer has a duty to inspect the property.

A buyer also has a responsibility to think. At least that's what the law seems to say when it holds that neither agents nor sellers are usually liable for opinions, or what is known as **puffing**: "Yessir, this is the best bargain to be found in this town. This entire area is likely to become the most popular neighborhood in town in a few years." Our society extends little sympathy to those who swallow such hype and build their foundations on untested strata.

One of the most confusing gray areas for all parties in the question of disclosure has been the unfortunate specter of AIDS. The Washington State Human Rights Commission specifically forbids real estate agents to conjecture about, discuss, or disclose the presence of the AIDS virus when selling a property, and neither the seller nor the buyer can legally ask about its presence (some states, however, require disclosure). Likewise, an appraiser cannot take AIDS into consideration. AIDS is considered a disability under the Washington State Law Against Discrimination.

**Discrimination** is not illegal per se. Requiring someone to have a real estate license to list property is a form of discrimination, but it is a legal form. A well-known case of a landlord refusing to rent to a black lawyer because "lawyers are troublemakers" was upheld by a New York judge as legal discrimination. (Seemed like a disability to me.)

According to federal law, an individual owner can also practice discrimination based on sex, race, etc., but only in a few specific circumstances, such as when renting a room in one's own home. In general, though, the Federal Fair Housing Act of 1968 is so comprehensive as to prohibit almost all forms of discrimination in selling or renting. These include race, color, religion, sex, national origin, disability, or familial status. The Washington Law Against Discrimination has *no* exemptions, so owners must consult with their attorneys if any questions arise. If both state and federal laws or state and county laws address a situation and the laws differ, in general the stricter rule applies.

Agents are held to an even higher standard than homeowners—absolutely no discrimination can be practiced by a licensed person—and from time to time anonymous "testers" from the Department of Housing and Urban Development (HUD) will call on agents and attempt to entrap them in discriminatory remarks or behavior. This may seem unfair, but it provides a good reminder to professionals that they must neither reopen old wounds nor inflict new ones. An agent who discourages a buyer because of race, religion, etc., from buying into a neighborhood is guilty of **steering**. An agent who tells owners they should sell because a religious group (or any of the other discrimination categories) is moving into the neighborhood is guilty of **blockbusting**. A lender who discriminates in making loans for properties in a particular neighborhood may be found guilty of **redlining**.

All communities feel that they have a need to address and control the general physical makeup of an area, such as what type and size of buildings shall be permitted. We call this method of control **zoning**. It is one of the most important and most complicated subjects that either consumers or professionals ever encounter. There are few topics that will draw so large a crowd and so many opposing views as a proposed change in the zoning of a lot or a block.

Few agents—much less consumers—ever develop any expertise on the subject of zoning, but it is still a topic that both parties should look into with each sale. A good place to start is with the tax records for the address. You might see a designation after the address that says "SF 7200." This means the property is designated for a Single Family residence and that lots on that block must be at least 7,200 square feet before a building permit will be issued. If a house is already standing and the lot is only 6,000 square feet, then we say that it has been **grandfathered**. If there is no house and no way to acquire any additional land, then you may apply for a **variance** to receive a building permit to build a house on this lot. Double-check any information from the tax records with the most recent zoning maps. As unfair as it may seem, it is unlikely that a city or county could be held liable for a mistake in the tax records. A variance is an admission by the authors of the zoning ordinances that they couldn't foresee all possibilities, but in most cases variances will only be granted for "small" deviations from the requirements.

Another common use of the variance is in the area of **setbacks**. A setback ordinance requires that **improvements**, i.e. man-made structures, be so many feet from property lines. If a new garage must be five feet from the neighbor's line, and the owner-builder wishes or needs to build closer to the line, then she may apply for a variance or work out an easement with her neighbor. An easement will most likely restrict the neighbor's use of that area of her property.

Grandfathered variances often carry a number of limitations. For example, a building may have to be demolished after so many years, or, if it is accidentally destroyed, rebuilding it may be denied. The people of South Carolina were shocked to learn after Hurricane Hugo in 1989 that many of their shoreline homes could not be rebuilt. A more common example of this problem is a small business located smack dab in the middle of a residential neighborhood. It was there when the zoning ordinances were passed, but it is now a **nonconforming use** and may face either a time limit or restrictions on enlargement, or on rebuilding if destroyed. It may face the loss of its current use when the property changes hands.

By virtue of its **police powers**, a community also has the right of **eminent domain** and the right to grant permits for **conditional use**. Eminent domain is claimed when the community condemns or takes a piece of property for the public good, such as a park or greenbelt, and compensates the owner. A conditional use permit might be granted when, again for the public good, a school is needed in an area of single-family homes.

One of the loudest outcries in the zoning wars occurs when a group of owners is told that they can no longer do something and that they will not be compensated for their loss of control or use. For example, owners on a block are told by the city that they can no longer erect any buildings at the west end of their properties because the city feels that this is a greenbelt that should be preserved for environmental reasons. If the courts rule that this was a **taking** by the city, then the city may be required to compensate the owners.

The **building code** is combined with and inseparable from the zoning ordinances. In fact, it is through the enforcement of the building code and the permit system for new construction or remodeling that much of the zoning system is controlled. A neighbor may complain about work that does not seem to be in keeping with neighborhood requirements, or a passing building inspector may see construction that requires a permit; if an investigation reveals that no permit was applied for or granted, then the inspector may **red tag** that project (or issue a **stop work** order). This invariably means that all work ceases until the permit has been granted. Of course, not all work requires a permit. Erecting a small fence or installing new kitchen cabinets does not typically require a permit, while installing a new window might, because by cutting a hole in the wall of a house we risk weakening the structure.

A **building inspector** is the person who has the authority to inspect new construction or a change in the use of a building, and then to issue a **certificate of occupancy**. This certificate is usually not required when you buy or sell a standing house, but if you intend to convert the house to a business or multi-family dwelling, the certificate is likely to be required and must be shown to all future purchasers. Savvy investors always ask to see this certificate for properties other than single-family dwellings.

If we happen to buy a house and lot in the city, and if that lot is large enough to equal two lots for that neighborhood, then we may **short plat** the extra lot and construct another house, or simply sell the extra lot, depending on the location of the original house. (A **plat** typically means a map showing property lines.) If the house straddles the proposed line between the two lots, then none of this may be possible. Just a few years ago, builders in Seattle would search out lots like this, demolish the house, and then erect two "skinny" houses, each 14'–15' wide, in its place. The uproar from the neighborhoods brought about restrictions on demolishing line-straddling houses, and this type of development quickly subsided.

Short-platting, which essentially means taking a shortcut through the red tape, is allowed when the developer intends to build on a relatively small number of lots, with the maximum being from 4 to 10 parcels in different parts of the state. In other words, if a developer bought 6 acres, and zoning allowed lots to be as small as one acre, the developer could short-plat the six-acre piece into six building lots. If she bought 12 acres, seeking 12 building lots, her permit application to create and plat these individual lots would probably require much more paperwork and research, and perhaps some form of Environmental Impact Statement.

One set of regulations that does not vary is the Washington Land Development Act, a consumer protection law that applies to the sale of unimproved lands in subdivisions of 10 or more lots, each of less than five acres. Remember the old scams of "lakefront property in Arizona, lots starting at only $1,500"? This law was passed to prevent such scams here. The Washington consumer must now be given a copy of a **property report**; otherwise the sale can be voided at any time. In any case the consumer has a 48-hour grace period in which to rescind the purchase.

A common misunderstanding is that consumers also have a 72-hour grace period on the typical **purchase and sale agreement** (**PSA**); they don't. (The right to rescind a contract for 72 hours was established more for door-to-door sales.) The PSA is often referred to in real estate slang as an **earnest money**. If you are from another state, you may have called this a **binder**. In any case, the PSA and the earnest money are actually two different things.

The PSA is a contract; payment of earnest money is an act of good faith that is not required to establish a valid contract. Some things, such as earnest monies and title insurance, are so traditional that consumers often assume they are required by law. They are traditional because, in general, they provide important benefits or protection for one or both parties. If an earnest money is included, and it almost always is, it can be cash, a promissory note, a check, or anything that the principals agree to. Most of the time it is cash or a check, and if the transaction involves a real estate agent, the broker of the selling agent is usually the one to deposit the money in a **trust fund**. If the amount is less than $5,000, the interest on the money will go into a state-controlled fund for housing and education, unless the buyer orders the agent to establish an interest-bearing account for the buyer. If the amount is over $5,000, the money's owner must be notified of the right to receive interest on it. The money can also be held by the lender or the escrow agent. Although the buyer could make out an earnest money check to the seller, most knowledgeable people would consider this somewhere between naive and foolish.

As the pressure builds for more housing in Western Washington, we are likely to see more of another type of zoning response: the **planned unit development** (**PUD**). A PUD is usually a large subdivision in which the houses are clustered close together to provide for more greenspace. If a buyer is looking for the type of residence known as a **townhouse**, she might find this in a PUD situation. A townhouse is similar to a condo in that it shares a common wall with one or more units, and owners may pay dues for maintenance and insurance of common areas. It differs from a condo in that it is more likely to have two floors, plus its own exterior entrance and private yard.

A type of housing that physically resembles the condo or townhouse, but which differs dramatically in use, is the **timeshare condominium**. The timeshare situation has provided more than its share of consumer abuse and high-pressure sales tactics, but it also meets the needs of some city dwellers. More information will be found in the Appendix under "Condos."

Timeshares are covered under the Washington Timeshare Act of 1983, which protects the consumer by requiring the sellers to provide detailed information on the development, and by allowing the purchaser seven days to cancel the agreement, either after signing the purchase agreement or after receiving the disclosure document, whichever comes later.

---

**TOGETHER ADD LAST?**

Washington is a community property state, which means that, generally, property acquired during marriage is jointly owned. Most consumers know this but don't know much about the details. Either party in a marriage may also own property "for his/her estate alone," either acquired during or before the marriage. My fishing guide has a sad tale to tell: He gave his second wife a check to mail for the mortgage payment on a house he owned before they married. She deposited the check in her account and wrote her own check for the payment. The divorce court ruled that the house had become community property. We catch more fish if we don't talk about this. (According to one legal opinion, this change in ownership would not happen in every case.) Partners or unmarried people can also buy property together, but their rights may be murky if they do not have an attorney advise them on how to take possession—whether as tenants in common (who can each **devise** [will] or sell their share) or as joint tenants (who would inherit each other's share). In addition, couples should have an outline of a buy-sell agreement in case things don't work out. In some transfers of property, a former partner or spouse may be asked to **quitclaim** his or her interest, if any, in the property, so as prevent any future claims by them. A quitclaim can be very valuable or totally worthless, depending on whether any interest existed or whether the property had any value (the liens may surpass the value).

---

There are three different types of ownership of timeshares, so the consumer would do well to investigate this acquisition thoroughly and to consult with an attorney with experience in this area. Many owners will tell you that a timeshare should be thought of as an expenditure, not as an investment; in fact, one type of timeshare ownership does not allow for the building of any **equity** in the property.

Equity is that portion of the value of any piece of real estate that is "unencumbered" by charges against it, be they a **mortgage** or other **liens**. We acquire equity by (1) making a down payment, (2) making payments on a mortgage ("equity buildup"), (3) letting a property appreciate, and (4) making improvements to the property ("sweat equity").

The word "mortgage" is so commonly used to mean a loan, or the balance of a loan, that many people are not aware that it originally meant—and still does—a document describing the terms of an agreement and serving as the lender's security.

MORTGAGE: THE DEATH (MORT) OF A DEBT OR PLEDGE (GAGE). THE SAME IDEA IS FOUND IN "TO AMORTIZE", TO KILL OFF IN EQUAL PAYMENTS.

A mortgage is a voluntary lien involving only two parties, the borrower (mortgagor) and the lender (mortgagee). (Mnemonic tip: Mortgagee and lender have two 'e's, borrower and mortgagor have two 'o's.)

Although the word itself remains in common use, the same cannot be said for the document, at least not the one typically used a few decades ago. Because it requires a **judicial foreclosure**—i.e. going to court to force a **sheriff's sale** of the property—and because the borrower may have 8–12 months after the sale to **redeem** the property, it is not a document that lenders prefer when they can instead use a **deed of trust** (**DOT**), or **trust deed**. Technically, the DOT is a three-party mortgage, in that the title passes to the buyer.

The DOT is presently the most common document for closing residential transactions in Washington. In the event of a default by the buyer, it allows for a nonjudicial foreclosure, i.e. a **trustee**, invariably an attorney, can force a **trustee's sale** (auction) simply by following a formula for informing the **grantor** (borrower) of the **beneficiary's** (lender's) intentions to take back the property.

Whereas a judicial foreclosure may literally drag through the courts for years, a DOT foreclosure will usually be over in a matter of around seven months, if the trustee is punctual. However, if a lender should wish to obtain a **deficiency judgment** against the borrower, a court action would ensue in either case. A lender might pursue a deficiency judgment if he feared that sales proceeds would not cover the balance due. Few lenders will make this effort, especially since **mortgage insurance** would most likely cover the lender's losses.

A third type of documentation for selling a property is the **real estate contract** (**REC**). The REC is used primarily in private transactions involving only the seller and the purchaser. This agreement seems to be known by over 50,000 other names, from **land contract** to **installment sale**. Though they are quite different, REC and DOT are used interchangeably in slanguage when discussing private transactions, or in advertisements where the seller means **creative (private) financing**. No buyer or seller should enter into either without discussing with an attorney the ramifications of these two different documents.

In the past, the REC was similar to the mortgage in that it required a judicial foreclosure, but as of January 1986, the seller can pursue a nonjudicial foreclosure if he waives his right to a deficiency judgment. This procedure can be completed in as little as four months, after which the buyer cannot redeem the property by coming up with the amount due.

Other than default by the buyer, i.e. failure to pay on time, reasons that a property might be foreclosed upon include **due-on-sale clauses** or a lien, such as property taxes that have not been paid in a timely manner and/or failure to keep the property insured.

A due-on-sale clause simply states that if the borrower **alienates** the property (to plain-talking folks like you and me, that means "sells the property," or "transfers any portion or interest in the property"), the balance of the loan is immediately due. If there is such a clause, then the chances of an **assumption**, i.e. taking over the owner's payments, are almost nonexistent.

A lien on a property is not necessarily a problem. Property taxes are the most common lien, and as long as they are paid on time, we encounter no complications. A mortgage is also a lien. But other liens, such as a judgment or a **mechanic's lien** (more accurately called a materialman's or labor lien), could even force us into a sale. A carpenter who has worked on a house but has not been paid must file the mechanic's lien within 90 days and foreclose within eight months. A judgment lien remains on a property for 10 years. The details of a judgment lien, too lengthy to be summarized here, are described in Tonnon.

Many of the terms used in real estate are not as clear as we would like, and are often quite different from their common or historical usage. One such example is the **homestead law**. This term conjures up pictures of wagons of pioneers racing across the plains to Yakima to make claim to 640 acres, then sobering up and racing back to civilization. In fact, homestead laws exist to protect the homeowner against some types of liens, in recognition that the need to provide shelter for a family is on a par with the payment of debts. A maximum of $30,000 of the value of the property is exempted; any amount over that could be awarded to the judgment holder. However, this exemption does not exist when the foreclosure involves or is due to any of the following: a mortgage or DOT, a mechanic's lien, child support, or a tax lien. What's left? In other words, the homestead law provides limited protection, primarily against judgment liens.

As you can see, liens are very important, and can be quite a complication, so it is very important that we learn all about them when a property changes hands by having a **title search** done. This is no game for amateurs. Even professionals manage to overlook title problems. But the most thorough title search has only temporary value; it tells us only what the searcher has found up to the moment. If we are going to be protected against things that may be recorded or discovered later in the day, then we will want at least a **standard policy of title insurance**. If we want to be protected against unrecorded liens or boundary problems, then we must pay for an **extended policy**.

Our primary interest in all of this is acquiring a **clear title**. This does not necessarily mean ownership without any liens. Property tax liens will always remain, although all taxes owed by the seller will need to be prorated and paid up to the day of transferring the property. Other liens may also be assumed by the buyer, with the buyer's knowledge and approval, provided that a lender does not object.

We are interested not only in whether we get a clear title, but in whether we get a title at all. In slanguage, we ask, "Does title pass?" If we use an REC, the answer is no. DOT? Yes. In other words, in the case of the REC, the property will remain in the name of the seller until all payments have been made. This can be a severe limitation on the buyer's use and enjoyment of the property, and can even prevent refinancing. It is one of many reasons why both the buyer and the seller must rely on legal expertise in the sale of properties. As we have already noted, the process of transferring property can be called "alienation." We have to wonder if the attorneys weren't indulging in a little humor when they chose this word, which certainly describes the mood of many a buyer and seller, even when everything is "perfectly legal" (oops, another oxymoron worms its way into the language).

# DRAFTING YOUR REAL ESTATE TEAM

**O**K, you're the new quarterback. You run onto the field and call the next play. You don't know any of the players, and they're not wearing numbers. You tell a tackle to go out for a pass, and a wide end to center on three. The whole team takes one look at you and goes out for a drink.

That's the way a real estate transaction can go if you don't know how to recruit your real estate team. You need to know the abilities and limitations of each of the players, and you generally have to accept the inevitability of working with some of them. On occasion, I have met a chip-on-the-shoulder macho-mouth who actually believes that he can totally avoid the players or treat them with contempt, and they'll still want to help him win. He'll be humble before we're finished with him.

But do you have to kowtow to the players? Will you have to abide by their whims? Of course not. You're still the quarterback. But plan on being pleasant for maximum yardage and, whatever you do, don't look for ways to get any of these players to work for free. Your motives will be obvious from the start and you'll just get what you paid for.

How big is the team? City teams will frequently involve 10 to 14 people, including the buyer. Small town teams may be half that size. Can a transaction come to pass that involves only a buyer and seller? It's legally possible, but I've seen consumers lose their shirts by not paying for the buttons. One of my former students avoided using an attorney and a title company, temporarily saving $600. Permanent losses amounted to $15,000. A friend chose not to have a $250 inspection. Permanent cost: around $20,000 (roof collapsed within six months). Those are just two of hundreds of examples of people behaving about as intelligently as someone trying to patch a leak in a yacht with paper towels.

## TWO RULES

**1. Ask somebody.** Don't make a move in real estate without conferring with somebody more experienced.

**2. Ask somebody *before* you make a move!** Funny, huh? I get calls every week from people who ask me, "Did we do the right thing?" In many cases one little phone call could have saved their bacon. Now even an attorney might tell them it's too late.

## A SUMMARY

Here is a list of most of the players. A more detailed description of their responsibilities will follow. They are listed in the order in which they would generally enter into the transaction or relationship with a home buyer.

1. **Real estate agent.** Could be either a listing or selling agent.

2. **Attorney.** If one is hired by the buyer.

3. **Structural inspector.** Ditto.

4. **Loan officer.** Takes the loan application.

5. **Processor.** Processes the loan application.

6. **Appraiser.** May be lender's employee or independent.

7. **Pest inspector** and/or **repair people.** Depending on what the appraiser or structural inspector finds.

8. **Title representative.** Orders title search of property.

9. **Underwriter.** Another lender employee. Decides if a buyer is a good risk for a loan.

10. **Closing agent/escrow person.** May be an independent attorney or escrow officer, or lender's escrow officer.

## A CLOSER LOOK

**Agents.** Since agents are involved in approximately four out of five transactions, it is probably to the buyer's advantage to learn the details of their qualifications and abilities (Chapter 3) rather than try to avoid them and limit yourself only to owner-sold properties. In Chapter 5, "Buyer Brokering," we'll go into detail on the legal obligations of the various agents, whose interests the agents must legally represent, and some strategies the consumer can adopt. For now we will just present an outline of the relationship the consumer is most likely to have with an agent.

If you are driving down the street and see a "for sale" sign in a yard, and underneath it is the name and home number of an agent, you have just learned the name of the **listing agent.** This is the individual who signed a contract with the owner, on behalf of the real estate company, to market the seller's property.

You may call this individual for information on that property, or if the area has a multiple listing service (MLS), then the odds are you can call any agent in the area and get information about the property ("Exclusive Listing" on the sign explains the seller's relationship with the agent. It does not mean that only that company can show the property. Explained in Chapter 14, "To List or Resist.") This is because if the listing company belongs to the MLS, it will have shared its information on that property via computer and bulletins. See Chapter 4, "Strategies for Buyers."

No matter which agent you call, if you wish to make an offer on that property, the agent who writes up your offer and presents it to the seller will be known as the **selling agent,** even if she is also the listing agent.

If the selling agent doesn't discuss whom she represents, and if she doesn't officially agree to represent the buyer, then she is assumed to be representing the seller. If she has a contract with the buyer to represent him, she is still the selling agent, but she would also be known as a **buyer broker** in this one transaction. This will be described in detail in Chapter 4.

The following would pretty much describe the traditional division of labor for the listing and selling agents in most parts of the state. The listing agent is in charge of advising the seller on preparing and pricing the property for the market, advertising, answering queries from other agents or consumers, providing access to the property, and representing the seller in negotiations.

The selling agent has probably already shown the buyers other properties, perhaps accompanied them on a visit to a lender, and once a suitable property has been found and an agreement has been negotiated, she will coordinate the activities between lender, appraiser, title company, repair people, and the closing agent. Unless some complication arises, the listing agent is no longer involved in the details of closing the transaction and can generally turn her attention to other clients.

**Attorneys.** Did you hear the one about the attorney who swam through a school of sharks, was substituted for a guinea pig, or was buried 40 feet underground? You probably have. This group has long been the focus of a great deal of black humor. You can substitute other occupations in these jokes, but unfortunately no one laughs as hard. I say unfortunately because it must mean we generally share a rather dim view of what attorneys do. Indeed, they are a very powerful group of people who could do a great deal more good. Sort of like body-builders: Despite all that strength and effort, nothing much is accomplished.

Like all groups, with the exception of pimps and hit men, there are some really wonderful members who can offer us a great deal of protection, and at a price that comes close to being a bargain. Sadly, attorneys are the most-likely-to-be-omitted members of the team. Consumers are terrified of any professionals who charge $100 an hour, no matter how fast they talk.

In Chapter 12, "From Offer to Closing" on contracts, you will see that I recommend using an attorney for "escrow," i.e. for drawing up the final documents and figures for the closing ceremony. If you're from Eastern Washington, you may look at me as if I'm crazy, since that's already the norm in much of that area. However, in Western Washington, either the lender's own escrow officer or an independent escrow officer will typically perform this service.

The point is, the cost for an attorney or escrow officer will generally be the same, but by choosing an attorney instead of an escrow officer to do the closing, the consumer can obtain some legal guidance. Some. You should never make the mistake of calling the escrow attorney *your* attorney. An escrow attorney is not normally going to takes sides. She can answer both parties' legal queries, but she would not normally be an advocate for either party. However, if the buyers had already retained her as an attorney, say for a will or partnership agreement, she could still handle the closing, as long as everything was disclosed to the seller and the seller agreed.

One of the most common questions I hear from my students is "Should we have an attorney?" The next question is "How do we find a good one?" The first question is relatively easy and can be answered with a straight face. Yes, theoretically, you should retain an attorney before you make or accept any offers, and then make each offer subject to your attorney's approval. But theory often takes a back seat to economy and practicality.

In transactions that include both lender-financing and agents, there are frequently so many safeguards in place that the vast majority close without any legal complications. But who wants to be in the minority? Also, after you read about the typical agent's qualifications you may not feel so secure.

Regardless of all these caveats, most of my own clients have chosen not to use an attorney, except the attorney used for the closing. However, if the transaction involves seller-financing, an assumption, or a dual agency, or if any other legal complexity arises, I insist that they visit the nest of a legal-eagle.

Some agents will do their best to keep you away from an attorney, but this isn't even in their own interest. They just don't have enough experience or good sense to know it. Why do they do this? Fear. Fear that the attorney will tell you the contract is no good, or that you should have negotiated something that was omitted. In other words, they're afraid the agreement will come unglued. Better now in the office than later in the courtroom, I say.

Agents have at least one legitimate fear: an incompetent attorney. Not just one who doesn't know much real estate law, but one who also steps out of line and talks about the neighborhood or price instead of sticking to legal issues, or who advocates a negotiating stance that is impractical. I have seen an out-of-touch attorney tell her client to play hardball with a builder, and then watched it backfire when the builder played harderball. The client did not want to pay that attorney's bill, and I certainly didn't include her on my Christmas card list.

I've taught real estate classes where as many as 10% of my students were attorneys. When I ask them why they are in my class, since I myself am just a lowly first-year law school dropout, they answer, "Because we don't know anything about real estate."

"Thank you," I respond. "Your fellow students needed to hear it."

The point is: Attorneys specialize. In fact, my inclination is to avoid attorneys who don't specialize. "Oh, you handle patent applications, DWIs, and real estate? Good, I was accused of being drunk when I drove my new perpetual motion machine across my neighbor's easement. You're just the person I need."

Even if an attorney does specialize in real estate, it could be years before he or she has the in-depth experience necessary to steer our ship through reef-ridden waters. So, a few gray hairs may be reassuring.

There seems to be one never-die myth out there: The lender will have your documents reviewed by an attorney, so you really don't have to worry about it. Nonsense! Any such review, if one ever takes place, would be to protect the lender, not you.

In conclusion, yes, you should consult a highly competent real estate attorney for every transaction, but especially for those situations where highly ethical and experienced lenders and agents are not involved, and doubly especially when either the lender's or the agent's qualifications are in doubt.

*Who?* If you are now convinced to budget a few hundred dollars for a good attorney, how do you find such an animal?

First, forget the referral systems. Local bar associations will frequently offer a referral service. Are you as skeptical as I am about indulging in this potluck?

I want my professionals to come highly recommended by someone I highly respect. The old word-of-mouth system is still the best strategy. But you may not believe that you know anyone who can help. You don't know until you've asked.

OK, you've asked 10 friends and not one has a recommendation. Next, you and I would probably ask a professional who would have a reason to know. Who would have the highest motivation to know a competent attorney, one who can prevent problems or salvage complicated entanglements? The obvious answer is a real estate agent. Since we know that many agents fear and avoid attorneys, we can accomplish two goals at once by seeking out agents wise enough to have found the best attorneys.

Now an additional complication: In theory, an agent should never recommend an attorney. One of Seattle's best-known real estate attorneys has even advised agents not to furnish a list of recommended attorneys. If we do we may incur liability for their actions. We also have a potential conflict of interest, since our recommendation can compromise the independence and interests of the consumer, especially if we recommend an attorney who courts the agent by avoiding any controversial positions. "Hand 'em the Yellow Pages," our legal expert seems to be saying.

I think I'm fairly idealistic about the need to avoid conflict of interest, but this Yellow Pages approach goes beyond my idealism and enters the realm of denying my clients access to practical information. Yes, it may be theoretically correct, but one of the most important services an agent offers his clients is the experience he's gained from the school of hard knocks, about who is and who isn't competent. I don't want to see my own clients get involved with second-rate professionals.

So here is the compromise I've worked out for myself: I tell my own agents never to "recommend" an attorney, inspector, or lender, but merely to say. "These are the names of professionals with whom we have had a good experience, but of course we can't predict or take responsibility for their future actions, and we urge you to make your own selection, either from among those we know or those your friends have recommended."

*When?* Find both the good agent and attorney just as soon in life as you can. Consult with both, if just for a very short visit, right at the start of the search. Then, when and if you make an offer, use the language the attorney gave you to make the offer, "subject to my attorney's approval by such and such a date." Just before closing, take the documents to the attorney for a final review. Three visits to the attorney = three to six hours = three to six hundred dollars = Peace of Mind.

**Structural inspectors.** Generally it is the buyer who hires an inspector to check a property for structural integrity and/or remodeling feasibility. Sellers rarely have an inspection prior to an offer, and even if they did, would a buyer want to rely on the seller's inspector?

Structural inspectors need X-ray vision and omniscience, but unfortunately they are human and lack both. And like humans in all other professions, their competence and education range from amazing to crazing. At this time, anyone who wants to inspect houses in the state of Washington can do so without having to meet any competency requirements. However, if an inspector who is not an engineer, architect, or building code inspector concludes, for example, that a beam in the basement is adequate for its load, he is in effect practicing engineering, which is as illegal as practicing medicine without a license. Enforcement is spotty to nonexistent.

In most parts of Washington a buyer wanting an inspection is most likely to turn to a friend or family member who has a little construction knowledge. That's understandable, but the war stories we can tell about these homegrown inspections would peel your paint. They range from amateur inspectors having overlooked major problems to having been so picayune that the buyer became terrified about a fairly normal house. Fathers who inspect for their daughters are the worst. Daddy has to be Daddy, even if daughter is the 45-year-old president of Engineers Conglomerate, Inc.

Only in the Seattle and Vancouver/Portland areas does it seem to be anywhere near the norm to have an inspection, and these cities' Yellow Pages have about 60 listings under "Building Inspection Service." The Spokane phone book has fewer than half a dozen listings in this category, and I was told of one Spokane inspector who had recently given up for lack of business.

One caveat in choosing an inspector is to avoid any conflict of interest. A contractor who stands to get work if she discovers a serious problem may "look

too hard." If you have to use a contractor, tell her she will not get any work at this time, and neither will anyone she recommends, unless you specifically ask her for a recommendation. Some inspectors make it a policy never to recommend anyone.

Of course, the most important requisite is competence—if we could just agree on what that is. I believe competence is a combination of experience and education. I have concluded that the best inspectors are generally civil engineers who have hands-on experience in residential construction and who have served an apprenticeship to another inspector. Out of the 60 or so companies in the Seattle area, a total of perhaps 12 inspectors from four or five companies fit that description. The rest of them can send their hate mail to the address at the back of the book. Postage due.

Quite a number of the contractors who do inspections often imply, or even state outright, that the engineers are just pointy-headed theoreticians who don't know a sawzall from a seesaw. But in my experience as a broker and an expert witness in lawsuits, the defendants have consistently been contractors who have experience but no formal education in engineering, and also no shyness in guessing about what they don't know. Thus it has long been my policy to influence my clients to use an engineer, or perhaps an architect, even though I know a couple of outstanding contractor-inspectors. There are several reasons for this: (1) my own liability if I recommend anyone not up to the challenge; (2) the lender's requirement of an inspection by an engineer if a structural problem is discovered by the appraiser; and (3) the occasional, unexpected problems that arise which only an engineer or architect is legally qualified to analyze.

Some years back, Washington's own Department of Licensing, with some prompting from engineers, urged all agents to recommend the use of an engineer. A battle royal ensued. The nonengineers sued the engineers (for interfering with their ability to make a living). The engineers countersued. The suits sit. Only the attorneys are smiling.

Many nonengineer inspectors have made an attempt to establish some legitimacy and professionalism in their vocation by joining a national organization known as the American Society of Home Inspectors (ASHI). It may be a small step in the right direction, but ASHI has no standards for candidates, and full-fledged membership can be gained without any formal education just by having done a certain number of inspections. That's a bit too much like my own profession, where we often learn our business at the expense of the consumer.

The great irony is that even if the state strictly interpreted the law to say that an inspection by a nonengineer constitutes the unauthorized practice of engineering, there simply aren't enough engineer-inspectors to go around. Why would an engineer take a job crawling under houses when he can work indoors with an electric pencil-sharpener and a chair that swivels?

*How much?* Engineers in the Seattle area generally charge in the $200–$350 range to inspect an average house, and the other inspectors usually follow suit. I have seen a contractor charge as little as $100, but the consumer got just what she paid for: gross incompetence.

*How long?* Most inspections will take from two to three hours. If you're there, you'll get an oral report on the spot. Many inspectors will deliver or fax a written report to you in 24–48 hours. In many cases your time restrictions in your contract with the seller may force you to accept or reject the house based on the oral report.

---

### 🏠  🏠  🏠
### CONTRACTORS' CREDENTIALS?

In the state of Washington, there are no competency requirements for contractors. No tests. No resumes. Just a bond. California is one of the few states that require a written test.

---

*When?* Generally, the inspection takes place within a few days after the seller and buyer have reached an agreement. Buyers often ask, "Should we ever get a house inspected before we make an offer on it?" That would seem to make sense, but what if someone else buys it while you're poking around in the attic, and what if you and the seller don't agree on the price after you've already paid for an inspection? No, probably best to continue the tradition of doing it after an agreement has been hammered out.

*What if it's bad news?* Expect some bad news; you're paying someone to look for it, and perfect houses are about as common as flying snakes. If it's *really* bad news and you can't live with the problems, then simply bail out (if the terms of your contract allow that). If you're lucky, you may be able to sell your inspection to the seller, but don't get your hopes up. Will you get your earnest money back? You should, if your contract included the proper language and you met the deadlines.

Will the inspector recommend repair people if there are problems that need correcting? As I mentioned before, some inspectors feel that to do so is both a potential liability and a compromise of their objectivity and independence. Respect this; it is idealistic.

*Who goes?* The buyers should be there, full of curiosity and dressed in old clothes. The seller should not be there. Daddy and friends should be at work.

How about the agent? Yes, if the buyer feels that the agent will help the buyer think of things to ask; no, if the buyer is the least bit concerned about the agent's ability to remain in the background and accept the findings with equanimity.

*Reopen the bargaining?* Don't get an inspection with the idea that you're going to pummel the seller with nickel-dime discoveries. Do it for the noblest of reasons, and for peace of mind. If the problems discovered are truly serious, then of course you are within your rights to return to the bargaining table.

*Hot-market problems?* Yes, often in Seattle's fast-moving market, where multiple offers are common, at least one of the bidders will not ask for a structural inspection, thereby gaining a bidding advantage. This is not to the seller's advantage, no matter what a seller thinks! A structural inspection protects a seller (and the agents) as well as a buyer. Show this paragraph to any seller who is looking at multiple offers. My expert-witness experiences have consisted primarily of situations where there was either no inspection or a poor one, and where the sellers did not fully disclose problems. A seller should actually insist on an inspection, especially since buyers are generally prepared to pay for them.

**Lenders.** You might already have made a commitment to a particular lender weeks before you make an offer. Many buyers just talk to several lenders over the phone and leave the choice until later. Once an offer has been accepted you must then make a formal loan application, if you haven't already done so. If Seattle's hot market remains at its feverish pitch, it may become commonplace to apply in advance.

The lender usually takes a good-sized check from you, in the $300–$500 range, to cover an appraisal, credit check, and preliminary title report. It is not unusual to have an inspection performed on or about the same day as the loan application. Therefore, you may want to ask the lender if you can make the application but put everything on hold until the inspection is completed and accepted. Most lenders will agree to hold your check until they're given the green light.

You have now added a lender to your team, but he will also be the leader of his own team, most of whose members you will never meet. Nevertheless, we should learn about the lender's employees, for reasons that will soon be obvious.

Before we do this, I want to reveal my own bias about a choice of lender; I hope the choice will not be based solely, or even primarily, on the lender's fees or interest rates. Many lenders are willing to negotiate a bit on fees and rates if the applicant has sufficient spine to ask them to, and has shopped around and knows the competition. Since all lenders buy their money from the same warehouse, it's rare to find any major differences among rates (the bigger difference is probably in fees). And what good is a great rate if a lender's incompetence somehow leads to a voided contract? From my viewpoint, the best measure in choosing a lender is their competency in the paperwork realm.

Why is this? Don't all lenders do about the same thing? Yes, just as all members of the NFL play football. But some do it much better than others, year after year. How bad can lenders be? I've seen two different lenders try to close transactions without revealing liens on the properties. I've seen a lender lose a client's entire file and then spend weeks searching for it, rather than admit the loss, fill out new forms, and keep the train on schedule. Quite a number of lenders are so bad about returning phone calls, keeping promises, and meeting deadlines that I honestly don't see how they stay in business. The S & L industry's problems did not come as any surprise to those of us who regularly work with lenders.

And, like choosing an attorney, the best practical way to find a good lender is to ask someone who has frequent contact with them and whose livelihood may occasionally depend on them. Attorneys and agents are two groups who meet these criteria. Appraisers are another group who often have insight into which lenders are the most reliable. They also know which lenders have the strictest requirements and the most conservative appraisal standards.

What type of lender? We have credit unions, savings and loans, commercial banks, mortgage brokers, mortgage bankers, and more. First of all, although credit unions are generally very fair with their members, they are not my first choice, simply because they usually don't handle enough real estate loans to become proficient with the details. This shortcoming often afflicts our friendly neighborhood banks as well. Just as I recommend choosing an attorney who specializes, I recommend going to lenders who specialize in real estate, the mortgage brokers and mortgage bankers.

The lender's representative you are most likely to talk with is called a **loan officer** (or **loan rep**). Most loan officers are actually commissioned salespeople. Their duties include explaining their types of loans, taking your application, and coordinating the communication with the appraiser, processor, etc. Unless the loan officer is also an owner, he or she will probably not have much to do with deciding whether you get your loan. In fact, once the application has been taken, many loan officers virtually disappear and a processor becomes the central figure or coordinator.

Here are six questions that you may want the loan officer to answer:

**1.** Are you a mortgage broker, or a mortgage banker? A broker may not have any actual money to lend, but instead has a working relationship with numerous lenders who do. The broker should know of many different loan programs, and match your needs with the most appropriate loan. A mortgage banker, on the other hand, may have his own money and still be able to broker to other lenders if the need arises. Theoretically, the broker has the lesser conflict of interest, whereas the banker might have a bit more control if the loan is "in-house." In reality, I have found outstanding lenders in both categories, and no consistently discernible difference in their fees.

Can a consumer be her own mortgage broker, i.e. by going directly to the lenders? Theoretically, yes, but so far I haven't seen any reason to do it; lenders do not generally reward this enterprising consumer by reducing fees or rates.

**2.** Are you approved for FHA "direct endorsement" or VA "automatic approval"? In other words, has this lender been qualified by those government agencies to make an FHA or VA loan without having to submit the paperwork to that agency? One less bureaucracy means several weeks saved on the loan processing and one less chance for a bureaucrat to meddle.

**3.** Where is your processing office? My own agents have found one lender much too difficult to work with because the processing office is located 10 miles away from the central office, which means that calls and paperwork must frequently be duplicated; all too often items in transmission seem to disappear or arrive late.

**4.** To what extent is your processing done by computer? The best processors I have dealt with are able to handle 70 – 80 transactions at a time, twice what the noncomputerized processors can juggle. The computerized processors should be best able to track incoming data.

**5.** How will you keep me informed of our progress? One lender sends out a weekly update that has proven to be so valuable and popular that it is probably one of the reasons this company has become a major lender in less than five years. Why don't other companies copy this method? Everyone thinks his mousetrap is the best.

**6.** Could I have the names and phone numbers of three or four buyers whose loans have closed in the last month? If a company agrees to do this, of course they will handpick borrowers they believe to have been satisfied. But they might be amazed to learn how many consumers will keep a thousand gripes to themselves until another consumer asks for an opinion.

Unfortunately, all the questions in the world may not expose a shoddy outfit. In the end, the best source of information is still someone who has worked with a lender on more than one occasion, and that person is an agent or attorney.

**Processors.** Processors are the lender's employees who assemble all of the documents required for a loan. They are the only team members worthy of sainthood. In my experience, if you really want to find the best lenders you will interview the processors, not the loan officers. Regrettably, there is no practical way to do this.

In my first year as an agent I kept relying on the loan officers for information. After a while I realized that some of them didn't really know the status of their own loans at any given moment—they were too busy trying to drum up new business—so I started calling the processors directly. That was when I learned who the truly important people are in lending.

After a year and a half, I found one of the best processors in the business, and wherever she worked, that's where I hoped my buyers would take their business. When she retired I went into a state of panic. Fortunately, her replacement soon proved to be her equal.

The processor's job is just what it sounds like: ordering the appraisal, informing all parties of work orders, verifying employment and bank accounts, requesting the title search, etc. Eventually she will assemble the "loan package." Once the package is complete, she will present it to the underwriter.

**Appraisers.** Appraisers are people who profess to be able to tell us what a property is worth, no matter what the rest of the world thinks. We might say they give us the "lie of the land." Until 1991, anyone who could afford business cards and a tape measure could be an appraiser, on the spot. One of my students drove me to tears one night when she insisted that she would get a "licensed appraiser" to tell her what the price of a house should be. When I told her for the third time that there was no such thing as a licensed appraiser, she said, "There must be!" I suppose it's hard to believe that someone with so much power isn't regulated, but this is common throughout American business.

Beginning in the summer of 1991, after years of nonregulation, all Washington appraisers must be tested and licensed. There won't be any "grandfathering"; i.e. no oldtimers will be assumed to be competent and automatically issued a license.

Usually within two to four days of receiving a loan application, the processor orders an appraisal. If the loan is FHA or VA, she makes a phone call to the appropriate government agency and requests an appraisal. The government clerk then looks up the address to see if an appraisal was done in the last six months. If one has been done, it is still valid and the lender must base any loan amount on it. Of course, in a fiery seller's market, an appraised value several months old may lag far behind the asking price, but until the six-month period has passed, we are stuck with that verdict. Few sellers know this. Instead they assume that a new appraisal will produce a new and better figure than they got when their last offer fell through, and they often accept a second offer without revealing that one just weeks or months earlier was voided.

If there is no prior appraisal, then an appraiser is chosen from an "approved" list and assigned to the job. He or she is not an employee of the government, but merely someone who has met the government's requirements, usually by having been in the business for at least five years and not being wanted in more than a few states.

If the loan is "conventional," then the lender can choose the appraiser. Some lenders keep one or more appraisers on staff, but many hire independent persons. Since a major responsibility of the appraiser is to keep the lender from loaning too much money on any one property, you would think that lenders would always want an independent appraiser. On the other hand, lenders have found it to their advantage to have a staff appraiser who will give the lender's needs immediate attention.

In addition to arriving at the market value of the property, the appraiser usually has to determine if any structural, zoning, or boundary problems exist. If yes, then we face one or more "work orders." Work orders can range from a $5 light switch to a $10,000 roof repair. Chapter 8, "Evaluating: Work Orders," gives details about this.

NOTE: More than one consumer has told me that her property was "inspected" by an appraiser, and therefore a separate inspection would be redundant. Appraisers typically spend 20–60 minutes at a site, and half of that time is spent rolling up the tape measure. Even if they could spend the time necessary for a thorough inspection, 95% of them do not have the training or background to perform this task.

In Chapter 6, "Evaluating: Price," we will examine how an actual appraisal is done.

**Pest inspectors.** A pest inspector may be called into a transaction either as a result of an appraiser's work order or as a requirement by the underwriter. The request for a pest inspection is often a reasonable admission by the appraiser that he suspects a problem but lacks the expertise to determine what it is, or the extent of it.

Pest inspectors do not have to have any particular credentials to do the inspection portion of their work, but if they apply insecticides or recommend a treatment, then they must be licensed by the Washington Department of Agriculture. Sometimes we see advertisements for "structural inspectors" who claim to be "licensed." The license to apply insecticides does not bestow the right to make structural conclusions. Only an engineer with a "Professional Engineer's (P.E.) Stamp," an architect, or a government building inspector is so authorized.

It would be ideal if highly competent pest inspectors had no potential conflict of interest, i.e. did not stand to gain by exaggerating a problem. But the number of pest inspectors who only do inspections is small.

The greatest advancement in this area has been the termite-sniffing dog. Unfortunately, these dogs are rare and expensive, and will most likely be sold and remain in the South, where there are both more termites and more people who pay dogs the homage they are due. Amen.

---

### REPARATIONS?

A number of consumers have asked me about the possibility of suing an appraiser or inspector if a problem surfaces later. Members of these professions, among others in real estate, generally see to it that language is included in their paperwork that makes them responsible only for remembering where they left their cars in the parking lot. If negligence is involved, however, the court may ignore such language.

Now ask any of the professionals if they are insured for their business behavior. Many agents carry E & O (errors and omissions) insurance, and it may be a criterion when you choose an agent, but in quite a number of these fields no such insurance exists. The members of those professions say, "Oh, we're self-insured." And probably self-approved, as well.

---

**Title reps.** This representative of the title company will be asked by the agent, lender, or closer to order a search of the legal status of the property and then deliver said search. As a group, these are the most cheerful people in the world of real estate. They obviously don't know what is going on.

The consumer almost never meets the title rep, but instead learns of any problems from the processor or agent. Maybe that's why these reps are so cheerful; they can let someone else deliver the bad news.

**Underwriters.** An underwriter assesses risk, and often is the main individual to decide whether you or I get a loan. Lenders frequently talk about the "loan committee's" decision, when in actuality the decision may have been made by an underwriter. Some lenders do have their loans reviewed by a select group of high-ranking employees, but those lenders who don't would like us to believe that a group of wise and fair-minded people passed judgment on our qualifications, that it wasn't made by just one person who may have been in a cranky mood or interpreted a rule very strictly.

Underwriters are frequently promoted to their positions after years of experience as processors. They need to to be extremely knowledgeable about the criteria of the secondary market (see Chapter 9, "Financing: The Basics") and the general rules of properly qualifying both the property and the buyer for a given loan.

When the loan package is complete and submitted to the underwriter, she will review it and say yea or nay, or, "Yea, if the following additional steps are taken." For example, she might note that the house has a crawlspace, but no pest inspection was performed, and thus insist on this step. She isn't just being petty. To some extent, an inspection offers protection for the buyer and seller, but the underwriter is also aware of the standards that must be met if the loan is to be sold on the secondary market.

The importance of an underwriter was summed up this way by a mortgage company owner when I asked him if he could overrule his underwriter: "Yes, but why would I? I pay her to make tough decisions."

**Closing agents.** In the state of Washington the principals involved in a real estate transaction can do their own closing, i.e. draw up the final figures and documents and record them in the appropriate hall of government. It's also legal to do your own dental work, which would probably be slightly more fun. Fortunately, very few people try to exercise this degree of self-reliance. Most gladly pay a qualified person to "do escrow." Who might that be? Either a licensed escrow officer—a Limited Practice Officer (LPO)—or an attorney.

As I said earlier, my own preference is to have an attorney do the closing so that when I ask a legal question I get an answer. But I know good agents who swear that attorneys as a rule are more likely to botch the final figures. So far, I've only caught one error—a mere $5,000 mistake—but it was the work of an LPO, not an attorney. Since many attorneys have the preliminary work done by an escrow officer anyway, I feel doubly sure that this combination is more likely to offer the highest degree of protection.

The cost of escrow is usually shared 50/50 by the buyer and seller, but this is based on tradition, not on any state requirement. On the other hand, both FHA and VA rules do address this area and specify who pays (the seller pays the entire amount in a VA transaction).

The sliding-scale fee of either an attorney or an escrow officer for a $100,000 house in Seattle averages around $600, whereas in the Spokane area the attorney's fee is more likely to be around $500.

## SUMMARY

Easily a dozen people may be involved in a modern real estate transaction. Transactions have become sufficiently complex to discourage all but the most determined from relying on themselves in the paperwork arena. Yet some of the professionals who would be offended if they were omitted from transactions have questionable credentials and go to some length to avoid liability for their actions. On the bright side, good help is available in every field, if the consumer looks in the right places and doesn't wait too long to find it. The best consumers still learn all they can for themselves about real estate, if for no other reason than to be able to recognize who is and who isn't competent.

# THE AGENT: INDISPENSABLE OR INDEFENSIBLE?

*Most people come into the business because they're undisciplined,*
*and fail for the same reason.* —Dave Page, broker

*Work with the best and starve the rest.* —Jim Stacey, broker

Agents are the people you hate to love, and the polls prove it. Agents consistently receive a 15% rating on trust and integrity except from the people they have just worked with. Then they earn closer to an 80% rating. Apparently, getting to know and working with agents raises people's trust and appreciation of them, if only temporarily. Other studies show that two years after a real estate transaction, consumers usually can't remember their agent's name.

What do I think of the hundreds of agents that I know as friends, antagonists, and students? I think they represent a cross section of America, ranging from outstanding humans all the way to slug slime. Some of my colleagues are as sweet and trustworthy as anyone on earth, but I have also known widow-muggers and an agent who used to steal all the prescription drugs in the medicine cabinets. My fishing partner is an agent, and neither he nor I has ever lied about the fish that got away. In fact, we've never had a fish get away. Really.

Yes, agents are more motivated by money than are many people, but they are also willing to work harder with less security in order to make it. Those who stick with this business must enjoy financial risk and adrenaline rushes, because their incomes rise and fall like a sprinter's chest. I've had to loan an agent gas money, only to see him receive over $20,000 in commissions a week later.

Agents as a group are not readers or good students (I know; I teach and administer their tests). Many of them feel threatened by a book like this because they think it makes them look bad. At the same time they are happy with the ridiculously easy educational requirements that they must fulfill to get into the business. Some worry about consumers knowing "too much," which may be an acknowledgment that their own knowledge is not very deep. Many didn't want to be interviewed for this book; perhaps they lacked confidence that they would be treated fairly.

As a group, agents are hard-working, a little bit creative but generally not deep or intellectual, a bit insecure but very interested in self-improvement and time-management, and more honest than most people give them credit for. A perfect cross section. And a great deal of the time they don't have any business doing what they do. The minute a Washington agent receives her license she has the legal credentials to sell a farm in Forks and a mall in Mt. Vernon. The state does not even have separate licenses for commercial and residential agents, though the work is usually as different as corn from cob. And what did the typical agent have to do to get that license? Typically, she spent 30 hours in a classroom, and perhaps the same amount of time studying for the state real estate exam (the equivalent of about two weeks of high school). It is literally harder to get a job clipping poodles than it is to become an agent, even though an agent immediately has the power to destroy a consumer's assets and peace of mind. Once agents are experienced and skilled, they can perform extremely valuable services; until then they should have to carry a hall pass.

One of the best-intentioned state laws is that an agent must be supervised by a broker, i.e. she must "hang her license" with a company. She may physically work out of her house but she must still answer to her broker, if the broker has any questions. A medium-large real estate office employs about 35 agents, but there are offices with over 100 agents, so some brokers have a devil of a time even knowing the names of all of their charges. In fact, one of the main reasons agents give for leaving a company is that their broker never had time for them.

One of the benefits and curses of the job is that the agent is technically an "independent contractor." This frequently encourages the attitude that the agent can do as she pleases, although that is not exactly the law's intent.

It does mean that she cannot be required to punch a clock, but it does not mean that she can ignore company policy or standards. Being independent certainly costs the agent, because she must pay all of her own Social Security, and "company benefits" may be limited to a heated workspace when the wind-chill factor is below 50 degrees.

Finally, at about the time an agent becomes valuable she quits; typically, less than 10% of agents stay with an office for more than two years.

## FINDING GOOD AGENTS

Agents are involved in almost 80% of the real estate transactions in this country, so avoiding them means limiting yourself to 20% of the available inventory. That's usually not the best course. Obviously, knowing good agents opens many doors for us. All puns intended. But there is no easy formula for finding them. If I said, "Only work with agents who have two years of experience," but your experienced agent proved to be unreliable or dishonest, you would have been better off with a new agent with integrity. Obviously, you want a combination of assets, some of which don't have a thing to do with experience or education.

There are two different considerations that are of equal importance if you are to have the optimum experience with agents: the agent's assets and your own behavior. It would be self-defeating for you to find a good agent and then behave in such a way as to make that agent want to run away.

First let's examine the search for the agent.

### TEN MEANS FOR MEASURING THE AGENT

**1.** Learn all the construction, financing, and contract terms you can. Unless you know the language, you won't recognize the con from the competent.

**2.** Go to open houses in a trial attorney's frame of mind, full of "stupid questions" that you already know the answers to. Act delighted when you get the right answer from the showing agent and just keep asking questions.

---

#### DISCLOSURE-ETHICAL BAROMETER?

You may remember that agents are required to disclose their allegiance (if any) to the seller prior to the purchase agreement. The earlier they do it, the more stars in their crown. The ones who wait until the last minute or don't do it at all shouldn't get your business.

---

**3.** Talk to friends who have bought or sold a property recently. Ask what kinds of complications came up, how they were handled, and if they would work with that agent again.

**4.** Ask for recommendations from professionals who encounter agents on a daily basis: loan officers, appraisers, and real estate attorneys.

**5.** Take note of the agents' business cards, or ask them what their level of training is, types of classes they have had, etc. Here are some typical titles and credentials found on business cards:

**Associate:** just an agent.
**Counselor:** just an agent.

**Associate Broker:** has broker's license, (2 years, 120 "clock hours," state exam), but continues as an agent (versus a broker-manager).

**Million Dollar Producer:** total value of all the properties agent sold in previous year—a good output in Walla Walla but can mean as few as two sales in Bellevue. Doesn't say anything about training, just energy or craftiness.

**GRI:** Graduate of the Realtor Institute—approximate equivalent of broker's training. Very few agents with less than two years of experience will have this.

**CRS:** Certified Residential Specialist—perhaps the equivalent of two GRIs.

**CRB:** Certified Residential Broker. Respectable.

**CCIM:** Certified Commercial Investment Member. Not likely to be involved in residential work.

---

### LOCAL AGENT?

One of the most frequently asked questions is how important is it to get an agent who lives or works in a given area. Obviously, there can be some benefits, but not nearly so many as in the good old days when an agent knew all the neighbors and all about the schools. Now we city agents probably won't even know which school your child will be bused to.

With the multiple listing service computer, however, we can pull up a ton of statistics on any area in a matter of minutes and become an instant expert. Just add water.

Here is a little study we did on a North Seattle neighborhood of around 10 square miles: Over a six-month period, 44 houses were listed by 28 companies, only 5 of which were in the area. The other 23 companies were located up to 20 miles away. No company showed any dominance of the area.

---

**6.** Take real estate classes, either for consumers or agents. Classmates or instructors will know of good agents. They might even be good agents.

**7.** Take advantage of the industry's referral systems. If you or a friend know a good agent who doesn't work in the neighborhoods that interest you, then ask for a referral. The first agent will probably receive a referral fee from the other agent, so he is motivated to both find you someone reliable and to keep in touch with that agent. You then have two agents you can ask for advice.

**8.** While still "shopping," make calls each day to any agents you are considering, either when you know they're not in, or with questions they will have to look up, and then note which ones are the best about getting back to you.

Promptness, reliability, and attention to detail are so important in our work that you can almost overlook some gaps in knowledge or experience.

**9.** Ask the agents if they carry E & O (errors and omissions) insurance.

**10.** Ask for references and ask how long the agent has been in the business, but keep in mind that the brighter agents learn 80% of their work in the first six months, whereas some of the worst agents I've ever met started their conversations with, "Well, I've been in the business for 20 years and I never heard of that." In the South, we called that showing your ignorance and being proud of it. A new, closely supervised agent is often better than these old mules who don't keep up.

**11.** Make sure in the larger cities that you only work with a full-time agent. Our neighbor to the north, British Columbia, thinks this dictum is so important that part-timers are not allowed in the business. But so-called free enterprise still reigns in Washington; "public experiment" would be a more accurate description. It is helpful, though, to be aware of the realities of the smaller towns. For example, in Dayton (Southeast Washington), a town of 2,500, where houses are slow to sell and the most expensive sale ever made in the town (through 1989) was only $85,000, I met an outstanding broker who survives because he combines residential and commercial real estate with his 300 acres of wheat farming.

BONUS: An agent who is also a homeowner may have more empathy with and understanding of the buyer's concerns (most buyers just assume that all agents are homeowners).

### COMPANY SIZE?

Some of the large realties have very good training programs; some don't. A company may be large because it's ruthless or because it's well-run. Some of the smaller companies have great brokers who supervise their agents like mother hens; some don't. A company may be small because it's ruthless, because it's young, or because it has a specialty. Size, then, is an unpredictable variable. So too is name recognition. Yes, larger companies usually do more business as a whole, but the volume per agent often doesn't correlate with the company's size.

Will larger companies be able to show the consumer more listings? In a multiple listing area we all have access to the same houses, with the only in-house advantage being first crack at new listings. Statistics indicate that small offices bring in just as many and often more listings and transactions per agent than even the best-known offices, some of which average less than one-fourth of a transaction per agent per month.

Do *not* place much importance on the size of the company or its name recognition. You are hiring an individual, not an institution. *Do* pick someone you like and intuitively trust; you're about to go through a very interesting adventure together.

## AGENT SERVICES

In Chapter 2, "Drafting Your Real Estate Team," the terms "listing agent" and "selling agent" are introduced, and in the chapter on buyer brokering that follows this one, these terms are explained a bit more. It is there that I make my case for buyers being represented by an agent, instead of the traditional method in which the selling agent represents the seller's interests, no matter how many weeks the buyer and agent spend together. Since buyer brokering, while preferable, is not always available, and in a few instances would be too complicated for the circumstances, here is a list of what the traditional agent can do for a buyer without placing him in conflict with his duty to the seller. The agent can:

**1.** Inform, but not advise. In general, an agent can explain financial options, repairs, etc., but not advise the buyer to take any particular strategy that in any way might conflict with the seller's goals.

**2.** Provide the names of lenders, inspectors, etc.

**3.** Arrange access to a wide variety of properties.

**4.** Provide tax and title information on a property, so long as the seller's interests are not compromised.

**5.** Provide information on prices and time-on-the-market of properties in an area. This is one of the stickier situations for the traditional agent, who may want to do this only if it shows the seller in a good light; a buyer broker would do this voluntarily or would be compelled to do it if the buyer requested it.

**6.** Provide information on schools, utilities, services, zoning, closing costs, and contracts.

**7.** Present the buyer's offer (in fact, Washington agents are required to present all offers).

**8.** Coordinate and/or monitor the loan processing and the closing of the transaction.

**9.** Send champagne, Christmas cards, and calendars as needed.

If you asked the agent, "What is the most important service you provide?" he might answer, "Keeping the buyer and seller at arm's length." No buyer would believe this to be important until she encountered a seller who started negotiations with, "The trouble with you is..."

### THE THREE MOST FREQUENT COMPLAINTS

The three most frequent complaints about agents (based on feedback by 5,000 real estate students) center on communication, and not so much on technical skills:

**1.** Not listening. "We'd like to see the *Forum*." "Fine, I'll be glad to show you the farm."

**2.** Calling too often. Not taking the hint to buzz off. Message-machine meltdown.

**3.** Not calling often enough. There's no doubt that on this one consumers share the responsibility. Phones have receivers at both ends.

### TEN COMMANDMENTS FOR THEE, YON BUYER

These guidelines were found inscribed on the ancient tomb of a hesitant buyer. Apparently, tensions between agents and buyers are nothing new, and buyers' mistakes and contributions to problems have long been recognized. Most of the commandments are as easy to understand today as when they were first written:

Thou shalt not take potluck with thy choice of agents, but shall choose as if thy fortune dependeth thereon.

Thou shalt keep thy face like unto a poker, showing no joy in the presence of an unknown agent who doth want thee to purchase today before sundown.

Thou shalt not believe that which sayeth "exclusive" because it meaneth not what thou thinkest.

Thou shalt not act as if yon agent is paid by the hour, and hath waited lo these many years for thy calls and questions.

Thou shalt not count thy coins in the presence of an agent unless he hath promised to represent thine interests.

Thou shalt not play one agent against another, denying that thou hath intercoursed around and viewed other dwellings with those agents.

Thou shalt not leave thy spine at home, but shall check for its presence every hour and speak truly that which concerns thee.

Thou shalt not sleep on a golden opportunity, because in the morning it will have been stolen from thee by thine enemies who seeth more clearly.

Thou shalt not broach the subject of thine agent's income as if it shall be thine income and shall purchase thee many goats and chickens.

Thou shalt not thyself be rude, because that which goeth around cometh around and will kicketh thee in thy butt.

Verily, verily, few things come to pass on this earth that are of one party's doings, but those things which blossom with abundance shall come of the joint effort of thy noblest intentions, and the rendering of that treatment which thou dost thyself desire, that thy roof shall shed water and thy taxes stay low for no less of a term than thy payments. Amen.

As we can see, the ancient scribes were long ago telling buyers to realize that "exclusive" meant the arrangement with the seller, and often had nothing to do with which agent showed the dwelling (see Chapter 14, "To List or Resist"). They also advised buyers not to confide in an agent unless the agent represented the buyer, and in general to follow the Golden Rule because it was believed even then that agents had the same feelings and needs for loyalty as buyers. Little has changed.

## COMPLAINTS?

If you feel that you have had unfair treatment at the hands of an agent, here are some possible remedies:

**1.** Start with the broker. Some brokers are apologists for their agents, but most want to maintain a good reputation and will make a genuine effort to solve problems. Don't start with threats; brokers aren't easily intimidated.

**2.** Call the multiple listing service. Each usually has a group of volunteers for fielding complaints.

**3.** Call the local association of Realtors, and hope the agent is a member.

**4.** Call the attorney general (branch offices in larger towns). Their city offices even have a booklet on the subject.

**5.** Call the licensing department in Olympia.

**6.** Call an attorney. But plant an apple orchard at the same time, so you'll have something to do until you get a court date. By all means, look into the possibilities of arbitration or mediation in your community; these avenues are often more practical than our logjammed courts.

## THE CAREER AND FEEDING OF AN AGENT

Have you ever considered becoming an agent? In California one out of eight people either now has, or has had, a license; in Washington only one in 180 presently has a license (about 25,000). Obviously, real estate is not quite as popular a hobby in the Northwest, although in the Puget Sound area the number of agents has grown faster than the population, increasing by 16% in 1989 alone. This reflects the seller's market that started in the late eighties. What it does not necessarily reflect is the wisdom of those who chose that time to become agents.

We often make emotional choices in our vocations, letting the headlines make decisions for us. If all those new agents had done a little research, they might have hesitated, because the statistics show that the people who made all that "easy money" in Seattle's housing market were the sellers, not the agents. When owners realized that it might make more sense to hold on to their rapidly increasing equity, the number of listings fell off by over two-thirds in a little over a year; at the same time more than 1,400 new agents joined the 8,500 already struggling to keep up. So the slices of the pie got smaller and smaller. In 1989 the average Puget Sound agent participated in fewer than 10 transactions. One of my own agents presented eight offers in one month that were beaten out by other offers.

Obviously, it wasn't as good a time to become an agent as it seemed. But then, no time is. Real estate is always at a challenging point on a cycle. I have seen agents come into the business when the interest rates were 14% and make over $50,000 in their first year. The majority, though, don't last two years.

As a broker, I have a vested interest in recruiting agents. Every good agent can mean another $20,000 gross to the office, but I know that if I recruit people who aren't cut out for it, I will waste a lot of time training them. So I may see if they're easily discouraged by telling them the horrors of the business, as I'm about to tell you.

This is what it's like: In the first place, you have the status of a hedgehog. No one respects agents, not even other agents. Not even their mothers. Most have been disowned. Strangers will call and ask about a house down the street and then tell you you're an idiot if you haven't memorized the square feet and property taxes. Inside your head, you'll probably agree.

An appraiser will call late in the day and want you to meet him the next morning at a house 30 miles away, just at the time you're supposed to be meeting new buyers. He'll swear it's the only time he can get there. You can't find the buyers' phone number to rearrange the appointment.

You've got $40 tickets to see Vazinski, the greatest dancer since Nureyev, when a buyer says she wants to make an offer on a house. She has a habit of making low offers that sellers won't even counteroffer. Your backup doesn't answer her page. No one wants the tickets.

You've spent two months on a duplex transaction when the appraisal comes in $15,000 low. The buyer backs out. You won't have another closing for six weeks and you've got less than $500 in the bank.

On Sunday morning you're snuggling with the spouse when the buyer who makes low offers calls and wants to know if you can show her a townhouse in 30 minutes. You suggest that she consider a cabana in California instead; she accuses you of being flaky. The spouse wants to know if you're free Monday evening for counseling.

Now why, oh why, would anybody put up with the invasion of privacy, the weird hours, the unpredictable income, and the demands by consumers who were cut out to be customs officers? Low self-esteem. That's got to be it.

That's why some of today's best agents were formerly nurses, military people, and teachers, especially liberal arts majors. Society has told us, judging by our pay in those positions, that we're not valuable people and no matter how hard we work we will always be worthless. Therefore, if one is going to work hard without any respect, one might as well work in real estate, where the possibility of making good money exists.

Is there actually anything good about real estate besides the possibility of

making money? Actually, there is. We really do meet a lot of really fine people. I consider the weddings I go to each year a priceless bonus. The work is almost never boring, because no two days are ever alike, and no one ever masters all aspects of the business. Although we may be at the beck and call of an appraiser or lender occasionally, for the most part our time is ours. If we practice good business principles or think of creative ways to make a name for ourselves in the business, we'll be rewarded with a lot more than a letter from an administrator or a gold watch at retirement. If we don't have any demanding clients at any given moment, we can head to Victoria without asking for permission. We can buy a decent car and write off a big chunk of it on our taxes, and little by little we learn how to make our nest eggs grow into ostrich eggs.

As for the money, even though the average numbers look terrible, the competent and disciplined people who persevere typically make one and a half to three times the income they made in those liberal arts positions, by their second or third year at the latest. But don't forget, it takes some money to get started as an agent. You're going to have bills for drycleaning, gas, lunches, seminars, dues, etc. My recommendation to the new agent is to have six months of living expenses and a reliable four-door car. If after four months no income is in sight, quit. You're either in the wrong business or in the wrong company. Now you've got two months to find a salaried job and resume a normal life.

"Well," you say, "it was interesting, and I made a lot of friends." You could have gone to a party and done that a heck of a lot cheaper, but at least now you'll never yell "easy money" again at an agent.

## AGENT INTERVIEWS

I had the pleasure of talking to dozens of agents as I traveled all over Washington, getting their input and perceptions on many topics. I asked them if they would fill out a 60-question form on practices and attitudes in their area. Most were a bit shy about this, but I managed to get enough volunteers to learn some disturbing and reassuring things. Below is a summary of the highlights of a totally unscientific poll:

Average age of respondents: 45. Average education: 2.4 years of college, 86 "clock hours" of real estate training. Average week: 54 hours. All own a home; slightly over half own investment property. Half own a new car. Two-thirds thought agent entrance requirements were just right (rest said too easy), could not name one of the commissioners, and read fewer than two books a year on real estate. Only 20% had any training in construction, but almost all do recommend structural inspections. Only 36% had taken a real estate law class in the last four years. Few advised sellers to avoid FHA/VA offers, or encouraged the use of an attorney (20% admitted to "dreading" an attorney). Slightly over half felt that agents should be required to be full-time and that an appraiser's work orders offer a buyer adequate protection.

Fewer than 10% admitted to witnessing another agent practice discrimination, or felt that commissions were too high (over 90% thought they were just right or too low). Almost 20% said that they had formally represented a buyer in a buyer brokering situation.

Only one-third felt that the law requiring an agent to disclose his/her obligation to a seller or buyer was a step forward, while the remainder felt it was a hindrance or unnecessary. Three-fourths felt that the Department of Licensing did a poor to so-so job of keeping agents informed.

Two-thirds felt that being able to buy listed property with any inside knowledge was simply a "privilege" of the profession, whereas the remainder thought that guidelines and/or restrictions were needed. Slightly over half either had no opinion or felt that it was acceptable to receive referral fees from lenders, whereas 45% thought this was an "unacceptable" practice. If they could change anything about their brokers, they would want them not to compete with their own agents, to have better communication, to hire a secretary, and "improve his hairstyle."

Most shocking revelation from an agent: A broker at a competing firm tells his own agents he has only one rule—he himself is to get first crack at all new listings.

# STRATEGIES FOR BUYERS: ORGANIZING/SEARCHING/NEGOTIATING

This chapter explains some of the necessary technical and psychological steps required to become a successful home buyer. Then, we'll discuss euthanasia, in case you find that more appealing.

If you are buying with a partner who likes to do things impetuously, you may be able to use this chapter to make him or her aware that rushing into buying property is about as wise as rafting the Grand Canyon in a bathtub. Just around the bend is Cast Iron Rapids.

Do you know the follow-up line to "A little learning is a dang'rous thing"? It's "Drink deep or taste not the Pierian spring." Alexander Pope tells us to either concentrate on what we wish to do or not to bother starting. Along those lines, I say: Learn all you have time for about real estate before starting; it is frequently a challenging and complicated thing to buy a house. Like juggling greasy bowling balls. Barefooted.

## THE PSYCHOLOGICAL STAGES

Every stranger I meet in a social setting seems to feel obligated to tell me that he isn't in the market for a house at that time, but "if something really nice comes along, give me a call." No way. He can call me when he's good and ready.

It took me about six months in the business before I quit taking casual buyers seriously. I really thought that if I found something extra nice they might buy it, even if they had just passed up an opportunity on the Taj Mahal the week before.

These buyers are, at best, in the **contemplation** stage of the process. They are the tire-kickers, the lookie-loos every agent complains about. Actually, we shouldn't complain. They're sort of like the farm team, getting in lots of training before moving up to play in the majors, replacing those who have "retired." We just shouldn't spend too much time with them until they're devoted to the game.

I sit these consumers down and explain: "I find most consumers to be very considerate. They state right away that they don't want to waste my time. Good. We have at least one mutual goal. All the same, you may need some guidance at this time, and I certainly hope to get your business eventually, so let's work out a compromise.

"You talk to your friends and parents, go over your hopes and dreams, and attend some open houses. Call me when you have questions. At some point, you will decide either to stay in your present pasture or to hop the fence. That is, you may decide that indeed this is the time for you to buy.

"If so, congratulations! You have graduated from the contemplation stage, where you explore your hopes and needs, to the **comparison** stage, where the search takes place. At that point, you and I will probably start to spend a great deal of time together. Now that you have decided to buy, I can help you educate yourself as to what exists in your price range.

"Note that I said 'educate yourself.' I can teach you a lot of things, but the one thing I can't teach you is 'value.' That doesn't mean that I won't accompany you. It just means that your own observations and insights are vital if you are to build the confidence to make a commitment. And **commitment** is the name of the final stage of buying a home.

"In this final stage you may still have some doubts, and it's entirely possible that we'll run into any number of typical complications. But your reaction to problems will reveal how thoroughly you have completed the first two stages.

"If you're still not sure that you want the responsibilities of homeowner-ship—remember, there's nothing as certain as death and gutters—or if you're wondering if maybe there isn't a better home out there, then you may grab the first opportunity to kibosh your own transaction.

"Does this ever happen? Do people actually make offers even though in their hearts they're still not very confident that this is what they should do? All the time.

"When I was still a very impressionable agent I watched a supersalesman make sale after sale, from which a very high percentage of his buyers backed out. He had persuaded them to act before they were truly ready. Agents call this backing-out 'buyer's remorse.' If instead we called it 'buyer's prematurity', we might better understand it and quit blaming the buyer solely.

"Part of the agent's frustration is that he or she may know with certainty how great an opportunity a certain house is, and can't understand why the buy-er doesn't see it as well. But that's not always reasonable. The buyer may need more time to work through those stages of contemplation and comparison.

"Of course, if that buyer is still looking after six months, we may be dealing with someone who has sniffed too much glue. Sylvia Porter featured a couple in her magazine who had looked at more than 180 houses before buying; she made it sound as if they were the ideal consumers. 'Slow learners' is more precise. If I encounter buyers who reject all of the 30 best homes in a price range, I may refer them to an architect or a marriage counselor."

---

### 🏠 🏠 🏠
### SOUND MARRIAGE?

Can the status of one's marriage affect this house search? Of course. A husband once admitted that he kept backing out of offers because he wasn't sure he was committed to the marriage. First things first.

---

Where does all of this advice fit in if we're talking about a seller's market, as we've recently seen in Western Washington? If prices are going up two percent a month, one month of educating oneself is very expensive tuition. The obvious answer is that as long as prices continue to climb at a swift pace, then the first mistake would be to dilly-dally. If I had a nickel for all the buyers who wished they had bought sooner, I could buy my Christmas presents at Nieman-Marcus. On the other hand, some buyers will pay more than is necessary—thousands above the nearest offer—out of panic. And those who purchase at the end of this seller's market will pay the record price and won't be able to sell a year later at a profit, as some of their friends have.

Obviously, we face a very difficult challenge: to move quickly through the first two stages—definitely out of our comfort zones at times—while trying to choose a house we won't be unhappy with, at a price we won't be embarrassed to admit, while hoping the house of cards isn't about to collapse. If you're looking for an easy solution to this dilemma, look elsewhere; I haven't found it.

### TIMING

The buyer has at least four questions to answer that relate to time:

**1.** When should I buy?
**2.** How much time will the process take?
**3.** How long should I look (how many houses)?
**4.** How long should I look at each house?

### I. WHEN?

First question: When should I buy? Answer: Now. Next question.

Oh, you want to be convinced? Well, there are no sure bets when it comes to our economy, but the nearest we can come to one is based on a bit of history: For nearly a century now, homes have appreciated by about 4.5% per year.

Let's translate that into a return on our investment (down payment) in a fairly typical transaction. If we make a 10% down payment we will gross a 45%

return, simplistically speaking, in just one year. If we make a 3% down payment, as we can do with an FHA loan, the return will be 150%!

I have learned a little bit over the years from my own experience, but even more from other people's experience, specifically their regrets over hesitating about one or more real estate opportunities. I have seen the pain on their faces as they silently calculate what those properties are worth today. Yes, there will be a few people who buy at the wrong time (like just before a city's economy collapses, which has happened in several Texas cities), but that's such a rare occurrence that only the supercautious are likely to consider it. But all this makes it even more important that you buy a property you will be happy in, just in case you have to wait for the next swing of the cycle to sell and move up or move on.

Overall, this old cliché is fairly valid: "Don't wait to buy real estate. Buy real estate and wait."

---

### FIVE YEARS AND STILL WAITING

Five years ago I met a buyer who was never quite satisfied. He once asked me, "How do I know that if I buy a house today, a better one won't come along tomorrow?" I answered, "But that will happen! There will always be better deals. At some point you'll just have to be content with your opportunity, or you'll be a tenant forever." He's still a tenant. I guess I should have lied.

---

Actually, the question about "when" can also be interpreted to mean "at what time of year" and "at what time in one's financial growth."

I don't think that the time of year is really all that important. Let's say you have to wait until fall for some event to happen: a birth, the reading of a will, a co-signer getting out of jail, etc. You may worry that people who buy in the spring or summer will have some advantage over you. Not necessarily. In some years more houses come on the market in the spring, but then more buyers also come out of the woodwork, so the proportionate number of available houses may not have changed. In one study I did, I found that the highest percentage of sales actually took place in the coldest months. One possible explanation for this is that Christmas sellers are the most motivated and thus offer the most realistic prices; many springtime sellers might be inflating their prices to see if some poor sucker from Dizzny-land, between planes, will pay the price.

Probably the more difficult timing question relates to one's financial readiness, i.e. "Should we wait until we have a bigger down payment?"

To properly answer this for yourself, you need to read the chapter on financing, but we can certainly examine a few principles at this point. The first thing I ask a buyer is, "Are you saving money at a rate that exceeds the appreciation of property?"

In other words, if the value of property in your area and price range is increasing an average of $500 a month and you're not already saving more than $500 a month, then it would seem to make sense to invest your savings as soon as you find a good property. But that's oversimplified.

In the first place, unless you're a vet eligible for a zero down payment, you usually have to come up with at least 6% of the price to cover your down payment and closing costs on an FHA offer, whereas around 15% is the ballpark minimum for a conventional loan (down payment 10%, closing costs 5%). So, regardless of appreciation in your area, you have to save until you come up with the typical minimum down payment and closing costs, or until you luck onto a seller who will accept creative financing.

Wait. There is one last factor. In a hot market, people who offer very small down payments are often at a distinct disadvantage if there are several offers on a house. The obvious question from "offended" buyers has been: "Why should the sellers care how big my down payment is if they will get all of their cash at closing from the lender?"

That's a fair question, but the seller has a fair answer: "The person with a large down payment is less likely to be turned down for a loan."

In Seattle, buyers have frequently made offers with 10% down payments only to lose out time and time again. After a few losses, those buyers have then mustered all of their resources (translated: their parents' money) and offered a much larger down payment than is required, just to finally be the victor in a bidding war. Sad but true.

## II. HOW MUCH TIME?

How far ahead should one start? How many weeks/months will all this take? Once again, the answer depends on many factors that only the buyer can determine. The chapter on financing will provide details on the time needed for different types of loans and contracts, but it is fairly safe to say that from offer to closing the vast majority of transactions require three to eight weeks. The tougher challenge is to guess how long it will take the buyer to become psychologically committed, get those finances in order, and find the desired property.

In a slower, saner market, where there is some give and take by both sides and less pressure to make snap judgments, a mature buyer may spend a month or two mind-wrestling before deciding to buy, and then two to twelve weeks in the serious pursuit. An immature buyer needs a lifetime. Usually someone else's.

In a hot market, the buyer may be so panicked that the contemplation stage lasts only a day or two; some buyers make offers within a week after they first contemplate buying a house. Of course, it may take several months and 5 to 10 offers before they are the *successful* bidders on a property. The greatest dilemma we in the profession observe occurs when a brand new buyer wins the first bidding war she enters. Just a week ago she was wondering if she should buy, and this week she's taking on a debt that seems as large as the national deficit. She may be swept by waves of buyer's remorse, but she has enough good sense to know that if she bails out she may have to spend $5,000 more next month to get a similar house.

If you're wondering what the shortest possible time a buyer needs to find a decent property, make the offer, and get it closed is, the answer is about three days—if the seller will accept creative financing and if at least one title company owes someone a favor. A big favor. One bordering on blackmail.

### III. HOW MANY?

How many houses should a buyer look at? How many calories should one consume? How often should one bathe?

I bet that almost everyone has an answer for the last two questions, at least an answer that satisfies their own needs. But once we've got the answer for ourselves, most of us know we have no business telling anyone else what to do, unless we're sharing food and a small house.

Nevertheless, I know from past experience that most first-time buyers want some idea of how many houses most buyers look at before making a decision. Why? They are basically insecure and seek reassurance that they are moving at a safe pace.

Every year the National Association of Realtors polls recent buyers on their experiences, and one of the questions focuses on how many houses the average buyer looked at. The answer has frequently been in the 9–15 range. That surprises me. Most of the buyers my agents and I work with would answer that they looked at 10–50 on their own and another 10–20 with an agent. So in our experience the range is 20–70, with 35 being a believable average. Why the difference? Perhaps because I teach real estate classes and as a result my brokerage attracts buyers who are a bit more self-protective.

Anyway, the answer is that there is no answer, despite what they taught me in my first real estate class. The answer there was nine. If after showing a buyer the nine best houses I could find, they hadn't made an offer, they obviously weren't motivated, or else I hadn't properly used one of the 17 different closing techniques. Back to Tommy Hopkins' boot camp in Persuasion Without Violence.

Okay, but what if the second house you look at is gorgeous? And in a hot market you know you have to make a decision within 30 minutes? It is possible to make the offer and then continue looking at other houses, either to confirm your choice or to learn that you moved too quickly. But when you do this you get into some very tricky legal and ethical questions. For example, can you use the five days the sellers agreed to for a structural inspection to do further research? And if after your research you then back out, will you get back your earnest money, and do you have to give the seller the real reason—that you found a property you liked even better? It has been done, but please ask your attorney and priest for guidance. And don't tell them I urged you to do it.

### IV. HOW LONG INSIDE?

How long should you spend in or around each house? Doesn't that depend on how much one likes the house? Not necessarily. In theory, we can learn more from a house we hate; we might do well to linger and take meticulous notes that will help us formulate our priorities.

When I show houses to buyers I tell them not to linger on my account; if they hate a house, they don't need to look at every room to avoid hurting my feelings. Yet I rarely see a buyer just walk in, take a look, and say, "Let's go." Part of the explanation for this is ordinary curiosity—isn't it fun to be able to observe other peoples' lifestyles? And another reason is that many buyers are making a conscientious effort to imagine solutions to each house's shortcomings.

So how long is long enough? Stay as long as you like or as long as you are still learning something, but don't be surprised if you feel a little rushed if the sellers are home (especially if they're eating). You may also feel unsure about what the heck you're looking for, or how to organize your analysis. I've had my students spend 10 minutes in a house and then I've hit them with questions such as whether the outlets were grounded, whether there was a dryer outlet, was there a fan in the bathroom, etc. This makes them aware of how helpful a checklist can be. On the other hand, I don't want them evaluating the house just based on a checklist. There are such things as ambience, Gemütlichkeit, and other intangible considerations that look silly on a list.

As for the best use of time, I believe that three 10-minute visits to a house usually reveal more than one 30-minute visit. The time in between visits is priceless for evaluating what we have seen and realizing what we haven't seen. Unfortunately, this three-trip approach is often a luxury denied in a seller's market. One 10-minute visit may be all we get. One of my agents recently described a house over the phone to an out-of-town buyer who then told him to make an offer for her. He then videotaped the entire house and put the tape on a plane that afternoon so that she could decide before midnight if she wanted to go through with the purchase. She did.

## MAKING LISTS

Whenever I sit down for the first time with new buyers, at least half of them pull out a tattered notebook page filled with their list of all the requisites of their dream home. If it's typed I know I'm in trouble. Too demanding, you can bet.

I do my best to look at this list with respect, and I am very cognizant that one of the most common complaints about agents is that we don't listen. But I can't wait for them to leave so I can gleefully shred that list. Who do these people think I am, their architect? The lender who will loan them a million dollars so that they can find or build a house that has all of these items under one roof? Arrrggg!

When I was a brand new agent a young couple gave me such a list—12 things they wanted—and I looked for six weeks until I found a grand old house that had every one of those items. No, they whined, it was too big. But it was *exactly* the size they had asked for! Grind teeth, stare at sun, imagine ancient tortures.

Of course, I was learning my profession, just as they were learning what they really wanted. I had taken their list too literally. Never again. I told subsequent buyers who handed me a list to take it back and tell me which were the three things that couldn't be eliminated. Might as well introduce reality right at the beginning. I also learned that no matter how hard I listened, the house that most excited people was often not the one I expected, and often not necessarily the best-built or best-priced. My own strategy then became one of showing people as many of the houses that came close to their expectations as they had time to see (remember: I was originally trained to show a buyer a maximum of 9 to 12 houses).

Am I saying that lists are a waste of time? Au contraire. Lists are invaluable. But it isn't the list itself that's valuable; it's the *making* of the list. The exercise of the brain. The examination of the values. The ordering of the priorities. It's a mistake for a buyer to take the list too seriously, as I did as a new agent; as you look at properties, your priorities change. An item that once seemed a necessity may not even be an option in that price range; so going to look at a few open houses first may tame our wild horses.

Occasionally there is a buyer who has a unique combination of needs that must be met, and within his price range. That's the challenge: "within his price range." I think of the man who collected antique cars and wanted a house with a four-bay garage in a neighborhood of older houses where the typically small garages were now used for storage. It took him a long time to quit expecting everything he had on his list.

One of the primary checks on house searching is exhaustion. There is nothing quite like it to bring a man to his senses. Few other things do. A mugging at gunpoint and child support, I'm told.

So by all means make a list. Then make three lists: one with three items, one with four, and one with five. Give an agent all three. That will demonstrate your priorities like nothing else could. And if you're a couple, then do this list-making separately the first time. Then try to prioritize and eliminate some of the items. Remember, there's very little stigma to divorce in our society, so complete agreement isn't absolutely necessary.

## SEATTLE'S CHILI-PEPPER-TABASCO MARKET:
## TOO MUCH OF A GOOD THING

Before a red-hot seller's market actually happens, agents long for it, believing that at last buyers will "quit wasting so much time" and the commissions will flow like a river.

But here's what has really happened in Seattle's hot market: At first, listings were relatively plentiful and they sold lightning-quick. A listing agent's biggest challenge was to get the listing, not to market it. Prices rose quickly. Multiple offers became the norm in the better neighborhoods.

The media had grist for their mills. Everyone who had ever thought about becoming a real estate agent decided this was the time. But the owners who had been thinking about selling began to realize that if they sold now, they would just be caught up in the desperate search for a replacement.

So the number of listings dropped by almost 70% in a little over a year, while the number of agents rose by about 20%. A smaller pie cut into more slices. Woe.

What is the worst thing about our seller's market? In the long run it may lower the percentage of homeowners. In fact, our entire nation has seen a significant fall-off in the percentage of young homeowners in recent years. This is bad news, since homeowners are more likely to vote, care, participate, and have bake sales. If it weren't for assistance from parents, the fall-off would be even more dramatic. Thanks, Mom and Dad.

## SPEAKING OF CHECKLISTS:
## GETTING ORGANIZED

**1. Start a notebook.** This can prove invaluable, especially if later a lender, seller, or agent says something contrary to a previous statement. Record addresses of every house you see; give this list to any agent you start working with. Write down terms you learn and insights about yourself and real estate. Compile names of plumbers, painters, etc., from friends' recommendations. Cut and paste ads and clippings. Save this for your grandchildren.

### FEELING SQUEEZED OUT?

Prices are going up faster than an empty ski lift. You thought you were making a good living until you talked to a lender. He asked you not to occupy a parking spot too long. You'd gladly put 50% of your monthly income into a house payment, but no lender is about to agree to such a ratio, and you can't come up with a big enough down payment to get those monthly payments down around the 30% mark. Don't give up. A few minutes ago I received a call from an elated young woman, a waitress, who had just bought a house. Two months ago she was ready to give up, but she persevered, adjusted her sights, and kept talking to lenders.

The first thing I tell any discouraged buyer is to look ahead 10 years when rents will more than equal today's house payment. That should keep you motivated. Then I insist on a major attitude adjustment. Repeat after me:"I will buy anything I possibly can that will appreciate. I will not be picky. This is just the bottom rung of my ladder.''

A year's appreciation on even a low-quality home is likely to equal or exceed any amount you could possibly save. In five years you may have enough equity to buy into that preferred neighborhood. OK, but you still have to buy the first rung. Let's get to work!

**1.** Talk to twice as many lenders as do buyers who make twice as much money. You need twice as much help. Ask them to explain "state bond,'' PLAM, and 80-10-10 programs. Keep asking questions. Take yes for an answer.

**2.** Tell your parents you're sorry you ever talked back to them. Can they help? Can relatives help?

**3.** Make a list of everyone you know. Who might need the tax benefits of a real estate investment? If you occupy the property and make the payments, they would be your "co-borrower,''and receive all or most of the tax benefits. You have to come up with a 10% down payment for this arrangement, but if you find the willing Samaritan you'll find the money.

**4.** Refinance any possible asset, from furniture to vehicle. Borrow against a trust, retirement plan, or IRA. You may have to qualify for both payments, the loan and the mortgage, but if you make a good salary and are just short on cash, this strategy may help.

**5.** Moonlight. But whatever you do, document the source of every dime. Lenders are very leery of unexplained money; the Feds can seize property bought with drug money.

**6.** Deliberately seek out elderly owners/sellers who own "free and clear," and can therefore participate in seller-financing. Some of this information can be found in the tax records. Explain your situation without embarrassment or pleading. They remember what it was like.

Now, do it! Ten years can pass all too quickly, and you can too easily end up saying, "You know, if I'd just bought something, anything, 10 years ago...."

**2. Adopt a reasonable degree of skepticism.** One of the old Greeks said: "In skepticism is the beginning of wisdom." But in cynicism we find too much of a good thing. Balance. Confirm every important piece of information. (I own several respected books on real estate that have serious mistakes in them.) Assume that everyone means well but is imperfect.

**3. Line up your resources. Now.** Buyers have told me their folks will help on the down payment, but the folks haven't said how much they will help. A few parents don't or can't come through. Get a commitment and an amount today, not after you find the property. See the information on "Gift Letters" in Chapter 9, "Financing: The Basics".

**4. Order a credit check on yourself.** Look in the Yellow Pages under "Credit Reporting Agencies." Prices to run a credit check in Seattle range from $15–$70, depending on the thoroughness of the credit check. If you have a common name, the more expensive report may tell you if others with the same name have debts that may complicate or delay your mortgage application. This type of report will be ordered by the lender, but you won't be allowed to see their copy, so if you expect *any* complication get your own, now. We occasionally see debts reported that were actually paid off over a year earlier.

**5. Pay off debts, if appropriate.** You won't know which debts to pay off, or why, until you have talked to a lender or two and told them which type of financing you will pursue. It isn't automatically in your best interests to pay off all debts, so their input should help.

**6. Pre-prequalify.** Actual prequalifying—getting a formal approval for a loan before finding the property—was very rare in Seattle before 1989, but once multiple offers on properties became almost the norm, buyers started trying to find every advantage. Pre-prequalifying can be done over the phone, free, by telling a lender or two how much you make, your bills, etc. You may even go so far as to request a letter from them, which does not usually represent a commitment unless you go in and make a formal application. A few lenders offer the plastic approach, an actual credit card, which does amount to a promise. For some reason, this has not exactly swept the industry, but some forms of pre-offer commitments are bound to become more popular.

**7. Order subscriptions to all local papers.** This is explained in "The Good Search," in this chapter.

**8. Consult a financial planner or CPA.** That is, if you have any doubts that homeownership is to your advantage. Finding a financial planner who is not actually a salesperson for bonds, insurance, etc., can be very difficult; these sales-people generally have not impressed me as being knowledgeable enough about real estate and taxes or possessing sufficient objectivity to be good counselors.

**9. Determine "cash-out" times.** Some buyers intend to sell stocks or cash in CD's or some other asset for their down payment, but sometimes they wait too long, trying to collect interest right up to the last minute. They risk voiding their entire contract. For a few dollars more. Hang 'em high.

---

### RENTER'S DISEASE?

Some buyers will have to accept "moving down" in order to buy their first house, or will have to adjust to a payment that is larger than their rent. Some will insist on keeping the house payment the same as their rent, even if they have to make an enormous down payment. This is sometimes an absolutely foolish use of money; I speak as one who believes money should work and not sit idle.

Here is the best advice I can give you: Make the first house you buy absolutely the best you can afford, or at least one you will be content with for years to come. Buyers frequently accuse agents of pressuring them to move up in price, thinking the agent is doing it just for a bigger commission. Perhaps, but maybe the agent is simply conscientious and knows he has already shown them everything that's cheaper. In any case, it is to my industry's advantage if you ignore my advice. The person who buys too small a house will have to sell it and buy another. The more mistakes you make, the more commissions we make. So forget what I just said.

**10. Keep eyes and ears open for a good agent.** See Chapter 3, "The Agent," for details on finding the good ones, and Chapter 5, "Buyer Brokering," for how to conduct yourself in the presence of an agent. A good agent will prove invaluable, whereas a bad one can put your entire savings at risk. Don't take potluck; CHOOSE.

**11. Visit open houses.** Early visits, before you are ready to buy, will help you gain insight into your priorities, help you discern value, and can introduce you to one or more agents you may want to interview later.

**12. Take/carry agents' cards.** Two different goals. First, keep the cards of agents you meet. Every buyer later has a question or an observation, and can't remember who the agent was. Glue the cards into your notebook. Second, once you have selected an agent to work with, you can present one of his/her cards to the agent hosting an open house, and that agent will usually back off and adopt a more helpful tone.

**13. Make mental adjustments as soon as possible.** If I said, "I will pay you $10,000 to live in a tent for six months," many people would ask, "Could I stay a year for $20,000?" Yet many first-time buyers have a very difficult time accepting that the first house they buy may not be as grand as they would like. Remind yourself: (1) I'm building equity and credit; (2) my parents didn't start at the top either; (3) no one has invented a ladder without rungs.

**14. Budget for professional assistance.** Buyers often budget $5,000 for immediate improvements to a house, but not so much as $500 for an attorney to make sure that their contract is a valid one. Good attorneys and structural inspectors are just plain cheap insurance; their total bill rarely amounts to one percent of the price of a home. We frequently pay five percent or more of a car's value *every* year for car insurance.

**15. Line up your professionals in the beginning.** I've seen buyers make an offer and then find out that their preferred attorney was on vacation, or that an inspector wasn't available for over a week. Ask them about their schedules and how much notice they need.

**16. Establish a contingency plan at work.** If you need to leave work on short notice to see a house that just came on the market, make sure you have already cleared this with your boss and co-workers. If you don't think this sort of urgency ever exists, or that such swift responses don't pay off—well, Hoss, you don't know nothin' about life in the big city.

**17. Spend a few lunch hours at the county seat.** In Seattle, for example, a buyer could visit the following departments and learn how to derive these bits of information: (1) Engineering and/or Building Department—location of sewer lines or septic tank, property lines, and any permits for past remodeling; and (2) County Assessor—zoning, property lines, age of house, price paid, etc. (The King County Assessor offers a 30-minute class every morning at 8:45 in the Administration Building. Just show up.) P.S.: Many real estate offices subscribe to a service for this tax information; some may allow their buyers to use it.

**18. Expect pressure.** This is another of those mental adjustments that simply needs to be faced. Some agents apply pressure; many don't. But the serious pressure that can't be escaped comes from other buyers, and the hotter the market the higher the pressure. It's a good time to buy tapes and books on retaining the mellow.

**19. Accept that the other side has a point of view that differs from yours.** Buyers often get angry when an ad proves to be misleading (counting a bedroom in the basement is a universal buyers' complaint), or because a seller rejected their "perfectly reasonable offer." Imagine if you were that seller: Wouldn't you advertise that basement bedroom and try to get every dollar you could? You know what happens to your nose if you lie.

**20. Know your legal status with the agent.** The vast majority of agents you encounter are legally representing the seller. You may be able to trust them to tell you the truth, but you have no business confiding in them. If one says, "I will represent you," get it in writing. See the chapter on "Buyer Brokering" for a detailed explanation.

**21. Establish the role your parents and friends will play.** Parents and friends often have a way of second-guessing decisions that can drive the professionals involved absolutely mad. They want to protect you, but they often base their remarks on myths, ignorance, or cynicism. In one case, a friend told a buyer that state law required that all transactions close in 30 days. He was wrong, but it really startled that buyer and it was hard to "prove" that no such law existed. If you are going to ask the opinion of friends and parents, then have them look at lots of houses with you so that they too will recognize value. (Have them get to know your agent, if there is one, to keep the mistrust to an acceptable level.) We in the industry prefer that your friends and family not even know you've bought a house until the housewarming invitation arrives.

**22. Maintain control of the search.** This may sound silly, but it wouldn't if you knew that many agents are trained to "take control." Fortunately, this attitude is more talk than reality, for two reasons: (1) many agents disagree with this outlook, and (2) few of those who do believe in the Control School have the ability to do it. All the same, be sure to look at houses and the surrounding neighborhoods without an agent present, if time and circumstances allow, even if you have an agent you trust completely. Agents will just naturally select the most scenic route. Finally, don't ever sit home and wait for an agent to call. Get out there and make it happen!

**23. Call on your inner strengths and utmost maturity.** A significant percentage of transactions are extremely trying, for months on end. A dozen people or more may be involved in handling your transaction; one or more of them will drop the ball on one or more occasions. Just state what you expect them to do. Don't yell the *first* time. Don't screw up your own karma by being rude to agents or anyone else. And finally, do remember what this is all about: You set out to buy a house and create a home, not to acquire a set of appliances or a chandelier. Don't lose sight of the mountain just because of the grain of sand in your shoe.

**24. Spend some time honing your bidding and negotiating skills.** Those who have the backbone, the knowledge, the creative solutions, and the decisiveness are the most likely to come away with the prize. For a warmup, there is no better practice field than half a dozen garage sales or furniture auctions. Or a week in Mexico. See the section on "Negotiating" in this chapter.

**25. Above all, be extremely honest.** No one has ever found happiness by lying. No one has ever profited by lying and managed to enjoy that profit with a song in his heart. And when liars are discovered, as they almost invariably are, there are righteous SOB's like myself who will delight in embarrassing them. It's not worth it. It's easier to be honest. Honesty is the greatest business gimmick in the world; honest businesspeople can spend half as much on advertising because they get twice as much repeat business.

## A HOT-MARKET STRATEGY

All of the preceding organizational guidelines are meant to prepare a buyer for any type of market, but here is a tactic that we rarely, if ever, saw in Seattle before 1989. A buyer walked into an open house hosted by the seller himself, and liked what he saw. As he spoke with the seller he learned that offers from other buyers were forthcoming. The price was $115,000. This aggressive buyer said, "I will offer you $119,000, plus $1,000 that I will write out to you on the spot, yours to keep, no matter what, if you accept my offer this minute. I will also deposit $10,000 in an earnest money account, yours to keep, if I default on the contract."

The seller accepted. This was one of the rare times when a buyer took control of the situation in our seller's market. In many instances the buyers have just let the sellers collect the offers and accept the one they liked the most, or counter-offer all of them, or give all bidders a deadline to present their highest offer. When this happens, we see many buyers pay $15,000–$35,000 over the asking price.

## THE GOOD SEARCH
### OVER A DOZEN AVENUES IN ADDITION TO THE TRADITIONAL OPEN-HOUSE VISITS

No buyer is likely to employ all of the following methods, just as no buyer should rely on only one of these approaches. Pick and choose; it's your buffet. But a balanced diet will keep your mother happy.

**1. Start with a swing on your own grapevine.** Tell everyone you know or meet that you are in the market for a house. Consider offering a finder's fee for information that leads to a successful transaction. Pay any resulting debts or your valves will stick. P.S.: Your "finder" can only tell you about an opportunity; any involvement by a friend or relative in negotiating or such could bring a charge of accepting a commission without a license.

**2. Start subscriptions to all of the local papers.** Especially those little neighborhood papers. You see, many people who sell their own properties don't understand that to sell their property for the best possible price they need to draw the largest possible crowd, which almost always means some serious advertising. They scoff, they buy cheap little ads, and they hope for a miracle. Pretend to be the answer to their dreams.

**3. Compile a list of local real estate publications and the days they are stocked.** Every town of any size in Washington has stands in restaurants and convenience stores that contain free real estate magazines, some for FSBOs (For-Sale-By-Owner) but most with only listed property (partial list in Appendix–"Resources"). One drawback: Due to the lagtime between listing and publication, many of the best properties will be long gone.

**4. Check to see if your local paper has a "bulldog" (weekend) edition.** This is the Saturday version of the Sunday paper. The ads are the same. Get a copy as soon as it hits the stands (often across the street from the newspaper office). Go through the ads, looking especially for "Just listed" or "First time available." Now get moving and take advantage of your head-start over less knowledgeable buyers.

**5. Do your own advertising.** I know some very successful investors who keep a simple ad running in a few of the cheaper publications, which is where people with FSBOs often place their own ads. "My wife and I would like to buy a house. We wouldn't mind having to do a little fix-up." Nothing threatening about that, is there?

**6. Oil your bicycle chain.** I had driven by a house near mine at least 1,000 times before I noticed that it had palm trees in the front yard, a startling sight in Seattle. Walking and bicycling around neighborhoods allows us to see more (vacant houses, for example) and makes it easier to approach people in those neighborhoods. "Hi, what a nice neighborhood! If I had the chance to move into this neighborhood, I'd sure jump at it....Know anyone who's been talking about selling?"

**7. Learn how to look up the owners of properties, vacant or otherwise.** If you visit your county/city offices (see #17, under "Speaking of Checklists"), you will find out much that you need to know.

**8. Stop at those garage sales.** I'm not sure it's efficient just to drive around

---

### GET YOUR LICENSE?

Folks frequently ask if they should get a real estate license to facilitate their search for a home or investment property. They're asking the wrong guy.

Yes, the license will provide them with lots of information. On the other hand, an agent has to disclose her status whenever she makes an offer (and she cannot get around this by having her brother-in-law buy it for her), so some sellers will respond with suspicion.

The crux of the question for me is an ethical one: How would you respond if your neighbor said, "I'm thinking about going to med school so I can get my drugs at a discount"? Is that someone you would want as your doctor? As your agent? As your neighbor?

Agents should have the right to buy real estate, of course, but those agents who put their desires above the needs of the sellers and buyers they are supposed to be serving should look for another line of work. A practical solution for brokers is to require the agent to notify his or her colleagues of an opportunity, and then give all of the buyers they know so many hours to act. Thereafter, the agent can buy it, provided that the seller is represented by an agent from another office.

to garage sales, chatting to see if the hosts are moving or know of anyone who might be, but as long as you're just driving by, what the heck. Besides, it's another opportunity to practice your negotiating.

**9. Consider a mail-out.** This requires access to tax records or a reverse directory. I've seen some enterprising buyers mail out 500 preprinted postcards, pointing out that "no commission will be involved." Someone always calls.

**10. In Seattle, consider subscribing to "FSBO Data Service"** (phone: 782-3914). This bargain service compiles a list of all the FSBO ads in the last 30 days from 18 newspapers in the Seattle area. Prices start at $35. Some real estate offices also subscribe to it, mostly in the pursuit of listings, but those who represent buyers may also offer it to their buyers.

**11. Investigate "repos" and foreclosures.** This trail is one of the steepest and rockiest a buyer can attempt. It is so complicated that it cannot even be covered in this chapter. My only encouraging observation is that since it's so tiring, most hikers will fall by the wayside; those who persist may eventually be the sole bidder on a property. But, I have known lots of bright people who have succumbed after many months of trying.

### AND NOW, WORKING WITH THE INDUSTRY

**12. Ask for the grand tour of the real estate office.** Every office has a different policy about the degree of involvement it allows or expects of its buyers. There are also multiple-listing rules to consider, so what is allowed in one area or office may not be acceptable in another. In any case, here are some of the ways that agents learn of properties, especially when they belong to a multiple, and apart from tips they get via the grapevine and from friends both in and out of the business:

**A. The computer and daily bulletin.** Most offices will probably depend on the computer to stay on top of the market, especially since it can be updated several times a day. In only a minute or two the computer can print out a compilation of all the properties listed in the last 24 hours. The computer can also be programmed to print out listings by criteria, such as "two-bedroom ramblers with a garage, under $87,500." The bulletin is delivered by courier to each office and often contains information on real estate courses and legal rulings as well as listings.

**B. The weekly catalog.** This is simply a compilation of information about properties for sale in the vicinity of the real estate office, with pictures. In a hot market this catalog loses some of its value. But houses that haven't sold after weeks or months are perhaps overpriced, and a buyer may want to consider making a "reasonable offer" on one of them.

**C. Brokers' opens.** This is a traditional method of marketing a new listing. The listing agent holds the house open for several hours on a weekday so that other agents can have easy access. Agents have commonly offered everything from fried chicken to lottery tickets to encourage other agents to take a look and bring back their buyers. When the market is slow, the food is great. And vice versa. No buyer who walks in off the street is likely to be ejected, so if you have time during the week, ask an agent about the possibility of visiting these properties.

**13. Follow the truck.** This is a joke. Someone suggested—some desperate buyer in Seattle—that a buyer should find the location of one or more of the companies that put up the yard signs for the real estate offices and follow their truck as it leaves in the morning. Isn't that crazy? Can you just see this convoy wending its way down a narrow street? Don't take this seriously. Really.

**14. Finally, think of something no one else has.** Here's a winner in this category. Someone approached a liquor store clerk and offered a fee for the name and address of every person who came in asking for moving boxes. Even if they were just tenants, it was one more house in transition and just maybe that landlord would be in the mood to sell at that moment. (Write me if you think of something equally clever.)

---

**CONFIDENTIAL! TOP SECRET! WELL, SORT OF.**

All information published by a multiple-listing service is considered confidential and is to be used only by its members in the fulfillment of their jobs. In other words, agents are not supposed to give or loan any of the catalogs or bulletins to consumers, or provide information to a buyer that could compromise the interests of the seller, etc.

But as one Seattle comedian said: "I had so many of those listing books in my trunk that I could get traction on ice."

## NEGOTIATING

Stop and think: How long has it been since you negotiated something?

My bet is no more than 12 hours. Oh, were you trying to think of when you last bought a car or attended a garage sale? We negotiate every day. Every time you start a sentence with one of the following phrases you're probably negotiating: "Would you mind—?"; "Will you—?"; "What if instead—?"

Therefore, even if you have engaged an agent who will present and/or negotiate your offer, you will still be negotiating with someone every day, including that agent, the lender, etc., so it pays to know the basic principles of this body of knowledge. In fact, negotiating is just a civilized person's method of fulfilling needs and desires.

This is a *very* brief presentation of those principles. For a more thorough discussion, see the books mentioned at the end of this chapter.

## THE PRINCIPLES

**1. Primum non nocere.** Or as the physicians say, "First, we do no damage." Or as a professional negotiator once summed it up, "Just shut up." Amateurs think that negotiating amounts to talking their fool heads off. The pros know that it starts by being quiet and observing principle number two.

**2. Listen.** This is a very real challenge for those of us who are full of answers and other ingredients. Studies have shown that the average man starts formulating an answer in six seconds, whereas women wait 20 seconds. Try this exercise in *active* listening: When someone finishes a statement, stay quiet but count to yourself; notice that by the time you count to 10 most people will have begun to tell you more.

**3. Ask questions.** Did you find it hard in the above exercise to just listen and not to comment? Good. You're becoming aware that negotiating takes practice. Now instead of commenting, start practicing the art of gentle questioning. It has been said that the most sure way to attract a lover is to ask about them, not to talk about yourself.

**4. Show the benefit.** The amateur says, "I am offering this because I want—." The pro says, "You are hoping to accomplish such and such; this offer is designed to help you accomplish that." Don't talk about your needs. First find out theirs; then point out which ones you are fulfilling.

**5. Tell the truth.** Do you have a perfect memory? If not, you cannot lie without eventually entangling yourself. Even if the wound heals there will *always* be a scar. Ask any deceived lover. Ask me. No, better not.

**6. Be specific.** Sure signs of the amateur: round numbers and splitting the difference. Contrast this approach: "Your price of $97,800 was an excellent asking price, but our research has shown that this size house typically sells for $93,500. In fact, the Bradford property on Vine is now available at $93,450. But since your house has an exceptionally well-maintained yard, we are prepared to offer $94,850, which is 97% of your asking price. At that price we can make the 20% down payment you wanted. We can also close in 30 days as you requested." We complimented the seller, showed several benefits, gave a specific price and specific reasons for our offer. The seller is now challenged to give reasons why he shouldn't accept.

**7. Have an alternative.** In the above example we mentioned the "Bradford property on Vine" and even pointed out that it is cheaper. The buyer who does not have an alternative, or cannot act as if he does, may be the seller's puppet. In theory we can say that a buyer should always act indifferent, but in fact many sellers have deliberately sold to the buyer who showed enthusiasm and indicated he would cherish that property. We need to react appropriately after we learn what the seller wants.

**8. Reject the offer, not the person.** And accept rejection as an impersonal response. The difference between amateurs and professionals is the number of bullets we dodge before we return fire. When that moment comes, amateurs make excuses for their anger, whereas professionals just take a walk and, if possible, turn over the negotiations to someone else.

## DOWN WITH THE PUT-DOWNS

A number of the get-rich gurus of real estate have advised buyers to destroy the seller's confidence by pointing out flaws in the property. There is no riskier strategy. You would not believe how touchy sellers can be, or how quickly they can storm away from the negotiating table.

In fact, it may not even be wise to talk about your remodeling plans, since even this can be seen as criticism of the seller's castle. Be sensitive, and *never* refer to "all that money" the seller will receive.

**For further research:**

1. Gerard Nierenberg. *The Art of Negotiating.* New York: Cornerstone, 1981. $5.95, 182 pages.

2. Gary Karass. *Negotiate to Close.* New York: Simon & Schuster, 1985. $16.95, 219 pages.

# Buyer Brokering: The Most Confusing Subject

*If it sounds too good to be true,*
*you just don't understand it yet.*

—Jim Stacey, *broker*

*DISCLOSURE—In Washington, an agent must fully disclose who he or she is representing. This disclosure must be made prior to preparing a purchase and sale agreement. The agreement must contain a statement that confirms that the disclosure was made....Usually the agent is working for the seller. Without this disclosure, many buyers might fail to recognize that although the [selling] agent may spend more time with the buyers in helping them locate the house they are looking for, the agent's main duties and loyalties are to the seller.*

—Alan Tonnon, *Washington Real Estate Law*

**B**uyer brokering is a legal relationship between a real estate agent and a buyer wherein the selling agent represents the buyer's interests and must strive to attain the best possible price and terms for that buyer. The only issue that seems as confusing as buyer brokering is teenage sex. It can seem so appealing, even compelling, at the time, but there just has to be some reason not to—uh, you know. Or wouldn't everyone else be doing it? Or are they, and just not telling? Will you be the first in your crowd or the last? Will everyone laugh? Or will you wear a smile that makes everyone wonder?

I have some good news: There is no great moral issue with buyer brokering. No guilt. No support payments. It is simply a business arrangement. An agent legally takes a buyer's side. The morning after, the vast majority of buyers feel pleased, even if they can't remember the agent's name. Of course, it is limited to consenting adults.

When I wrote my first article on buyer brokering in 1985, I wrote more from theory than experience. I had just started to act as a buyer's agent as well as a listing agent. This approach to working with buyers seemed to make sense, but there weren't a lot of oldtimers to interview. Anyone who had done it—fewer than one percent of agents— was pretty much viewed as a radical in our very staid, traditional industry. Some of the most traditional brokers even seemed to attach a moral stigma to it, as if they were in the real estate business to be missionaries. Later on, I began to realize how threatened many brokers are by change, and so for a while I felt that I had a mission to help my colleagues see that buyer brokering is simply another way to do business, another way to be one step ahead of the crowd in the offering of services. After encountering some buffalo-brain resistance, my missionary zeal disappeared and I turned to educating the public instead. It pays much better.

I won't pretend to be totally objective, nor will I conceal the complications of buyer brokering—it's not without its problems. But after five years of owning a company in which buyer brokering has comprised over 80% of our business, you may not be surprised that I find it to be a viable and respectable enterprise.

Let's start with a review of the traditional real estate agent's relationship to the buyer and seller, followed by the first questions that usually come to the buyer's mind, and then I'll provide a little history of how this all came about.

## REVIEW

Jane, an agent with Traditional Realty, approaches a seller with a marketing plan. If Jane and the seller reach an agreement on the plan and compensation, Jane has become the seller's listing agent and the seller has become Jane's client. At the same time, Jane is also working with buyers on another transaction in which Bob from Second Realty is the listing agent. On this transaction Jane is called the "selling agent," the agent who writes and presents an offer for the buyers.

Bob and Jane are both members of Typical Multiple Listing Service, which observes the tradition of subagency, meaning that if one agent takes a listing all other agents in that multiple promise to work on behalf of the seller when they present an offer. Therefore, as Bob's subagent, Jane owes as much loyalty and service in "fiduciary duties" to Bob's seller, whom she has never met, as she does to her own seller, who is an old friend of hers. Bob's and Jane's offices will most likely split the commission paid by the seller.

Even though Jane has spent over a month working with her buyers, legally she can only treat them as *customers*, which means that she must be forthright with them but she cannot represent their interests in any way that clashes with the seller's.

She may tell them of good lenders or explain financing options, but she cannot recommend (without the seller-client's consent) any option that would cost the seller or put the seller at any kind of disadvantage. She is even supposed to discourage them from pursuing something that is to their advantage—such as VA financing in which the seller must pay the entire escrow fee—if she knows that it will cost the seller.

Later, a couple who lives on Jane's block comes to her and asks her to represent them as a buyer broker. Jane asks for and receives permission from her broker. She now must tell every seller she encounters in searching for a home for her neighbors that she is representing the buyers solely; she must "sever the chain of subagency." Now she can and must tell the buyers about the best kind of financing options, negotiating strategies, etc., and exclusively represent their interests in all future negotiations. Jane is still known as the selling agent, but she is also a buyer broker in this one instance. Tomorrow she may return to a traditional selling agent and/or listing agent role.

## WHEN IS BUYER BROKERING THE MOST APPROPRIATE?

Buyer brokering is almost always the best arrangement for the buyer (see "Complications" below), but for the agent the road is not so clear. In the first place, many brokers still refuse to allow their agents to practice buyer brokering, even if at times it means a total denial of common sense (see #3 below). In the second place, the agent must avoid involving herself in any "dual agency relationships" if at all possible (more on this later). Finally, if she is new to the business and doesn't have a broker who understands buyer brokering, an agent may be safer if she sticks to the traditional approaches for the time being.

There are a number of instances, however, in which the "experts" agree that an agent is probably on the best legal and ethical track if she does practice buyer brokering. These instances occur when:

**1.** The buyer is a friend—possibly even just a friendly acquaintance, such as a neighbor.

**2.** The buyer is referred to the agent by other agents, buyers, or acquaintances.

**3.** The buyer is a relative. This should be obvious, but I have seen an agent at a traditional company present an offer for her son while stating that she was representing the seller. This would amuse a jury and could lead to a finding that she also represented the buyer "by implication" in an illegal dual agency.

**4.** The buyer has engaged in other business, academic, or social relationships with the agent that might compromise the agent's ability to represent the seller's interests—for instance, when an agent has a longstanding working relationship with an investor but pretends to put the seller's interests first.

**5.** The buyer is a professional investor who has sought out an experienced agent and expects a very high degree of loyalty.

## TYPICAL QUESTIONS FROM BUYERS

**Cost.** The first question from every buyer is, "Will it cost me anything?" If the property you buy is listed, the seller has probably already agreed to pay a "selling office commission (SOC)," no matter who the agent represents. So in that case you wouldn't need to come up with any more cash. Of course, it can be argued that the commission is built into the price and that you are already paying part of the commission whether you're represented or not as a buyer. If more buyers realized that every month $30–$50, or more, of their payments were paying off that commission, the demand for buyer brokering would grow even faster that it has.

If the property is not listed, then the fee is negotiated with your individual agent. Personally, I don't like to work for free, but I also want my buyer-client to experience every possible benefit of buyer brokering, so first I ask the unlisted seller (via the contract-offer) to pay me a commission that has already been negotiated with and agreed to by my buyer. If the seller refuses, I then ask the buyer, "Would you like me to add my fee to the price, so that I get my fee from the seller's proceeds?" (This, of course, increases the buyer's loan and monthly payments.) Or I ask, "Would you prefer to pay me directly with a check?" Most sellers will pay a reasonable commission, and most lenders know they are also financing built-in commissions. According to my manager, about 6% of our For Sale By Owner (FSBO) buyers have paid us directly, and we have added our fee to the price about 12% of the time. This means that around 82% of the time we have received our fee from the seller's proceeds without any increase in the property's price.

**Legality.** "Is buyer brokering completely legal?" Of course. Occasionally, one of our buyers has encountered an agent who said it wasn't. We don't know whether that agent was just ignorant, or if he was a prevaricator trying to "steal" a buyer. Although it is completely legal, buyer brokering does generally require more knowledge of real estate law, and this may encourage lazier, less-principled agents to "skip all that hassle" by telling a buyer that it isn't legal. Most of the agents doing buyer brokering are a cut above the average (my biased opinion, obviously), and are often more concerned with legalities and trying to keep a healthy balance between greed, service, and principles.

**Loyalty conflict.** "How can it be legal to work against someone's interests (the seller's) and still get paid by them?" Ask the attorneys; they do it all the time. Nothing ever sticks in a human's craw as much as paying an ex- spouse's divorce attorney. Anyway, the American courts ruled in the 19th century that payment alone does not establish a duty; however, a court might interpret a payment as establishing a duty if there were no other "proof" of which party was the client. With this in mind, the buyer broker is likely to insist that the buyer sign a contract. In addition, in Washington an agent must have a contract to make a claim for payment. I think that buyers too should want a contract; then they would know what they were getting, in detail.

**Differences.** "How different is it from traditional real estate?" As different as mediation or arbitration is from traditional attorney practices, only, ironically, the buyer broker more closely resembles the attorney than the mediator. In other words, traditional agents are often just trying to play the middleman and "put a deal together" any way they can, even though they're supposed to "take sides" with the seller, whereas the buyer broker actually takes the buyer's side. We can see tangible differences later in a comparison of how the two different contracts are written.

**Atmosphere.** "Are there any problems with reactions from sellers or other agents?" Occasionally, but no more problems on a percentage basis than with the traditional approach. I think the buyer's biggest concern is always "Will the seller not want to accept my offer because the agent is representing me?" Perhaps one seller in 25 dissents, and we have had sellers accept another offer rather than ours. Whether buyer brokering was the main reason, we'll never know. However, we do know from a government study that the majority of sellers have mistakenly assumed all along that the selling agent was supposed to represent the buyer, and many a seller has said, "I don't see how what you're doing is any different." Since that's the type of acceptance the buyer broker wants the seller to feel, we're not going to sit there and say, "You'd better not take our buyer's offer; we're going to be working against your interests." We certainly don't try to make the seller feel that we are the enemy.

Keep in mind that I can and do switch hats at any time and become a listing agent, so I know the point of view from the listing agent's and seller's side as well. In fact, on my last listing the selling agent was a buyer broker. I read the offer closely and told my seller I saw no reason not to accept it. The only difference I anticipated was that if later we had to negotiate a work order or any other item, I couldn't assume that the selling agent would be on my seller's side.

We have encountered pockets of hostility from individual agents who couldn't or wouldn't express their reasons for not cooperating with buyer brokering. I don't think it could be "on principle," because the most principled agents either practice buyer brokering or accept it as a viable alternative. I think the dissenters are just worried that it's going to mean less money for them or that it will expose the shortcomings of the traditional approach. On the other hand, many a listing agent has actually made the negotiation atmosphere as genial as possible by reassuring her seller that she represents the seller's interests and the selling agent represents the buyer's interests. Many a seller has then remarked, "Seems fair to me." It does to me too.

Very infrequently we see a listing in the Puget Sound area with fine print that reads, "Seller will not pay agent representing a buyer." We suspect this is the agent's idea, because sellers generally just want to sell; they don't give a lot of thought to theory about the fine points of the law. Keep in mind that Washington law requires that the agent present all offers, so this listing agent would still have to give us a chance to present our offer. As buyers' representatives, we would ignore this fine print and ask for a commission anyway, or deduct the amount of the selling office's commission from the price and collect the commission from the buyer. This situation has been so rare that we have never had occasion to present an offer to such a seller, but if ever we do, we won't be surprised when the listing agent ends up with egg on his face. He is not doing his sellers a favor to discourage any offers; the agent and seller should welcome all offers and then decide if they want to play ball. A good buyer broker will do everything possible to present the offer to the seller in a professional and effective manner, and avoid antagonizing either the seller or listing agent.

**How common?** "Will I be able to find a buyer broker in my area?" Four years ago some of our industry's leaders predicted that in five years buyer brokering would constitute half of our business (a remarkable coincidence, considering the fact that exactly half of the consumers are buyers). The change has been nowhere near that fast, although apparently there has been a 3,000% increase nationwide in the number of agents practicing it. A recent *Realtor* study concluded that over 30% of the nation's offices now have one or more agents offering this service. There are, of course, different levels of involvement in buyer brokering: agents who do it on a regular basis, agents who do it only when asked, agents who would do it if their brokers would let them, and agents who don't want to or don't know how to do it.

In the first category, I estimate the "regulars" number from 75 to 150 (up from 5 or 6 in 1986) of the 10,000 agents in the Puget Sound area, but hundreds more have done it occasionally and/or are willing to. In Spokane and other Washington towns, with the exception of the Mt. Vernon–Anacortes area, I haven't found much evidence of buyer brokering—at least no one who openly advertises it.

**Amount of compensation.** "Will the buyer broker work for a flat fee or a reduced fee?" As I said earlier, I believe that most of the agents who practice buyer brokering are a cut above the average—even a bit idealistic, given the level of competition in this business—so they are usually the last ones to try to make their fortune on any one transaction. I'm not going to print any numbers about what I charge or what I think anyone else should charge, but in general, I want to be paid approximately what I would receive if I were performing in the traditional manner. Many buyers ask me to work for a "reduced fee." I answer this way: "If I work against your interests, the seller will pay me 700 pieces of lagniappe, but if I work for your interests you want me to keep 400 and give you 300? Have I summed it up correctly?" Most buyers look a bit embarrassed when they hear it put this way. As much as I like my buyers, I'm not that inclined to become the main contributor to their favorite charity—themselves. I tell my buyers that I am almost as motivated by money as the next guy, so they shouldn't try to see how much of my motivation they can take away. If anything, they should consider paying me a bonus if I save them money. That usually stops most talk about working for a reduced fee.

As to whether we do buyer brokering on a percentage basis, by the hour, or for a flat fee, that's open to negotiation and there's no objection to any combination of these approaches.

**Conflict of interest.** "If my agent is receiving a percentage of the price, why would she be motivated to negotiate a lower price?" Personally, I consider this a nonissue, but it does deserve an answer.

If a buyer broker saved a buyer $5,000 on the price, in most instances this translates into a "loss" to the agent of anywhere from $80–$200. If the agent still stands to receive, say, a commission of $2,500, most agents are going to think more about what they will get than what they won't get. Since the agent wants the buyer's repeat business, doing a good job and having a happy buyer (who also sends his friends) will more than make up for any so-called loss. I tell any buyer who doubts my ability to negotiate aggressively on his behalf that: (1) perhaps there is too little trust for us to enter into a relationship, but (2) if he feels that it really isn't a matter of trust, just human nature, then he can swing the advantage to himself by simply offering me a bonus, a percentage of anything I save him. Then he knows I'll be motivated to negotiate aggressively on his behalf. My integrity isn't for sale for $80–$200. My bottom line is $10,000. Heck, I've got my principles.

**Saving money.** "Will a buyer broker usually save me money?" That's as impossible to answer as "If you had driven to work via a different route this morning, would you have been in a wreck?" We can be excellent negotiators, but we can never really prove that we did anything that turned out to be unique. We can only conjecture. We probably do save some money for a significant percentage of our buyers, but I don't dwell on this. My emphasis is on the differences in the service, relationship, and contract.

In a seller's market, as we've had in the Puget Sound area, paying more than the asking price can become commonplace, so saving a buyer money may require that we concentrate on getting some other concession from the seller. Unfortunately, many buyers seem to be as hung up on the price as sellers are, instead of looking at the beneficial terms, net costs, or some other savings. That's one of the reasons I've concluded that it takes both bright consumers and bright agents to do buyer brokering. Some dogs can't learn new tricks, no matter how many biscuits you put in their bowl.

**A service difference.** "What's an example of a service difference?" A traditional agent may not want to tell you about an unlisted house that sounds right for you. She risks your going directly to that seller and leaving her in the cold. But a buyer broker is legally and morally obligated to tell you, and would have no reason *not* to tell you, since you've (probably) agreed to see that she gets paid no matter what the status of the house is.

**A relationship difference.** "What's different about the buyer-agent relationship?" One of the main differences is confidentiality. The traditional agent doesn't dare get caught not telling the seller everything he knows about you, the buyer, from your income to your intentions for the property. But the buyer broker has a legal duty to disclose only that information which the buyer has authorized. The buyer doesn't have to watch everything he says around the agent. Celebrities frequently want this arrangement but don't understand that only a buyer broker can offer it. Don Johnson ("Miami Vice") even sued an agent for telling the seller he was the buyer. Why? The seller knew immediately that the buyer was wealthy and could afford the seller's price.

**A contract difference.** "Does the buyer broker use a different purchase and sale agreement?" He or she can use any contract that the buyer wants and the broker agrees to, but one of the buyer broker's goals is not to upset the entire applecart when all that's needed is just a bag or two of fruit. Remember: We don't want to establish an adversarial atmosphere with the seller or listing agent. Such a tactic may work for attorneys who are getting paid by the hour and have a different degree of leverage, but in real estate the seller could too easily take offense and ignore our offer, so we have to walk a little more gingerly. My own approach is to use the front pages of the most common local contract and add a page or two of attorney-approved verbiage that asks for a number of benefits and protections for the buyer. Later in the chapter I'll provide some examples.

**The seller's market.** "What good is a buyer broker when everyone is paying more than the asking price?" The question presupposes that price is the only thing that matters or is negotiated in a contract. It also presupposes that everybody pays more than the seller is asking and that all buyers would pay the same amount over the asking price. That's a few too many jumps to the gun. You either want a relationship based on trust, in which the agent agrees to keep your confidence and write a contract that favors your interests, or you don't. If you do, the fact that it's a seller's market is irrelevant.

**Retainer fees.** "Will a buyer have to come up with any money up front?" Possibly. Agents in the Puget Sound Multiple Listing Association enjoy the arrangement of having the seller pay the selling agent, no matter who the agent represents, if the seller didn't previously make an exception in the listing contract. Thus, most of the time, agents are paid from the seller's proceeds, and the buyers put out no more cash than they normally would for down payments and closing costs. Nevertheless, as a businessman I must say that retainer fees have their place. I may ask for a retainer fee that (1) is refunded or applied to the buyer's costs if the buyer completes a transaction, or (2) is forfeited by the buyer if she decides after some time to quit looking or changes our relationship in some other drastic way.

My reason for taking the retainer fee is to test the buyer's sincerity (I don't want to waste time with someone who is just "thinking about buying") and to ensure that I will receive some compensation for my time if after a couple of weeks the client decides to fire me or to quit looking or whatever. An agent on a residential transaction might ask for a retainer of no more than $100–$500; in large commercial transactions a retainer of $10,000 might be nominal. In any case, retainer fees are usually quite negotiable, and many agents will never ask for one.

**Firing the buyer broker.** "Can a buyer enter into a contract with a buyer broker and then fire him?" You may not be able to, if you don't put it in your contract, but that's one of those things you want to think about. The buyer broker should also be able to fire the persnickety impossible-to-please buyer. One concern for the buyer in this case might be whether any retainer fee is to be returned. I would advise any agents who are contemplating taking retainer fees to make these fees partially or fully refundable for a reasonable time, for the sake of fairness and good business practices. About six to eight minutes should do.

**Consumer involvement.** "Why should a buyer have to pay an agent a fee, as you might have to do with a buyer broker contract, if the buyer found a FSBO property?" Because the agent isn't being paid to be a cab driver. Although finding good properties depends in part on skills and serendipity, a good deal of it is just time-consuming driving. The real work and expertise are in the areas of advising a buyer on financing, contracts, work orders, pricing, etc. That is when I become the most valuable. First-time buyers in particular place too much emphasis on finding a property, forgetting that if the financing is funko or the contract is cockeyed all the discoveries in the world might be in vain. When a buyer has been a successful searcher and saved me a good deal of time, I might offer rebates or discounts, but the search is not the most important thing I have to offer. This should all be covered in the contract between the buyer and agent.

**Consumer complication.** "If a buyer broker will give a buyer a discount if he finds his own property, then why shouldn't a buyer just drive around with another agent until he finds what he wants and then go to the buyer broker?" Because he'll go to real estate hell. But that comes later. On this earth we have to deal with the agent who drove him around. That agent may claim to be the "procuring cause" and demand a healthy percentage of any commission or a placating "tip," so there goes any "rebate" to the buyer. And there's another issue here: Buyer brokering looks sleazy when it's abused in this way, and that's exactly the image we're trying to get away from. The abused agent may now tell the seller that buyer brokers can't be trusted. In other words, if we don't keep the idealism and integrity intact, we'll lose in the long run. And short run. I hear that in real estate hell everything has a lock on it. Everything. Rusted shut.

**Exclusivity.** "Does the buyer broker expect the buyer to look at houses with her exclusively?" That's up to the individual agent, but if you're asking me, yes. If you look with four agents, three won't get paid. I don't ever again want to be one of those three, so I personally require exclusivity. Most of us are content to have one doctor or one dentist at a time, so why do we need more than one agent? Loyalty for loyalty.

**Limited choices.** "But wouldn't a buyer who is looking with only one agent have less chance of finding his dream home?" My first response to that question is: Is there only one property in the world that could ever satisfy all our needs? I think lots of buyers who swear they found the perfect house are just saying that they found all they needed when they were finally in the mood to buy, or ufficiently tired of the chase. Second, it often takes time, several days or even eks, for a buyer and an agent to "click" and come to some quality communi- n about their goal. That's hard enough to bring off with one agent, much number of them. Third, the buyer seems to have reverted to thinking of nt as just a property finder instead of a professional negotiator/coun- tract writer, etc. This is the kind of buyer we have seen get into deep horse-heap and then yell for help. Fourth, the better the agent the more likely she will be to insist on loyalty, so if you want quality you must accept this trade-off. Last but not least, in an area served by a multiple listing association everyone has access to the same listed homes.

**Pocket listings.** "But in a seller's market, won't even more agents than usual 'pocket' a listing, or delay turning it in to the multiple listing service (sandbagging it)? How are we going to learn about those listings if we don't work with several agents?" Do you know which agents they are? Of course you don't. Will they have just the very house you wanted? Perhaps. Will you be able to trust that this is the only way in which they bend the rules? Do good things happen to us when we join forces with the corrupt?

**Larger companies.** "The larger companies seem to get more listings, so they may stick to traditional real estate, but wouldn't we learn about more new listings with them?" First, all buyers and sellers should be reminded that in reality they work with an individual agent more than with a company. Second, this buyer has reverted once again to emphasizing only the search for the perfect property. Third, the larger companies attract more buyers and sellers, so they may not be able to offer any larger slices of the pie than the medium and small offices do. While the size of the company is essentially irrelevant, the ability of the individual agent is extremely relevant. Ironically, one of the most common complaints from buyers is that an agent showed them only his own listings, yet we have some buyers who turn right around and audition for the role of "The Manipulated Buyer." Of course, the traditional agent can't depend on his buyer's loyalty, so he may be all the more inclined to create pressure that serves his own interests, not those of the buyer.

**Broker objection.** "Why would a broker ever feel reluctant to allow her agents to practice buyer brokering?" First, buyer brokering often requires additional legal training, so the broker may be worried about the extent of her own legal knowledge or that of her agents. Second, it may seem to threaten a part of the company's income, since the company can't "double-end" as many transactions; in the Puget Sound area a company sells its own listings about 35%–40% of the time and does not have to split the commission in those cases. Some brokers may worry that if buyers thought they shouldn't call the listing agent, the company would lose some of those in-house sales. They apparently don't realize that buyer brokering could make up for any such losses. I remember one broker who at first thought buyer brokering was a communist conspiracy. He then took the time to listen. Within a few months he had more than 30 agents practicing it. Quick learner.

Personally, I don't think the public will make any big changes any time soon; buyer brokering will probably continue to appeal only to about the same percentage of consumers who wear a helmet when they ride a bicycle.

**Broker appeal.** "Why would a broker want to do buyer brokering when there is money to be made in traditional real estate?" I'm a businessman, perhaps a bit more idealistic than most and not as idealistic as some, but one who believes that time is precious and efficiency should be a goal, say four days of every week. The real estate industry is extremely inefficient; we waste more time before 9:00 a.m. than the army does all day. We often spend as much energy as makeup artists do, with the same goal and results: a better image, but no lasting improvement in ability. I want my agents to waste the least amount of time possible, so that they can devote more time to their education, families, and clients, yet have a better batting average and produce more income per agent. Call it idealistic business. It can only happen if the agent and the buyer are mutually selective and have agreed to work as a team.

## TWO COMPLICATIONS

Misbehavior on the part of the buyer broker may be imputed to ("blamed on") the buyer. If a buyer retains an agent as his representative, and the agent harms the seller through negligence, dishonesty, etc., the seller may sue the agent *and* the buyer. In the traditional scenario, the agent works with the buyer as a subagent representing the seller, and the seller may not be able to name the buyer in a lawsuit. Moral: If a competent, squeaky-clean buyer broker is not available, the traditional subagency approach may be the best one for the buyer-customer to take.

Another complication is "undisclosed dual agency." It is likely to occur when an agent *should* represent the buyer, but instead chooses the traditional subagency routine of representing the seller. To understand it, let's review the correct relationship between an agent and a buyer:

**Single-agency** is not a complication, but the ideal. Single-agency occurs when the agent owes fiduciary duties and loyalty to one party in a transaction—the client. The other party receives only customer-level service.

**Disclosed dual agency** occurs when the agent represents both the buyer and the seller and owes them the same duties, such as full disclosure and confidentiality. These duties can quickly conflict. An example of a legal dual agency is when the buyer is a friend of the agent and the seller is the agent's mother, and everyone knows it and agrees to an "informed consent" for the agent to practice dual agency. The informed consent must be in writing and must be very explicit about how the agent can no longer take sides, and about what problems and alternatives may exist. Then the agent must play win-win, act as a facilitator or mediator, and bring the parties to a fair compromise.

**Undisclosed dual agency** can occur when an agent sells her own listing to a friend without telling the seller of her relationship with the buyer. The seller may sue for damages and rescind the contract, even if there are no damages. The agent I mentioned earlier, who made an offer for her son without getting an informed consent from the seller whom she purported to be representing, is a candidate for a suit for damages and rescission, as well as disciplinary proceedings and loss of commissions.

In 1989 one of America's largest commercial real estate firms was ordered to pay $15 million in damages to a seller for practicing undisclosed dual agency. The company had listed the property and then sold it to a buyer who already owned adjoining property and planned to construct a shopping center. The agent knew this but did not disclose it to the seller.

Dual agency, disclosed or undisclosed, is an agent's nightmare. In either case, it takes only one unhappy party and an eager attorney to send the game into overtime. Every broker should own and discuss with her agents the reference books on agency issues mentioned in the Appendix—"Buyer brokering."

## CONTRACT DIFFERENCES

A most naive agent wrote a letter in 1989 to the *Seattle Times*: "We [traditional] agents can do anything for the buyers that buyer brokers do" (paraphrased). No, they can't. Not legally. Dual agency, you know. Rescission of the contract is often the seller's automatic right if the agent does anything in opposition to the seller's interest.

Here are some differences we might see in the contract used by a buyer broker. The actual language is omitted to prevent both consumers and inexperienced agents from playing jailhouse lawyer. Both should see an attorney or experienced buyer broker for specific language and details.

**1. Financing.** The agent naturally seeks the most advantageous financing method for the buyer, considering the size of the buyer's down payment, ability to qualify, etc. The agent then tries to persuade the seller that this method is appropriate.

**2. Title search & insurance.** Additional language may be incorporated requiring that a copy of the title search be sent immediately to the buyer, with an escape clause and/or provisions for the seller to provide extended title insurance if certain complications exist.

**3. Phrases repeated.** Because some sellers may later swear that they were not aware of an obligation, phrases that address common sticking points may be repeated deliberately in an addendum that requires a seller's separate signature.

**4. Closing agent.** Buyer brokers are more likely to persuade all parties to use an attorney instead of an escrow agent.

**5. Deadlines.** All deadlines (loan approval, closing date, etc.) are determined with the buyer's preferences in mind. Provisions for reasonable extensions may be included.

**6. Closing costs.** With the guidance of a CPA, the buyer broker may try to divide the closing costs so that the buyer receives the greatest tax savings.

**7. Inspection clause.** Even the most traditional agents will include this clause or addendum, but a buyer broker may add language that gives the buyer greater leeway to reject the inspection without penalty. It is common to negotiate for more time for the buyer to look over the inspection.

**8. Possession.** Occasionally a seller is reluctant to leave the premises or to leave them in good condition. Language may be included for assessing fines or withholding payments when this occurs.

**9. Earnest money.** Language may be included that delays the deposit of the earnest money until some event has occurred, such as the structural inspection.

**10. Included items.** The buyer broker typically takes more pains to list exactly which items are included in the sale and to stress that appliances and such be in good working order.

**11. Repairs.** The buyer broker tries to persuade the seller to perform repairs and/or ensure that the buyer's contribution to the repair effort will be reimbursed in the event of a voided contract.

**12. Rescission.** The buyer broker may include language to provide for the prompt return of the buyer's earnest money in the event of a voided contract, without having to get the seller's signature.

## A LITTLE HISTORY

Once upon a time, commercial agents found themselves working with buyers who asked for the agents' devoted efforts searching and negotiating for many months. These agents thought of ways to make sure they got paid for their time. They devised up-front fees and made contracts with the buyer. Residential agents only thought about things like this from time to time. We assumed that the traditional relationship with the buyer (Be nice; hope they'll be loyal) was here to stay.

Then, in 1981, the Federal Trade Commission completed a study (not released until 1984) that revealed that over 70% of buyers believed the selling agent was their agent, whom they could confide in. So the FTC told the real estate industry: "Clean up your act. Start disclosing your loyalty to the seller."

Although James Warkentin and other attorneys in the eastern states had been teaching buyer brokering throughout the seventies and and early eighties, the real impact wasn't felt until the publication in 1984 of *Home Buyers: Lambs to The Slaughter?* by Sloan Bashinsky, an Alabama attorney and broker. The book sold well but failed to receive any awards from the real estate industry. It did, however, convince many buyers to investigate their options more aggressively, and taught them not to confide in a traditional agent.

In 1986 the Washington real estate commissioners held public hearings, led by John Reilly, a Hawaiian attorney and expert on buyer brokering. On April 1, 1987, Washington's disclosure law went into effect. Almost 2,000 agents flocked to meetings to learn more about this "frightening" mandate that required agents to be candid.

In 1989, Barry Miller, a Denver broker and educator, formed the Real Estate Buyer Agents Council (REBAC), a national educational and referral organization for buyer brokers and consumers (see Appendix). By 1990 about 30 states had passed disclosure laws, nearly the same number of states as have representatives in REBAC.

## WASHINGTON'S DISCLOSURE LAW

Washington's disclosure law is still widely misunderstood. Many consumers think it makes buyer brokering legal for the first time. Wrong. Others think it requires agents to represent sellers. Wrong. Some think it means the agent just has to be up-front and reveal who is a client and who is a customer, prior to the signing of the purchase agreement. Right. The disclosure law was simply a catalyst in the ongoing process of improving and increasing the options and awareness of the Washington buyer. It has also provided the buyer with the opportunity to gain some insight into an agent's values and attitudes, depending on whether he or she agrees with and consistently practices disclosure.

# EVALUATING: PRICES

This chapter focuses on the various methods used to price real estate, and the following two chapters consider highly related matters: evaluating the assets and problems of a property. Imagine for a moment a sunburned man trying to pick blackberries in a poison ivy patch, and perhaps that will give you some idea of how overwhelmed I feel in trying to separate the above subjects—prices, repairs, value—subjects so intertwined that all separations are arbitrary and are made here merely to create chapters of a manageable size.

In other words, if the reader is to achieve the maximum comprehension of the relationship of prices to assets or problems, and vice versa, then all three chapters should be read at least once. Reading one chapter three times will probably not prove as effective.

### IS THERE SUCH A THING AS A "FAIR PRICE"?

Why do some cars cost more than houses? Why do diamonds usually cost more than dishwashers? Why do bad movies cost as much as good ones? Obviously, the factors that determine prices are not always logical, are not necessarily tied to function, and are hardly ever in our control to the extent that we would like. It's all very confusing. Anyone who insists on prices being fair will eventually ask the bartender for a double hemlock on the rocks.

The best that we can hope for is to understand how a reasonable seller goes about pricing his house, how a buyer judges whether it's a reasonable price, and how an appraiser concludes whether the seller and buyer are talking turkey or babel.

### THE BALLPARK

This 1,500-square-foot house is priced at $120,000 but the one on the hill is $190,000. If size isn't a factor in this case, what explains the difference? First, we look to see if there are any tangible, emotional, or cultural factors, such as a view, a greenbelt, waterfront, zoning, noise, commuting considerations, or a substantially larger lot. If not, the explanation most likely has to do with education and politics.

Most of us want to live around people like ourselves who, even though they may not vote the same, share many of our opinions on how humans should conduct themselves. We often start with the assumption that people who can afford what we can afford will believe what we believe, and so we buy a particular house in a particular neighborhood, not because we get the most house for the dollar, but because we want to be politically and culturally comfortable. We may also be influenced by our belief that with each passing year we should reward ourselves for our accomplishments at work and in raising a family. So we make a move that in our minds is a move up the rungs. In reality, we could often stay put, spend half as much on remodeling, and get all of the tangible improvements that we tell ourselves we are moving for. But in our self-esteem and self-reward system it would not be the same.

Nowhere does our pricing scheme tell us that if a house costs more, it's worth more. Or that it isn't. How do we define "worth"? Do we automatically get more square feet, fewer cracks, better insulation, or higher amperage? Of course not. "Worth" is perception, it is belief, it is faith. We merely get a house that most people who know the neighborhood would say is worth just about what we paid for it (or a little less, if they bought their own house over five years ago). Our whole system of pricing is a subjective exercise that can either be ridiculed or said to be quite sensible, depending upon whether the judge is a disinterested party.

Now my analysis of motivations and pricing reflects just my opinion and may be torpedoed by any other observer, but of this much I feel confident: Anyone's analysis will prove that pricing is a much more complicated fact of life than the casual observer thinks. This brings us to one of my pet peeves: the belief that there is such a thing as an "accurate price" and that the system of paid appraisals can determine what that price is. The appraisal system is only slightly more defensible than one that judges poetry by weighing it (which one of my better professors did). Nevertheless, the appraisal system is deeply entrenched and, absurd though it may be at times, our present challenge is to learn how to work with it while hoping for a better system in the future.

## WHAT IS AN APPRAISAL?

An appraisal is one person's opinion of a property's value on the day it is appraised. "Value is what a reasonable seller would accept, and what a reasonable buyer would pay, both parties being informed of the marketplace and neither being unduly motivated to act hastily."

The opinion must be supported by data, which the appraiser chooses carefully in order to demonstrate that the conclusion verifies that the data was properly chosen and verifies the conclusion determined by the data, and which indicates that if a dog chases its own tail long enough, it is its own grandpa. Most appraisers are very careful not to prove themselves wrong.

The primary purpose of the appraisal is to protect the lender. If the lender does not loan more money than the property is worth, then in the event of a repossession the lender should be able to sell the property for at least the balance of the mortgage.

A second accomplishment of the appraisal is an assessment of the general condition of the property, which can also protect the lender from several other problems. If the property were repossessed, the lender would want the property back in the best possible condition; thus the appraiser is authorized to call **work orders.** Work orders must generally be completed before a loan is made (see exceptions in Chapter 8). And by ensuring that these repairs are done, the lender is somewhat more likely to have a satisfied new owner who is less likely to discover expensive problems that could lead to a default by the new owners.

In addition, the appraiser's site visit can help to prevent fraud. If, for example, a buyer and seller were in collusion and, say, agreed on a price for a vacant lot which could only be justified if there were a building on the lot, the lender might not suspect that the lot was vacant (lenders rarely visit a site). Then the buyer and seller could take the loan money and run. This type of fraud occurs only when the appraiser is also involved in the scheme, which has only happened a few hundred times (back east mostly, where corruption is an official state religion).

A final benefit of the appraisal is that it may prevent panicked, naive, or grasping buyers or sellers from agreeing to a price that would have an unconscionable effect on them. For this preventive to work consistently, however, the appraisal system would have to include checks and balances. Such an improvement will only happen when there is a threat that the industry's own members' checks might bounce.

## WHO DOES APPRAISALS?

Before the summer of 1990, the answer was, "Anyone who wants to." In the first century of Washington's statehood, it was open range: "Watch out for appraisers on the road." No licensing has been required for 101 years. No required courses. No proof of competency. The only checks on the system have been the lenders, who have had a vested interest in seeing that thorough work was performed, and real estate agents, who stood to lose their commissions if the appraisers tossed a sabot into the gears. The lenders have tried to hire the best appraisers, and the agents have tried to get the worst ones fired.

The best news about the new licensing requirements is that no "grandfathering" will take place. All appraisers must take state exams which will be administered by the Department of Licensing.

There are a number of professional organizations for appraisers, some of which have established lofty goals and standards, and some of which have just established lofts. The two most widely respected designations for appraisers are the "MAI" (Member, Appraisal Institute), for those who chiefly do commercial appraisals, and "RM" (Residential Member).

## WHO PAYS? WHO PICKS?

"Who pays for the appraisal?" is one of the questions most often asked in my classes. When I answer that it is traditional for the buyer to pay, the next most frequently asked question follows: "Then do we get to pick the appraiser?" Wouldn't it be nice if life were so fair? But, no. If the buyer applies for a conventional loan, then the lender chooses. Some lenders have staff appraisers; others prefer to hire independent appraisers. There are advantages to each system: while the staff appraiser is generally more available and perhaps more polite to all parties, the independent appraiser, at least in theory, upholds the doctrine of reaching an independent conclusion. In reality, neither type of appraiser is very independent, since both depend on the good graces of the lender for future employment.

If the loan is an FHA or VA type, then not even the lender gets to pick the appraiser. The loan processor makes a call to the appropriate bureaucracy and the appraiser is assigned from a list of "approved" independent appraisers, some of whom enjoy demonstrating just how independent they can be.

If no lender is involved and if an appraisal is being done merely at the request of one or both of the parties to a transaction, then of course the buyer and seller can negotiate on the choice and payment of the appraiser.

As this book goes to press, appraisals for the government agencies cost $250, whereas conventional appraisal prices are "a function of the marketplace" (the typical range is $300–$350).

**Special circumstances:** In a few instances lenders do not require an appraisal, or will accept an abbreviated appraisal—a "short form," a "drive-by," or a "windshield" appraisal. As the name implies, the appraiser may never get out of his car. This may sound a bit shocking, but if the appraiser knows the neighborhood his appraisal is likely to be about as "accurate" as the more convoluted appraisals, which can be as jury-rigged as Grandma's gate. In fact, if I were to suggest an overhaul of the present system, I'd suggest that two appraisers do drive-by appraisals; if their results are more than 3% apart, then a third drive-by or a full appraisal is called for. This system could cost as much as the present one, but it would introduce more "checks and balances."

The circumstances in which no appraisal is required are typically when a down payment of more than 25% is offered, and the loan is a "portfolio" type, meaning it will not be sold in the typical secondary market (see Chapter 9, "Financing: The Basics"), or the owner is refinancing and has at least 25% equity.

## HOW IS THE APPRAISAL DONE?

The typical in-city appraisal for a home loan—the "market data" approach —will require about 20–60 minutes of the appraiser's time at the house, where he measures the square footage and looks for structural problems. Hold it! Before one assumes that the appraiser gets paid $250–$300 for no more than 60 minutes of work, let's learn the whole story. One appraiser tells me he often requires nine hours to do all the paperwork for one appraisal, and must then split the fee he receives with his boss. Easy money? It ain't necessarily so.

The appraiser must find three "comps," i.e. three properties similar in size, neighborhood, and amenities. Depending on the type of loan, the comps should have sold within the last few months (often six) and should be located within so many blocks or miles of each other (typically one mile, but up to three). The appraiser is not expected to inspect the interiors of these comps. Some make the effort of calling the former listing agent for a description of the interior.

The appraiser must now glean all available data on these comps, from tax records, multiple listing files, and, as noted, by making calls to the listing or selling agent. As soon as photographs of all four properties (subject property plus three comps) have been made, the paperwork begins in earnest. Detailed forms are filled out which compare the features of the four properties. Below is an abbreviated outline of what a few lines of such a form looks like:

| ITEM | SUBJECT | COMPARABLE #1 | | COMPARABLE #2 | | COMPARABLE #3 | |
|---|---|---|---|---|---|---|---|
| Address | 242 Walnut | 123 Maple | | 231 Vine | | 321 Oak | |
| Sales Price | $100,000 | $102,000 | | $104,000 | | $98,750 | |
| VALUE ADJUSTMENTS | DESCRIPTION | DESCRIPTION | ADJUSTMENT | DESCRIPTION | ADJUSTMENT | DESCRIPTION | ADJUSTMENT |
| Lot size | 6,000 SF | 5,000 | +$1,000 | 6,000 | | 6,000 | |
| Garage | One car | One car | | Two car | –$1,000 | One car | |

**Explanation:** An actual appraisal would have many more lines of comparison, but in this little exercise we will just compare the sizes of the lots and garages. As you can see, the subject property has a pending sale at $100,000, whereas the three comps have already closed at the prices quoted.

The lot of Comp #1 is 1,000 square feet smaller than that of the subject property, so we see a +$1,000 adjustment. In other words, if all other items between the subject property and Comp #1 were identical, the most accurate price for the subject property would be $103,500, ignoring for the moment the other two comps. Now look at the garage comparisons. Comp #2 had a two-car garage, so we should subtract $1,000 for this advantage from its sale price of $104,000; now if all other things were equal, the subject property would be worth $103,000, ignoring the other two comps.

So far, based on just these two lines of comparison, we might conclude that the price on the subject property is a little low. But obviously we don't have the whole picture.

**Typical flaws:** In the first place, who says that a two-car garage is worth exactly $1,000 more than a one-car? The appraiser does. How about the 1,000 square feet of lot? If the lots are worth around 25% of the total value, then each 1,000 square feet would be worth more like $4,000 on a strictly prorated basis, but the appraiser might opine that the first 4,000 square feet constitutes 90% of the value. On the other hand, if the appraiser preferred to give more credit for the extra land, he could do it, subject only to the scrutiny of his own boss or the lender's underwriter. In other words, the appraiser can jockey the num-

bers and fairly easily justify any price within 5% of the subject property's price. Is this done? Do dogs love fire hydrants?

Another built-in flaw of this appraisal system is that the appraiser cannot know intimately the condition of a comp at the time it was sold. Four months prior to the day he takes pictures of it, it may have looked like a "before" property for "This Old House." Now it may be all dolled up, replete with blooming roses.

Seattleites are now experiencing another phenomenon that affects the current appraisal system: appreciation so rapid that it can be measured on a monthly basis. If a comp sold four months ago, and appreciation is 1.5% per month, then we might need to adjust that sold price by around $6,000. In a depreciating market, of course, this consideration goes into reverse.

Many appraisers admit, off the record, that they see their job as simply making sure that the buyer and seller aren't totally bonkers, and unless there is a very obvious variance in the value and price, they make the data fit the conclusions. This is known in the business as the MAI appraisal, "Made As Instructed."

## WHAT ABOUT LOW APPRAISALS?

A low appraisal can be a nightmare for everyone, even though at first a buyer might salivate at the opportunity to reopen negotiations with the seller. This *is* a possibility, but in many cases the seller has become so psychologically locked into the agreed-upon price that flexibility just means something to do with aerobics. (It may be two to four weeks from the day of the offer to the day we learn of the appraiser's conclusions; in that time the seller has counted and fried his chickens over and over again.)

If an agent was involved, she may try to head off the low appraisal at the pass by giving the appraiser data on comps that she used for helping the seller determine the asking price. This must be done delicately. Some appraisers are grateful for the input; some get on a high horse and sit on the saddlehorn because they think the agent is trying to compromise their independence.

If in the end we still have the low appraisal, then someone, agent or consumer, has to go to work. It is possible to have another "fee-paid" appraisal done, if the buyer or seller is willing to spend the money. If this appraisal is favorable, it is turned in to the lender's underwriter for adjustments. The underwriter could also direct the original appraiser to take another look, if the agent or consumer has provided pictures and data of other comps that indicate a second look is in order. Miracles are not guaranteed, though. One of my own agents had occasion to provide an appraiser with data that indicated a higher price could be justified; even though the appraiser agreed, he refused to adjust his original conclusion. "My data can beat up your data anytime!"

The effect of a low appraisal is this: Since the lender only loans a percentage of the value, if the appraisal is $5,000 low and the seller won't come down on the price, the buyer may have to come up with $5,000 more for the down payment. In instances where the buyer is still willing to pay the seller's price but cannot come up with the extra money, some buyers look for a creative solution. One such approach is known as the "side addendum." In this situation, the buyer may agree to buy the appliances separately, or make out a promissory note to the seller for monthly payments or some future lump sum. This is extremely risky. Such an agreement may violate the terms of one's loan (all debts must be reported, and every additional debt makes it harder to qualify for a loan), and it may void the entire agreement. Consult your attorney.

## CMA: THE AGENT'S APPRAISAL

Depending on which agent you talk to, CMA stands for "Competitive Market Analysis," "Complimentary Market Analysis," or "Church of the Most Adjustments." The CMA approach is essentially the same as appraisers use with comps, plus a CMA has its own unique set of flaws and benefits.

In the first place, there is no standard way of doing CMA's or interpreting the data. Every company and every agent simply strives for the most appealing and commonsensical approach. An agent may use three comps or ten, and may use any period of time or distance from the subject property that can be defended.

In many cases, the agent uses only listed properties for comps, not having been trained in doing research in the tax records which would provide the information on owner-sold properties. A perfectly good comp next door may be overlooked.

The most obvious advantage of the CMA over the fee-paid appraisal is that many agents include properties that have *not* sold, as well as properties that are presently on the market and in competition with the prospective seller. By looking at the properties that did not sell, we can get some idea of the cut-off price for buyers of that type and size of property.

The CMA is often used as a marketing gimmick—"Get your free red-hot Market Analysis right here!"—and it certainly provides the agent with an opportunity to show off her knowledge of the market. It is also a major contributor to the inefficiency of the real estate industry. Many an agent has spent four to six hours preparing a CMA for a homeowner who then proceeded to sell the house to his neighbor or friend, using the agent's data. Some agents refuse to do the CMA until they are reasonably sure that the seller intends to list with them.

**Mark of stupidity:** The seller who chooses to list with an agent because the agent's CMA indicates a higher potential price than another agent's CMA is the world's biggest sucker. If the seller finds differences in the suggested sales prices between several different CMA's, then those differences should be studied and resolved as a separate issue. An agent and a real estate company should be chosen because of their marketing plan. Period. The best plan will get the best price (see "Strategies for Sellers," in Chapter 13).

### DON'T AGENTS OVERPRICE?

This question has not been examined for common sense. What must the questioner be thinking? That if the house sells, the agent will make a little larger commission? Overpriced properties don't sell; the agent doesn't get paid *at all.* The average Washington homebuyer will not make a decidedly low offer on an overpriced property; he will simply walk away. Only experienced investors are accustomed to making take-it-or-leave-it offers.

No, the majority of agents do not deliberately name an unrealistic price. A small minority do, just to get the seller in a greedy frame of mind. When a property is overpriced, the explanation is more likely to be one of the following:

**1.** The seller insisted the property is "worth every penny." The agent most likely agreed to list it at that price, thinking/hoping the seller would soon see the light.

**2.** The seller played one agent against another. "Well, Jane at XYZ Realty thinks we can get $10,000 more."

**3.** The agent made an honest mistake, because he was trying to do exactly what the law says he must: get the seller the best possible price. Since pricing is not a science, experiments at higher prices are inevitable.

If the public has a legitimate concern in the area of pricing, it should be that relatively rare cad who deliberately underprices a property, especially an elderly person's house, just to pick up a quick commission or to sell it to a friend or, worst of all, to buy it himself. If he's caught he may be liable for the difference, at the very least. Look after thy neighbors, especially the white-haired ones.

### TIPS, TRIVIA, MISCELLANEOUS

**1. Be self-reliant.** Since the appraiser's conclusions are one person's opinion and are only as accurate as that person is competent and conscientious, it is important for both the seller and buyer to have looked at lots of properties, as impartially as possible, to build confidence in case they sail into the winds of a low appraisal.

### 2. Never rely on the appraiser's "inspection."

*Many an owner I have met in distress,*
*who now is forced her naivete to confess:*
*"I thought an appraisal meant I was protected,*
*but the termites and leak sites went undetected."*

Appraisers as a rule have little or no training in construction, and even if they did, their visit to the site is short and they are concerned with catching only the most obvious problems, which may not be the worst problems or even be actual problems. We know of a Seattle appraiser who called for a new roof when the present roof was only a few months old. That's what happens on a dark day in old Cloudtown.

**3. Don't count on an appraiser being liable.** Right there in one of the contracts you sign will be some exculpatory language, saying that the appraiser's sole responsibility is to change his oil and get a tuneup twice a year. There will probably have to be an unbelievably gross example of negligence before you can attach any liability to an appraiser.

**4. Don't base decisions on old spouse's tales.** Or, "A myth is as good as a mile." The damnedest myth, one that will not die, is the lie that FHA appraisals are automatically harder, stingier, meaner, tougher—what have you. Maybe this was so before I got into real estate. Maybe it's true in one town or county. But as a rule, there is no truth to it. The secondary market, which affects almost all loans, has come so close to standardizing the expectations that the differences between appraisals is accounted for by the different personalities doing them. Yet if an agent has a bad experience with one FHA appraiser, she may tell her sellers to avoid FHA offers. She is in all likelihood doing her sellers a disservice.

**5. Ask the seller about previous offers.** One complication that happens

---

### WHAT A LAUGH!

From time to time you'll see an ad for carpeting or some building material that reads: "Meets FHA standards." I am one former contractor who can tell you that the retailer could just as well have phrased that ad: "Meets the very minimum standards; probably adequate for your tenants but certainly not good enough for a discriminating person like yourself."

with FHA and VA offers occurs when we discover that a previous FHA or VA offer was made and an appraisal completed in the last six months. If the transaction never closed, a low appraisal may be the reason. The seller, not knowing that any future offers will be cross-checked by the address, then accepts another FHA offer, thinking that another appraisal will be done and surely this time the appraiser will get it right. Don't assume the agent knows this. Many don't.

**6. Investigate the zoning.** One of the old standby theories of appraising is that the price should reflect the "highest and best use." This theory, which is not applied quite as strictly as it was a few years back, means that if a corner lot could bring more with a filling station on it than a single-family house, then the price should reflect that. I bought a single-family house that was eligible for re-zoning as a business; if the appraiser had bothered to learn or mention this, it is possible that my loan would have been refused, or processed by other standards. Usually a call to the county assessor's office, or the zoning department in the larger cities, or possibly to a title company, will provide this information. Many real estate offices have this information in their microfilmed tax records.

**7. If different, expect difficult.** The appraisal system works relatively smoothly in a suburb where the ticky-tacky boxes differ from one another only by the toys in their driveways, but try buying a solar-heated, earth-sheltered house of 3,000 square feet at the end of a lane, two miles from the nearest house. Where will the appraiser find comps? Vail and Moose Jaw. If a bank agrees to lend on this property, don't be surprised if it requires a substantial down payment.

**8. Increase your choices.** If you know of an appraiser who comes highly recommended, and you are applying for a conventional loan where you may be able to choose the appraiser, ask the appraiser to submit a resume to your lender. Some lenders will consider your request.

**9. "Just the facts, Ma'am."** We have been talking so far about the market data approach—the use of comps—for pricing owner-occupied properties. We are about to discuss two other legitimate methods, but first we should examine two ways *not* to price a home:

**A.** "I paid $110,000 and I put $30,000 into it, so it's got to be worth at least $140,000. Now car-owners would never expect anyone to believe that a car's value increased by the amount they put into it, but homeowners make this totally illogical statement with conviction. Must be trying to convince the dubious spouse.

**B.** "The county appraised it for $82,000, so I guess I'll ask for that." You do and your granddaddy will open his casket. County tax assessments are notorious for being nothing more than ballpark figures. I've seen a few that were 50% of the market value, and a few that were 125%. Sure, use these figures in your offer or ads if they're helpful, but don't believe them yourself.

## OTHER APPRAISAL METHODS

The market data (or "sales comparison") approach to appraising owner-occupied homes is most likely the only method the average consumer will see, but if our homebuyer should someday become an investor she needs to be familiar with the cost-replacement method and be able to apply some of the techniques of the income method.

The cost-replacement method is just what it sounds like: We determine the square footage, we determine the price to build (or rebuild) a square foot, and we dust off the calculator. This method is useful for new houses in a new suburb, or if a fire has swept an area and we can now appraise only from original blueprints. Or it may be useful in appraising something large, unusual, and commercial that is unique, one-of-a-kind.

The income method (or capitalization method) also relies on comps, as our owner-occupied market data method does, but not in exactly the same way. Remember: This is an oversimplified explanation. Let's say that we are buying a triplex, which has a total income of $1,400 per month ($16,800/year). In our research of rental properties that have sold, we find only two duplexes and a fourplex. With a little calculating, though, we can see that the average selling price was 110 times the monthly income, or 9.167 (110÷12) times the annual income. Using either of these factors, known as "Gross Rent Multipliers," we multiply the respective factor of our triplex to determine the market value of this property. Either way—110 times $1,400 or 9.167 times $16,800—we get $154,000.

What can go wrong? To start with, the rental incomes for either the subject property or any of the comps may be low for the neighborhood. This could easily skew the results. Could the rents ever be "too high?" It is possible, such as when a slumlord crowds every possible tenant into a shelter, although the more common situation of a too-high rent projection occurs when the seller fudges the figures, painting the rosiest possible picture. One sign of high rents is rapid turnover.

It is also possible that the appraiser or consumer won't get the whole truth from the owners of the other buildings. For example, the owner of one duplex reports that his monthly rental income is $750, while the other duplex owner reports an income of $925. But owner number one didn't want to mention a tiny, illegal studio in the basement that brings in another $200. If we don't know about that studio we may wonder why he paid so much for his property.

The income method is a good place to start, but it is obviously as flawed as any of the other methods in this imperfect world. It certainly behooves the investor-buyer to independently ascertain every possible figure. In fact, it is common for investor-buyers to make their offers subject to inspection of accounts and leases, and verification of all income statements.

### TWO FACTORS THAT MAY COME INTO VIEW

An appraiser cannot just look at a house and lot without also looking at the neighborhood. That's obvious. But the appraiser must also look at how well the house serves its occupants.

If a lovely house sits on a manicured lot, but next door there's a rendering plant and across the street there's a car lot and behind it a busy highway, we have a few reasons to say that the property suffers from "External (or Economic) Obsolescence." Its highest and best use may no longer be as a house. These factors may force the appraiser to turn to her thickest manuals to determine how to evaluate that property.

On the other hand, we may have a house that fits in perfectly with its neighborhood but suffers from bad design: the only bathroom is on the second floor, the wiring is inadequate by today's standards, and the bedrooms will not accommodate a queen-size bed. Here we have an example of "Functional Obsolescence," which the appraiser will no doubt mention and point to for adjustments of the final value.

### AND HOW LARGE THE DIFFERENCES?

The vast majority of appraisals conclude that the buyer and seller are paying/receiving just about what they should. A tiny percentage of the appraisals come in noticeably higher, but a larger percent come in low, even in an ordinary market and quite commonly in a fast-moving seller's market.

Occasionally we find someone willing, or forced, to pay for a second appraisal. It is at such a time that we realize how much of a charade this whole system can be. I have seen two different appraisals (on two different properties) conclude in each case that the proper price would be $100,000 higher (or 31%–49% higher) than what the buyer and seller had actually agreed to. Each of these properties had been on the market for many months, so obviously buyers who would pay what the appraisers thought was correct were lost in some other part of town. One of my own agents sold two *identical* apartment buildings to two different buyers who used two different appraisers who reached two different conclusions: $130,000 and $150,000.

One may assume that these discrepancies are more likely to occur in the higher price brackets. That is a fair assumption. An asking price of $5 million may suddenly drop to $4 million without even a pause in the polo game, but an asking price of $100,000 is not nearly as likely to drop by 20%, so we may feel that we have a better grip on prices in the middle-class ranges. Even here, though, variances of 20% are not unheard of, and 5%–15% variances are a part of every agent's life.

Somewhere out there is an appraiser who owes me a refund. Imagine a 17% difference in two appraisals on a $60,000 house. He did. Another reason to just say no to drugs.

# EVALUATING: VALUE

**R**emember: This chapter is complemented by the next one, on work orders (repairs, especially those called by an appraiser). Very little space here will be devoted to the obvious (are the carpets dirty, is the sink dripping?). No sense in insulting your intelligence. *Nothing in this chapter or the next one is meant to facilitate or encourage you to buy a home without having a professional inspection.* My purpose is to help you decide if you want to make an offer, if the assets outweigh the problems, and if there are concerns that you should include in your negotiations.

As you start to evaluate a house, stop and write down all the things you like about it, because now we are going to look at many of the reasons you shouldn't like it. You might forget why you ever even took a second look, so occasionally glance back at the assets and benefits, and repeat after me: No house is perfect.

## GOOD BUY...?

Good buy or good-bye? Which is it? To decide this you may have to examine everything from the bathroom outlets to the zoning across the street. When the new homebuyer first starts looking at houses, the challenge of performing a thorough evaluation can seem overwhelming. Some new buyers make offers that never quite come together, or if their offer is accepted they may find some way to get out of it; in many cases this is because they have no confidence in what they're doing. They blame someone or something, without admitting or realizing that they simply haven't learned how to do a reasonably thorough evaluation and balance of the pros and cons.

I demonstrate this in some of my classes. Thirty to forty of us stand in front of a vacant house. On the command "go," we rush into and around the house, and in 10 minutes the uninjured return to the front yard for an oral test: "Are the upstairs outlets grounded, does each gutter have a downspout, did each downspout have a drainblock, is there a dryer outlet?"

Well, of course these questions stump almost everyone, but somehow I know the answers. The point is: If they had known what they were looking for, as I did, they would have seen more in 10 minutes than most people see in 10 hours.

Quite a number of my former students have gone through the extended list in this chapter and made their own lists, condensing theirs to the 20, 30, or 40 items that most concern them. My purpose here is to provide the most complete list that I can, because I have no way of knowing which of these items will be important to you or to a particular site. Another option for you to consider is one that I am working on myself: Make a cassette tape that guides you through and around a house. If I see you at an open house wearing your headphones, I'll know you got this far.

---

### NONCONFORMIST?

The most radical nonconformists in our society don't buy houses, they occupy them. Maybe even burn one occasionally. But even they, by middle age (myself included, at this point), may begin to see the benefits of nest eggs and cozy corners. But do we longtime rules-breakers want to buy an unusual house that says, "We're different"? That's up to you; it is not my intent to persuade anyone to conform to the tastes and values of any group—we always need people who break the rules, who have a vision. My aim is merely to make everyone aware of the risk of buying a nonconforming house. Trying to find a buyer for that geodesic dome could be a snap, or in a slow market it might take years. The safest route is to buy a mainstream house and fill it with furnishings that say, "Someone unique lives here." I started off as a fan of "radical" Steve Baer's "Zomeworks," read everything that Ken Kerns wrote, and worshiped the ground that Bucky Fuller built on. But I bought a house just like my grandma's. But just you wait: Someday I'll build a tamped-earth house with bottle-glass windows. And leave it to somebody who deserves trouble.

---

### THE YUP AND COMING NEIGHBORHOOD?

A year or two ago I was asked to teach a class on how to discern which neighborhoods would make the best future investments. That proved to be the hardest teaching challenge I've faced, next to asking a group to rappel off a 130-foot cliff at night. It is also a subject that can bring out the most superficial, egotistical grandstanding imaginable in those of us who know just enough to be dangerous, so I had to practice a little self-discipline. Like a chokehold. I swore I'd teach the principles of analysis without mentioning a single neighborhood.

Of course the students wanted me just to tell them which areas to buy into. But since Seattle itself has over 90 distinct neighborhoods, and there are many surrounding suburbs, where would we start? You should always start practicing your powers of observation right in your own backyard. One of my boyhood heroes was Sherlock Holmes; with one look at your boots, this man could discern your profession, your income, and your mother's maiden name. Perhaps you should start with the Holmes series to learn how to learn to see. But don't read *Hound of the Baskervilles* late at night.

As an English teacher I once asked my students to write a paper on what they might deduce from the appearances of their fellow students. Very few of them even noticed the shoes that were then popular with fraternity boys, the dried clay on some of the art students' shirts, or the knee-banging slide rules hanging from the belts of engineers (does this date me?). If it weren't for this

little classroom challenge, my students might never have taken a second look at anyone who didn't appeal to their libidos. I must admit that when I started to teach the class on neighborhoods, many of my own conclusions were based solely on intuition, so I too had to train myself to look and think about those things that make a neighborhood a candidate for getting-better-with-age.

An aside: I realize that this is a sensitive area, in that we are touching on the subject of gentrification, the displacement of the working class by the middle and upper classes. However, the opposite of gentrification is slumification. Is it possible for a neighborhood to take the middle road and never become distinctly worse or distinctly better, or is change inevitable and ongoing? No matter what I write here, these processes are going to happen, but when they happen seemingly overnight the result shocks and concerns us, as it should. This book will not promote or stop gentrification, and I don't have the omniscience to know if it *should* be promoted or stopped. Perhaps the best we can hope for is a good balance between our hopes and ambitions and our caring and compassion. In other words, let's keep our greed under control; wealth is a state of mind.

In any case, these are things we should look for or examine to determine if a neighborhood is likely to bask in tomorrow's sun:

**1. Architecture.** The styles that will be popular in the near future are those styles we venerate now, not those we denigrate. The safest styles will be those of houses built before 1930. Even the plainest of them often have more genuine character than our most expensive modern examples of Neo-chateau de Origami.

When I say "we," I am thinking about the types of people who make good urban pioneers (UPs): young professionals with the energy (if not always the time) to take on, or tolerate, or even find "charming" the problems of old plumbing and such.

"We" is also an essential concept, in that for a neighborhood to begin the road back to prosperity, it must appeal to a number of buyers. We're not looking for anything weird or out of the ordinary; in fact, mass appeal at the young professional level might be a leading guideline. This means the neighborhood should have a minimum of houses that are out of place as to age or style.

**2. Present condition.** Even though we may envision many improvements in a neighborhood's future, I can't envision too many UPs moving into a neighborhood where the transmissions on the lawn outnumber the tricycles. If some ordinary pride of ownership isn't already visible, skip it and let somebody else be the first.

If you ever took a sociology class you may have studied how a city grows in concentric rings, and how the inner ring(s) will often become slumified and then eventually be revived as the value of the downtown property is realized. What was probably not mentioned is how neighborhoods also reflect historical events or influences that very few people are aware of. For example, many buyers have told me that they wanted to avoid a particular neighborhood just north of my office. They sensed that something wasn't quite up to par, but they couldn't put their finger on it. Well, years before any of those buyers were born, that neighborhood was at the edge of the city limits (it is now three miles inside the city limits). Because it was outside the city limits many of the houses were built to the owners' standards but not to any code. There were no sidewalks, which tends to leave the area looking unfinished and encourages people to park cars on lawns.

This leads to the question: "Wouldn't that make the neighborhood a good long-term investment? When sidewalks are installed, won't those properties increase in value?" Yes, they will increase some in value. But no, it probably won't happen in our lifetime. The property owners have to petition the city for the sidewalks, and many of those owners are landlords who live elsewhere and would not want an assessment that could be $5,000 or more. It's a bad-odds bet.

Speaking of negative perceptions, I heard a tip from an insurance man once: "We're a little more cautious about neighborhoods with clotheslines. Those people can't afford dryers and may not be inclined to take care of things as well as we'd like." I guess they'd really be concerned about pigs in the backyard. "Ma, get that Hampshire outta sight! Here comes the Mutual of Enumclaw man."

**3. Size.** Young professionals venerate the family and privacy, and they like entertaining their friends and having office space at home. That means they usually want three or four bedrooms, dining room, hallways, basement, upstairs, "country kitchen," and preferably lots of closets (often missing, however, from even the best of old houses). Does that sound like a small house to you? Doesn't to me either. Very few houses under 1,200 square feet are likely to make the list, so, ideally, there should be only one or two houses this small in a block.

**4. Location.** It's possible that the kind of neighborhood we're talking about is 20 miles out in the country, but I believe that one of the main reasons a transitional neighborhood will become valuable is that these owners will be only minutes from work but a memory away from traffic jams.

For years I've been telling everyone that Seattle's traffic would help revive the downtown condo market; I wish I'd listened.

🏠  🏠  🏠
## THE DREGS OF DRUGS

If you bought a house in 1980 that had been used for drug dealing, your greatest concern might have been a former "customer" knocking on your door at midnight. But now that houses are being used as laboratories to manufacture methamphetamines, the danger of drugs might not be so obvious. Some no-smell chemicals permeate the wood, carpets, and drywall, and their presence might not be realized or guessed at until the new owners experience rashes, headaches, and dizziness. The Department of Ecology and the police are just beginning to confront this nightmare, and we in the real estate industry know only enough to run the other way when we know that a problem exists. At this time, the best advice I can think of is this: Strike up a conversation with the neighbors about the house's history, but be extremely careful what you ask. You don't want to start a rumor any more than you want to swallow one.

**5. Safety.** I could drive a buyer to several close-in neighborhoods that nicely satisfy the four criteria already discussed, but said buyer would see something else she hadn't sought: bars. Bars on the windows, bars on the doors, and probably bars on the corners. From time to time in Seattle's seller's market we have encountered a decent house at a decent price that didn't sell in its first week on the market. More than once, a chat with the neighbors revealed that the drug activity next door was the problem.

A drive through such an area at night and at other times when most people are home from work may tell us things that aren't obvious at high noon. Besides any obvious hell-raising, we should look to see if parking is a problem and if the after-dark walk from car to house is short. UPs like to drive nice cars, which stay nice longer when parked in a driveway or garage. So all things being equal, I would give a bonus point to the neighborhoods that have yards wide enough to have driveways, or alleys that allow backyard access to a garage. Notice the origins of cars; the more foreign-made cars we see, the more likely the neighborhood is well into its upswing.

**6. Shopping.** Shortly after the upward changes in a neighborhood begin, we are likely to see some changes in the types of shops on the edges of these neighborhoods. If truffles, sugarless baked goods, and risque greeting cards can be bought in those stores, the neighborhood is on its way. It can't be said with certainty which is the chicken and which is the egg, i.e. whether "progressive" businesses lead or just follow their clientele. In any case, we should always patronize the last remaining mom 'n' pop grocery store so that when we have a Twinkie craving, our need can be met.

**7. Present marketplace.** If there isn't pressure from the marketplace, the changes in most neighborhoods will be fairly slow, no matter what the conditions or opportunities are. As long as average buyers can still afford houses in less speculative neighborhoods, and the commuting times are bearable, they are not going to be too compelled to become urban pioneers. The speculator, of course, is trying to predict that a shortage of affordable houses is just around the corner. So many factors are involved in such speculation that few of us can or should make any predictions. The best that most of us are able to do is to buy early in a cycle, and we can do this by reading the newspapers and doing enough analysis to feel confident that the limb we're going out on is reasonably strong.

---

### OLD OR NEW?

I love old houses, but occasionally I do covet those new-house conveniences—built-in vacuums and such. But I couldn't afford any new house that matched the quality of my old house's woodwork and leaded glass. And patina? Patina can't be imitated. It's important that you know what you like. This sounds simple, but many a buyer has looked at old houses for months before realizing that she wanted a "carefree" new house, or even a condo.

Unfortunately, new doesn't guarantee carefree. I've seen houses selling for half a million dollars that had a dozen problems, ranging from serious to inexcusable. One of the very real risks of a new house is that many of the problems won't surface until long after any warranties have expired, if they were even covered to start with. Contrary to popular myth, Washington does not require builders to provide warranties. Know the business history of the builder. Check references of buyers from several years ago.

The answer to a common question, "Should I have an inspection of a new house?" is no. You should have *two* inspections—one as soon as there is something to inspect, and one just before closing. Some inspectors do a short second inspection without charging.

## THE BIG PICTURE

A number of things that are pointed out in the following pages don't have a thing to do with whether the house you are evaluating will allow you to enjoy it thoroughly. Children grow up as healthy on a fir floor as on an oak one. But in selecting a house, do keep one eye on the future; someday you'll probably sell this structure, and then you'll be glad you bought what people as discerning as yourself want.

We'll start by standing across the street, trying to put everything into perspective and to see if the house seems to be on the level—literally.

_____ **1.** Is there any new construction in sight (assuming we're in a settled neighborhood)? In any case, make a note to check the zoning, both for this street and the one behind it, or whichever streets will most influence the house's use and comfort.

_____ **2.** Is there off-street parking? If the street is an arterial, this concern is twice as important.

_____ **3.** Any nearby schools? At first I thought this would be an asset, but a closer look and interviews with residents convinced me otherwise. Litter, noise, and traffic are very common problems.

_____ **4.** Underground utilities? Great! A bonus.

_____ **5.** Nearby park? Can be a bonus, or can have the same problems as a school. Ask the neighbors.

_____ **6.** Are the noise levels acceptable? Careful: Neither overreact nor underestimate the effect of noise on resale. In Seattle, where we're not so likely to sit outdoors, this may not be so significant as in Spokane, where one has more outdoor-sitting weather. Arterials (marked by broken yellow lines in some communities) are often major influences on a house's value. But then there are major arterials and minor arterials. If you really want to determine the extent of the influence, look at the tax records and note how many of the houses are owner-occupied along several blocks of that street. Compare the percentage with that of nearby nonarterials. It is not unusual for a heavy arterial to have twice as many rentals as a nonarterial just one block over.

If street noise is a factor, it can be diminished noticeably. The most effective (but probably least cost-effective) response is a brick or stone wall. A solid board fence is almost as effective, heavy hedges are not too far behind, and storm windows (more than insulated glass) will also help quite a bit. The most cost-effective measure is weatherstripping, since noise primarily enters through openings, not by penetrating walls. Some of my friends swear that blown-in insulation helps, but I haven't found any data confirming that. Also see #13.

_____ **7.** Is there a bus stop in front of the house? This can severely limit parking, so it could be a noisy negative factor for almost everyone except those hermits who neither own a car nor have any visitors.

_____ **8.** Is the subject property noticeably larger or more expensive than any other property on the street? Be very careful. Sometimes oversized houses sell very quickly and sometimes they don't, depending a great deal on how charming they are.

_____ **9.** Is the roof (ridge line) straight? Hold up a clipboard or book for comparison. If there is a sag, the important thing is to find out why (ask your friendly engineer).

_____ **10.** Is the roof steep? A steep roof can double and even triple the labor cost for a new roof. But flat roofs still elicit a negative reaction from many buyers, even though modern roofing materials, such as the rubbery "torch-down" EPDM, seem to be very promising (though not cheap).

_____ **11.** Is the chimney straight? The top four to six feet of many of Seattle's chimneys have had to be rebuilt because winds from the south blow rain into

---

**ROOF PITCH**

12/12

8/12

4/12

HORIZON LINE

A roof's pitch will be a factor in how long it lasts, how likely it is to leak, and how expensive it is to repair.

To get an idea of a roof's pitch, hold book vertically and see which line comes closest to matching the roof's angle. Anything less than a $4/12$ pitch (rises 4 feet every 12 horizontal feet) requires special application to be waterproof. Roofers increase their labor charges as steepness increases, starting as low as $6/12$. Above $12/12$ the cost could even be doubled.

the mortar and create a softening and settling effect. After 60 years it is not unusual for a chimney to appear ready to topple.

_____ **12.** Will the yard be a challenge to maintain? Note the condition of retaining walls; large cracks or any bulging or leaning may mean soil movement, which can be a tough problem to deal with.

_____ **13.** Are there many steps? This can affect everything from the delivery of a refrigerator to the chances of selling the house to anyone over 40 or anyone who ever played football (bad knees). But being above the street a bit can help the noise levels if the house is on an arterial.

_____ **14.** Is the driveway challenging? I discovered on moving into a new house that it took almost an hour to negotiate a steep narrow portion with my trailer. Kept the house; sold the trailer.

_____ **15.** Is the lot at the bottom of a substantial hill? If ever a spring will account for water in the basement, this is a likely location to see it happen. See "Wet basement" in Chapter 8, "Evaluating: Work Orders."

_____ **16.** Does the yard generally slope away from the house, on all sides? Note under decks. Soil (or a paved area) that is sloped toward a house is a major factor in wet basements.

_____ **17.** Do we have "solar access," or could construction next door eventually put us in the shade? I haven't heard of any Washington cities guaranteeing that sun or view won't be blocked (unless an easement is privately negotiated). Oregon has shown a little more progress in the area of solar easements.

_____ **18.** Is the area prone to landslides? A few calls to insurance companies may answer this. Several times my buyers have had to pay for very expensive soil tests (required by a lender or insurance company).

_____ **19.** Is the house well-located on the lot? In reality, a house that sits near one edge provides the most yard, but for resale the traditional centering is best. A house at the very back of the lot is usually the worst value (most people want backyards).

_____ **20.** Can desired sideways enlargement/remodeling be allowed? Ask your engineer or county building inspector for an explanation of "setbacks." While checking for zoning, also investigate easements, since these can prevent you from even adding a deck. You may have to turn to a title company or county building/engineering department for easement information.

_____ **21.** Is the driveway shared? A "common easement" driveway is one of the

---

### SWIMMING POOLS

This is one item that is perceived differently across the state. In the heat of Yakima it may be a blessing, but in Seattle it may make a house harder to sell. Seattle owners rarely get a return on their investment. But resale is just one of our concerns. Everyone knows about the liability—all the signs and fences in the world won't necessarily prevent intruders, accidents, and lawsuits. And then there can be problems that aren't found in any book: One couple built a pool over a septic tank, which stopped the tank's "action"; in another transaction, the insurance company felt that the pool made the house more likely to slide down the hill, so they required extensive soil tests. Hey, the city pool's looking better all the time.

---

worst headaches an agent has to deal with, and it truly affects resale (see Chapter 8, "Evaluating: Work Orders," and Chapter 12, "From Offer to Closing").

## MOVING CLOSER: THE EXTERIOR

Remember: many items you might expect to see covered here, such as the roof, gutters, etc., will be found in Chapter 8, "Evaluating: Work Orders." Although an appraiser can name any defect as a work order, most of the concerns in this chapter are more likely to worry the buyer than the appraiser.

____ **22.** Is there quite a bit of vegetation close to the house? Burglars hope so, but this can also be a problem for painting, interior light, and the siding and mortar, such as when ivy grows into cracks and even under the shingles. Tall trees on the south side, especially evergreens, can mean endless moss and needle-clogged gutters, as well as life in the dark lane.

____ **23.** Is there at least a foot of roof overhang for each story? This is a rule of thumb that generally suffices for protecting the foundation, siding, and sills from rain. The Cape Cod–style house has no eaves to speak of, but it still holds up and sells quite well in most cases; it just may require a little more upkeep of windowsills and the like.

____ **24.** Are the soffits in good condition? A soffit is the underside of any structural member, but most carpenters would probably think of the area right under an eave (or the enclosed area over the kitchen cabinets). Peeling paint in this area can be a sign of high humidity in the house. More on this under "Work Orders."

_____ **25.** Is the mortar in all brickwork hard and intact? Don't start pulling out big chunks, but do scratch a place here and there with a key or nail. If it is sandy-soft, you might be in for a tuckpointing job (very labor-intensive).

_____ **26.** Are the brick surfaces the original surfaces? In other words, have the bricks ever been sandblasted, etc.? Some owners think this is the correct thing to do, but it can lead to deterioration of the brick ("spalling"). A diplomatic, discreet question to the owner may help you learn if they were sandblasted.

_____ **27.** Are decks built up high enough to allow work to go on underneath them? No one thinks about this when building a deck, but one house needed the soil under its deck recontoured to keep the basement dry, and it meant having to completely remove the deck. Low decks (surface less than 18" high) can be especially prone to rotting/moisture problems.

_____ **28.** Is there metal flashing at the roof's edge and along the tops of windows, exposed doors, etc.? A house can get along without this if the builders did a good job to start with, but when amateurs install new windows or such, they often leave gaps that rain can enter. Caulking is at best a temporary substitute.

_____ **29.** Are there any louvered metal or solid plastic plugs in the siding? In some parts of the country the one-inch louvered plugs are called "painter's plugs," implying that they allow the wall to breathe and the paint to adhere longer. In Washington, though, plugs usually signify that urea formaldehyde or cellulose insulation was blown into the walls. Many experts feel that insulating the walls of an older home is a bit of a risk, due to possible condensation problems, but urea formaldehyde has the added problem of a "health scare" (see box). Ask the owner (this is often addressed in the offer; see Chapter 12, "From Offer to Closing").

_____ **30.** Is there an 8"-thick concrete wall foundation? Many buyers have discovered the hard way that if their plans for the house include adding a story or finished space upstairs, the building codes usually require 8" of concrete or some expensive reinforcement alternative.

_____ **31.** Are the materials used in renovations in keeping with the age and style of the house? Aluminum windows, wrought iron railings, indoor-outdoor carpeting, poodles wearing ribbons, Grandma wearing a miniskirt.... Many buyers are turned off by modern materials installed in old houses.

_____ **32.** Are the bottom edges of the siding straight? Checking for straightness

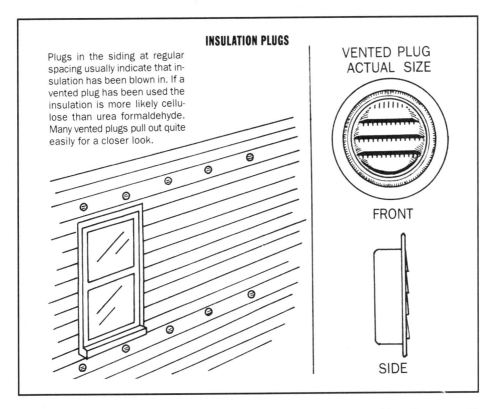

**INSULATION PLUGS**

Plugs in the siding at regular spacing usually indicate that insulation has been blown in. If a vented plug has been used the insulation is more likely cellulose than urea formaldehyde. Many vented plugs pull out quite easily for a closer look.

VENTED PLUG
ACTUAL SIZE

FRONT

SIDE

is a quick but unprofessional way to detect any noticeable settling along a wall. If you know how to tell if a 2 × 4 is straight, you'll know how to "shoot this line."

____ **33.** Is the siding material or pattern something that your friends would like? If not, resale is a concern. The most common negative comments concern aluminum siding, especially the wide type with the fake wood-grain. There's nothing intrinsically wrong with it; it just makes a lot of noise when the temperature changes, and dents if you hit it with a marshmallow.

____ **34.** Are stair risers consistent and no more than 7" high? If you find yourself tripping on the steps, others will too, long after you have gotten used to them. Building codes recommend the 7" riser (exceptions are possible with a knowledgeable design). Long runs of steps without a landing (at 10' intervals or so) can be quite dangerous; they are also a code violation.

____ **35.** Are there frayed wires running to the house or garage, or are wires hanging low or near windows? Some problems I've observed: (1) wires to garage frayed, possibly from overheating; (2) decks and windows too near wires (minimum: 10' from deck surface, 3' from any window that opens).

## UREA FORMALDEHYDE

It may be many years before we know the whole story about urea formaldehyde's (UF) health hazards, but we know with certainty that it had a drastic effect on house values in the early eighties. Houses that had it installed lost an average of 14% in value before it was outlawed in 1982 (now it's legal again, but the building industry doesn't seem interested in using it).

UF is accused of being everything from a carcinogen to a pre-allergen (sensitizing people so that they become allergic to a lot of other things). If you are already allergic to many materials, you may want to err on the side of caution. However, most air tests seem to indicate that if the work was done a decade or more ago, the "parts per million" (ppm) of UF in these insulated houses is no higher inside the house than in the backyard.

It is now a matter of course for agents to see that owners get the lab tests done and show the results to prospective buyers, who have pretty much quit reacting so negatively to UF insulation.

The story with new houses and mobile homes may still be unsettling. Houses built with paneling and lots of particle board and plywood (UF is found in the glues) may have ppm's that disturb sensitive individuals. One way to determine the risk of allergy is to test the level of UF where you presently live and compare it with the level at the desired property; this is not cheap ($150 per house, give or take, unless you collect the air samples yourself). One study of mobile homes showed an increased likelihood of throat cancer, but another study denied that the evidence was conclusive.

"Low-fuming" plywood is one response by the builders to this concern. It emits less UF because it was manufactured at a higher temperature. The words "low-fuming" are stamped on the plywood, but if the plywood is already covered up, we have to get proof from the builder. (By the way, that new carpeting and pad, and all of your new wrinkle-free clothing, most likely contain UF. It's in hundreds of products, and that's one reason many allergy doctors think we should be paying more attention to it). For an excellent study of UF, asbestos, radon, lead, and similar problems, see Appendix—"Environment" (*The Healthy Home*).

## LET'S GO INSIDE: THE FLOOR PLAN

_____ **36.** Is the entry disruptive or supportive of life in the living room? When someone enters, must they walk through a conversation to get to other parts of the house? The smaller the living room, the more noticeable every interruption. A separate hall is all too rare but definitely a bonus.

_____ **37.** Are the different areas of the house separated or buffered for noise and privacy? Some prefer a totally open floor plan. Just make sure it fits your desires. A one-story house may not buffer noise as well as a two-story house.

_____ **38.** Would everyday coming-and-going tasks be smooth? Imagine (or even walk through) bringing in groceries, taking out garbage, and getting ready to go to work.

_____ **39.** Would you have the degree of control over heating and cooling that

### SQUARE FOOTAGE

I cringe every time I hear consumers bring up square footage. We don't really judge candy bars by their weight or cars by their wheel base, so what is this concern with square footage? Yes, it tells us a little about a house, but so little that I have rarely even asked for the number. The best use for square-footage data is usually in comparisons of new houses in a subdivision, or a condo. Even then, if the condo or smaller house has a better floor plan, square footage should be pretty much a nonconsideration.

One of the major problems with square footage is that very few people know how to determine it, so the numbers can be very inaccurate—even a full 100% miscalculation is not that unusual. Tax assessors often include every foot under the roof, basement and all, whereas the appraiser is supposed to consider only the "gross living area," which is defined as "the total area of finished and above-grade residential space" (from _Appraising Residential Properties_). Not even a finished basement or attic is supposed to be included. If someone gives you a number, you need to ask who did the measuring and by what standards before you try to interpret it. Oh yes, building departments have even a third approach for permit considerations, which requires very technical knowledge involving headroom and wall heights. Can I persuade you just to rely on some other yardstick?

you like? This has been a criticism of open plans and split-levels. There is no zone-heating control, and are often lots of drafts.

_____ **40.** Would furniture-moving be so difficult that only professionals could do it? Especially pay attention to stairs. Many a queen-sized box spring has met its match in a stairwell.

_____ **41.** Are the stairs well located? Do you have to go through a private space to reach them? Not good. If plans include finishing an attic, do the stairs allow for the best use of that space? Most common mistake: stairs that are at the end of a narrow attic, making it difficult to construct separate bedrooms.

_____ **42.** Ideally there should be at least a half-bath on every level. Important for resale.

_____ **43.** Is the bathroom convenient, for guests as well as for those 4 a.m. toe-stubbing trips we all make? Worst possible location: Bathroom requires visitor to walk through a bedroom. Second worst: Off the kitchen.

_____ **44.** Is there a linen closet for the bathroom?

---

**BATHROOM DEFINED**

**Quarter bath:** commode or sink
**Half bath:** commode and sink
**Three-quarter bath:** commode, sink, and shower
**Full bath:** commode, sink, and tub (with or without shower)
**Outhouse:** none of the above, but more reading matter

---

_____ **45.** Are the main bedrooms at least 115 square feet, plus closets (minimum recommended for double-sized bed)? The minimum legal size is 70–80 square feet in many areas, but rooms that small are serious drawbacks these days (they make good offices, however).

_____ **46.** Is the kitchen a dead-end or a crossroads? Lots of old kitchens have as many as four entrances/exits, which means limited wall space for counters and cabinets, plus all the disruptions.

_____ **47.** Is the headroom on all levels both legal and comfortable? Low ceilings are "depressing" to many people. Building codes generally require at least 7'6"

---

**RANDY NEWMAN WAS RIGHT**

Short- to medium-height people may not attach enough importance either to legal or psychological headroom. But when it comes time to sell, if limited headroom has eliminated tall buyers, there will be fewer buyers at your auction. A person under six feet shouldn't be able to touch the ceilings.

---

ceilings in living areas and 7' in hallways, kitchens, and baths. Some communities may allow 6'8" basement ceilings for rec rooms, etc. There are many code exceptions to the above, and measurements often require technical knowledge. If headroom is less than 6', the basement is technically a crawl space.

____ **48.** Is there 6'6" headroom at all points on stairs? Few things are as difficult to correct. Another code requirement.

____ **49.** Is there easy access and plenty of storage for the tools or gear that matter the most to you?

### INTERIOR STRUCTURE AND SYSTEMS

____ **50.** Are floors reasonably level? This can affect resale as much as water in the basement. If a problem is widespread, the repairs can be very complicated, requiring anything from "pressure grouting" (lifting a corner of a house) to repairing windows, doors, and cracked plaster afterwards. It's important to have an engineer determine if damage is recent or old. If the house is only a few years old and has settled, ask yourself if you really have to have this house.

____ **51.** Does the plaster still have its "key"? The material that oozes behind the lath strips when plaster is applied to them and dries is the key that locks the plaster to the strips. If a drip occurs within the wall (as from an ice dam or roof leak) the keys soften or break off. A gentle push reveals this; the plaster will feel loose. Drywall swells and stains if there has been a drip.

____ **52.** Are there stains or raised grain on windowsills? The condensation from an aluminum window can be so great that it works its way into the wall below the window and rots out that wall in a few years.

____ **53.** Are the wall materials cosmetically pleasing? Cheap paneling or "beaverboard" (sometimes found in poorly done attic rooms) will need to be

🏠  🏠  🏠
## A BRIEF KITCHEN ANALYSIS

**1.** The stove, refrigerator, and sink constitute what is known as the "work triangle." The sum of the sides of this triangle should be at least 12' and no more than 22'. Although the enormous "country kitchen" is a favorite, it is often very inefficient, especially when a table ends up in the middle of the triangle.

**2.** Is the work triangle free of through traffic?

**3.** Is there 3'–5' of counter space between each of the work centers? (Some overlap is considered acceptable.)

**4.** Is there counter space for groceries to be loaded into the refrigerator?

**5.** Is there 9'–14' each of base and wall cabinets?

**6.** Are there electrical outlets at least every 6' feet along the counter?

**7.** Is there a quiet exhaust fan? (Downdraft fans, as found in kitchen islands, are often almost useless.)

**8.** Is there sufficient lighting? Window openings should total 10%–20% of the floor space.

**9.** Is there a dishwasher? Important for resale. If a dishwasher is built-in, is there a chrome vent on the counter just above it?

replaced when your time comes to sell, if you want the best price. Cracked plaster may not be beautiful, but it isn't necessarily anything to worry about, so don't overreact to this minor fault. People get crow's-feet; houses develop cracks. The repairs are relatively simple. For houses.

**P.S.** We found one house with perfectly straight, vertical hairline cracks in the new drywall. Reason: Remodeler had "textured" the wall without bothering to tape the cracks first. Cheap.

____ **54.** Are there electrical outlets on all walls, especially on the second floor? (It's harder/more expensive to add them upstairs.) And never assume that because the outlet plates are the three-hole, grounded type that the outlets are actually grounded.

____ **55.** Does the bathroom have a "ground-fault-interrupter" (one of those outlets with a "test" button)? If a bathroom has been remodeled recently and does not have a GFI, the remodeling was done without a permit, since these are now required for bathrooms and outdoor outlets. They trip in $\frac{1}{40}$ of a second if shorted out, and prevent electrocution. See "GFIs" in Chapter 8, "Evaluating: Work Orders."

_____ **56.** Does the bathtub water drop to a trickle when the basin is filling and the commode is flushed? Galvanized pipe was meant to have a life of about 20 years, but we find houses 70 years old where the original is still in use. Drops in water pressure are common, due to scaling (sediment/rust buildup). Replacing pipe is very expensive if a plumber does it, time-consuming if you and I do it. If you do it, do the horizontal runs first; these have a tendency to be the most clogged.

_____ **57.** Is there any woodwork near the shower? In the days before taking a shower became the norm, it was common to put a window just above the tub. This is an invitation to a dry-rot disaster.

---

### A TOOLBOX?

Several books have been written on how to do your own structural inspections (which no amateur should do; even professionals lack objectivity when inspecting their own purchases). These usually include a list of tools you should bring to the inspection—a screwdriver, a level, and even an ice pick. An ice pick!? Now let me tell you, most sellers are not going to welcome anyone carrying an ice pick into their homes. "Destructive testing," i.e. the probing, cutting, or scraping of any materials, is considered *rude*. It is done only with permission, and permission is requested only when the problem seems *very* important. Just as doctors can detect a great deal without exploratory surgery, engineers know how to detect most problems without opening a wall.

You and I can even tell a great deal about how level things are just by lining up doorjambs and lintels to see if they are parallel. Tapping on window sills with our knuckles may tell us just as much as stabbing one with an ice pick.

A professional inspector's tools are few: a strong flashlight, outlet tester, screwdriver, level, and possibly a gas detector (for checking a furnace). Many things, even water pressure, can be evaluated by professionals and amateurs alike with just our natural tools—our eyes and ears—if we know what we're looking for. I have needed binoculars less than once a year, to get a look at some part of a roof or chimney.

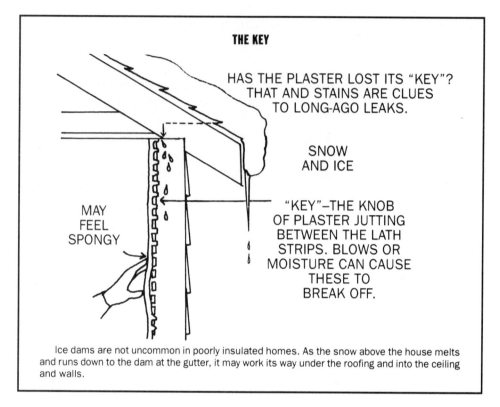

THE KEY

HAS THE PLASTER LOST ITS "KEY"?
THAT AND STAINS ARE CLUES
TO LONG-AGO LEAKS.

SNOW
AND ICE

MAY
FEEL
SPONGY

"KEY"–THE KNOB
OF PLASTER JUTTING
BETWEEN THE LATH
STRIPS. BLOWS OR
MOISTURE CAN CAUSE
THESE TO
BREAK OFF.

Ice dams are not uncommon in poorly insulated homes. As the snow above the house melts and runs down to the dam at the gutter, it may work its way under the roofing and into the ceiling and walls.

____ **58.** Is there a quiet fan? Noisy fans don't get used, so moisture may not be dealt with adequately. See "The Trouble with Moisture" in Chapter 8, "Evaluating: Work Orders."

____ **59.** Is the wall above and around the tub solid, caulked, and free of mold? The area around the built-in soap dish is especially vulnerable. Here it is easy for water to penetrate the wall. Tap all around the soap dish to see if the wall is sound. Then look for floor movement by concentrating your weight at the tub corners and at the base of the toilet. Dry rot in the floor can even be the result of a "sweating" toilet tank or a toilet that rocks on its base.

____ **60.** Is the house generally free of signs of "deferred maintenance"? Examples: a doorbell that doesn't work, dirt in the heat registers, missing switchplates, switches that don't work, fixture handles that don't match, stains around tubs and sinks, missing or dirt-packed furnace filters, etc.

### CHECKING UTILITIES, DOWN BELOW AND GARAGE

____ **61.** Are there any deposits of white salts ("efflorescence") on the foundation walls or basement floor? These are caused by the movement of moisture through the concrete, leaching minerals to the surface. These and/or stains on walls or supports indicate moisture problems that need investigating.

_____ **62.** Is there any standing water in a crawl space? A very serious concern. See "Dealing with Moisture" in Chapter 8, "Evaluating: Work Orders."

_____ **63.** Is the furnace relatively modern, or is it a classic "octopus"? Older furnaces are often relatively inefficient, and if one wishes to install a new furnace, the bill can take quite a leap ($1,000–$2,000) if the heating ducts are wrapped in asbestos.

_____ **64.** Were furnace ducts and piping installed correctly? This evaluation requires technical knowledge, but one obvious and common flaw is the notching of the bottom of joists or beams to install these pieces. This can be vvwvwvery serious damage.

_____ **65.** If the floor joists and pony walls ("little walls" resting on the concrete stem walls) are not concealed, has any type of triangulation been used in the

---

### CHECKING FURNACES/HOT WATER SYSTEMS

Inspectors vary in how thoroughly they investigate furnaces. Some use mirrors and "gas sniffers," while some just take a glance. In the summer it is all too easy for everyone to forget to check the thermostat. This is your wake-up call.

Lenders sometimes require the buyer to sign a statement indicating that they have checked out the furnace, etc., and accept it in its present condition.

One inspector reports that furnaces installed in crawl spaces tend to have a noticeably shorter life than those installed in basements, possibly because of condensation and rust.

Old-fashioned radiators should alert us to look for asbestos (used to insulate the steam pipes).

Water heaters are rarely inspected closely. It is simply not practical to spend $100 in time dismantling a $200 item that is going to wear out anyway. The best investment of time is five minutes, spent every three to six months, opening the bottom spigot and draining off about five gallons; this may prevent sediment buildup and prolong the water heater's life.

construction, i.e. angled braces, angled subflooring (houses built before 1950 or so), and "cross-bracing" between the joists? Many houses have survived decades without triangulation, but some knowledgeable buyers expect these features. "Racking"—the subtle leaning of a house due to wind—is sometimes revealed by doors and windows that are hard to open/close, and has been observed when the pony walls are not braced. Amateurs often confuse this racking from wind with settling.

Ask your inspector if the sill plates are bolted to the foundation, and if in his/her opinion this truly provides any advantage in the event of an earthquake.

____ **66.** If the garage and house share a door, is it a self-sealing door with an automatic closer? And the room that shares that door better not be a bedroom! Don't underestimate carbon monoxide (car exhaust); it doesn't provide any warning or second chance.

____ **67.** Is every wall or ceiling shared by the garage and house covered with drywall? This is required for minimal fire protection.

---

### EARTHQUAKE DAMAGE

I noticed that a charming 50-year-old house had its share of unevenness, but there were a few too many cracks in the plaster and foundation. After a while I realized that there was a pattern to the cracks, all radiating from one point. This house had experienced earthquake damage in the late forties. It took a courageous buyer, with many skills, to buy that one.

---

## CONDOS/CO-OPS

Everything under kitchens, bathrooms, etc., to be inspected in a house should also be done here.

____ **68.** Was the building originally built to be a condo or apartment? The older "conversions," although sometimes very charming, are generally harder to sell. The reasons range from not having washer-dryers in the unit to not being built to modern noise standards.

____ **69.** Are the bedrooms remote from sources of noise? Underground parking and hallways make great echo chambers but poor companions. One of the

---

## COLORS

OK, the dining room is turquoise. So what? Is that the only problem? To reject a house for that reason alone seems a bit hasty. Agents suspect people who give color as their reason for not liking a house of having a hidden agenda.

Unless we're talking about the bathroom fixtures. Then the concern is legitimate. But there's still hope. We can decorate with accessories until the day comes for the total bathroom overhaul, or we can change a fixture here and there as money allows. As for the tub, if it's cast iron and there's no need to demolish the walls, then coloring the tub in place may be the best response. It may be best to replace the lighter, cheaper tubs. Remember: People who do the most creative things and take the most risks reap the most rewards and are the life of every party, even more than harmonica players.

---

problems with condos is that you don't get to spend a night in them before making an offer, so you need to imagine all the problems you can. Make an effort to visit in the evening to see if you can hear neighbors upstairs or next door. Try to stay long enough to hear a neighbor's toilet flushed; if you hear a pipe gurgling in the dining room wall, keep looking. Listen, and even sniff, at the vents; these sometimes carry everything from a neighbor's conversation to cigarette smoke.

_____ **70.** Is there secured parking and secured ingress? Well lit? These rate fairly high for resale.

_____ **71.** Is the building generally free of high-maintenance perks that you may not use a great deal? If it has a pool and a clubhouse, these should be important to you; otherwise you will be subsidizing someone else's fun. Inspection of common areas reveals a great deal about other tenants as well as the management. Also be aware that a unit without a balcony or patio gets lots of sneers from buyers and has diminished future resale value.

_____ **72.** Are the windows double-glazed or thermal? This is a concern because the individual owner may not be allowed to make any changes.

_____ **73.** Are the hallways and elevators clean? What, no elevator? Hmmm, how many floors up must you carry the groceries? Anyway, check out the general cleanliness and decor, inside and out.

## A PRIMER ON INSULATION

With few exceptions, thickness equals effectiveness, assuming that air gaps are practically nonexistent. So look in the attic and see how deep the insulation is. It takes 8"–11" of rock wool, cellulose, or fiberglass to meet the requirements or recommendations in most of Washington. If fiberglass with a foil or paper face has been installed, the face must be toward the warm side. An extremely common mistake is to install it facedown in a crawl space. This can trap condensation. Another common mistake is to install fiberglass between rafters without allowing space between the insulation and the roof surface for air flow (to vent moisture and hot air).

Insulated siding provides minimal payback in heat savings. The most cost-effective measures are weatherstripping, ceiling insulation, and floor insulation (especially over crawl spaces). The least cost-effective are storm windows, insulated glass without a "thermal break," and blown-in insulation in walls of old houses. Removing an electrical outlet plate and looking into the wall with a flashlight may reveal whether the cavity is insulated. It's a good idea to insulate/weatherstrip all outlets and plumbing on exterior walls.

Some financing methods allow adding on the cost of insulating. Ask your lender.

____ **74.** Is there an on-site manager? Good managers are an enormous asset. Who else will let the phone installer in? Smaller buildings may not be able to afford them.

____ **75.** Is there plenty of convenient, secured storage?

____ **76.** Is there parking for friends? There rarely is, but we can dream, can't we?

____ **77.** Does the unit have a central vacuum, and if so who has the responsibility for repairing it?

NOTE: If you are preparing to purchase a condo or co-op, the points discussed above should be combined with those discussed in Chapter 15, "Mondo Condo."

## ASBESTOS

Asbestos has not affected house values to the extent that urea formaldehyde insulation did, even though its dangers are better confirmed and seemingly much worse. The primary impact of asbestos has been in commercial real estate, although residential buyers do ask about it, and several times a year an agent may see a transaction disintegrate because of it.

Asbestos is found in more products than most homeowners suspect: sheet flooring, furnace insulation, siding, roofing, attic insulation, ceiling textures ("popcorn" or "cottage cheese"), and even in plaster.

Before doing any remodeling, any material that will be cut, drilled, or sanded should first be tested for asbestos (and lead, as well, if it was painted before the 1980s). Tests are usually not expensive (see "Laboratories—Analytical" and "Laboratories—Testing" in the Yellow Pages). When a Georgia homeowner had new heating ducts installed, the walls of his home were found to be almost 50% asbestos. The house was condemned by the state.

If left alone, asbestos *may* be no more or less of a problem than the bottle of bleach under the sink, but once asbestos is released into the air the problem is serious. The fibers are so microscopic that no filter commonly available to the amateur is capable of removing them. When negotiating on this item, one strategy to consider is requiring the *professional* removal of the asbestos so that some suicidal seller doesn't try to remove it himself.

### RADON/FORMALDEHYDE/LEAD

Radon is public enemy number one, according to *The Healthy Home* (see Appendix—"Environment"). Unfortunately, testing for radon, formaldehyde, or lead is not usually an option available to a buyer. Most sellers do not want to wait for the lab results. The good news is that radon and formaldehyde can usually be dealt with for no more than a three-figure sum. Lead is another story. It can require the same level of expertise and expensive equipment to remove as asbestos. Take all of these concerns seriously, and pay special attention to lead if you have young children and the house was built before 1979.

# EVALUATING: WORK ORDERS

**What are work orders?** Work orders are requirements for any changes, repairs, or inspections of a property that, when completed, make it less likely that the new residents will encounter physical or legal problems with the land or the improvements thereon. Whew! Catch your breath. Work orders may be required by an appraiser, pest inspector, or building code inspector, or any representative of the lender, including the underwriter and the insurers of the loan (private mortgage insurance). Work orders may even be called at the last minute by the lender's inspector who checks on the completion of the first set of work orders.

**Why does the lender require this process?** By eliminating the majority of, or most serious, problems from a property, the lender makes it less likely that the buyer will default. If the buyer encounters an expensive repair just after moving in, she might do anything—walk out, refuse to make payments, or sue the lender or the seller.

In addition, the vast majority of loans made today will be sold tomorrow in the secondary market (explained in Chapter 9, "Financing: The Basics"). Since the investors who buy these loans will never set eyes on the properties, they require assurances that the properties have met minimum standards of habitability.

**What if the buyer and seller are willing to sign a waiver?** Tough. The lender would still be vulnerable. If the buyer defaulted and the lender had to foreclose and repossess the property, the last thing the lender would want is a property that needs repairs.

**Does this system then assure the buyer that no other repairs will be needed?** Not at all. The appraisers are not generally trained in construction, and typically they spend no more than 50–60 minutes on the site. It usually takes an engineer several hours to thoroughly inspect a house, and even then no one can say that all problems have been discovered. Most contracts include fine print that relieves the lender and appraiser of responsibility for any future discoveries; the stated purpose of the appraisal is to determine the maximum amount of the loan.

**Who must pay for any work orders?** No one. Well, maybe. If no mention was made of the work orders when the purchase and sale agreement was negotiated, then there may not be any way to require anyone to pay for them. The word "may" denotes that not all legal experts agree on this. Some say that a seller *would* be required to provide a habitable house by making "reasonable" repairs. In reality, very few agents or consumers are willing to be a test case in the courts, so the typical scenario involves negotiations *after* the work orders are called. In a slow market, with a motivated seller, we frequently see the seller volunteering to absorb the costs (or at least biting the bullet). Even agents have been known to pay for minor repairs when the principals are bickering over them. Now don't get any ideas, you ragpickers.

The better the market, and the better the house, and the more the buyers want that house, the more likely it is that the buyers will pay for some or all of the work orders.

If no agreement is reached, the buyers are usually refunded their earnest money and they begin their search anew. This often happens after a month or more has been spent on this transaction.

---

### JAILHOUSE LAWYERS DO IT AGAIN

See Chapter 13, "From Offer to Closing," for an explanation of the requirement that a seller correct building code violations. This is commonly misinterpreted by amateur contract readers to mean that sellers must perform work orders.

---

**Then shouldn't work orders be negotiated in the original agreement?** Yes, but. Several buts. Your attorney may tell you that if some agreement isn't reached on the work orders in the original contract, the contract might be null and void if work orders are called and no one is willing to pay. As noted, not all experts agree. But to be practical, that is the most likely result.

I have been urging agents to negotiate work orders up front for years, but I have not made too many believers. Here are some of their "buts":

**1.** BUT if we do, we'll scare the buyer to death. He's not really all that sure he wants the property anyway, so if we start talking about the cost of a roof, he may just walk away. ANSWER: Better he walk away now than a month from now.

**2.** BUT if we wait, the buyer and the seller will probably be more committed to the transaction, and surely then we'll get a compromise out of them. ANSWER: There's a grain of truth in that. Have you been making all of your Gamblers Anonymous meetings?

**3.** BUT if the appraiser reads in the contract that the seller has agreed to pay for a new roof, the appraiser will be sure to call the roof. So let's pretend we don't expect any repairs. ANSWER: This is based on an unfair assumption that appraisers are lazy, whimsical, and lacking the ability to make independent judgments. We have no proof of this. Furthermore, the appraiser doesn't always see the PSA.

**4.** BUT even if we had to negotiate the work orders up front, no one has ever been able to anticipate an appraiser's calls with complete accuracy, so we could still end up with an unenforceable contract. ANSWER: Another grain of truth. And yet, with a little more effort on the part of sellers and agents, the vast majority of work orders could be predicted and a reasonable amount for repairs agreed to, without even naming any specific repairs or problems. The alternative, waiting for the appraiser, should be called "contract gambling" and could be a new game in Las Vegas. Better there than in real estate. Buyers are advised not to gamble. If you want a repair or change, negotiate it. Don't count on the appraiser calling it.

---

### OUT WEST

In general, the Washington homeowner can legally do just about any repair needed or imaginable. However, a neighbor may not. If I get the proper permits, I can change my electric panel, but my neighbor who knows twice as much as I do cannot work on my house, at least not for a fee. Not unless she is a licensed electrician.

One of the few areas where building departments draw the line is the sewer. What's inside the house is our bailiwick; what's outside they feel they must control.

---

**When must the work orders be done?** In general, the work orders must be completed prior to closing, but there are several important exceptions. One would be when a rehab loan is the financing vehicle; in this case the buyer, or persons employed by the buyer, does the repairs and often has as much as six months after closing to complete them.

---

## 🏠 🏠 🏠
## A FRUSTRATION EVERY TIME

When the appraiser calls the work orders, the process is usually one of checking off a box for that item on a standard form, and possibly, just maybe, a few words will be scribbled in the margin explaining what the appraiser expects. This paper is relayed to the lender, who may then send a copy to the agents and/or seller. It is museum-rare for anyone to understand from this form what the appraiser observed or expects. For example, "fix dry rot in the basement" can turn out to be a spot smaller than a golf ball in a doorjamb. We often have no choice but to fake a diplomatic mood and call the appraiser for an explanation.

---

If weather is a factor, as it often is with roofs and exterior painting, the lender may agree to a holdback of two to four months. Is there a catch? Yes—the party responsible for the repairs must usually deposit a sum equal to 150%–200% of a written estimate of the cost. The estimate must generally be on the letterhead of a licensed or otherwise qualified repairperson.

Can the person who pays for the repairs use someone other than the person who gave the estimate, or do them himself? Yes, in instances where the lender or local building codes do not prohibit this.

The greatest exception or solution to work order problems is the waiver. A waiver in this instance means an expert's opinion that the repair is not needed. Since the expert may incur some liability for making such a statement, this opinion may not come cheap. In fact, some of Seattle's better roofers have lately been charging in the vicinity of $250 for a written "roof certification." A few years ago such an inspection could be had for $50–$70, but some of the lenders' underwriting rules have been tightened, and the roofer must now guarantee, not merely opine, that the roof has five remaining years and any repairs will be made at his expense.

The expert must inspect and then write a report that is delivered to the underwriter, who may then confer with the appraiser and personally inspect and photograph the roof; if all is in order, the waiver may be granted.

Some work orders can never be waived. For example, a waiver for a pest inspection requires proof that none was needed, which requires a pest inspection for said proof.

### ABUSE OF POWER?

Many offers in the big city include a structural inspection contingency. Listing agents generally accept this (such inspections can lower their liability as well as the seller's), but they hate like fleabites for the appraiser to learn that this inspection will be performed. Some agents request that the inspection contingency be written on a separate addendum that is not submitted with the PSA to the lender. Why? Because some appraisers will then request/demand a copy of the report, even though many inspectors specify right on the report that it is only for the eyes of the paying customer.

The appraiser may then call work orders based on someone else's observations and conclusions. This causes resentment and accusations that these appraisers are either lazy or going overboard. Wait. Let's look at it from the lender's and appraiser's viewpoint. If the goal is to do the best possible job, then it does seem that this could be a step in the right direction. But before we give more credit than is due, we must note that there is no consistency. If the goal is so noble, then lenders should start requiring inspections in every case, by *competent* inspectors, and arranging for a shared or discounted cost since there would be a shared benefit. Just daydreaming; don't mind me.

## THE MOST COMMON WORK ORDERS

There is no such thing as a complete list of work orders; an appraiser can always come up with something no one would have imagined. Likewise there will always be structural problems resulting from unpredictable coincidences. However, the following alphabetical list is almost guaranteed to eliminate, head off, or prepare the seller or buyer for 95 percent of the Hydra's heads.

As noted elsewhere, these work orders are as likely to be called by one kind of appraiser as another. In other words, differences between conventional, FHA, and VA appraisers are very small and are more likely explained by their personalities and backgrounds than by any requirements of their institutions. Agents who sell only a few houses a year may have a bad experience with two appraisers representing the same type of loan and then conclude that all FHA appraisals or VA appraisals will involve that complication. This is unfortunate inductive reasoning, because they may then tell their sellers to avoid FHA offers or VA offers. This problem seems to be as persistent as mosquitoes.

**Access to unfinished spaces.** Attics and crawl spaces require "head and shoulders access." This allows checking for insects, dry rot, etc. A trapdoor of no less than 24" × 30" should be provided, and even one this small will no doubt raise a hue and cry. An appraiser is within her rights to suspend the entire appraisal and not return until access is provided (suspension is rare, though; in fact, I have seen appraisers entirely overlook lack of access). In addition, if we need to get up into an attic, government agencies require their appraisers to carry only a 4' ladder, so be prepared to deal with this shortcoming. *What* is a 4' ladder good for?

**Basement floor** (also see "Wet basement"). If a sleeper floor (a wooden floor laid right on a concrete floor) is not vented, the appraiser can either declare it unfinished space or call for vents. One or two 4" × 12" vents, as used for furnace ducts, would probably suffice for a bedroom. This is a rare call.

**Bathroom, etc.** Since water is the primary enemy of the structure, followed by wind, sun, and children, in no particular order, it follows that the home of the enemy is the bathroom (although basements and kitchens compete for this honor). Bathroom candidates for work orders may include and require: (1) either a fan or a working window; (2) an intact shower-surround if the tub is being used as a shower; (3) caulking of tub at floor and wall, and of the shower-surround and soap dish; (4) replacement of any torn/damaged flooring.

**Broken, missing, or damaged anything.** Broken windows, plaster, or steps fall into this category. An ordinary crack in a window or in the plaster is not too likely to be a call, but unpredictability is the name of the game. Missing siding, railings, splash blocks, and downspouts are pretty much sure things. Missing doorknobs and switchplates are strong maybes.

We have had appraisers require that every room have at least one window that opens freely for fire safety. (Might I suggest keeping it shut at all other times to prevent the city miasma from diluting the formaldehyde and asbestos?)

**City or code inspection.** If the appraiser sees anything that she suspects of being a "serious" code violation, she can call for an inspection of the entire structure by the local authorities. They in turn can call more work orders than Santa's elves could complete in a month, so this can be a serious event. But it is not common.

The last one of these inspections I encountered cost $165 in Seattle, which included one free reinspection. Items that might trigger this inspection include improperly installed woodstoves (the majority of them, in my opinion), post-and-beam foundations or floor joists using substandard materials, a wobbly deck, etc.

Once the inspector is on the premises, everything is fair game. I've even seen them require better locks and peepholes in exterior doors.

**Cracked foundation.** Here is one reason I commonly recommend using an engineer for an inspection, rather than someone who has simply decided that inspecting houses is a good way to make a living. If the appraiser sees a crack, which is very common, she can require a "certification," which is nothing more than a statement by an engineer that everything seems to be stable. A copy of the engineer's original report may even suffice. All such cracks should be grouted to prevent the entry of insects and water.

If a corner or wall has actually broken away and settled, then we most likely have a whole different story. I have seen several houses like this that have been occupied for 40 or more years after the damage. Everyone still reacts, however, whether it is the appraiser or prospective buyers. The cost of these types of

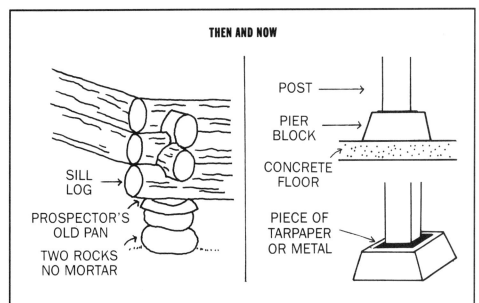

**THEN AND NOW**

SILL LOG

PROSPECTOR'S OLD PAN

TWO ROCKS NO MORTAR

POST

PIER BLOCK

CONCRETE FLOOR

PIECE OF TARPAPER OR METAL

Just as with a candle wick, moisture wicks its way up through stones or mortar by capillary action, and dry rot is the eventual proof of this process. Much of this capillary action can be halted by a "mortarless gap," a pier block set on a concrete floor or pad. An improvement on this is to put tarpaper between the pier block and the wooden post.

The prospector's pan has been replaced by galvanized termite shields, but termites long ago proved that they can crawl around such barriers. The perfect system eludes us. It is not lethal chemicals, which eventually end up in our water.

"repairs"—such as "mud jacking," where cementitious grout under pressure is used to lift the foundation—is usually so large that most owners just find a way to live with the problem.

**Crawl spaces** (also see "Earth-wood contact"). Crawl spaces are supposed to be at least 18" high (24" if they contain "mechanical" devices, e.g. a furnace), and yes, you can be required to dig one to that depth. There is supposed to be 1 square foot of ventilation for moisture for each 300 square feet if the crawl space has either a concrete floor or is covered with plastic; otherwise, 2 square feet per 300 square feet. Ventilation usually consists of ordinary open-mesh vents at the corners. Do not use louvered vents; they can be rejected (the appraisers say these can get clogged with spiderwebs and grass clippings. And Donald Trump will depend on his social security).

If your house is properly insulated, you won't want to close up any of these vents in the winter. Especially in the winter. That is frequently when the removal of moisture is most important.

If there is *any* debris, and vapor barriers (ordinary plastic) are not in place, you can bet that a pest inspection will be called. Technically, the pest inspector can call for an eight-mil plastic, which is a lot more expensive than a four-mil but looks identical when it's already lying there. If you catch my draft.

**Driveways.** See "Easements."

**Dry rot/insect damage** (also see "Earth-wood contact" and "Pest inspections"). Is there anyone out there who hasn't already heard that dry rot is a misnomer? I didn't think so. But just as a refresher, rotting does require "intermittent wetting," plus "germs" of some kind. A house is an excellent candidate for dry rot because of the frequently changing humidity and temperature. See "The Trouble with Moisture" illustration in this chapter.

Check each of these structural members: the sill plates (the 2 × 4s or 2 × 6s lying flat atop the concrete walls in the basement), all pieces of wood in a post-and-beam foundation, all pieces in a deck or exposed porch plus any outdoor steps, all sills and jambs in basement windows and doors, the rafters and the roof deck (the wood surface the shingles are nailed to), and finally the soffits and rafter tails (area between gutter and siding).

There are no big secrets to this inspection: a *strong* flashlight, a screwdriver or knife or even a drill with a ¼" bit, nails and a hammer (sometimes just rapping on wood with knuckles reveals corruption), and possibly a mirror to look at tight spots.

In addition to crumbling wood, we are looking for any series of holes, especially those with little piles of sawdust at the entrances, and for "mud tunnels" (tubes on a foundation wall in which termites travel back and forth to the earth). Large beams that appear perfectly sound can be completely hollow, able only to bear their own weight; driving in a drill bit or a nail can reveal the problem immediately.

**Earth-wood contact.** In many cases, work orders addressing "earth-wood" are not necessarily implying that any damage exists, just that preventative measures must be taken. No wood is supposed to be within 6" of the ground. Technically, an exception is made for pressure-treated wood, but many builders and inspectors will tell you that this is still not a good idea. Once this wood has been cut, the "wounded" area is as vulnerable as nontreated wood, and not all treatments are meant for long-term exposure.

Common earth-wood problems involve the bottom of outdoor wooden steps that are resting on bricks or what have you, wooden siding that comes almost down to the ground, and posts in post-and-beam construction where dirt is piled up around the pier block.

Any of these situations will trigger a call for a pest inspection or for specific items to be corrected, or both. If siding or such cannot be raised, or the dirt cannot be lowered without creating a little moat around the house, then the

---

### GFI'S: WHERE'S THE CUTE IN ELECTROCUTION?

Electrocutions kill hundreds of people in their homes every year. A large percentage of these deaths could easily have been prevented. For some years now we have had requirements that areas where electrocution is most likely to occur—bathrooms, garages, and outdoors (and, in some parts of the country, kitchens)—be protected by a device known as a Ground Fault Interrupter (GFI), also known as a Ground Fault Circuit Interrupter (GFCI).

The GFI works by detecting a short and by turning off the circuit in $\frac{1}{40}$ of a second. Unfortunately, the first GFIs were not easy to install. (Remember the outlet that has the "test & reset" buttons, which should be tested *every month* by hitting the test button while a hairdryer or razor is running?)

But now the good news, the *great* news: Someone has invented a plug-in variation. No installation is required, and I have found them for as little as $4 at Pay'n Pak. At any price they are a bargain, especially where children live.

bottom pieces may have to be replaced with "cement board," aluminum, vinyl, or pressure-treated wood (always take pictures of pressure-treated wood for proof, showing the stamp prior to painting).

**Easements for maintenance.** An appraiser might note that a house sits right on its property line, making it difficult, if not impossible, to erect a ladder and paint that wall. A work order might be called for the seller to acquire an easement from the neighbor, in which case an attorney would be needed. This is a very rare work order.

**Electrical outlets.** Appraisers generally move so fast and concentrate so much on the biggest items that they don't pay much attention to outlets, but occasionally they mention a broken or missing plate. The real hazard is with ungrounded or improperly grounded outlets, and any seller or buyer can determine easily enough whether this situation exists. Go to the hardware store and say, "I want one of those little yellow plugs, you know, for testing outlets, and one of those adapters, too, you know what I mean, for two-hole outlets." The clerk will know what you want and think you were once a famous athlete and treat you with respect.

**Electric panel.** This work order candidate is a hair-puller and one of the two most expensive of the common work orders. It also remains one of the two most difficult areas for predicting an appraiser's reaction (the roof being the

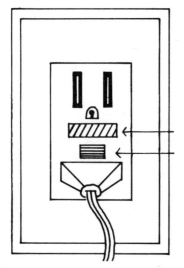

### GROUND FAULT INTERRUPTER (GFI)

The GFI is a very important safety device that is required for all bathroom, garage, and outdoor outlets in new homes. Some parts of the country also require these in the kitchen. It shuts off a "shorted" circuit in $\frac{1}{40}$th of a second.

GFIs should be tested every month. While a hair dryer or other appliance is running, push the black "test" button. The appliance should stop. Then, when the red "reset" button is pushed it should resume.

RESET BUTTON
TEST BUTTON

A homeowner is not normally expected or required to replace the outlets in an older home, but now that some very cheap plug-in versions of GFIs have been invented, this important safety margin is available to everyone for just a few dollars.

Note: A Ground Fault Circuit Interrupter (GFCI) is the same thing.

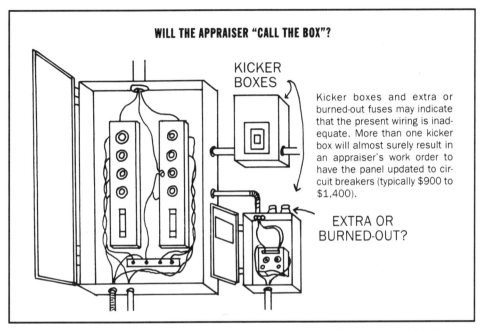

**WILL THE APPRAISER "CALL THE BOX"?**

KICKER BOXES

Kicker boxes and extra or burned-out fuses may indicate that the present wiring is inadequate. More than one kicker box will almost surely result in an appraiser's work order to have the panel updated to circuit breakers (typically $900 to $1,400).

EXTRA OR BURNED-OUT?

other unpredictable and expensive item). Twice I would have bet my banjo that the panel would be called, once because it was outside in the weather and once because it was a totally decrepit set of fuses behind a wooden panel (a code violation), but both times FHA appraisers said, "Looks OK to me."

The appraiser's major focus is usually on whether the panel (the amperage) is adequate for the size of the house. There is actually a formula for this that can be found in handyman paperbacks on doing your own wiring. Appraisers, however, don't use any formula for making their calls, with one exception:

---

### ELECTRIFYING TRIVIA

1. Appraisers don't usually require that wiring be updated. The wiring is usually left alone; only the panel is updated. The old knob-and-tube system of wiring is not intrinsically dangerous, as long as the right size fuses are used, the insulation is intact, and it is not constantly "pushed" to its limit (usually 15 amps) by modern appliances.

2. A pile of burned-out fuses tells a story. Look for this around a fuse box. Also make sure that fuses larger than 15 amps haven't been screwed into the slots for appliance circuits.

If the panel has more than one "kicker" box, then it is supposed to merit an automatic call. Otherwise it's pretty much their gut-call.

You may save money by doing some work orders before they are called; the electrical panel is not one of these. The main reason some sellers do this one before the house is sold is to make more buyers feel good about the house; many buyers are needlessly intimidated by fuses.

Costs for this repair, including permits, will probably be in the $900–$1,400 range.

**Environmental concerns.** These generally get very little notice from appraisers, and sometimes not all that we would hope for from inspectors either, but then there are many complications. To detect lead, radon, formaldehyde, and asbestos we need to do separate lab tests; cost of testing for all four might be $300–$450, or more.

Very few work orders for asbestos were called before the late 1980s, even though asbestos was often in plain sight or strongly suspected. Until around 1978, it was wrapped around heating ducts (a soft white tape, in many cases), around steam-heat pipes (a dirty-white "blanket"), and sprayed onto ceilings ("cottage cheese" texture). In some cases, it has even been mixed into plaster. One of my own agents recently had the underwriter, *not* the appraiser, call for "either professional removal or encapsulation" of asbestos on basement pipes, based solely on the engineer's report, which stated that the asbestos was "friable" (fragile, tattered, etc.).

Radon does not seem to be as common a problem on the western side of the Cascades, but testing for it in Spokane has become almost commonplace. "Pockets" of radon have been detected in the Columbia Gorge and in south King County.

Lead in old paint is always a concern, especially for those of us who scrape, heat-gun, or sand the stuff; lenders who make FHA loans require that buyers of any house built before 1978 sign a form indicating they are aware of the risk. Everyone with young children should have the paint tested.

See Chapter 8, "Evaluating: Value," for details on formaldehyde, and the Appendix—"Environment" for the book *The Healthy Home.*

**Flooring—kitchen or bath.** An obvious tear in a vinyl floor can result in a call for a whole new floor covering. The appraiser is looking for places where frequent wetting would lead to more problems. The edges of flooring should be secured and caulked or covered by molding. Any softness or swelling of the floor below the area of a tear may indicate water damage.

Many tears can be repaired sufficiently to pass the appraiser's scrutiny, so the seller should visit a floor covering store for patching materials before the appraiser gets there.

⌂  ⌂  ⌂
## THE BOX WE OCCUPY

Homeowners who don't understand some of the principles and goals of insulating and ventilating have occasionally been their own worst enemies, such as when they close attic or crawlspace vents in the winter to "keep in the heat." Instead, you should think of the house as three "units." The roof/attic (which we need to ventilate, but not heat), the crawlspace (ventilate like the attic; of course, a finished basement may require both insulation and ventilation), and the box we live in (which needs both insulation and ventilation). The vents are there for the removal of moisture, which is just as much, if not more of a concern, in the cold months. See "The Trouble With Moisture."

One sure sign that a homeowner doesn't know the basics: insulation is installed between the joists with its paper or foil face on the "cold side." This vapor barrier face should either be installed toward the warm interior of the house or slit in many places to prevent condensation of water vapor in the insulation, which will dramatically lessen its effectiveness.

**Gutters.** The lowly gutter has left many homeowners nostalgic for the days when they were carefree renters. They are easy to ignore until patches of rust or moss tell our neighbors what they've suspected all along: We're too cheap to buy a ladder.

The homeowner who is guilty of deferred maintenance may be bug-eyed to learn that it can easily cost $500 for a new set of gutters. The do-it-yourself alternative usually costs no more than $125–$200. But the complications of deferred maintenance in this area can be much more significant than any problems with the gutters themselves; if the eaves or rafter tails require repairs and painting, we are talking about a labor-intensive job that offers few shortcuts. And if missing downspouts or splash blocks, or just poorly routed runoff water, result in a wet basement, then we might as well forget about getting the best possible price for the house unless we take care of these problems right away.

In general, there must be a splash block at every downspout; this is one of the most common calls. See "Unpainted surfaces" and "Wet basements."

**Hot water heater.** See "Leased equipment" and "Pressure relief valve."

**Insulation.** At this time there are no requirements that we insulate *standing* houses, only new ones. So appraisers note only if a home is insulated, and to what extent. This can affect their estimate of maintenance and utilities costs, which can have some bearing on how much the lender will loan.

If a buyer wishes to insulate after purchasing the house, the cost of doing so can be added to many loans. There can be a complication involving the electrical panel: If a full 200-amp panel is installed, the local utility may require a written statement that the new owner does not intend to install electric heating; otherwise, the owner may have to bring the house up to the utility's insulation standards.

If the attic has been insulated, then the likelihood of a call for "roof jacks" becomes a near certainty. See "Roof ventilation."

**Leased equipment.** Washington Natural Gas leases hot water heaters and conversion burners on furnaces. FHA and VA loans require that the seller *purchase* (or *replace*) any leased equipment by the time of closing. Only conventional loans permit a buyer to assume the payments on leased equipment. I prefer leasing a heater; then I never have to worry about it.

Once the requirements of the lease have been fulfilled—e.g. a minimum of one year of payments—the owner/seller can replace the leased equipment. This will almost certainly be cheaper than purchasing the utility company's equipment. One homeowner in Seattle replaced his conversion burner and water heater for $450 (labor included); the gas company wanted over $1,000 for the similar units.

**Peeling paint.** See "Unpainted surfaces."

**Pest inspection** (also see "Crawl spaces," "Dry rot," and "Earth-wood contact"). I have mixed feelings about telling a seller how to avoid the expense of this inspection. In the first place, it's not an expensive inspection ($65 is a common price), and if there are pest problems, we don't want to conceal them. On

---

**COMMON COMPLICATION: PESKY INSPECTIONS**

If you are a seller and are debating whether to get a pest inspection before you put the house on the market, you probably should get one if you have a crawl space, no matter how clean it is. The reason is that at the last minute, the underwriter or someone at the private mortgage insurance office may see that the house has a crawl space and call for a pest inspection, even though the appraiser thought it looked OK. Last-minute delays like this imperil the entire contract.

the other hand, if the house has a full, dry basement where sill plates (the horizontal lumber on top of the concrete wall in the basement) are visible and easily inspected, and if the attic has been well ventilated and can be easily inspected, then the pest inspection might be a needless expenditure. But I have seen homes that were professionally inspected undergo a major remodel during which we discovered concealed termite damage. I'm telling you, there's no guarantee of finding termites without using a termite-sniffing dog.

There are at least four things that may prompt a call for a pest inspection: (1) debris in a crawl space; (2) no vapor barrier or vents in the crawl space; (3) earth-wood contact around outdoor steps or such, especially where some portion of the structure is concealed; and (4) firewood, stumps, or beauty bark up against the house. Buried timbers (often found in retaining walls) are to insects what an aircraft carrier is to navy pilots: a base for attacking the nearest target. And, oh yes, that old window in the shower often provokes a pest inspection. At the very least, it should be covered by a plastic curtain.

The pest inspector can call work orders in addition to those called by the appraiser, so this inspection is not to be taken lightly.

**Plumbing.** In general, plumbing work orders are few and far between, except for the PRV (see below).

**Pressure relief valve (PRV).** This is a brass valve, smaller than a fist, on the top or side of a water heater, that is essential for preventing explosions. If the thermostat malfunctions, the water can reach boiling, turn to steam (which occupies 1,200 times the volume of water), and blow the house and occupants into the next county or the next life. A number of people in King County have died this way. Stay in a motel until this valve has been installed.

If the valve exists but does not have a venting pipe to direct the flow of "exploding" water, the appraiser will call for its installation as well. If the heater sits on a concrete floor, the appraiser may be satisfied with a venting pipe that runs to within 6" of the floor. If the floor is wood, or the heater is not in the basement, the rules of venting can be a bit more complicated; the pipe must usually

---

### AND YOU THOUGHT YOU DID DUMB THINGS?

PRVs have a bad habit of leaking and needing to be replaced. One homeowner didn't like the leak, so he just soldered a cap on the relief valve. Reinventing the bomb.

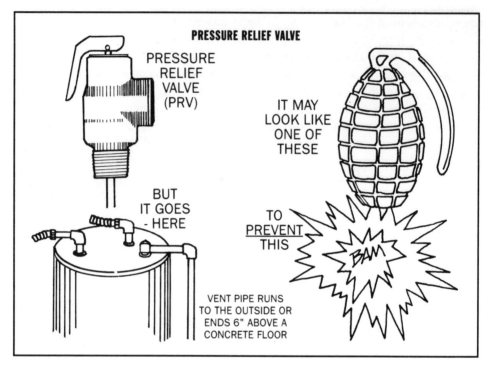

PRESSURE RELIEF VALVE

PRESSURE
RELIEF
VALVE
(PRV)

IT MAY
LOOK LIKE
ONE OF
THESE

BUT
IT GOES
- HERE

TO
PREVENT
THIS

BAM

VENT PIPE RUNS
TO THE OUTSIDE OR
ENDS 6" ABOVE A
CONCRETE FLOOR

be run to the outside. A trip to the plumbing store should provide sufficient information.

**Roof—surface.** Some roofing materials are rejected automatically by appraisers—"rolled roofing," for example, won't be accepted by FHA or VA. Even if a freestanding garage has rolled roofing, a new shingled roof may be required *unless* the seller is willing not to include the garage and its value in the appraisal. This rule is rarely enforced. As for composition shingles, if the pebbly surface is so eroded that the underlying surface of tar shows, it is likely that a whole new roof will be required. Badly cupped shingles also may result in a call (see "Roof—ventilation").

Three layers of roofing material is not usually allowed, unless the first layer is the original wooden shingles with one layer of composition roofing over it; then a third layer may be installed. Otherwise, if a "shovel-off" is required, the cost of a roof often doubles. Since very few roofs cost less than $2,000 for a single layer without a shovel-off, and many cost $4,000 or more, the number of layers is a legitimate concern.

Here's a tip: For probably less than five percent more money, an owner can install a 240-pound composition roofing material. The usual weight is 220 pounds per 100 square feet. This heavier material provides five to eight more years of use, if it is vented correctly.

Can just half of a roof be done? Don't count on it once the appraiser has visited. It wouldn't set too well with most buyers, either. But if a seller can find a shingle of matching color, and if only the southern side (the "weather side")

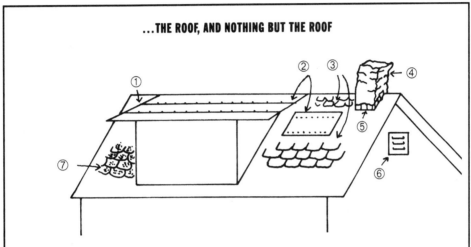

### ...THE ROOF, AND NOTHING BUT THE ROOF

1. The shed dormer has a pitch of less than $4/12$. "Hot tar" roof may be needed. The gable dormer (below) may sacrifice headroom but it offers better rain repellency.
2. Rolled roofing will most likely result in an appraiser "calling the roof."
3. Cupped composition shingles have been "fried like bacon" from heat build-up in the attic.
4. The chimney leans to the southwest, from whence cometh the wind-blown rain that softens the mortar.
5. Flashing is often the most likely culprit when a leak occurs.
6. Tests have shown that gable vents are not effective; the entering air drops to the attic floor and pockets of very hot (and/or moist) air remain at the peak, frying the shingles and rotting the rafters. In addition, if not screened properly, insects may invade. Ridge vents are the best solution, with properly placed roof jacks a close second choice.
7. Dark patches may indicate erosion of the granules, indicating the roof has very little remaining life. In addition, if moss has grown sufficiently to lift the shingles or fill a gutter, it is a safe assumption that no maintenance has been done in at least 10 years.

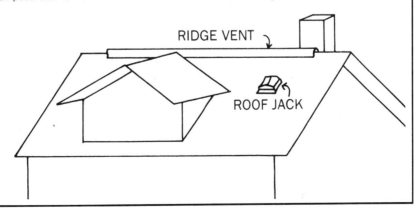

RIDGE VENT

ROOF JACK

is on its last legs, then a seller might want to consider doing it prior to putting the house on the market.

As for wooden shakes or shingles, these should be free of all moss and debris. There are companies that clean and revitalize these roofs at a relatively low cost ($250–$300); check references with past customers, because some companies have been known to do more damage in the long run (walking on roofs can cause more damage than years of weathering). Show some concern for our environment by asking what kind of chemicals they use.

Don't forget fire concerns. The shingle industry claims that modern chemical treatments have made wooden shingles as safe as composition shingles, but the fire that swept through and destroyed a Spokane subdivision jumped from wooden roof to wooden roof. Even *if* treatment renders wooden shingles safe, if the shingles are not of the very best grade or are not applied correctly, they can last a very short time (six to ten years). Fiberglass shingles have the best fire rating ('A,' vs. 'C' for wood and asphalt), but fiberglass often looks lumpy when it's applied over other layers, so consider using either the heavier fiberglass grades or asphalt shingles.

The appraiser's goal or standard is to be reasonably sure that the roof has at least five years of life remaining. Some appraisers tend to err on the conservative side; we actually had an appraiser call for a new roof when the present one was brand new. That's Jesse Helms–conservative. If you feel that your roof has five years but the appraiser doesn't, you can hire a roofer to inspect and

---

### THE TROUBLE WITH MOISTURE

The trouble with moisture is that the danged stuff won't stay put. It insists on moving as water vapor to drier air, be that in the attic or walls or the great outdoors. That could be to our advantage except for one other pesky trait: it can condense on surfaces that are a mere 10° cooler than the air containing the water vapor.

We may see and wipe up the pool of water on the bathroom window sill, but the slow dry rot of roof and wall sheathing from condensed water often goes undetected until the damage is extensive and expensive. The solutions are obvious: (1) prevent water's entrance into the basement or crawlspace; (2) remove water vapor caused by showers and cooking with professionally installed fans and vents.

See "Don't Vex that Vent" and "The Wet Basement."

write a guarantee. Since the roofer takes quite a risk, these written guarantees can cost $250 and up.

The likelihood of a call for an inspection or new roof goes up dramatically with a flat roof. More than one owner has mopped on gallons and gallons of "tar" prior to the appraiser's visit, just to give a flat roof the appearance of longevity. And twice I have seen an appraiser take someone's word that their flat roofs were fine without taking a look.

If buyers knew how frequently appraisers don't even glance at the roof, they would be much more inclined to take this item into their own hands and get their own inspections. Don't blame the appraisers; remember, the government doesn't want them to get more than four feet off the ground. Since a roof may have problems even when it appears to be perfectly sound, the lender might also have the buyer sign a statement at closing accepting the roof in its present condition.

**Roof—ventilation.** This is one of the most frequent and saddest of work orders. Although it is usually not expensive to install or add vents to a roof, the fact that they have not been there or were inadequate often means that a whole new roof will be needed much sooner than otherwise. Simple vents can eliminate both high-temperature and high-moisture problems. One sure sign of poor ventilation is the curling of the bottom edges of composition shingles; they are curling from heat just as surely as if they were sizzling strips of bacon in a frying pan. On a summer day, an unvented attic can reach a temperature of 145°, "cooking" a 20-year roof right down to a 10-year roof.

The work order will call for the installation of "roof jacks." These are metal or vinyl vents that look like upside-down cake pans and are often placed near the ridge and the lower edge of the roof. They cost $6–$8 apiece and take no more than 20–30 minutes each to install. Roofers or insulation contractors are likely to charge about $30 each, which includes the vent.

No single vent can work very well. There must be a vent where air enters (as in the soffits near the gutters) as well as where it exits (at or near the ridge). See "The Trouble with Moisture," above, for the optimum number of vents.

The most efficient venting system is the ridge vent. It costs a little more, but in the long run it is a better investment.

**Sinks, tubs, and frequently wet surfaces.** It is easy to understand why a seller may hesitate to install roof jacks (dangerous) or dig out a crawl space (dirty), but there is no defensible reason for a seller in good health not to maintain or repair easy-to-reach places where trouble *will* happen without routine maintenance. And why leave another item undone that is bound to be a turn-off for the buyers?

First, get out the bleach and eliminate the mildew. Then caulk, caulk, caulk, caulk, caulk, anyplace that water can enter and cause problems. But caulk neatly. Include: soap tray in shower wall, bottoms of tubs and toilet, wall sides of tubs and showers, edges of linoleum/vinyl if not under a toe strip, and edges of sinks in counters (unless they have a good "hoodie rim").

If there is a shower nozzle over the tub but the walls are just painted plaster, the appraiser usually requires a new "tub surround." This can run from as little as $25 in materials to $500 or more for an installed job. See "Pest Inspections" regarding a window in the shower.

**Smoke detector.** This may qualify as the most seriously neglected work order, at least in Seattle, where UL-approved detectors must be in every dwelling —battery powered are acceptable if installed before 1980, but "hard wired" are required thereafter. Check local ordinances.

**Stained plaster, ceiling tiles, etc.** Stains can reveal a leaking roof or plumbing, or severe condensation problems, and can mean that extensive and concealed damage exists. On the other hand, stains can be virtually meaningless, merely indicating a former, temporary problem. The appraiser is not likely to require that anything be done about the stains themselves. He is just more likely to order further inspections.

If the seller is sure she is not concealing a serious problem, then she should paint over the stains. Many stains must be sealed before they can be painted. Shellac is one such sealer, and I have had mediocre success with aluminum spray paint. Also, Beadex has a product made for this purpose, "Texture Fresh."

**Stairs.** This area is not usually addressed by the appraiser. Perhaps it should be, but the emphasis of the appraisal is generally on value and marketability, not on safety. The appraiser may call for a city inspection if a code violation, such as a missing hand railing, is suspected, but it usually takes more than this to get his attention.

On behalf of clumsy real estate agents everywhere, I would like to ask sellers to go beyond what is required, and do what is right. At least two Seattle agents have taken bad falls on stairs—one on a broken step concealed under carpet (the seller *had* to know of this) and one due to a basement door that opened into and over the stairs without a landing and had no latch (the agent's fall resulted in several days in the hospital). No, an agent will probably not sue you, but a buyer surely will. It's awfully hard to sell a house that's tied up in court.

**Unpainted surfaces.** Even drywall or interior woodwork must usually be painted, the reasoning being that if they aren't, they are very vulnerable to damage. But the major concern in this area is usually the exterior, and this is one

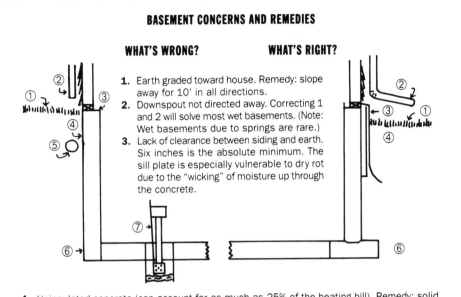

## BASEMENT CONCERNS AND REMEDIES

### WHAT'S WRONG?        WHAT'S RIGHT?

1. Earth graded toward house. Remedy: slope away for 10' in all directions.
2. Downspout not directed away. Correcting 1 and 2 will solve most wet basements. (Note: Wet basements due to springs are rare.)
3. Lack of clearance between siding and earth. Six inches is the absolute minimum. The sill plate is especially vulnerable to dry rot due to the "wicking" of moisture up through the concrete.

4. Uninsulated concrete (can account for as much as 25% of the heating bill). Remedy: solid insulation on the outside, covered by a vapor barrier which *must* be covered by aluminum or vinyl to prevent deterioration from ultra-violet rays.
5. Drain tiles may actually *increase* the leakage problem in a basement. Remedy: see 1 and 2.
6. Lack of footing (a serious problem for the owner who wants to add a floor). Remedy: buy a house that has a separate footing to start with. How do you know? Either drive a steel rod or warm up the shovel.
7. Sump pump indicates drainage is a persistent problem. Appraiser may call for structural inspection and expensive repairs. Remedy: see 1 and 2.

area where a seller should not wait for the appraiser. There might be only 10 square feet of peeling paint on one exterior wall, but to an appraiser that spot looks like the whole house. What could have been one afternoon of scraping and painting might turn into a $1,500 paint job when the appraiser calls for the entire house to be painted.

The owner should pay special attention to window sills, the undersides of eaves and soffits, and the south or southwest sides of the house. Also note the corners of the house, where rain often enters; all gaps in the siding should be repaired or caulked.

A study in New England showed that appraisers added an average of around $8,000 to the value of well-painted houses.

**Wet basement.** The solutions to a wet basement—and their costs—can vary from no-sweat to severe anxiety attack. In one situation a VA appraiser refused to accept a sump pump as the solution to a wet basement, even though the sump pump had already been doing an adequate job for at least 10 years.

The repair estimates ran over $3,000, and the deal died on the vine. This was one of those rare basements that have a serious problem with a spring.

Many problems that are attributed to natural springs are actually due to downspouts that saturate the surrounding earth and to soil that is not sloped away from the house for 10'. (Research has shown that proper grading of the yard is much more effective than any kind of buried drainage system, some of which contribute to the problem.)

Sump pumps are not usually rejected outright, but they usually cannot be added once the appraiser has visited. If a sump pump is still needed after you have attended to downspouts and grading problems, then it should be installed before the appraiser arrives.

Another problem area can be a sidewalk or any paved area that abuts a foundation and forms a "cold joint." Water may leak into the basement at this junction. Building supply stores carry products that can seal these joints.

**Woodstoves.** These should often trigger a code inspection. Installing a stove is not easy; there are no intelligent shortcuts. Call the local building department or fire department for help.

Allow me to give one illustration of why it is so important to follow the code specifications. When the wooden stud in the wall behind the stove is relatively new, it has a kindling temperature of around 450° F. After it is subjected to many hours of drying temperatures, its kindling temperature can drop down to around 185°, so a wall fire, the kind that smolders and kills us in our sleep, becomes much more likely.

Here are some of the sure signs that the woodstove installation was not inspected or done with a permit: the stove or pipe is within 18" of any wall, the hearth in front of it is less than 18" deep, a fireproof "shield" has been glued directly to the wall instead of being suspended with an air gap, the pipe is within 12" of the ceiling (if it turns and enters the wall near the ceiling).

As for fireplaces, there can be numerous problems and hazards, but they evade the casual inspection. An experienced chimneysweep or structural inspector needs to give this hallowed amenity a going-over.

## ADDING INSULT TO INJURY

As if we didn't have enough to worry about and pay for, the buyer or seller has to pay for a reinspection if any work orders are called. The cost ranges from $40 to $70. Of course, that's only if everything was fixed correctly. If not, the inspector will repeat and so will the bill.

# FINANCING: THE BASICS

## THE CATEGORIES

There are four basic categories of financing a home: cash, loans, assumptions, and seller-financing. They form the acronym CLAS, and from here on this is a CLAS act!

My students sometimes look at me in disbelief ("There must be more than four!"). Well, if I said there were only two kinds of animals, those that eat people and those that don't, we could find hundreds of goblins in each of those categories. And so it is with financing, except that we can crossbreed monsters and useful animals much easier. But once a student of real estate thoroughly understands the big four, the only limits to financing a home are one's creativity and the big house at Monroe.

### I. CASH

If you can read without moving your lips, you know what cash means—"all cash to the seller at closing"—but cash can be confused with "cash-out," which is in itself confusing because it is often used in two different ways: (1) to pay the seller in full with either the buyer's personal cash or the lender's cash, or (2) to make a "balloon payment" at some later date that equals the balance owed.

"That's right, Mr. Seller, I'll pay $10,000 down and make payments at 10% on the balance, and execute a cash-out in five years." Obviously, this is not the same as "cash."

Who pays cash? Buyers who are "moving down," such as the elderly or "empty nesters," frequently want the security of a free and clear property, even if it means leaving themselves cash-poor. They are the source of hundreds of horror stories about financial crises, but many of them have a hard time accepting counseling, especially from someone half their age.

Investors occasionally pay cash. Naive or first-time investors may pay cash when it isn't even necessary, possibly because of the ego factor. But knowledgeable investors will pay cash only when it means a substantial savings in price or is the only way to acquire the desired property (for example, a fixer that would not be eligible for a typical loan).

Recently we have seen a third group enter the Washington market with the ability to pay in full: those who have sold their more expensive properties in other states and immigrated to the Northwest. Many Washingtonians have griped; none have turned them down. Well, maybe one or two.

Who shouldn't pay cash? Everyone who doesn't have to. To pay cash is to risk all. To pay cash could be to lose leverage if a problem is discovered after closing. To pay cash is to be unable to grab an opportunity that is discovered the day after closing. To pay cash can mean to find oneself owning the property but not having any funds for repairs. To pay cash can mean to lose interest on those funds and on tax benefits.

---

### RENTER'S DISEASE

Five years ago, the buyer of one of my listings used a combination of her own money and her father's to make a $44,000 down payment on a $58,000 house so that she could assume an old low-interest loan of $14,000. Unless she had lots more where that came from, I consider what she did a very foolish use of money. She could have bought several low-maintenance rentals in addition to her own house, and today she might easily have a nest egg of $200,000 or more. She apparently suffered from a malady I call "renter's disease," in which the only thing that matters is keeping the payments as low as possible.

---

The advantages of paying cash include being able to close the transaction in just a few days and keeping the closing costs quite low, since only a few fees, such as escrow and recording, must be paid. See the sample closing costs at the end of Chapter 12.

Many beginning players assume that "money talks." That's sometimes true, but in many residential transactions it has no bearing on the final price. If there are multiple offers on a property, then a cash offer that matches all other offers probably has a distinct advantage because the seller knows the cash buyer won't have to withstand a lender's scrutiny. But frequently, especially in a seller's market, cash buyers pay just as much as borrowers, and sometimes more, because they are so well-off that they are willing to pay well over the asking price to make sure they get the property.

## II. LOANS

"Loans," as used in this book, means monies borrowed from a financial institution. Institutions as a rule are relatively conservative in their policies, so people who don't meet their criteria but still need to borrow money may have to turn to private lenders, who are often found in the classifieds. These private loans aren't particularly hard to understand, but they are expensive, and sufficiently risky that the buyer should consult an attorney.

Institutional loans generally fall into four categories: conventional, conventional-portfolio, Federal Housing Administration (FHA), and Veterans Administration (VA).

The general benefits of loans are: (1) they offer financial leverage (controlling a lot with a little, exactly what a tool is supposed to do); (2) they take time to process, which may be used to get our house in order (in every sense); and (3) the lender's standards and steps afford a bit of protection for all parties (e.g., a lender requires title insurance, which some scrimping consumers might skip, only to lose everything later).

Some of the disadvantages of loans are the same as their advantages: They take time, and we must jump through hoops. One disadvantage of loans that has no apparent benefit is that they are expensive.

### CONVENTIONAL LOANS

A conventional loan is any institutional loan that is not guaranteed or warranted by a government agency such as the FHA or the VA.

A conventional loan may be the common, no-name, fixed-rate type of loan, or it may be an adjustable-rate loan, or a second mortgage, or any one of dozens of hybrid programs, some of which resemble a sculpture created by six preschoolers using oatmeal and catsup. Some hybrids are actually quite sound and can be very much to the buyer's advantage. But since they have not yet been through the test of time and are difficult to explain, most buyers stick to financing arrangements that are easier to understand. Of course, a buyer's motivation to learn about alternative financing methods is enhanced in direct relationship to increases in interest rates.

For a conventional loan the borrower may turn to a mortgage company, a savings and loan, a mutual savings bank, a credit union, or a commercial bank (the type we usually mean when we say "my bank").

The buyer usually pays a fee of $450–$550 upon application, for an appraisal, a credit report, and a "down payment" on a title search. Little or none of this fee will be refundable if the transaction fails to close. A loan officer takes the loan application, but a loan processor orders all of the above steps plus numerous other documents, ranging from a "verification of employment" to sundry statements that verify the borrower's debts and assets.

Another employee of the lender, the underwriter, is well versed in the standards that the buyer and property must meet for loan approval. The underwriter gauges the degrees of risk and makes many decisions, including who will inspect any repairs that need to be done or whether a "hold back" will be allowed on exterior repairs that are difficult to complete in cold or rainy weather.

Overall, the underwriter is trying to ensure that the loan will meet the standards of, and can be sold to, the "secondary market." Her criteria for granting a conventional loan will normally be provided by two of the three agencies that constitute the majority of the secondary market: the Federal National Mortgage Association (FNMA, or "Fannie Mae," which is supervised by HUD, though privately owned) and the Federal Home Loan Mortgage Corporation (FHLMC, or "Freddie Mac," a creation of the Federal Home Loan Bank System).

The third agency is the Government National Mortgage Association (GNMA, or "Ginnie Mae," also directed by HUD but concerned with FHA and VA loans, not conventional loans). This agency is the source of "quotes" on points for FHA and VA loan discounts.

## ADVANTAGES OF CONVENTIONAL LOANS

**1.** There are many lenders to choose from.

**2.** There are as many different types of loans as there are hungry loan reps.

**3.** The lender can choose the appraiser.

**4.** If the first appraisal proves to be a major roadblock, a new appraisal *may* be ordered (for an additional fee). However, if FNMA standards must be met, the first appraisal must be included and an explanation for ordering a second appraisal must be given. It might be easier to make a new loan application with another lender.

**5.** Most conventional loans do not require any fees (points) for discounts (as do many FHA and VA loans). We simply don't get a discounted conventional loan, unless we wish to "buy down" the going rate of interest.

**6.** The lender does not have quite as much federal meddling to contend with, and therefore may be somewhat more flexible.

**7.** Conventional loans are often obtained a little more quickly than government-backed loans—but don't count on it.

**8.** Many sellers and agents express less fear and loathing; FHA loans still have a bum rap from the days when they were substantially more complicated.

**9.** Once the buyer acquires equity equal to 20%, by payments on the principal and/or appreciation, it is possible to waive the mortgage insurance payments. And the buyer who makes a 20% down payment is not required to pay for mortgage insurance. This is not possible with the FHA, which always requires mortgage insurance.

**10.** Larger loans can be obtained than with FHA or VA loans. See "Jumbo Loans" below.

All in all, the advantages of capitalism are apparent. If the money isn't loaned, the lender doesn't make any money, so the lender is motivated to be both accommodating and efficient. Lenders make more money if they are efficient. Only government employees make more if they are not.

---

### THE SECONDARY MARKET

The secondary market has had an enormous impact on the mortgage industry over the last 20 years. Since the lender may be able to "sell" his loans to one of the secondary market agencies and thus recover his money to loan it all over again (often making much of his profit on the servicing of the loan), it has meant a greater availability of mortgages. The secondary market agencies derive their money from individual investors and from industries such as insurance companies, who buy mortgage-backed securities from them.

Since investors want a minimum of risk, and since these investors never meet the borrowers or see the houses, both the borrowers and the houses must meet criteria that steadfastly limit the risk for the investor. This means that the standards of appraising and qualifying for a loan have become relatively uniform across the nation.

---

### DISADVANTAGES OF CONVENTIONAL LOANS

**1.** Their minimum down payments are larger than with most government-backed loans. Five percent is the minimum conventional down payment for owner-occupied property, and 30% is usually required for rental property.

**2.** They can be the most expensive loans, with closing costs often as much as 5%–6% of the loan.

### JUMBO LOANS

Conventional loans are usually your ordinary five-and-dime loans. But if they get large enough, they fit the category known as "jumbo," which somehow justifies the lender charging more or requiring more of a down payment. Don't look for logic in any of this.

A glance at 43 jumbo loan programs showed that for loans between $187,450* and $500,000, minimum down payments ranged from 10% to 25%, with little consistency. So if you borrow large amounts, you should expect to make a healthy down payment and pay a fraction of a percent more in interest. See "Loan Origination Fee" in Chapter 10, "Financing: Details."

*The cut-off amount for a jumbo loan changes every year.*

**3.** Fixed-rate loans are, for the most part, never assumable; adjustable-rate loans may be, with the lender's permission.

**4.** The loan may be denied if the house is so substandard as to be worth less than the lot it occupies.

**5.** It generally takes more income to qualify for a conventional loan than for an FHA or VA loan of the same size, *if* a low down payment is being made.

**6.** The separate and independent company that issues the mortgage insurance can reject the marginal borrower, even if the borrower meets the lender's standards.

### CONVENTIONAL LOAN: PORTFOLIO

Just as the purely conventional loan described above might be called the "loan of the middle classes," we may refer to the portfolio loan as the "loan of the exceptional cases." Here are some examples of people who might be interested in and qualify for a portfolio loan: someone who is unemployed, or underemployed, or occasionally employed, but who has substantial savings or some other source of money, such as a trust fund; someone who has less than a year of employment in the same field (or two years of self-employment) but possesses professional credentials that lenders feel promise success; someone who can qualify for a conventional loan but fears that some complication with the house or situation will be discovered under the closer scrutiny of the more conservative lender.

POINTS

We frequently use a term that seems to be the single most confusing concept in financing: points, or discount points.

First of all, a point is slang for one percentage point. If a buyer must pay one point to "buy down" the interest rate from 9.25% to 9.0% on a $50,000 loan, this means the buyer will have to pay a fee of $500. Points paid to a lender are charged on the loan amount, not on the price of the home.

$$\left(\begin{array}{c} 50000 \\ \times\ 1\% \\ \hline = \$500 \end{array}\right.$$

The points concept seems to be best understood in my classes when I call it a "bribe." The lenders might not be too enthusiastic about this description, but if it helps the consumer understand, then so be it. "Pssst, hey, Mac, I can see that you get a 10% home loan, but it'll cost you three points up front. Deal?"

If a lender is presently making conventional loans at 10.5% interest, then buyers applying for FHA or VA loans may expect those loans to be around 10% (actually, only VA loans continue to have any preset interest rate). Since the lender is not reimbursed by the government for granting a loan at a lower interest rate, the consumer will have to pay for the lender's "losses." If a buyer wants an even lower interest rate, say 9.5%, the lender will charge even more points. Such a loan is said to be "bought down," or "discounted."

Can you follow this statement? "It usually takes anywhere from five to eight points to buy down one point"? It means that if we pay 5%–8% of the loan amount, in cash, at closing (the points vary according to the lender's confidence about the economy), our interest rate will be reduced by a full percentage point for the life of the loan. See, that wasn't hard.

Points can and do change on a daily basis. A lender gets her quotations (recommendations) from a wire service in New York. Once she has the quotation in hand she is free to make her own adjustments and quote a higher or lower fee to the consumer, according to her best guess about the direction of the economy and her desire to compete with other lenders.

A loan origination fee (LOF—the basic fee for processing the loan and obtaining the interest rate) may also be described in points: "Their LOF is a point and a half." But this charge is not related to the daily quotations. It's just a set fee for that one lender, on that particular loan.

One basic philosophy of the portfolio loan is that the borrower is required to make such a substantial down payment (often 25% or more) that the lender is well protected in the event of a default, and therefore relaxes the standards. In some cases, credit checks and appraisals may not be required.

Equally important is that the lender will not sell the loan to the conventional secondary market, and therefore neither the borrower nor the property must meet the secondary market criteria. In a true portfolio loan, the lender just loans his own money, i.e. "puts the file in his portfolio," and subsequently has that much less money to loan until it's paid off. Nowadays, though, the loan may be allowed to "season," or run its course for a year or two so that the borrower establishes a record of reliability, and then it may be sold on a secondary-secondary market (institutional buyers such as pension funds).

It is common for portfolio loans to be adjustable-rate mortgages (ARMs), which do not appeal to everyone and which in some economic cycles lose their advantages over fixed-rate mortgages. Since portfolio loans might seem to appeal to those borrowers who enjoy an unconventional lifestyle, you might assume that they are more expensive, i.e. have higher closing costs. This is often not the case at all, so they are always worth investigating.

## FHA LOANS

The FHA was founded in 1934 to stimulate the construction industry and to stabilize the mortgage market. Congress got lucky on this one. The primary activity of today's FHA is the insuring of loans.

A borrower may go to any mortgage lender who, in addition to conventional loans, also offers FHA loans *and* has "direct endorsement" or "in-house clearance." Lenders with such a qualification can keep the paperwork entirely within their own walls; they no longer have to send all applications to an FHA office. Since 1984, when this program modification went into effect, the time for closing FHA loans has been noticeably reduced. Four to six weeks is almost always enough time to allow between offer and closing.

The FHA 203b loan is the main mule in financing the moderately priced home. It has been with us for so many years that it is a very routine loan for many lenders, and one of the best friends a first-time buyer can have. Let us pray that the government does not try to improve it.

The FHA has tried to implement other loan programs that are similar in flexibility and creativity to conventional "alternative financing"—Graduated Payment Mortgages, Growth Equity Mortgages, and even their own version of a rehab loan (203k)—but some of them have virtually collapsed under the weight of FHA-imposed "guidelines." The FHA does offer a viable ARM, but very few lenders ever mention it. It should be investigated by more borrowers.

### ADVANTAGES OF AN FHA LOAN

3 – 3°⌐⌐

**1.** The qualifying standards are more lenient at low down payments than conventional loan standards, unless the borrower has many children.

**2.** The minimum down payment for the "standard" FHA loan (203b) almost always works out to be less than 3% of the price.

**3.** The loan can be easily assumed or "wrapped" when it is time to sell (provided that the loan is over a year old and the buyer intends to occupy the property).

**4.** The closing costs are often no more than 3% of the loan.

**5.** The buyer (as well as the seller or a third party) can pay discount points, if necessary, to strike a deal.

---

### 🏠 🏠 🏠
### PAR IS A BIRDIE!

Some lenders rarely volunteer this information, but with FHA loans it is possible to pay *no* discount points. One can simply close the transaction at the "par" interest rate. When I obtained approval on an FHA loan in 1987, I asked my lender what the points were that day. He said, "Nine percent is par, eight-and-a-half requires a point and a half." Since my loan was for $91,000, that meant I would have to pay 1.5% of $91,000 ($1,365) to get the lower interest rate and a reduction of $32.49 on my monthly payment. In 42 months I would recover the $1,365 (tax considerations ignored); in that time I could take that money, fix up my basement, and rent it out for $4,000 a year. Pay the points? No way!

---

**6.** The FHA does not have the conventional loan's prohibition against lending when the lot is worth more than the house.

**7.** The entire down payment can be a gift from relatives, if the relatives will sign an unconditional gift letter. Conventional loans require that a down payment of at least 5% of the purchase price be the buyer's own money (unless the donors will make a gift that equals or exceeds 20% of the price).

## DISADVANTAGES OF AN FHA LOAN

**1.** Every area has an FHA loan limit (which changes every couple of years, so check with a lender). The loan limit in the Seattle area, $122,450, is behind the times, and will fall further behind each month until the seller's market slows down.

**2.** Mortgage insurance must be paid, no matter how large the down payment (unlike a conventional loan, which "excuses" this obligation with a 20% down payment). This insurance adds almost exactly 0.5% to the note rate, i.e. if the loan is granted at 10% the payment should be calculated at 10.5%.

**3.** Unless the lender has an approved appraiser on his staff, there is virtually no choice as to the appraiser; it is potluck in a government mess hall. If you get stuck with an incompetent appraiser, an impossible list of work orders, or a low appraisal, you may be stuck for six months, until that appraisal expires. You may have to apply for a conventional loan, attempt a seller-financing arrangement, or find an underwriter or agent who knows the tricks of the trade to circumvent the appraisal.

**4.** At a time when the market is very busy, a shortage of FHA appraisers can cause delays of a month or more.

---

### FHA DOWN PAYMENTS

From time to time a newspaper reporter writes a story about financing, and attempts to give the formula for the FHA down payment. It is usually obvious that the reporter interviewed a lender who didn't have the time or patience to explain it. Neither do I. I mean, I don't have any patience with it; it is obviously the concoction of a bureaucrat who was told to "create work."

We agents will often tell you that the minimum FHA down payment is 3%. We know then that if you have at least that much, there shouldn't be any problem, because the actual minimum amount will almost always be in the 1.5%–2.5% range. It amounts to a sliding scale, with the most expensive loans requiring the largest down payments. If it is important to you to know exactly how much the amount is, then ask a lender for a chart or a printout of down payments, or tell them the price and wait five minutes for the calculations. See "Typical Down Payments" toward the end of the next chapter.

---

**5.** Work orders are reinspected by an FHA inspector (not the original appraiser), and this inspector, who charges for this "service," can require a whole new set of work orders.

**6.** If complications arise—for example, if some part of the house's construction is the least bit out of the ordinary—the lender may turn to the FHA for a waiver or ruling. Once a borrower's papers leave the lender's office for the FHA office (as happens with a lender who does not have direct endorsement), the prospects of a prompt reply grow dim. Many lenders swear that FHA paper-pushers vindictively return a file to the bottom of the heap if any inquiries are made about it. So you wait. A month's delay is not unusual. Fortunately, this situation is.

**7.** "Secondary financing" is now allowed (as of July 8, 1985), but there are numerous restrictive guidelines. For example, a balloon payment may not come due before 10 years. An example of secondary financing on a $75,000 house would be a $5,000 down payment with a $60,000 FHA loan, plus a seller-financed "second mortgage" of $10,000.

**8.** Some sellers believe that to accept an FHA offer is to subject their home to unreasonable appraisal standards. This is not true with a typical home. But stubborn sellers may not listen, and you may have better luck making them a conventional offer.

**9.** The discount points that lenders charge for "favorable" FHA loan rates are sometimes erratic.

**10.** In years to come, if you sell the property on an "assumption," you may still have "secondary liability," unless you require the buyer to formally assume the loan. Check with your lender for the FHA's latest requirements for a "release of liability" from any buyer assuming an FHA loan.

---

### FHA LOAN LIMITS

For 1990, loan limits for a single-family home are as follows: King/Snohomish County—$122,450; Pierce County—$94,550; Yakima County—$83,350; Kitsap County—$80,200; Thurston County—$79,800; and all others—$67,500.

THE VA LOAN

As with FHA loans, the Veterans Administration does not actually loan money. It just guarantees repayment of losses sustained by the lender (the vet may still be on the hook). If the borrower defaults, it is the VA (or HUD, in the case of FHA) that handles the repossession and disposition of the property.

An eligible veteran can purchase up to a fourplex, but he must occupy one of the units. In other words, an investor is not supposed to exploit his VA eligibility to buy purely investment property. What will the VA do if he doesn't occupy the property? Make him repeat basic training?

No, seriously—they can call the loan due.

I have been assured that VA loans are made with a minimum of sweat and tears in areas surrounding military bases. This has not been my experience in this city. The VA loan presents the highest percentage of complications of any of the types of loans I've discussed here. One of the most serious problems is that VA officials often imitate telephone poles; everyone else is trying to communicate, but it's all over their heads and they officially don't care. They have treated many homebuyers with the same indifference they applied to Agent

Orange victims. When problems arise, they often refuse to explain or even to speak to any agents or lenders; they will speak only to the veteran, who then has to relay the information to a lender or agent or someone who has the expertise to solve the problem. I saw a vet turned down for a loan because the VA used a credit check that was two years out of date. It took us weeks to get the information from the VA; in the meantime, the vet and his wife and infant slept on a friend's floor.

### ADVANTAGES OF THE VA LOAN

**1.** No down payment is required for a loan up to $184,000 on a single-family home as long as the property appraises at the sale price (larger loans are available; see your lender for up-to-the-minute information).

**2.** The seller can pay all of the buyer's closing costs, so that not one dime is needed by the vet for the transaction. (The vet/buyer may have to write a check for an earnest money deposit, which can then be refunded at closing.) The seller can also pay a buyer's closing costs on an FHA loan, but the requirements are a bit complicated.

**3.** The VA loan can be freely assumed once the loan is over a year old; yes, that means a non-vet can assume it. (This does affect the veteran's eligibilty for future VA loans, however.)

**4.** There is no prohibition against secondary financing, so on a $72,000 house a buyer can obtain a $60,000 VA loan, the seller can "carry the paper" on $10,000 (or the buyer's parents could loan him $10,000), and the buyer can put $2,000 down. The possibilities are limited only by the creativity and flexibility of the principals.

**5.** As with FHA loans, the VA uses a more liberal qualifying method. At least it is more liberal if one has no dependents.

**6.** No escrow fee is charged the buyer (the seller is charged the entire amount).

**7.** Closing costs are relatively low, usually around 3.5% of the loan amount.

**8.** Both permanent and temporary buy-downs of the interest rate are possible. See your lender for the latest information.

### DISADVANTAGES OF THE VA LOAN

**1.** The zero-down-payment feature can mean less of an emotional commitment to the property and payments.

**2.** The VA "Automatic Approval" is not as efficient as the FHA's direct endorsement plan. VA loans must still cross a desk in the VA office, where the staff frequently puts all phones on hold so that they can catch up on their work. Lenders may even be told not to inquire about the progress of a file, so its status may be a mystery for a while.

**3.** It is widely believed that only the seller can pay the discount points, but in reality a third party can pay them. A California court has ruled that even the vet can pay them, but this belief is still a stumbling block. And who wants to be the precedent-setter in Washington?

**4.** There is no "par" option as with FHA, so if the seller's price is inflexible, then the estimated amount of the points must be added to the price, which makes a low appraisal more likely.

**5.** A low appraisal requires the buyer to come up with a down payment, unless the seller will reduce the price; this frequently becomes an emotional sticking point.

---

### LOCK-INS

One of the complications of the FHA-VA system of discount points is that in many cases we buy a pig in a poke; we may not know until a few days before closing (once loan approval is granted) how many points the lender will charge us for a certain interest rate. Since the number of points fluctuates from day to day, whoever is paying the points may "gamble" for a few days, hoping to catch the number at its nadir. Once the choice is made, we usually get a "free 10-day lock-in." If we close within 10 days, that rate is guaranteed.

Competition in the marketplace has encouraged many lenders to offer lock-ins of 60 days, which become more meaningful in an unstable economy where it is not uncommon for points to double overnight. Lenders may or may not charge for this perk, so the borrower will just have to inquire.

One of the most bitter moments in lending comes when the loan doesn't close until the 61st day, or the points drop from the original lock-in. The buyer will swear that the lender deliberately dragged his feet, or that he should have to offer them the lower rate. A meek buyer does not do well in either of these situations.

**6.** See the FHA disadvantages, numbers 3, 4, 6, 8, 9, and 10.

## LOANS FOR FIXERS

In general, when an appraiser calls for repairs, they must all be completed before the transaction can close. With a "rehab loan," however, the lender allows up to six months after closing for completion of any work. The buyer may also be able to borrow the money to do the work, and may even be allowed to do the work himself (some lenders require that a licensed contractor do it).

Rehab loans are generally expensive (closing costs of 6.5% are not unusual), and the lender practically becomes a partner in some enterprises, watching over the proceedings. Structural inspections are *de jure*, and written estimates by contractors are likely to be required even if the buyer is doing the work. If the buyer has "money left over" after the work is done, it can be used for a vacation or party, but not for reducing the payments on the house. Once the bank loans money, they don't want it back without all of its interest.

Rehab loans usually come under the heading of "Conventional Loans." In the past, lenders in the Seattle area have found the FHA rehab loan (203k) too cumbersome, but Security Pacific recently found a way to cut through the red tape. Their loan is noticeably cheaper than conventional loans but severely limited in size. In King County the limit for one unit is $122,450. In Pierce and Kitsap counties the limits are even more restrictive—$94,550 and $80,200, respectively. Security Pacific has offered a conventional program all along that is not nearly so limited, but it is also more expensive; the very fact that these programs exist proves that the lending industry has a heart. There couldn't possibly be enough profit in them to justify the lenders' extra work and risk.

If you wish to see what options are available in your own community, call a number of lenders and ask about rehab, construction, and bridge loans.

## III. ASSUMPTIONS

An assumption is nothing more than taking over someone's payments. I lied. Nothing is that simple in real estate. Not only are we likely to face some complicated documentation, but we almost always must address the question of what to do with the seller's equity. Of course, buyers want the seller just to give it to them, but sellers want us to give them either a down payment equal to the equity, or as much cash as we can muster and then make payments on the balance of the equity. In other words, you may be making two payments, one to a lender or private noteholder, and one to the seller.

If there is to be an assumption there must have been a previous loan (or an "extension of credit," as in the case of seller-financing), but we still look on the assumption as a separate category of financing because in most cases the

### FmHA WHO?

The FHA loan is well known but FmHA financing is not. FmHA stands for the Farmer's Home Administration, an agency within the U.S. Department of Agriculture that assists home buyers in rural communities of less than 20,000 inhabitants. Its low-interest loans are very appealing, although in Washington's smallest towns and slowest real estate markets, where alternative financing is welcomed, agents said they didn't know of anyone ever qualifying for or receiving this assistance. "Too many restrictions."

When I received the FmHA booklet provided by the National Association of Realtors, I understood. The FmHA program is for the farm, all right. I'd call it the *"keep* 'em down on the farm'' program. Some of the limits of this program include: a house for a family of three cannot be larger than 1,008 square feet, nor have more than one bathroom. Garages, decks, patios, and even fireplaces are among the many prohibited amenities. A dishwasher could get the buyer shot at dawn. In order to qualify a family's assets cannot currently exceed $7,500.

With FmHA, a legitimately poor family could find a reasonably-priced house that meets its needs, but never be able to thread its way through this government needle. Wish I could say I'm surprised. Regardless, if this program might meet your needs, look 'em up in the phone book. Who knows? Maybe they're as lonely as the Maytag man, and will try extra hard.

lender's decision-making time was in the past. Now there can be an agreement solely between the buyer and the seller.

With many assumptions the buyer just takes over the seller's payments without any change in interest or terms, so when a buyer is faced with two houses that are priced exactly alike, the one with the assumption may actually be thousands cheaper in the years to come. Yet I have seen buyers choose a new loan over an assumption because the new loan had an interest rate half a percent lower, even though the closing costs for the new loan are so much more than the cost of the assumption that it could take six to eight years to recover the difference. (Of course, many buyers will sell before they break even.)

As of early 1990, the following loans can usually be assumed with few restrictions: FHA 203b loans, VA fixed-rate loans, some private loans and conventional adjustable-rate mortgages (ARMs). Most other conventional loans cannot be assumed, but the seller, agent, or buyer would be mistaken if he did not investigate that possibility. Some conventional lenders are very cooperative and will allow an assumption even when they don't have to. They may or may not increase the interest rate. But they can charge a substantial fee, even 3%–4% of the loan amount, for doing a relatively small amount of paperwork.

---

### UNRECORDED? DON'T DO IT!

Buyers and sellers occasionally try to close transactions without recording them and notifying lenders of the sale, so that the lender can't enforce the due-on-sale clause. Since an unrecorded transaction could allow the seller to sell the property twice, or encumber it in some other way, it is a very risky strategy, so risky that—well, just look for another way.

---

Most lenders are not so cooperative. Some give an oral commitment to allow an assumption of a conventional loan and then withdraw the promise at the last minute (do get it in writing). On the other hand, some lenders say that a mortgage cannot be assumed, hoping the seller will not investigate and expose their bluff.

In general, if there is any chance of an assumption, buyers, sellers, and agents should work with an attorney from day one. Only an attorney will have the expertise to defy the lender if the lender tells the seller that a prepayment penalty will be charged. The assumption has none or few of the safeguards of acquiring a new institutional loan, and must often be done through the mail, so it pays to have very knowledgeable assistance.

## ADVANTAGES OF ASSUMPTIONS

**1.** The closing costs can be less than 1% of the price. Where the conventional lender might charge $500 for the paperwork alone, the FHA charge is only $45 (of course, this is not the only closing cost).

**2.** More of each payment goes toward the principal than with a new loan.

**3.** There are fewer years before the assumed mortgage is paid off.

**4.** The buyer *may* not have to qualify for the payments ("yes" with conventional loans and FHA loans made since 12/15/89 and VA loans made after

3/1/88; "no" with some older FHA and VA loans, and those seller-financing arrangements where the seller or noteholder doesn't require it).

**5.** The closing time can be very short, 10–20 days.

**6.** The seller may agree to some very flexible/creative terms on her equity.

### DISADVANTAGES OF ASSUMPTIONS

**1.** There simply aren't enough of them (pursuing only assumptions means limiting one's choices).

**2.** By not having to qualify with a lender, the buyer may take on unrealistically high payments.

**3.** If the buyer has not actually assumed the first mortgage but is just making payments to the seller and trusting the seller to make the payments, the buyer could lose everything. See "Contract escrow" near the end of this chapter.

**4.** Assumptions processed through the mail can take months to close.

**5.** There may be onerous terms related to the seller's equity portion. She could stipulate such a short period for a balloon payment that the buyer has insufficient time to establish credit, etc.

---

### SUBJECT TO—

The phrase "buys the house subject to the mortgage" may sometimes mean that the buyer will not formally assume the old loan. This can be a perfectly legitimate way to close a transaction, but it is also used by some wheeler-dealers to take advantage of unsophisticated sellers. Take any such offer to an attorney. Rapidly.

---

### SELLER-FINANCING

Seller-financing is often called "creative financing," and that alone should tell us that understanding its ramifications is a challenge. It may be an arrangement solely between the buyer and seller, or it may also include a lender for some portion of the price. Most people think of seller-financing as an arrangement whereby a seller extends credit to the buyer on any balance owed after a down payment has been made. The buyer then makes payments on the balance directly to the seller. This is not a loan by the seller (no money changes hands);

it is an "extension of credit" by the seller. If anything, it resembles a "loan of the house."

The interest rate, period of time, and frequency of payments can be as creative as the buyer and seller are clever and agreeable.

**Example of a buyer's offer:** "The purchaser will pay at closing 5% of the price, and the seller will carry the balance at an annual interest rate of 9%, amortized for 30 years, with the balance coming due in 10 years. If the purchaser makes a good-faith effort in the 10th year to secure a loan, but fails to do so, the seller will grant a 12-month extension so that the purchaser can reapply or sell the property. The purchaser will keep all taxes and insurance current, and furnish proof to the seller on an annual basis."

**Explanation:** If this is an $80,000 property, the buyer will pay the seller $4,000 at closing. The payments on the $76,000 balance at 9%, amortized (spread out) for 30 years, will be $611.51. In 10 years the balance will be $67,966.61. The buyer will then have to secure a loan for this amount, sell the house, use the 12-month extension to reapply, or renegotiate with the seller (often the best option).

## REMINDER: DOCUMENTS USED IN SELLER-FINANCING

Many different terms are used to mean seller-financing: contract, contract for deed, land contract, creative financing, hold the paper, carry the paper, real estate contract (REC), and deed of trust (DOT).

Although REC and DOT are used interchangeably, they are actually two very different documents, or legal frameworks, for establishing a transaction and the responsibilities of all parties. Neither document is used solely for seller-financing arrangements (institutional loans in Washington are usually closed with a DOT), but seller-financing almost always uses one of them. (An old-fashioned "mortgage" would be the other option.)

Perhaps the most important distinction between the frameworks is that title "passes" with the DOT but not with the REC. Title is an "imaginary concept," a legal status, somewhat like the right to the "pursuit of happiness"; the courts can uphold it, the legislature can defend it, and we can even get insurance for it (title, not happiness), but it remains an intangible right or series of rights. The complications in this area can get tangible very quickly, however. Here is just one worst-case scenario: A transaction on Dogg House is closed with an REC so title does not pass; the property will remain in the name of the seller until the mortgage is paid in full. The seller makes a number of errors in his business and loses a lawsuit. He has little money, so a judgment is filed against all property in his name. After three years the winner of the lawsuit is tired of waiting and forecloses on Dogg House. The buyer (occupant) may not even know that any of this is taking place until it is too late.

Buyers and sellers are reminded once again that they need the best legal advice they can possibly find, right from the beginning.

### COMPARISON OF REC AND DOT

**1. Costs**. No differences in buyer's closing costs, which are usually about 0.5% of the price of houses in the $50,000–$100,000 range.

**2. Time to close**. No differences. They can close as soon as the title has been "searched," old-loan figures are computed for pay-off figures (assuming the old loan is not being assumed), and the down payment is on hand. About 2–14 days, in most cases.

**3. Practical differences**. None for the buyer. The buyer can usually remodel or sell the property in either case. But if a buyer wants to remodel or refinance, she probably won't be able to get a loan on a property that is not in her name, as is the case with the REC.

**4. Technical differences**. With the REC, the buyer has "equitable title" (can occupy/use the property without restriction), but the property remains in the seller's name. Also, a purchaser with an REC may be able to get a forfeiture set aside by the court.

**5. Costs of foreclosure**. Probably about $800–$1,200 for a DOT and $500–$750 for an REC.

**6. Time for nonjudicial foreclosure**. About seven months in the case of the DOT, if the seller or trustee keeps the hoop in motion. The new REC may require as little as four months. If the seller wishes to sue the buyer for a "deficit judgment" because the property is now worth less than the balance owed on it, a judicial foreclosure must be pursued in either case. In the meantime, the buyer can probably live rent-free at the seller's expense for several years while the seller's grain of sand moves slowly through the court's hourglass. That is one reason why most sellers or lenders do not pursue the judicial judgment.

The REC required a judicial foreclosure until January 1986. Since that time, the advantages/disadvantages of the REC and DOT have not been so clear. Consult an attorney to determine which is best for either party. More on RECs and DOTs in Chapter 17, "Foreclosures."

### ADVANTAGES OF SELLER-FINANCING

**1.** The buyer's closing costs are generally as low as any financing arrangement, frequently less than 0.5% of the price of the property.

**2.** The buyer may be able to make a very low down payment. Three percent of the price will probably cover the seller's closing costs on an unlisted property. On a listed property the seller's closing costs are usually in the 8.5%–10% range, so a small down payment is not likely, unless the brokers and agents are willing to defer their commissions. Fat chance.

**3.** The creativity and flexibility of the terms can be a work of art.

**4.** The buyer does not have to qualify for a loan (but smart sellers often require a credit check, verification of employment, personal references, and a net worth statement).

**5.** The closing time may be as short as 2–14 days.

**6.** The seller may favor this arrangement if she understands its tax benefits (if any; there won't be in every case).

**7.** The buyer can request a "right of first refusal" in case the seller should later wish to sell her "paper interest" in the property. This can result in an opportunity to buy the seller's interest at a substantial discount.

### DISADVANTAGES OF SELLER-FINANCING

**1.** The safeguards of the loan process—appraisal, work orders, and even title insurance—are often omitted. A buyer could even allow his homeowner's insurance to expire, and lose everything in a fire (a seller can and should require regular proof of insurance, and payment of property taxes).

**2.** The buyer may take on an unrealistically large payment.

**3.** A seller has at least three reasons to be wary of seller-financing:

  **A.** It is a preferred arrangement of bargain-hunters and those with a poor credit history.

  **B.** If later the seller requires immediate cash, she may have to sell her interest in the property to a private investor at a substantial loss (discounts of 30%–50% are common).

  **C.** The seller will have to bear the cost of repossessing, and might not receive a single payment for four to seven months—or more. See the explanation of deficit judgments above.

**4.** See number 3 of "Disadvantage of Assumptions." Also, see "Contract escrow" below.

## CONTRACT ESCROW AND OTHER PROTECTIONS

Entering into an assumption or a seller-financing transaction without legal advice is as dangerous as wearing a fur coat to a Greenpeace meeting. Ask an attorney and/or lender for an explanation of the three items below, and for the steps necessary to acquire these simple protections.

**1. Contract escrow (or "true escrow").** An account/service for collecting and disbursing funds. Instead of sending money directly to the seller, the buyer pays a service that, in turn, pays all appropriate parties. Such a service is also important for holding a "fulfillment deed" when a real estate contract is involved. Fulfillment deeds are especially important when the seller is out-of-state and/or elderly.

**2. An estoppel letter.** A lender's promise not to "accelerate" a loan, i.e. call it due if a buyer should want to assume it.

**3. A release.** A lender's release of a seller's responsibility on an assumed loan.

## MONEY AND TIMING

There are three moments when money usually changes hands during transactions involving loans. They are:

**1. Earnest money.** A good-faith deposit usually made by a buyer when she makes an offer. It is usually held in a trust fund until closing, at which time it may be applied to any of the costs charged the buyer or seller; the buyer must be given credit for it, or it can be returned to the buyer at closing.

**2. Loan application.** A fee paid the lender to cover a preliminary title search, credit check, and appraisal. Usually made within five days after seller accepts buyer's offer.

**3. Escrow/signing.** The time at which the down payment, if any, and the closing costs are paid, usually with one certified or registered check (money can also be "wired"). Don't ever show up at signing with a personal check unless you have been told it's OK.

# FINANCING: DETAILS

If you have read the previous chapter, or in a former life mastered the basics of financing and can recall the nuts and bolts without going into a trance, we can sally forth into the seemingly endless details. To make this chapter more accessible as a reference, it is structured as an alphabetical glossary.

For complete definitions of all real estate terms, see Alan Tonnon's *The Complete Guide to Washington Real Estate Practices* (Appendix—"Language and Law").

## ABBREVIATIONS USED BY FINANCIERS

| | | | |
|---|---|---|---|
| **APR** | Annual Percentage Rate | **P&I** | Principal and Interest |
| **ARM** | Adjustable Rate Mortgage | **PITI** | P&I plus Taxes and Insurance |
| **C/O** | Cash-Out | **PMI** | Private Mortgage Insurance |
| **F/C** | Free and Clear | **PTS** | Points |
| **GEM** | Growing Equity Mortgage | **RAM** | Reverse Annuity Mortgage |
| **GPM** | Graduated Payment Mortgage | **REO** | Real Estate Owned |
| **GSI** | Gross Scheduled Income | **SAM** | Shared Appreciation Mortgage |
| **LOF** | Loan Origination Fee (loan fee) | **VOD** | Verification Of Deposits |
| **LTV** | Loan To Value, or LTVR (ratio) | **VOE** | Verification Of Employment |
| **MIP** | Mortgage Insurance Premium | **VRM** | Variable Rate Mortgage |
| **NOI** | Net Operating Income | | |

**Acceleration clause:** requirement that the balance of any remaining debt be paid immediately if payments are missed, taxes are unpaid, etc.

**Addendum:** any addition to a contract; the terms of financing are often included in an attached financial addendum. It can be a blank piece of paper to start with or any one of dozens of preprinted forms.

**Adjustable rate mortgage (or variable rate mortgage):** the interest and payment are adjusted at set intervals to reflect some economic barometer. Intervals are most commonly one, three, or five years. The rate of interest is the sum of a "margin" (the lender's profit, which is fixed) and an "index" (the chosen barometer, such as "T-bills" or "11th District Funds," which fluctuates). Generally, ARMs are capped, which means they can only rise (or diminish) so much at any one adjustment; they may also have a lifetime cap. The consumer must compare a number of ARMs at different lenders to get some idea of what is available or advantageous. If you do not plan to be in a house a long time or when the economy is in flux, ARMs are always worth investigating, but insist that the lender provide an estimate of a worst-case series of payments for five years.

**Adjusted basis:** the cost of a property plus any capital improvements and the costs of financing, minus depreciation. A figure the owner's accountant will provide if the consumer provides receipts.

**Alienation:** see "Due on Sale."

**Alligator:** an investment that has a negative cash flow (is eating us alive).

**Amortize:** to spread out payments so that a debt can be retired ("killed," as in "mort"; see "Mortgage" and "Factors"). A business calculator or a book that contains amortization tables must generally be used to figure this out. If we borrow $90,000 at 10%, for 30 years, each of the 360 monthly P&I payments will be the same ($789.81). But each month more of the payment will go toward the principal: $39.81 the first month, $40.14 the second month. The 277th payment will be the first payment in which more than half applies to the principal. As of the 283rd payment (23 years, 7 months) we will have paid slightly over half of the principal. By the final payment we will have paid $194,333.19 in interest on the original $90,000 debt.

**Annual percentage rate:** a figure that must be provided by lenders in advertisements or statements and which assists the consumer in understanding the real cost of the loan and in comparing it to other loans. For example, if two loans have a 10.5 APR, we can surmise that over the life of the loan they will each cost us about the same. However, one loan has a note rate of 9.875% and the other has a note rate of 10.125%. That would almost certainly mean that the loan with the lower interest rate has higher closing costs to make up for the lender's "losses" on the monthly payments. The person who is cash-poor may prefer the loan with the higher interest rate and lower closing costs.

**Assessments:** often used to mean charges or estimates of value by a government body. "My property is assessed (valued by the county) at $168,000, and I have an assessment (a bill from the county for an improvement) of $4,400 for the new sidewalks."

**Balloon:** a final or substantial payment, defined by some as a payment that is at least twice the normal monthly payment.

**Basis:** the cost of a property plus the costs of financing, commissions, capital improvements, etc. See "Adjusted Basis."

**Blanket mortgage:** when two or more pieces of property are used as security.

**Bridge loan:** an interim loan, as when for example, buyers have bought a new house but have not yet been able to sell their own home.

**Buy-downs:** payments to a lender to acquire a lowered interest rate temporarily or permanently. A 3-2-1 buy-down means the interest rate will be three percent lower the first year, two the second year, etc. A 3-2-1 buy-down might cost the sum of its parts (6 points, i.e. 6% of the loan). These are offered by builders in slow times to assist buyers in qualifying.

**Call:** a privilege reserved by the lender to make the loan come due at some future date, often for the purpose of raising the interest rate. To be avoided.

**Cap rate:** investor talk for return on one's investment. It is arrived at by dividing the net operating income (NOI) by the cost of the property. An oversimplified way of comparing properties or determining if they are worthy of buying. If a building's NOI is $19,200 per year ($1,600 per month), and the investor desires a cap rate of 10, then she will offer no more that $192,000 for that building.

**Capital improvement:** an improvement with a life of more than one year, such as a new roof or a garage. An important distinction for tax purposes. See "Repair."

**Cash out:** used interchangeably to mean paying the seller all monies due either at closing or some future date, with either the buyer's personal money or the lender's money.

**Closing costs:** charges by the professionals involved in effecting a loan and/or a closing, as well as charges by any other debtors, including the government or judgment-holders. A table of closing costs is provided at the end of Chapter 12, "From Offer to Closing."

**Cloud (on a title):** a lien or encumbrance that needs to be removed in order to have a clear title.

**Co-borrower:** someone who actually shares the property and the liability. Must be a resident if less than a 90% down payment.

**Depreciation:** the loss in value of the improvements (buildings, driveways, etc.) as they age and wear out. Since in reality real estate commonly appreciates in value, depreciation is often called the "phantom write-off" as it pertains to taxes. Residential rental property is presently depreciated by the straight-line method for 28.5 years. If the improvements (not the land) are worth $142,500, this amount divided by 28.5 equals $5,000. $5,000 times one's tax bracket equals

the "tax savings" for one year, e.g. 5,000 times 0.28 equals $1,400, which would offset a negative cash-flow of $116 per month. Commercial real estate is depreciated over 31.5 years.

**Down payment:** a partial payment that primarily serves as an inducement for the lender and/or seller to do business with that buyer. See the table of down payments near the end of this chapter.

**Due-on-sale clause:** a requirement by the lender that if there is a transfer of ownership (an "alienation") the balance owed be paid immediately. Sometimes called "Clause 17." This clause prevents assumptions without the lender's approval.

**Encumbrance:** any debt or condition attached to a property that may affect its transfer to another owner or its use by the present owner. These can range from easements to mortgages. See "Lien."

**Equity:** that portion of the value of the property that is unencumbered by a mortgage or judgment or any other debt. Equity is acquired by any of four methods: the initial down payment, payment toward the principal ("equity buildup"), improving the property ("sweat equity"), and appreciation due to economic forces that drive the prices of all houses higher.

**Equity skimming:** a fraudulent purchase of a property, often by pretending to assume the mortgage and then selling or renting the property very quickly, taking any monies offered by the naive and vulnerable.

**Factors:** numbers (decimals) that can be used to calculate amortized payments when one lacks the proper calculator or set of tables. For example, the factor for a 30-year 10% loan is 0.00878. If one borrows $90,000, this amount times 0.00878 equals $790.20 (the real estate calculator says $789.91, so we are only 39 cents off, or 99.96% accurate). On the other hand, if we want to have a payment of $700, we divide 700 by 0.00878, and the result, $79,726.65, is the amount we'd have to borrow at 10% to achieve that payment. Obviously, we would have to come up with a substantially larger down payment ($10,273.35 more) to get that lower monthly payment.

| Interest Rate | 15-Year Factor | 30-Year Factor |
|---|---|---|
| 8.0% | .00956 | .00734 |
| 8.5% | .00985 | .00769 |
| 9.0% | .01014 | .00805 |
| 9.5% | .01044 | .00841 |
| 10.0% | .01075 | .00878 |

| | | |
|---|---|---|
| 10.5% | .01105 | .00915 |
| 11.0% | .01137 | .00953 |
| 11.5% | .01168 | .00990 |
| 12.0% | .01200 | .01029 |
| 12.5% | .01233 | .01067 |
| 13.0% | .01265 | .01107 |
| 13.5% | .01298 | .01145 |
| 14.0% | .01332 | .01185 |

**First mortgage:** the mortgage with the highest priority in the event of a forfeiture or sale.

**First-time buyer's program:** a Washington state program that provides for a tax credit and/or a reduced interest rate for some buyers who have not owned property in the last three years. There are limits on the buyer's income and on the number of loans available in different areas. "Target" areas, with lower-income properties, usually provide more loans. These schemes come and go like butterflies: very pretty, but never around when we'd most like to see them. They require staying in contact with the lenders who have elected to participate in them. Details in the Appendix—"Financing."

**Gift letter:** a form sent by the lender to Mom and Dad for their signatures, attesting that the money they provided Junior for his down payment is a gift, not a loan which would count against him in his efforts to qualify.

**Graduated payment mortgage:** artificially low payments are made in the first years, so a deficit (called "negative amortization") occurs. In other words, the amount the borrower owes increases during the period of low payments. Eventually the payments must rise to a point where both the original loan and the accumulated debt can be paid off at term. This loan is designed for the person whose income is bound to grow. One example is the FHA 245 program.

**Gross scheduled income:** investor talk for "rent." The total of all income for a building, including parking fees, etc.

**Growing equity mortgage:** a fixed interest rate but with scheduled increases in payments. The extra amounts are applied to the principal, thus shortening the term of the loan, often to a range of 13–17 years.

**Impounds:** advance payments collected at closing to ensure that funds are always available for taxes and insurance.

**Improvements:** the buildings and such on the land. See "Depreciation," "Capital Improvements," and "Repairs."

**Interest only (straight mortgage):** no payments are paid toward the principal, so no complicated amortizing or computation of the balance is required. A good method for some short-term seller-financing schemes. For example, if the seller extends credit on $60,000 at 10% for five years, 10% of $60,000 is $6,000, which when divided by 12 gives us a monthly payment of $500. At the end of five years we still owe $60,000. If we had amortized this over 30 years, the payments would have been $526.54, and the balance at five years would be $57,944.59. Amortized calculations require either that both parties be skilled or that one trust the other to be correct, so "interest only" eliminates those complications.

**Internal rate of return:** investor talk for compounded interest received on an investment. If we invested $50,000 and in 6 years received in return $100,000, naive people would say we doubled our money. In reality, we made about 12% per annum, compounded. Time must never be omitted from our considerations. If instead of 6 years it had taken us 20 years to gross that $100,000, we would have received a pitiful return of about 3.6%. See "Rule of 72."

**Lien:** a charge or debt attached to a property, such as property taxes, judgments from lawsuits, and county assessments.

**Loan origination fee:** the lender's primary charge for making the loan. Often stated in points: "The LOF is two points" (a charge equal to 2% of the value of the loan).

**Loan to value:** the percentage of the value of the property that a lender will loan; this figure is the reverse of the down payment, i.e. if the LTV is 80, the down payment must be 20%.

**Lock-in:** the securing and guarantee of an interest rate for some period of time. Also refers to a time in a loan when no prepayment is possible.

**Magic money:** private mortgage insurance that allows buyers to make small down payments. A play on the letters "MGIC" (Mortgage Guaranty Insurance Corporation), one of the larger insurance firms.

**Mortgage:** literally, the death (mort) of a debt or pledge (gage). Usually means a loan or balance owed on a property; it can also mean a legal instrument (like a Deed of Trust), which is used infrequently in Washington's residential real estate.

**Mortgage banker:** a person/institution that specializes in home loans. This banker "sells" his own loan programs.

**Mortgage broker:** a person/institution that may or may not actually have money to lend, but does have the ability to deal with any number of lenders and to process loan applications.

**Mortgage insurance:** payments to an institution which has insured the lender against losses on a loan in the event of a default (this is *not* life insurance on the buyer). The only benefits to the borrower are that small down payments are made possible and the likelihood of a lawsuit for a deficit judgment becomes quite small. Conventional mortgage insurance is called Private Mortgage Insurance, and is usually collected as a one-time premium at closing and in monthly payments. It is collected if the down payment is smaller than 20%, and it may be extinguished once the purchaser has acquired equity equaling 20%. With a down payment of 5%, the premium at closing is 1% of the loan; with a 10% down payment, the premium is 0.5%, so the borrower saves a substantial amount by making a larger down payment (gets an "immediate return of 10%" on that extra down payment). FHA mortgage insurance is called a Mortgage Insurance Premium. It is a one-time payment at closing. The buyer may borrow it and add it to the loan, in which case the amount is 3.8% of the loan. If the borrower pays it in cash (probably not wise), the amount is 3.661% (2.344% on a 15-year loan). The 3.8% premium raises the monthly payment the same as if the note rate were 0.5% higher. The VA loan has a "funding fee," which is noticeably less. With no down payment, the vet is charged a 1.25% fee. The fee is lowered with larger down payments, and drops to 0.5% for down payments exceeding 10%.

**Negative amortization:** the increase in a debt to a lender by making payments that do not fully cover the P&I payments. A buyer borrows $70,000 at 10% for 30 years; the amortized payments should be $614.30, but the loan allows the borrower to make payments of $550 for the first year, or $64.30 less than owed. At the end of the first year, the borrower would owe $70,771.60. See "Graduated Payment Mortgage."

**Net operating income (NOI):** what remains from the rents when the bills have been paid. If a fourplex provides a monthly gross scheduled income of $2,000, but the utility bills are $400, the NOI is $1,600.

**Note rate:** the actual interest rate on which loan payments are calculated, as opposed to the APR or a temporary "teaser" rate that is used in advertising or for initial payments.

**"Or more" clause:** a statement declaring that the borrower reserves the right to pay more than the minimum monthly payment without any penalty for prepaying. Buyers will want this option included in every type of financing.

**Prepayment:** making early payments on the principal. Many loans allow this (FHA & VA always do), but it can be denied in other financing arrangements if the language does not provide for it. See above and "Prepayment Strategies" at the end of this chapter.

**Principal/interest/taxes/insurance (PITI):** the components of the lump-sum house payment we mail off each month to some distant state. This should really be called PITIM, with the M standing for mortgage insurance, which is always required with an FHA loan or with a conventional loan when the down payment is less than 20%.

**Private mortgage insurance:** see "Mortgage insurance."

**Promissory note:** an I.O.U., a promise to pay, a negotiable instrument if made to the "bearer." Signed by borrowers as the mortgage note, but also used by some buyers as an earnest money, instead of cash or a check. Builders often use this note to avoid tying up their cash, and wheeler-dealers use it for their own good reasons. Insisting on a large promissory note is one strategy available to a seller who fears a default by the buyer; instead of a suit for damages, the seller may simply try to collect the note. See an attorney when a note is involved.

**Purchase money mortgage:** often used to mean seller-financing, in that the seller extends credit for some portion of the price. But this term means so much more than that, and has so many legal ramifications, that it confuses more than it clarifies. The method is not necessarily to be avoided, but an attorney is essential to explain the details.

**Refinance:** an application for a new loan that can either consolidate several loans or provide the borrower with cash and/or a lower interest rate. The rule of thumb is to refinance the present loan when a 2% reduction in interest rate can be acquired, but the borrower must run all of the numbers (taxes included) to see how long it will take to recover the costs of the new loan. It is unusual to break even before two years have passed.

**Regulation Z:** see "Truth-in-lending."

**Repair:** an effort to maintain a building or property that does not increase its value, as opposed to a capital improvement. Important for the purpose of determining tax benefits on income property. See a CPA for advice about whether an effort is an improvement or a repair.

**Reserves:** see "Impounds."

**RESPA:** Real Estate Settlement Procedures Act, a federal law that requires the lender to furnish an informational booklet and a statement of estimated settlement costs when someone applies for a first mortgage.

**Reverse annuity mortgage:** the "golden years" mortgage. Actually, this is not a mortgage, because the homeowners are not making payments; instead they are receiving payments from a financial institution, either until death or to some agreed-upon age, often 100, at which time the property may be sold.

 **Rule of 72:** a rough measuring device for estimating the return (the interest or the time to "double") on one's investment. If we invest $10,000 at 12%, 72 divided by 12 equals 6, so we can conclude that in six years we will have a total of $20,000. If instead we want $20,000 in 4 years, we divide 72 by 4, which equals 18. We know that we have to find an investment that pays 18% if we are to acquire that amount that quickly.

**Second mortgage:** a loan on a property that is in a "junior," or inferior, position to a first mortgage in the event of a default and repossession. Institutional seconds are useful when the buyer is assuming the first mortgage and the seller wants her equity cashed out. Institutional seconds are often loaned for no more than 15 years at an interest rate that is higher than first mortgages. Seller seconds are whatever the buyer and seller agree to, within the bounds of usury.

**Settlement costs:** closing costs. See "RESPA" and "Truth-in-lending."

**Shared appreciation mortgage:** can be either institutional or private financing, with the lender or seller providing some benefit (often a very low down payment) in exchange for sharing in the appreciation when the property is sold.

**Subordination:** assuming an inferior position in the collecting/paying of debts. A builder wants to get a construction loan, but the land is still in another person's name; the builder may be required to get the landowner to subordinate his interest to the lender before a construction loan can be made. This procedure has been used in numerous real estate frauds, so an experienced attorney is essential when this word surfaces in negotiations.

**Tax credit:** a dollar-for-dollar benefit. If we are allowed a credit of, say, 10%, and we have spent $5,000 on that item, then we will be able to deduct $500 from our tax bill. Other than the occasional first-time buyer's program, day care is one of the few tax credits presently available.

**Tax deduction:** if an item falls into a deductible category, such as a repair of a rental property, then that amount is combined with all other deductibles and is subtracted from the income on that property to arrive at the amount subject to tax.

**Term:** the time allowed for a loan.

**Triple net lease:** a lease that essentially requires the tenant to pay for everything except the owner's Christmas gifts, from property taxes to maintenance. Can also be called a "net lease." With a double net lease, the tenant pays for everything except property taxes.

**Truth-in-lending:** a set of federal regulations requiring lenders to provide information to consumers, especially in advertisements, so that they may make informed decisions. Among other things, the annual percentage rate must be disclosed.

**Usury:** an interest rate higher than the law allows. Residential (owner-occupied) loans are usually covered by this law, but loans for investments are not. But there are many exceptions. The typical usury limit is four points above the most recent 26-week Treasury-bill auction. Agents often receive bulletins that contain the usury limit, so they can bring you up to date.

**Wrap:** or wraparound. A financing method that typically consolidates a first mortgage (that does not have a due-on-sale or acceleration clause) with seller-financing. For example, the seller has a $70,000 FHA loan at 9%, and $50,000 in equity (total price: $120,000). The buyer puts down $10,000. The seller then requires one payment for the $110,000 balance, with payments figured, say, at 10%. The seller makes the payments on the FHA loan, and keeps the difference as profit. The seller's actual rate-of-return (yield) on his $40,000 extension of credit is 11.7%.

## TYPICAL DOWN PAYMENTS

**Conventional loans:** 5%, 10%, or 20% for owner-occupied; often 30% for nonowner-occupied.

**Conventional, portfolio:** often 25% or more.

**FHA:** for convenience, the down payment is described as 3%. In reality, it requires some fancy calculating which is beyond the scope of this book, and the actual final percentage is usually less than 3%.

Here are some sample FHA down payments at different prices:

| | | | | |
|---|---|---|---|---|
| Price | $44,000 | Down payment | $250 | (0.6%) |
| Price | $65,000 | Down payment | $1,400 | (2.2%) |
| Price | $85,000 | Down payment | $2,200 | (2.6%) |
| Price | $100,000 | Down payment | $2,750 | (2.75%) |

**VA:** no down payment up to $184,000 for a single-family home; larger loans are available for multifamily (up to a fourplex), but the vet must occupy one of the units.

**Assumptions and seller-financing:** these are totally dependent on the circumstances, amount of equity, etc. But most sellers want a down payment that covers their closing costs. If they are selling without a commission, closing costs are likely to be at least 3% of the price.

### PREPAYMENT STRATEGIES VS. 15-YEAR LOANS

If a loan has no prepayment penalties or prohibitions, the borrower may want to pay it off early. There are advantages and disadvantages that often require an explanation by a CPA or financial planner; it is not something you should do without counseling. Prepayment often fits the needs of middle-aged buyers who want to time their retirement with the retiring of their mortgage, but in many other cases it may be to the buyer's advantage to continue making monthly payments.

I have an FHA loan, so I can pay early without any complication. However, there is a provision by my lender that payments of less than $100 can be refused. Each month my office manager makes out a *separate* check for $100 "for principal only." This amounts to a tax-free savings account of $1,200 each year at 9%, compounded, and should shorten my 30-year loan by around nine years. That first year's extra $1,200 will "be worth" the saved interest, equaling $6,725 by the 20th year.

Much has also been written about the Canadian, or bi-weekly, mortgage in which the monthly payment is simply cut in half and then made every two weeks. This creates one extra monthly payment over the course of a year. Some people have offered to set these up for consumers for a "mere $500." They can usually be set up for the cost of a mere stamp. No "outside expert" is likely to be needed. A simpler approach might be just to make two payments in whatever month the loan started, or whenever the timing is right, such as during a month when one receives a bonus. Prepayment plans like these will retire most 30-year loans in 15–20 years.

Many borrowers elect to apply for a 15-year loan at the outset. The monthly payments on a 10% loan are about 22% higher than for a 30-year plan. At first glance, 15-year loans seem to offer an extra benefit or two, such as a slightly lower interest rate, but analysts have concluded that when the tax benefits are considered, these loans are not necessarily advantageous. Personally, I favor a 30-year loan which has no prepayment prohibition. If I want to "convert" it to a 15- or 20-year loan by making extra payments, I can do this. If in an emergency I need that extra money one month, I don't have to send it in. The problem with a voluntary, self-imposed plan is that it requires persistent self-discipline. Or an office manager.

# QUALIFYING FOR A LOAN

### THE LOAN APPLICATION

Qualifying for a loan, writing a book, and riding a bike across the Rockies—these are three similar ordeals I have experienced. They are similar in that no one made me do them, every day I had to do more than I wanted to, and I finally had to accept unpredictable problems as predictable. Each of these efforts delivered me to a desired place and provided a wonderful sense of accomplishment, but when they were finished I was glad to rest. Of the three only one—the loan—had a distinctly unpleasant element: it was essentially out of my control.

If you have read any of the chapters prior to this, you know that there are so many people and complexities involved in real estate law and financing that it's a wonder so many loans are approved and closed. This may best be explained by the fact that most loan officers are paid only on commission: no loans, no income. Let's keep it that way. Now if we could just figure out some way to put legislators on an income-for-results plan.

Since for the most part we lose control of the loan process, it is all the more important that we do our part as letter-perfect as possible. And the more we know about the other players' parts, the better we can accept and deal with common problems.

The applying part of the loan process has certainly undergone some changes in Western Washington in the last five years. At one time it was common for an agent who was holding an open house to "impersonate" a loan officer (and maybe it still is). He would sit there with a calculator and soon have complete strangers telling him everything about their finances. He would tell them, with no doubt about his conclusions, how much of a loan they could qualify for.

Every time I did this and then saw a buyer get turned down for a loan I'd told them they would get, I began to wonder if I had any business trying to be so helpful. Then another element entered the picture: Both agents and consumers began to pay a little more attention to the agent's obligations to the sellers, and a very serious question surfaced. Does an agent representing a seller have any business inquiring about the finances of the buyer? I came to the conclusion that he does not. On the other hand, agents who were representing the seller had an obligation to ensure as best they could that the buyer would qualify.

To resolve this dilemma, I began to ask that buyers I met with "prequalify" before making an offer. If I represented them as a buyer broker, I went with them to a meeting with the lender. If I represented the seller, then I would not

go to the meeting unless the buyers were so open and trusting that they weren't concerned if I knew about their finances. When I did not go with them, I was content with assurances from the loan officer that these buyers would in all likelihood qualify for the property or price range they were considering.

Until 1989, informal prequalifications—often done over the phone—were about all the buyers were doing until they actually had an accepted offer. Then the formal application would be made, usually within five days after the offer was accepted, at which time the buyer paid for some of the initial steps in the loan process—the title search, credit check, and appraisal.

But as the seller's market in Western Washington really began to take off in 1989, buyers began to take more interest in being truly prequalified, formal application and all. Since multiple offers on many of the best listings were common, agents began to stress the need for the buyer to look like the sellers' knight in shining armor. One of my agent's buyers found a loan company that not only would guarantee that the buyers would qualify, they would limit the appraisal to a "drive-by only to confirm value," and thus there could be no delay in closing. The buyers showed this letter to the seller, who gladly accepted their offer. The appraisal was done after the buyers moved in (and only because the lender needed an appraisal in the file).

In Eastern Washington this degree of competition for properties does not usually exist, but prequalifying will always make the seller feel more inclined to accept or consider an offer, so it is worth investigating in all markets.

## FOUR LEVELS

There are essentially four levels of prequalifying. They are:

**1.** A ballpark number (loan amount) furnished by an agent or by using the formulas in this chapter.

**2.** An informal (unpaid) interview with a lender, by phone or in person. This offers no commitment.

**3.** A letter from a lender stating that if all the information furnished is verified, the buyer should qualify for a loan of so many dollars.

**4.** A letter (or even a credit card, in a few cases) from a lender that says the buyer has definitely been approved.

## WHAT TO BRING

The methods and standards of different loan programs require that buyers furnish different pieces of information about themselves. Instead of going into all the differences I will list those documents that a buyer most likely will need. A phone call to the lender will usually provide any missing pieces of the puzzle.

**Documents for the loan application:**

**1.** Photo I.D. (driver's license is OK).

**2.** Social Security card, or a certification of the number (try an official document containing the number, such as a tax return).

**3.** Credit information—account numbers, balances, and payments for credit cards, furniture, appliances, etc.

**4.** Current mortgage, if any, including name, address, and account number.

**5.** Copies of leases, if buyer is a landlord.

**6.** Bank account information, with account numbers, branches, and phone numbers.

**7.** Names and addresses of all employers for the last two years.

**8.** Current pay stub. One of the most unpredictable areas is overtime. Some lenders will accept overtime as reliable income; some will not. Take all the proof to be found.

**9.** Divorce decree, especially if there are children.

**10.** Documentation of any income other than employment, such as child support, trusts, royalties, etc.

**11.** List of all major assets, such as stocks and bonds. Supply copies of certificates and/or serial numbers.

**12.** A copy of the purchase and sale agreement plus all addenda, if applicable. It should include the legal description of the property.

**13.** DD 214 papers, or certificate of eligibility, if a vet and applying for a VA loan. Call the VA office early in the game to get the certificate.

If you are self-employed, take all of the applicable documents I listed above, plus the last two years' tax returns, with all schedules. Expect to furnish profit-and-loss statements and a current balance sheet. These may require a CPA's signature.

Finally, as a tip to those who have what might be called a common name (more than three of you in the phone book), be prepared to furnish the details of your whereabouts for the last two to five years. In credit checks and title searches it is not uncommon for judgments to be discovered against someone with the same name. The lender will need proof that this is not you. I've seen borrowers get very irritated about this, as if the lender were questioning their integrity. Stay cool and do what you have to do.

## DON'T BE STUMPED

Lenders often ask, "Can you tell me how much your personal belongings are worth? Just a number for this line." A hint: Don't take this too seriously. I have seen couples discuss this, with feeling, while the lender waits. Just a number. A guess. A ballpark figure. A stab in the dark. A wild shot. But no, borrowers want it to sound impressive, so they try to think of everything. OK, double it then. Pick a number. Add four zeroes. No one is coming over to look in your closets. No one. Trust me.

## ARE YOU SELF-EMPLOYED?

I used to think that if someone were self-employed, he or she would know it. But in lending situations, it's not always that simple. Of course, you can start with your income forms: If you receive 1099s you are considered self-employed; if you receive W-2s, you are employed by others, in most cases. However, it is possible to receive a W-2 and be technically self-employed in the eyes of the lender—for example, if you own a certain percentage of a corporation for which you work.

Not only should anyone who is self-employed, or might be classified as such, speak to a lender as soon as possible, he should also talk to his accountant for a review of "addbacks." Self-employed types like to take all the tax deductions they can, such as from depreciation for rental property. A figure such as this can usually be added back into our income for the purposes of qualifying. Depreciation of cars and office furniture may not be eligible, however, since the lender may feel that these items will eventually have to replaced. Other eligible addbacks are deductions for Keoghs and IRAs. Add those figures to the bottom line on Schedule C and there's a good chance you'll arrive at the figure the lender will use for qualifying.

## JOB LONGEVITY

In general, lenders feel the most comfortable with borrowers who can show at least two years of full-time employment with the same employer. The lender shows the most resistance to the short-term self-employed, and to those who have made a career change. A career change means a move into an unrelated field. A recent college graduate who has continued in the field for which she trained is probably better off with one year of employment than the self-employed person is with several years of self-employment. In general, buyers can change jobs within the same field during the loan process without any complications (though the lender does expect to be informed). But if you are considering a career change, buy the desired real estate before the big move if at all possible.

## THE HISTORICAL EXPLANATION

I'm so used to working with lenders that I sometimes forget that many consumers are puzzled or curious about where lenders get their "rules." Why will lenders only allow a certain percentage of one's income to be spent on housing? Are the rules really rules? Do all lenders have the same rules? Do they ever consider one's sincerity and put the rules aside?

In the first place, some rules are rules and some rules are guidelines. It takes about two lifetimes to learn which are which. All loans that are sold to FNMA, FHLMC, or GNMA must have an appraisal in the file. That's a rule. Buyers making down payments of less than 10% can spend no more than 25% of their income on housing. That's a guideline. But if lenders want to give you a reason why you were turned down, suddenly it's a rule.

Where did these guidelines for qualifying originate? On a chart, so to speak. If we charted all borrowers by the percentage of their incomes going to housing, and then cross-referenced to the percentage of late payments and forfeitures, we would see how the late payment–forfeiture line begins to accelerate after some point in the percentages. After years of watching these charts, lenders have come to some conclusions about where their degrees of risk begin to accelerate noticeably.

Yes, all lenders know the guidelines, but they also have their own personal philosophies about risk and generosity, so a borrower who gets turned down by one lender and then gives up is making the mistake of believing that all lenders are alike. No, all politicians are alike; lenders are as different as the many shades of gray.

Although lenders can introduce some flexibility into the qualifying process, they won't normally carpet the horse's stall. If they want to sell that loan on the secondary market, they're going to have to give convincing reasons why they showed any mercy. But there are limits, i.e. percentages that a lender dare not exceed even if such a decision seems illogical. A friend of mine encountered such a situation: She had been making payments for four years on a 14% mortgage, but when she tried to refinance her loan at a 10% rate, the lender said she didn't qualify (insufficient income per the formulas, even for payments at the 10% level), even though she had never missed or been late on the payments at 14%. So yes, there are times when sincerity, good looks, and even being a stockholder won't be enough.

## ROOMMATES?

If a borrower might not qualify for a house payment, is it possible that the lender will consider the rental income from a roommate? Call and ask. The most recent trend is not to give any credit for roommate income. Some lenders consider it a sign of being too close to the edge.

Whatever you do, don't blurt out anything about the house you want to buy having a separate apartment from which you will receive rent. Investigate the zoning for that area and find out if that "mother-in-law" (MIL) apartment is illegal. Appraisers have been known to call for the removal of the separate cooking facilities so the house will conform with local laws. MILs are illegal throughout King County, although there may be as many as 20,000 of them.

## SHARING LIFE?

I once met a young couple who in the 1970s had wanted to buy a house. However, an agent had told them they wouldn't be able to get a loan since they were unmarried. Instead of being appropriately skeptical, they believed her. Too bad. Perhaps they would have encountered some resistance then—that was a long time ago, before television and penicillin, wasn't it? There is little problem today, with the exception of VA loans. To qualify for the latter, both partners must be vets or they must be married to each other. One of the worst complications is the need for two credit reports instead of one, so there is an extra charge (typically about $70). Otherwise, go for it! (Many of my friends have had an attorney draw up a partnership or buy-sell agreement. It's nice to have some discussion of "what if?" Drawing up a contract forces couples to deal with some questions they would naturally like to avoid, such as who gets the property if they split up.)

I have even seen a lender tell a young couple not to get married during the qualifying process, and it didn't have anything to do with the lender's feelings about matrimony. Since the woman wasn't working, and therefore would be a dependent, her partner's salary alone wouldn't be enough to qualify them for the loan. So he applied and received the loan as a "sole proprietor," and several months after they moved in, they had a wonderful wedding.

## THE APPLICATION INTERVIEW

I forgot. I left one item out of the list of things to take to the application: your checkbook. The application process usually goes like this:

**A.** A discussion of what your plans are, what size payment you hope for, types of loans, etc. Good loan officers are masters at putting one at ease when talking about money, so this is often less painful than people expect. Did you know that a study only a few years ago showed that most spouses didn't know the other one's income? We are only beginning to be comfortable with talking about income; we still sometimes treat it as if it were an inherited disease.

**B.** A decision as to whether to go ahead and make the application, or to talk to other lenders first. If the decision is to go ahead, then the lender must (1) fill out a good-faith estimate of your closing costs (never lose this! You will want to take it to the signing ceremony for a comparison), and (2) provide you with a little booklet that satisfies the RESPA requirement that you be informed of your rights (see Chapter 10).

**C.** The signing of a check for the initial steps in the loan application. A typical range is $350–$550, to cover the credit check(s), appraisal, and title search. Very little of this amount will be refundable, but you can ask a lender to hold your check and the processing until you call and state that some step has been completed, such as the structural inspection.

## EDUCATING OURSELVES

It takes more spine than most people ever possess to negotiate with a lender on interest rates or closing costs, but all the spine in the world won't do you any good if you don't know what the competition is offering or asking. If no one else in town is offering a benefit or discount, then that lender doesn't have to match it. So first you have to know that someone out there has a better deal.

How do you find out what other lenders are offering? You have to be able to understand their language. If you still don't know such abbreviations as LTV, LOF, etc., then you're going to have a hard time reading their literature. Make sure you learn most of the language in Chapter 10, "Financing: The Details."

Some information may be gathered from newspaper ads or phone calls, but this doesn't usually tell us very much. What a consumer really wants to see is what she isn't supposed to see because of Regulation Z. This federal truth-in-lending regulation says that if a lender advertises a loan, then the whole truth about that loan must be told. Lots of details. In order to skip having to print all of those details and to effectively communicate their programs to people who can recommend them, lenders distribute newspapers and flyers ("rate sheets") to real estate agents, with a statement on the banner that says, "Not intended for the public: for real estate agent and broker use only."

In the Puget Sound area there is a great little newspaper called the "Western Washington Bulletin" that has dozens of ads and articles and line-by-line comparisons of loan programs. Many agents give it little attention, often because they already have preferred lenders, but it could be a great tool in the hands of a consumer who intended to find out what the typical lender was charging for a certain kind of loan. So ask an agent for a copy; I don't think one would mind pulling it out of the trash can. In other areas of the state you might ask an agent to save the different rate sheets for you for a week or two.

## LONG-TERM DEBTS AND INCOME

Before you attempt a do-it-yourself qualification, you have to understand the concept "long-term debts" (LTDs). These are bills for items that require numerous payments, and although they may be important items, such as a car, they are often debts that can be "erased" by paying them off. Furniture, appliances, vehicles, and boats are frequently found in this category. Credit cards and child support will also be included; obviously, child support or day care is not an item that one can spuriously dispense with, but credit cards are an item that we have more control over. However, since most of us have "bad habits" with these little keys to the good life, lenders assume that we will use them, and therefore unless we have absolutely no pending charges, the lender will assume that the minimum allowable payment will be made each month. Strangely enough, utility, food, and clothing bills are not normally figured into this formula.

For FHA and VA loans, any debt with six or more remaining payments is deducted from that portion of income that you might use for housing. Again, this is a guideline, not a hard and fast rule. The guideline for conventional loans is 10 months.

I have seen buyers attempt every imaginable strategy to lower their LTDs, from making extra payments to transferring a debt into a relative's name. Most loan officers even suggest some strategies—within the law, of course. The point is, these efforts should be made as far in advance of applying for a loan as possible.

## GIFT LETTERS AND PRIVACY

If a parent or friend loans the buyer any money toward the house, the loan payments will be viewed by the lender the same as payments to the TV store, the car dealer, etc. Lenders especially fear any "unsecured" loans that could become liens on the property.

If a parent or relative is willing to sign a gift-letter form stating that the amount is truly a gift, then the lender is covered and doesn't have to reduce the buyer's borrowing ability. What happens after that is unlikely to be the lender's concern. However, many parents and relatives don't wish to enter into any subterfuge, so they face a very real dilemma: either sign the gift letter or see their relative not qualify. At this point, many buyers have asked me, "Well, how does a lender even know where I got that money?"

Ah, yon naive buyers. A lender is going to thoroughly investigate one's bank accounts, savings, stocks, etc. When I tell buyers this, a few of them act miffed and reply that they didn't think those things were any of the lender's business. But wouldn't you feel the need and right to know those things before you made the decision to loan someone many thousands of dollars? In other words, a borrower can't make an issue of financial privacy.

So where does this leave you with the loan or gift from friends or relatives? Lenders only go back so far in investigating one's finances, i.e. recent deposits, so if you inquired about local customs and found that lenders only checked the previous three months prior to the loan application—well, you get the idea.

Anyway, months before the loan application you should be sure to "return" the interest on any gifts, eh?

### STRETCHING IT?

Some borrowers want to know if the lender will look ahead and see that the actual monthly house payments will eventually be "reduced" by tax benefits accrued from interest deductions, and will therefore increase the amount that will be loaned. No. All of this has already been considered, and that would be cutting things too close.

However, some of the short-lived programs that originate with the state (so-called state bond programs) will allow this projection, even though they are already relatively generous. Buyers should take the initiative and recognize that their margin of safety may become very thin; they must take extra steps to practice good money habits if they participate in any of these programs.

### ARE THEY ALL THE SAME?

I have had many a buyer call two different lenders and end up with two different loan amounts for which they supposedly would qualify. They often differ by 10% or more, so it pays to shop. On the other hand, some of these more "generous" loan officers didn't deliver when it came time to cash in the chips. It also pays to be skeptical.

## QUALIFYING—CONVENTIONAL LOANS

| Down Payment | "Front-end Ratio" | "Back-end Ratio" |
|---|---|---|
| Less than 10% | 25% | 33% |
| 10% or more | 28% | 36% |

As noted before, if you make a humongous down payment, 25% or more, it is not unusual for the lender to make the loan, "no matter what," as long as the property comes close to being worth the sale price. These guidelines, then, are primarily for the middle masses who make down payments of 20% or less.

At this point, review the abbreviations LTV, PITI, and PITIM in the previous chapter, as well as "factors" for determining payments.

The buyer who desires a 5% down payment will encounter the strictest criteria. The PITIM should be no more than 25% of her gross income (before taxes and Social Security deductions). This is often called the "front-end ratio." If her income is $4,000 a month, then $1,000 must cover all components of her payment.

The lender's next step is to double-check that this borrower has her financial life in order, by the lender's standards (back-end ratio). So we must now total the house payment and all of those long-term debts discussed above, and this total must not exceed 33% of the borrower's income. Or we can total the LTDs and subtract them from the 33% figure of $1,320. Let's say she has a student loan, a car payment, and credit card payments that total $370. This leaves her with $950 that can be applied to her PITIM, not $1,000 per the front-end ratio.

Now let's figure out how much money she can borrow. You must subtract the monthly amount of the property taxes and hazards insurance. Let's say those are $80 and $25, respectively. So you subtract $105 from $950, and the result is $845. Feed this amount into a calculator, or divide by the appropriate factor.

If the interest rate is 10%, then you should use the factor for 10.5% (0.00915), because that is approximately the effect of the monthly PMI premium. You divide $845 by the factor of 0.00915 (30-year loan) and get the figure of $92,350, which is the amount of the loan for which she would qualify.

It's that simple. Almost.

If our buyer makes a down payment of 10% or more, then the lender's risk is supposedly reduced and thus the ratios can be liberalized to 28% and 36%. I say "supposedly" reduced because one study concluded that forfeitures are explained by "changes," such as divorce or loss of employment, that are frequently unrelated to down payment. However, the lender has a response: There is more risk that a lender will lose money in a forfeiture with a small down payment, because with so little equity the closing costs alone may put the lender in a hole.

Of course, that's what the PMI is all about—to cover the lender's losses. Even so, the lenders want to keep the risk low, as they see it.

Some lenders use ratios of 28% and 33% for those making a down payment of less than 10% (or, as they say in the lending business, an LTV above 90%), but if the more conservative 25 and 33 figures are used, you shouldn't be disappointed.

Once again, these ratios are just guidelines, and many exceptions are made for people with excellent credit, large savings accounts, other assets, etc. In fact, the ratios are increased for larger loans, called "jumbo" loans, because those who have an income large enough to be in this price range should easily have sufficient income to take care of life's necessities. Even ratios as high as 37% and 43% are considered for loans approaching $500,000.

NOTE: One final consideration that has surfaced lately is the requirement that conventional borrowers have the equivalent of two house payments in the bank after the down payment and closing costs are paid (in the case of a 5% down payment, three payments may be required).

### QUALIFYING—FHA

FHA qualifying standards have recently been changing on the average of once an hour, so it wouldn't hurt to call the lender and see what the standards are for the next 60 minutes. VA standards are similar, but they are even more likely to require the assistance of a loan officer, so the formula below may only give the vet a rough idea of what his or her chances or limits are.

Some lenders may still use an approach called "residuals," especially if the borrowers have a large brood. If they use this method, have them explain it to you. If not, be glad you don't have to add this complication to your life, even though some believe it to be more generous than the ratio method.

As with the conventional method of qualifying, the FHA has begun to use front-end and back-end ratios, only their numbers are 29% and 41%, respectively. The 41% figure is an absolute rule that cannot be exceeded. Considering that you may be making a down payment of only a few percent, these percentages are fairly liberal. However, both the FHA and VA consider child care an LTD, while conventional lenders do not, so if there are children, the conventional method may be more liberal. You (or the lenders) must simply run those numbers.

In the above conventional 5% down payment situation, our buyer qualified for a loan of $92,350. By the FHA's formula she would qualify for a $1,160 payment (PITI) and a loan of about $115,000 (at 10%). But keep in mind that the government programs, though worth pursuing, invariably have complications. Don't go out there making offers until you've talked to a lender or two.

## MAKE TOO MUCH?

Can you make too much to qualify for an FHA loan? Not presently, but watch the newspaper. Congress has been toying with this one for a long time. As for the loan programs administered by the state, yes, you can make too much money to qualify. A "participating lender" can explain both income limits and "target areas," towns or neighborhoods where there are fewer limits or restrictions in order to encourage purchases in these less-desirable areas.

# FROM OFFER TO CLOSING

## THE PURCHASE AND SALE AGREEMENT
### SIGNING AND PAYING

L et me tell you how far I got in law school: not very far. I had been teaching rock climbing for a living when I halfheartedly decided to become an environmental lawyer. I was in no mood for classes so boring that even the instructors fell asleep, and by the fifth month I was so overcome by revulsion that I couldn't go back. I still wonder what they did with the things in my locker.

I tell you this to let you know that if you find the law a bit of a bore, I understand. On the other hand, I know it's something we would all like to master if we could find an efficient way to do it. Finally, I want to make this point: What you are about to read is not legal advice. It may be practical. It may explain things. But it is no substitute for having an attorney advise you on what to do or how to do it.

We have touched on attorneys before, noting that their one unquestioned but involuntary contribution to the world is being the subject of a great deal of sardonic humor. Yet each of us knows attorneys who are decent and noble beings and who simply bear the curse brought on their vocation by their greedy or ruthless colleagues. Well, I know one, anyway. I also pointed out that the experienced specialist is the only one sufficiently qualified for our needs, even though some of them sometimes recommend a strategy that is impractical, no matter how correct, and which may backfire because it doesn't take into consideration how the other side may feel. It's important for the consumer to know when not to take their advice.

I mentioned earlier that there is a cheapskate's way to involve an attorney at no extra cost, but that the degree of protection is minimal. We will review this when we come to that point in the contract. If money were no object, we would all hire an attorney before we did anything that involved a contract, but since for many of us that could mean a daily expense, we have to limit ourselves to the most important situations. This is one of them.

## SOME SELF-RELIANCE

Even if we have the best attorney in town, some of us still want to be as self-reliant as possible, able to plot our own strategies and then have the attorney merely confirm that we're on an acceptable course. We also want to know enough of legal theory and language to understand what we're told by the attorney. The challenge for us self-reliant types is to remember that we don't know it all. I had a student in my last class who failed this challenge. He was a middle-aged man who obviously knew some law, but he had some of the screwiest ideas! He said things in class that the other students might have gone out and attempted in the belief that he knew what he was talking about, if I hadn't challenged him. We've all heard about people like this, but we're not always lucky enough to recognize someone who is half-cocked. All I can say is, maintain a healthy degree of skepticism. Always get that second opinion.

If you want to build your own library of books on real estate law, please see the books listed in the Appendix. I've already mentioned both of Alan Tonnon's very serious tomes. If paying $20–$35 for a book on this subject stubs your toe, perhaps I haven't convinced you of the seriousness of this topic: We're risking a pound of flesh, at the minimum.

## THE VALID CONTRACT

Before we get into the specifics of a purchase and sale agreement (PSA), we need to review some generalities. Since no one can ever master every word or line of every printed contract or addendum, we need to be able to apply and answer some general questions. No matter how careful we are about a detail or two, if we don't have an enforceable contract to start with, our effort is in vain.

You've probably heard it said, "The law is an ass." That's because the language of contracts is often a pain in the law. Only a jackass would use the word "alienation" to mean to sell or "transfer interest" in a property. The same is true of using the word "severability" to indicate that if one part of a contract is invalid, then that part may be severed and the rest of the contract upheld. We can gripe, and in our lifetime we may see a little improvement, but the point is that we laypeople can quickly get in over our heads, so let's not get cocky. I've had to referee some awful fights between laypeople who were sure they knew what a phrase meant.

McLaw. Since I don't have an eidetic memory, I need mnemonics to remember what I wish I would never forget. One such mnemonic is "McLaw," for five of the components required for a valid real estate contract.

M is for **mutuality,** or a meeting of the minds. This is an area that sellers especially need to understand since they frequently show preference for offers that seem "simple." But the contract that seems simple may ultimately require some complicated unraveling. If I said, "I will pay you one hundred dollars for your porch swing," you might start unhooking it. But I didn't say whether I would pay you in one lump or two, or fifty. And what about, "All appliances to remain"? Sellers like that sort of language, but only the most naive negotiators are so sloppy. We need to state exactly what and why: "All of the following appliances are to remain and are to be in good working order at closing, and they are of nominal value and are being left merely for the convenience of the buyer and seller: the 22-cubic-foot almond Amana refrigerator,..." To make sure our contract stands up later, we need to put a good bit of starch in it right at the beginning.

Keep in mind that it is not just what we discuss, but also what we omit. If we work out an agreement between the parties as to what and when they will pay but fail to mention the steps or penalties if payments are late or missed, then we may not have a valid contract. Or it may take a court interpretation and considerable expense to assess its validity.

**C** is for **consideration,** i.e. something of value that we exchange. It can be money, services, goods, property, rights, options, and/or promises. In fact, the consideration that creates most contracts, including the PSA, is an exchange of promises: "I promise to sell and you promise to buy...." Many people think the earnest money is consideration. It may or may not be. We'll see later what category and purpose earnest money serves.

**L** is for **legal objective**. We have to set out to do something that is legal to start with. Wanting to buy a tractor is a legal objective, but getting someone to steal the tractor and "sell" it to us is not, so we could never successfully sue the thief if we gave him the money and he didn't deliver the tractor. In other words, we have to work within the law. We must never assume that just because two people totally agree to do something, that makes it legal. For example, a landlord might get a tenant to agree to give up some right, but our state law says that some tenant's rights can be waived only if the tenant's attorney agrees, *in writing.* This is unlikely, so the agreement would be unenforceable.

**A** is for **ability** (some say "capacity"), as in ability to understand and perform. This eliminates the mentally incompetent or disturbed or retarded, the intoxicated, minors, and all of our friends and relatives who have bought into pyramid schemes. We should confine our dealings to that minority known as SASMs—sober adults of sound mind.

The trickier questions about ability often revolve around status and timing. For example, if I offer to sell you my neighbor's house for $200,000 and you agree but I don't come through, I may not be able to escape responsibility just because I never owned her house. If I had the time to acquire it and didn't, well.... I also didn't necessarily do anything illegal by offering to sell something that wasn't mine, if it could be acquired, *unlike* that old universal hook, the Brooklyn Bridge.

**W** is for **written,** an element that is not required in all areas of commerce. States often enact laws that set some dollar limit on oral agreements, such as $5,000; any amount over that requires a written contract if you are going to ask the state for help in enforcing it. The state of Washington decided long ago that real estate was too important ever to be transacted with an oral agreement. I think this gives the knowledgeable consumer a great tool: The person who wants to "just shake on it; whatsa matter, don't you trust me?" can be told that it's to his advantage to put the deal in writing because otherwise Washington law may later invalidate the whole effort.

The above five McLaw components are necessary general requirements. There are also specific requirements, which change from time to time and about which there are arguments as to their necessity or method of fulfillment. Examples of these specific requirements include but are not limited to: a legal description of the property, signatures, the closing date, prorating of taxes, and copies of all documents to all parties. The fact that there are so many of these items and so many different points of view about them should persuade us not to play the jailhouse lawyer.

## THE *#@+!# ^ & STANDARD CONTRACT!

There is no more dangerous idea in the world of commerce than that there is such a thing as a standard contract. "Oh, there's no use in reading all of that fine print; it's just a standard contract anyway." There is a Bureau of Standards where one may find the standard inch, the standard kilo, and perhaps even the standard of living, but they will think you a deviant if you ask to see the standard contract. What is the point of this point? We have to read every contract. And we have to ask questions before we sign one. We dare not assume anything.

## THE WEIGHT OF THE WORD

Now that I have persuaded you to read that fine print, or "boilerplate," I'm going to turn right around and admit that in some situations a judge might rule that some portion of the fine print is inapplicable or unenforceable. This can happen when the fine print is "unconscionable," i.e. excessively unfair to one party. It can also happen when additional phrases have been added to the contract, either written or typed, which modify or even contradict the fine print. In general, our changes or additions will be given greater weight in the eyes of the court; those changes are more obviously negotiated, and they are more likely to fulfill the meeting-of-the-minds requirement.

## WHEN DO WE HAVE A CONTRACT?

"Connors is back in top form, but McEnroe has pulled out all the stops. He's not about to lose his first match on the seniors tour. McEnroe serves…Connors loses his glasses but manages to return it…McEnroe adjusts his pacemaker and makes it to the baseline…you're not going to believe this, folks—the ball bounces off McEnroe's walker and right back to Connors! But the referee rules it's out of bounds. McEnroe's nurse is trying to restrain him.…"

Now, students of real estate, if every time the ball was struck by a racket someone had signed the PSA—first McEnroe the buyer, then Connors the seller—at what moment did we have a contract? Or do we have one at all?

A contract requires three actions: Offer (the buyer signs), Acceptance (the seller signs), Notification (the buyer learns of the acceptance). Thus, when McEnroe saw or heard that ball coming back, we had a contract.

What if Connors counteroffered? *Any* change constitutes a counteroffer. So if Connors caught McEnroe's serve and then served with a new ball, that would constitute a counteroffer. Now it's up to McEnroe to accept and notify Connors.

And so it goes. Is this important? To those of us who occasionally send long-distance offers through the mail or by fax, it can be dog-eat-dog important. It is not at all unusual for an offer to be in the air when another one is presented over the phone. This is one of the reasons agents have nosebleeds. Until that moment of notification we hold our breath and sit near the bartender.

Here's a scenario that can cause people to regret their hesitancies for years to come: The seller has counteroffered by changing only the date of closing.

---

### JUST THE FAX, MA'AM?

Is a document that is sent and returned with signatures by fax a legitimate document? Some of the best-known real estate attorneys around Seattle take the position that it is, but attorneys in other fields tell me that they have no precedents that provide them with any confidence about this. Just to make sure, some principals are making sure that actual copies are sent and signed even if faxed documents are already in the file. That's good, but we mustn't ever forget that the real secret to keeping contracts together is meeting people's needs. If they're happy, we can send notes on toilet paper with a carrier pigeon and limit our legal costs to birdseed.

The agent drives to the buyer's house with the PSA. The buyer is not disturbed by the counteroffer but wants to think about it for an hour before signing it. The seller however, calls the buyer 10 minutes later and withdraws the offer, having received a better offer in the interim. Our buyer is out of the picture.

This buyer could have accepted the offer on the spot, immediately notified the seller, and left the other buyer waiting on the porch. Yes, our buyer would have had to make a quick decision, but, frankly, at this point the buyer is usually better off than the seller because it is common for the buyer to include some contingency in the offer that allows him to get out of the contract.

Fortunately or unfortunately, it is hard to hold a reluctant buyer's feet to the fire. Many is the time that a buyer acted unfairly and deserved to lose the earnest money, but kept every penny on a technicality. That is one reason we see more sellers in multiple-offer situations demanding nonrefundable earnest money. In a seller's market they often get it. (Of course, in a seller's market very few buyers are hesitant.)

## A TYPICAL SCENARIO

As a real estate professional I've experienced a moderately wide range of situations involving negotiations, but the majority were very similar, at least in the order of things. If an agent isn't involved, then everything in the scenario that follows may take place in a completely different order at a completely different pace.

First we start with the buyers' decision. They usually say they would like to make an *offer*. Notice that they hardly ever say they want to buy a house. That's understandable; this is big-time commitment. A little unsureness is acceptable. At that moment we sit down and start to fill in the blanks. This may be at the office, in a restaurant, or in the car in front of the property. I have written up a few offers in less than 30 minutes, but frequently we're going to need 90 minutes to two hours to go over all of the items that need to be decided. Once the buyers have signed and handed me the earnest money, they're likely to think I'm rude because I may leave in that proverbial cloud of dust. In fact, while they were discussing some item, I was probably on the phone to the seller and/or listing agent setting up the earliest possible appointment. If the property is listed I have to notify the listing agent. If she is not available, then I must notify her office so that they can send a representative in her place. One long-standing strategy is to give the listing agent enough time to get there but not enough time to call her own buyer and write up an offer. We constantly walk the line between fair-nice and competitive-cutthroat.

At this point many buyers ask: "Can we come along?" There is no answer that satisfies everyone. I have seen a book by one of those gurus of real estate theory who think they know everything, in which he recommends that the buyer "may want to take the agent along; he may come in handy." What a stupid statement! The agent is the professional, objective negotiator, and if he isn't he should be in another business. The buyer is nonobjective and probably an amateur negotiator, and if he's a typical male he's his own worst enemy. Our testosterone almost automatically disqualifies us from negotiator-of-the-year awards.

On several occasions I have asked a seller if the buyer (it was always a male buyer who wanted to be there) could come in—he was outside in the cold, cold car....Invariably the seller has turned as pale as a dollar bill in the dryer. Sellers don't want to meet the buyer. The buyer is the *enemy*. On one occasion a seller did let my buyer sit in the basement. On another a seller said OK, and it worked out very well. But in general, buyers who come along are placed in a most awkward position—waiting and wondering just what the agent(s) are saying. Moons ago I said not to take potluck in working with an agent; it's at moments like this that buyers wonder if they were selective enough.

MY *VADE MECUM*: The papers that I take with me when I present the offer are these:

**1.** The earnest money check or a copy thereof

**2.** The PSA itself and enough copies for everyone to read at once

**3.** Extra blank addenda or forms for a counteroffer

**4.** A printout of what the seller's net proceeds will be at that price

**5.** Any letters from lenders about the buyers' qualifications

**6.** Any documents required to support a point that I plan to make

Some agents take their personal resume. This is valid in that the agent's skills have great bearing on the likelihood of the transaction closing. A few agents take a portable computer to do research right on the spot.

If the seller accepts the offer, then I pick up the phone and call the buyers. This is the buyers' notification that establishes a contract. Then I meet with the buyers as soon as possible and get their signatures as proof of the notification. If the sellers have counteroffered, then I break the news, but not the details, over the phone and then meet with the buyers to see if they accept the counteroffer or want to make a counter-counteroffer.

The very first offer of my life required four trips across town between 8 p.m. and midnight. I began to wonder if a helicopter wouldn't make more sense. You may wonder why I didn't just phone the parties and skip all that driving. If there is one sure way to lose a negotiation, it is to make it as uncaring as possible, and the phone does exactly that. Once again we must walk a line, this time between being "cool" and "caring."

## MAKING CHANGES

Every agent has a preferred way to make changes on an offer when the buyer changes something at the last minute or the seller counteroffers. Usually we just draw a single line through the obsolete item, initial and date that change, and print the new term(s) nearby. Some attorneys recommend that a new form or an "official" counteroffer addendum be used, but not many negotiators go to that trouble, at least not for just a few changes. If an addendum is used, it should be cross-referenced on the other documents.

A common mistake of the layperson is to try to erase or obliterate a mistake or change. If a judge is ever called upon to "follow the paper trail" and interpret who did what, she will want to see every piece of paper and be able to follow the order of changes. Any obliterated or erased change may even require notarizing, so don't get too eager. One line is fine.

## PUT ON YOUR COAT...

It's time for a blank-by-blank study of a purchase and sale agreement, so put on your coat and go get one. It would be practically impossible to reproduce one that you could use in this book, and it might not be the document prevalent in your area or the one that your agent uses anyway. If you have an agent, then simply ask for a copy and study it at home, long before it's time to make an offer. If not, ask any agent or attorney, or simply pick up a form at an office supply store.

## BLANK BY BLANK

KEEP IN MIND: We have two points of view and two sets of needs to consider, so there is no absolutely correct way to do these things. The buyers want to reveal enough information to make their offer appealing and respectable, yet they still want to keep some cards close to their chests. The sellers, on the other hand, want to know *everything* about the buyers. We will see this conflict in the very first topic—names.

**1. Names.** The typical PSA starts off with the buyers writing in their "legal" names. In a very few cases, buyers don't want to reveal their identity. They might use a business name or write "undisclosed," or their attorney or someone else might sign with a power of attorney. But not only will our seller want to know who they are, she may want to know their marital status. I have had buyers at different stages in a divorce buy "for their estate alone." Invariably the seller became extremely interested and wanted assurances that the transaction would not end up in court.

If our buyers are investors they may want to write after their names "and/or assigns." This means they are clearly reserving the right to assign (transfer) their rights to buy the property to someone else if that proves to be in their best interest. Some attorneys say this is not necessary, that we always reserve that right, but since not everyone agrees, some buyers feel they should put it in to prevent any arguments. That phrase is a red flag to sellers. What is this buyer up to? They worry that some "unqualified" buyer may be substituted. So if it does not serve a purpose, the buyer may want to omit this phrase.

**2. Address and legal description.** By the time a transaction closes we must have a legal description or some equally detailed description of the property that makes it absolutely certain what is being sold and where it is. A common address will not suffice. An in-city legal description might sound like this: "Lot 9, and the east 4 feet of lot 8, Block 4 of Fuller's Addition, page 222, volume 7 of King County Records, Seattle, Washington." These features refer to a set of plats showing the layout of the streets and lots. A farm or large vacation site might require a description that fills a page or more. The legal description describes the actual layout and size of the property, or refers us to the record

---

### ASK FOR SOMETHING YOU DON'T WANT?

A common strategy in negotiating is to ask for something we don't really want, along with something we do want. Then when we give up the unwanted item, the seller may feel a victory and flex on the other item. In a seller's market, however, this idea must be used sparingly. In some situations ours may be one of six to ten offers, spaced 30 minutes apart. We only get one shot in many cases, and we know nothing about any of the other offers. Every out-of-the-ordinary request may put us at a disadvantage.

The likelihood of getting the seller to sign our offer without looking at any of the other offers is very small, especially if we don't provide some very substantial temptation for the seller to do so, such as a nonrefundable check. In other words, as galling as it may be for a buyer, this could be a time to be submissive. Just remember: The cycles of real estate are inevitable. Someday those sellers will be buyers, and you'll be the seller. Eat your bran, stay healthy, and wait.

---

where it can be found. Attorneys are not in total agreement about what sort of description will stand up in court, but it is good to have the legal description at the time of the offer. It is perfectly legal to add it to the offer later.

How does one acquire a legal description if no agent is involved? Start by calling the county assessor. It should also be found on the seller's deed, the title insurance, and the tax notices (but these notices are usually too abbreviated to be a good source).

**3. The price.** There is no big legal issue here. It is just one of the first blanks that we have to confront, and often the last one to be filled in. I will share one observation: Over the years I have heard many more people regret what they didn't buy than what they did buy. If they had it to do over, a lot of them would go back and make full-price offers, especially those who tried to save just a few percentage points (amounting to $10–$20 difference in their monthly payment). We all love a bargain, but it is not uncommon to pay full price and later find that you've got a bargain. Many buyers make silly assumptions, such as that all sellers pad their prices, etc. Don't think in cliches; just think.

How about making a low offer at first and then returning with a full-price offer if the first offer didn't fly? Sometimes this works. In a seller's market, though, this strategy is usually absurd; there is no second chance.

What if we make a full-price offer? Does the seller have to accept it? No. She can ignore all offers, but she may owe a commission, if the property is listed and the agent has fulfilled his obligation to bring her "a ready, willing, and able buyer." Few realties actually sue a seller, but they certainly threaten, and if necessary they will proceed to a suit.

What about multiple offers, all of them full price or over? Does the seller owe a commission on each of them? The question is one that the industry has tacitly agreed to ignore. Since the tradition of the industry is to serve the seller primarily, then it would look downright hypocritical if all of a sudden we started putting our thirsts above the seller's. So, like the gentlepersons we like to think we are, we congratulate the seller and move on to the next game in town.

Conclusion: Make a low offer if there are no other offers, or are not likely to be any other offers, and you feel that the seller is asking more than the market supports. But don't make a low offer to exercise your ego or earn bragging rights at the next picnic.

**4. Method of payment.** In the contracts most commonly used in Seattle, we find an inch and a half of white space allocated for this item. Five or six years ago I might have written in the down payment, method of financing, conditions for the inspection, and a list of the appliances. With a fine-point pen. Now I am more likely to write: "See addenda A, B, & C attached and made a part of this document." In other words, as I became more cautious and more detailed in my approach, I began to use a full addendum for each of the areas that I once crammed into that white space. The real estate industry has also adapted. For example, as we have come to see the wisdom of a structural inspection, we have composed a preprinted form, rather than let the average undertrained agent scramble a few words. One of Washington's most famous lawsuits (Cultum *v.* Heritage House) occurred when a rushed agent inserted this line: "This offer subject to a satisfactory structural inspection." Those words did not meet the requirement of mutuality. Who had to be satisfied? When? The court battle was long and expensive.

If a buyer works without an agent and has no preprinted financing form, she can do one of several things: copy language from another contract that seems to match her needs, ask a lender for advice, consult an attorney, or wing it. If she wings it, she can take the bare-bones approach and write "All cash to seller at closing," assuming that the seller will be cashed out with personal cash or a loan; or she may want to be more informative and write in the type of financing (conventional, FHA, etc.), the size of the down payment, etc.

But then it starts to get deep very quickly. What if the buyer is applying for an FHA loan at 9.5%, asking the seller to pay two points for the discount, and then just before closing the interest rate goes up? Is it possible for a consumer to know how to write language to address such situations and still keep a contract valid? I don't think so. If there is an inflexible, uncooperative seller, no consumer is likely to be able to write in the needed language.

**5. Financing contingency.** The next line on my contract form gives me the opportunity to check a box as to whether the offer is "conditioned" on the buyer acquiring a certain type of loan. Be careful. I have seen many agents check the wrong box, declaring in essence that the offer was not subject to the buyer

---

### FILL IT IN FILL IT IN FILL IT IN!

Years ago a very impatient and ill-tempered agent brought an offer to the sellers of a property I had listed. About half of the blanks and check-off boxes had been ignored. I was trained to fill in all blanks and boxes or draw a line through them. From her offer we couldn't tell what she had and had not discussed with her buyer, so we told her to come back with a more complete offer. She stormed out, went to a pay phone and called the sellers. She told them that I was too "picky" and if I were gone she would come right back with the original offer. The sellers instead filed a complaint against her and she got her comeuppance. But she was right about my being picky. Better me than a judge.

---

getting a loan, when it really was. At the very least this puts the buyer's earnest money in jeopardy. Double-check.

**6. Contingency contingency.** As we've seen, real estate slanguage requires us to relearn some portion of our everyday language. A contingency is any condition that must be satisfied, but in the local real estate swamp we traditionally think of "a contingent offer" as one where the buyers must sell their own property before they can complete the transaction. Of course, the financing and inspections may also be called contingencies, but to distinguish them we may say that the contract is "conditioned on" or "subject to" their fulfillment.

The contingent offer portion of the contract can be almost as complicated as the financing portion. A buyer may ask for 30 days to "sell" his house (i.e. receive a bona fide offer), or not specify any time element. The seller may accept a contingent offer, with or without a time limit (this may cause some question of legality), but counteroffer that the property has to be listed, viewed by her agent, etc. Most of the time, we include a "bump notice" provision that states that if the seller receives another acceptable (the seller defines this) noncontingent offer, the buyer may be notified and given as few as five days to sell his house or find financing. The seller may also require that the buyer not accept a contingent offer on his house, so that a chain of contingent offers isn't created.

Many buyers have asked me about the wisdom of making a contingent offer in a seller's market. There isn't any. Wisdom. In such a market you sell first, unless you can afford two payments. If you have to rent an apartment until you buy, so be it. A contingent offer has virtually no chance of being accepted in a seller's market.

**7. Asbestos/urea formaldehyde (insulation).** In this portion of the contract, we see little boxes once again. In order to check them off, we often have to "make assumptions." The buyer typically initiates the offer without knowing for sure if the house contains asbestos or urea, but we still mark the boxes for "none." This puts the burden on the seller. If she signs the contract without making a change, she warrants the house to be free of these substances. If she is not sure, or knows that those items have been installed, then she must either disclose their presence or write something along the lines of "seller does not warrant the house to be free of these substances."

**8. Condition of title.** Some forms include a blank where the buyer or agent can write that the title is to be free of all encumbrances except "none" or "those of record." I feel that either of those options can create an enormous complication, and that an attorney is absolutely essential for the language for any such blank. In the Puget Sound area we eliminated the blank some years ago and wrote language to the effect that the seller will deliver a "marketable title" and the buyer agrees to accept the recorded covenants, etc. As a buyer, I personally would never agree to this, or I would at least add a condition that I (my attorney) be given so many days to review the preliminary title search. This is an area where agents take a different tack when they represent a buyer: We may write in the title contingency, even naming a company that we know to be prompt. We then quickly order the title search, with a copy for the buyer's acceptance or rejection by some specified deadline.

Because this paragraph no longer has a blank, it typically gets the same attention as all other boilerplate: none. But it is one of the most important areas we deal with.

**9. Utilities.** The seller typically warrants/discloses that the property is connected to certain utilities. Too many assumptions are made. Buyers assume that any property in the city of Seattle is hooked in to a sewer. Not true. One agent even told me of a septic tank that was nothing more than a 55-gallon drum. Nowadays we tend to check these things more carefully, and some local governments require that wells and septic tanks be tested, pumped out, certified, etc. In Seattle a seller might be required by the lender to hook into the sewer.

**10. Leased fixtures.** We can lease such things as hot water heaters and conversion burners from one or more of the utility companies, such as Washington Natural Gas, but if our offer is FHA or VA the seller must acquire title to these items and pass them on to the buyer as realty, not personalty. Look on the hot water heater for a sign that says "Property of...." If the seller has had the lease in place for more than 12 months, Washington Natural Gas will allow him to replace the items with his own. Otherwise we pay the company some rather inflated amounts.

Leased fixtures make sense. They mean one phone call when problems ensue. So, on a conventional loan the buyer may want to look into assuming the lease.

**11. Closing of sale/date.** In the blank afforded for the name of the person the buyer chooses to be the closing agent, agents or buyers often write "buyer's choice." That's fine, except for one thing: The buyers typically forget to make a choice. The lender often makes it for them, and of course the lenders choose their own escrow department. In most cases, this won't create any problem, but I'm that picky guy who wants everything to be as secure as possible, so I'm going to write in the name of an attorney who handles lots of real estate transactions, perhaps even one who also has an LPO (Limited Practice Officer—a licensed escrow officer) on her staff. Most of the time, this won't cost us any more than the lender's escrow fee, but we have the cheapskate's advantage of having an attorney involved for *some* legal assistance. Remember: The lawyer is usually a neutral party, so the involvement may be minimal, but at least she is likely to tell us if we need to take additional steps and she can answer questions that the LPO cannot.

As for the date of closing, we write in whatever date corresponds to the time the lender has recommended, if there is a lender. Many buyers put in a date near the end of the month because this will require the least amount of cash for "prepaid interest." Discuss this thoroughly with the lender.

But while we're talking about dates, let's discuss one of the most important things that we have to do: Meet all deadlines. You may see or hear the phrase "time is of the essence" and think that it means that we need to move along at a good pace. So did I for the longest time, until I learned that in the courtroom it means meet the deadlines or the deal is dead (if one of the parties wants out).

So this is what I recommend: Once you accept an offer, go to the calendar and write in all deadlines, and mark the days prior to the deadline, because we must not wait to the last minute to start inquiring where things stand.

**12. Possession.** This is an area where hard feelings so often materialize needlessly. If we say that the buyer is entitled to possession on "closing," that means the day that the documents are recorded in county records—not the day they are signed—and the money is available to the seller. So don't plan on signing on a Friday afternoon and moving in that evening. Shoot for a Wednesday, or earlier, if you want to be in by the weekend. Some sellers want a few days of grace after they receive their money. This may mean "free rent" for them while the buyer is paying interest. That's up to the buyer's generosity. But what about the seller who just doesn't want to move out in a timely fashion? When we buyer brokers are representing a buyer we sometimes include language that says the seller has to pay so much a day. If the charge is high, we don't care if he stays forever.

**13. Agency disclosure.** This was addressed earlier. If the agent has not disclosed his/her duty before this, now is the time to make a notation. Many agents and brokers still do not take this area seriously, even after some incredible lawsuit judgments. If they won't take it seriously, then consumers have to force them to imitate the professionals they claim to be.

**14. Boilerplate by the barrel.** From this point on, much of the contract is that old "fine print" that we really do have to read. If we don't agree with it, then we have to take an addendum and write in our preferred actions. One of the items that is sometimes ignored is the requirement that a deed of trust and promissory note be attached to the PSA in all seller-financing transactions. Ask your attorney.

Note that in the boilerplate it is typical to call for a "standard policy of title insurance." If the buyer wants extended coverage, which has been discussed elsewhere in this book, then this item will need to be struck and additional language incorporated on an addendum.

**15. Earnest money receipt.** As we approach the point where the buyer(s) will sign the offer, it is time for another decision—the amount of the earnest money. In Smalltown, Washington, a $500 earnest money may not even raise an eyebrow, but in Seattle neither does a $5,000 one.

The range is quite large. Every real estate company has its own policy or recommendations, and it is always a negotiable item. The buyer's challenge is to risk no more than necessary while making it large enough to be convincing to the seller, especially if there are other offers. If the amount is over $5,000, the agent is required to disclose that the consumer is entitled to receive interest in a separate account.

As mentioned earlier, the earnest money is traditional, not required by law, and its legal category is "liquidated damages," not consideration (not all legal authorities agree on this). It is what the seller is supposed to receive, at the least, if our buyer defaults on the contract and causes damage to the seller by removing the property from the market, etc.

The earnest money is supposed to be deposited by 5 p.m. of the next business day, unless language is added that instructs the agent to hold it until some event or date has passed, such as the structural inspection.

It is traditional to have the buyer make out the earnest money check to the selling office's trust account, but it can just as easily be made out to an attorney's or lender's trust account. In no case is it ever to be commingled with company funds or touched in any way until the transaction is closed or voided unless the buyer and seller agree otherwise.

Although the earnest money is credited to the buyer's down payment or closing costs, it typically remains in the broker's account until a letter from es-

---

### THE TRADITION OF THE RESCISSION AGREEMENT

Whenever a contract "flips," or "goes sideways" as we say in the biz, the agents involved must go through the motions of tying up any loose ends. One of the most important is dispensing with the earnest money. Generally, before the broker dispenses this money, which in most cases amounts to returning the entire amount to the buyer, she sends the selling agent on the thankless errand of obtaining the seller's signature and agreement not to contest returning the money to the buyer. Sometimes it takes days to find the seller or get him to agree. And some never cooperate.

The rescission agreement is a valuable piece of protection for the broker (and the buyer) if the seller later feels that he was indeed entitled to the earnest money. However, it is not essential in every case. As the Washington Department of Licensing has noted, if a contract is "void on its face," e.g. if a commonsense reading by any halfway objective person would lead one to conclude that the contract was voided because a deadline had not been met, and the seller was not damaged, then the rescission agreement is superfluous. Superfine. It's still nice to have it in the file.

crow is received releasing it for application to the broker's commission. It's all very confusing, but the main thing is that the buyer does get credit for it.

The stupidest thing a buyer can do, in most cases, is to make out the earnest money check to the seller. This occasionally happens in FSBO situations. When wouldn't it be stupid? When it is the only way to get the property and the buyer is *extremely* confident that the property and title are without complication. Those are some tough standards.

If the contract is voided and a dispute arises as to whether the seller is entitled to the earnest money, then if a broker is holding the money he has these choices:

**1.** He can negotiate a compromise between the buyer and seller.

**2.** He can decide who gets what, and hope he doesn't get sued.

**3.** He can "interplead" the money to the courts, forcing the principals to take legal action. Since this often costs more than the amount involved, those who aren't caught up in the principle of the thing may come to their senses and accept a compromise.

**16. Signatures and time limits.** We now have "filled in the blanks," and perhaps written and attached an addendum or two. The buyers must now sign the offer. The agent hurries over to the seller's house to present the offer. The buyers will usually have written in a deadline, saying in so many words that "the seller must accept our offer by such-and-such time, or we will withdraw it."

How much time should the buyer give the seller? Some agents say, "Very

little." Others say, "Give them a week in writing, but don't leave the negotiating table until they have made a decision."

What if the seller accepts the offer *after* the deadline? Ask your attorney. That may constitute a counter-offer. In any case, if the buyers still want the property, and they proceed just as if the seller had accepted their offer by the deadline, I would expect most courts to rule that we have a valid contract.

Once the seller has signed, the offer is returned to the buyers, who then sign it a second time, acknowledging that they have received a "seller-signed copy." *Now* we have a contract.

## THERE'S SO MUCH MORE

An entire book could be devoted to just the first two pages of a PSA, and then another book to the various addenda that fill our file cabinets. So I have to stop at some point. But I want to close on a specific paragraph of the financing addendum that we use in the Puget Sound area. No phrase has ever provided more persuasive evidence of the need for professional help. Those significant 43 words in their entirety:

**Obligation to make repairs.** Seller understands that as a result of any city, county or other government inspection, seller may be required to make repairs to the property in order to comply with the housing code even if a sale is not completed."

Now tell me, what do those words say?

One of my students, a retired man who had actually done well in real estate, decided to sell one of his houses. He priced it himself at $89,000. He didn't ask anyone's opinion. It sold very quickly to a young couple who convinced the seller that they needed to move in right away. The couple moved in, without any deposit. The seller didn't ask anyone's opinion. In several weeks, the appraisal came in at around $96,000, with a monster of a work order for a whole new shake roof. *Now* the seller asked for an opinion. "Did I do the right thing? Can I get the buyers to pay for the roof?"

The buyers insisted that the "Obligation to make repairs" phrase required that the seller put on a new roof. An agent explained that work orders and code violations are not necessarily the same thing, and that the appraisal was not a government inspection for that purpose, although an appraiser has the right to call for such an inspection.

The buyers moved out in a huff. The seller put it back on the market, sold it again, and then discovered that the house had been insulated with urea formaldehyde. Eventually, all the problems were solved. No lawsuits. Just a bit less net profit than if he'd sought some professional assistance or opinions right from the start. This self-reliance thing can get out of hand, oh so easily.

## THE WEEKS GO BY...AT LAST, SIGNING

Between the signing of the PSA and the final documents—usually a deed of trust and a promissory note—many days or weeks will pass. Much of what goes on in that time is unknown to and seemingly out of the control of the buyers and sellers. Finally, a call should come from the closing agent with a time and place for final signatures at a signing ceremony (ceremony is a little misleading, but it sounds better than funeral).

At this point the buyers and sellers should make arrangements to pick up copies of all documents one or more days early for perusal and consultation, preferably with their respective attorneys.

By this time the buyers should have made arrangements for transferring all funds to cover the down payment and closing costs. Many buyers wait a day too long and put the entire transaction at risk. Two days of interest on even $20,000 is typically less than $10.00, but some buyers try to squeeze every penny. Will the mature spouse please stand up and knock the bejesus out of the obsessed one? Thank you.

If a "walk-through" has been agreed to, this should be completed within hours before signing, or even after signing but before recording.

Finally, it's time for the walk down the long hall. The chaplain will visit with us while they shave our heads. We take one last bite of pecan pie and...wait, wait! I'm in the wrong dream. No, I'm sorry, that long walk only happens if we show up at closing with a personal check. If we show up with a certified or cashier's check for the right amount, they will let us leave by the front gate. We're free, free at last, except of course for a little case of house arrest.

## SAMPLE CLOSING COSTS

The sample costs below provide a good idea of the types of charges that a buyer or seller pay at closing. However, closing cost calculations can be very complex, and can vary a great deal, so the figures below are only samples, not projections (figures below rounded off in most cases).

Sample number one: the buyer's and seller's costs for a 30 year FHA loan of $85,000 (property price $87,500). The buyer will be charged a 3.8% mortgage insurance premium, but it is financed and added to the loan amount. If the buyer chose instead to pay it in cash, the amount would be 3.661% of $85,000, and thus the closing costs would be substantially higher.

Sample number two: the buyer's and seller's costs for a conventional loan of $150,000 (property price $190,000, so there is no mortgage insurance premium because the buyer made a down payment of 20% or more).

These transactions will be closed at the end of the month, so no "pre-paid interest" will be collected on the loan. If the transactions had instead closed in the middle of the month, the buyers' costs would be higher by one-half month's interest on each loan.

### BUYER'S COSTS

| Category | Sample #1 | Sample #2 |
|---|---|---|
| Loan origination fee | $850 (1.0%) | $3,000 (2.0%) |
| Loan discount | * | $750 (0.5%) |
| Appraisal fee | $250 | $300 |
| Credit report | $70 | $70 |
| Flood certification | – | $5 |
| Assignment fee | 0 | 0 |
| Tax registration | – | $50 |
| Pre-paid interest | – | – |
| Hazards Insurance | $200 | $300 |
| Impounds** | | |
|     Insurance | $30 | $50 |
|     Property taxes | $120 | $300 |
| Escrow fee | $275 | $500 |
| Title insurance | $250 | $300 |
| Recording fees | $15 | $15 |
| Total | $2,060 (2.4%) | $5,640 (3.8%) |

### SELLER'S COSTS***

| Category | Sample #1 | Sample #2 |
|---|---|---|
| Excise tax (Seattle 1.53%) | $1,300 | $2,907 |
| Escrow fee | $275 | $500**** |
| Title insurance | $500 | $600 |
| Assignment fee | $ 5 | – |
| Tax registration | $55 | – |
| Flood certification | $ 5 | – |
| Recording fee | $ 5 | $ 5 |
| Total | $2,145 (2.5%) | $4,012 (2.1%) |

\* Points - either the buyer elected to take the "par" interest rate or the seller paid the points in this case.

\*\* Impounds - these are typically two months of pre-payments on hazards insurance and property taxes, so that the lender is assured that the buyer will never get behind in these areas. Property taxes for one half of the year may also be collected from the buyer or seller (in some pro-rated fashion).

\*\*\* No commission is calculated for these examples.

\*\*\*\* If the buyer sought a VA loan, the seller would be required to pay all (versus half) of the escrow fee, so this amount would be doubled.

# STRATEGIES FOR SELLERS

**A**s the *total* consumer in real estate, you need two points of view:

1. You buy a *house*
2. But you sell a *home.*

As a seller, you are faced with a challenge that is more than a mechanical process, more than a mere function of numbers. You must also be a creator of a pleasant atmosphere, a disseminator of a dream, and a representative of an enviable lifestyle.

> *When people buy homes they don't buy bricks and mortar, they buy lifestyles ...*
> *they don't only look at the property, but at the furnishings and people....*
> *If there is one rule for selling real estate it is this: Try to dress as you think*
> *the buyers would dress when they go to church.*
>
> — John T. Molloy,
> *Dress for Success*

Speaking of points of view, this chapter is written for both the owner who wants to FSBO (For Sale By Owner) and the owner who doesn't. Either way, most of the same tools and labors will be needed, but the FSBO must also do the things an agent normally does.

If you are undecided about whether to FSBO or not, but you are leaning toward it, I have some bad news for you: If you FSBO you may earn over $200 per hour for your effort. And what's so bad about that? Do you have any idea what people have to do to earn that kind of money?

---

**FSBO**

FSBO (fizz-bo or fizz-beau, not from the French). For Sale By Owner. verb. 1. To attempt to sell one's shelter without benefit of professional assistance. 2. To amuse the neighbors with handpainted signs. 3. To confound the neighbors if successful.

---

Ten-thousand-dollar commissions on Seattle houses have become commonplace, and even before this was true sellers were concerned about the relative size of an agent's fee, especially since it sometimes represents a major percentage of the owner's equity. Selling one's own property has probably been contemplated by just about every seller; in fact, a high percentage of listed properties were FSBOs first.

If you just follow one simple suggestion, I guarantee that you can sell your own home: Lower your price by $200 every day. Before long you will have a very attentive bunch of buyers, and one of them will make the first move. By now you're saying, "He's kidding, isn't he?" Well, yes. But I intend to make this point: *Anyone* can sell his or her property if the price is low enough.

I have actually heard more than one owner say that he sold his house for $10,000 less than its market value, and then brag, "But I didn't have to pay a commission!" In other words, they took all that risk and did all of the work an agent would have done, and then didn't pay themselves. And now they're trying to convince us they're clever people? Oh, feed me a slug.

Are we agreed that the idea is to get at least as much as an agent would get, or at least within a few percentage points of what that property should bring, while incurring the least amount of effort, stress, and risk? If we can't *net* more by FSBOing than by listing, then we should list it and let the agent worry about the problems.

As I said, just about every seller has contemplated FSBOing. Is it unusual for an agent to FSBO his own home? Yes and no. Lots of agents do it if they have the time, but I have also heard a broker admit he'd fire any agent of his who tried it (an agent must advertise his agent status to prospective buyers). So agents do it for the same reason nonagent sellers do it: to save money (agents usually have to pay a commission to their brokerage, though smaller). Is there any other reason? Some sellers think so.

Some sellers think that no one else could possibly show-and-tell all the fine points of their home. An owner with a show-and-tell mentality may be the last person who should attempt it. I have watched these sellers talk, talk, talk buyers out of buying. Pride goeth before a severe case of tunnel vision.

## THE PROS AND CONS OF FSBO-ING

**The Pros:**

**1.** You can save money. Obviously.

**2.** You have to do the preparatory work yourself anyway.

**3.** If you do your homework, you may even do a better job than the average agent would.

**The Cons:**

**1.** You will be tied to the house and to the phone for the time it takes to find a buyer; weekend trips are out.

**2.** You will probably save only a portion of the commission because you will have to spend the money the broker would have spent on advertising, and you may accept a low offer, rationalizing, "Well I don't have to pay a commission."

**3.** You may write a contract that doesn't see you through to closing or lands you in court later.

**4.** You will have to deal nose-to-nose with the buyer, the appraiser, the underwriter, et al.

**5.** There is virtually no chance that you will know the sleeve tricks of an experienced agent for dealing with the complications of low appraisals, work orders, lost job verifications, etc.

**6.** Many buyers are not eager to deal with a FSBO. I say this, with some surprise, after polling my consumer students. I knew that the aggressive bargain-hunters shopped FSBOs, and I had assumed that most buyers would do the same. My students, however, said that they are often too unsure of themselves as homebuyers to deal with another amateur.

In the end, we can't just say that there are more reasons *not* to do it than there are to do it. The money saved is a *big* factor, and in some sellers' eyes that is sufficient reason for doing the work and taking the risks. Think long and hard, and if you decide to FSBO, *commit* yourself to it; it's too important to do halfheartedly.

## THE SECRET OF THE BEST PRICE

Such a simple combination of efforts goes into getting the best price for your home that it seems silly to call it a secret, yet it has escaped many a seller and even some agents.

First we clean and prepare a house so that it appeals to the broadest possible range of buyers. One of the stupidest attitudes sellers take is, "It only takes one buyer." If only one buyer wants your property, then you have virtually no leverage with that buyer. If you have to sell, then that buyer is in control.

Second—and this is the part that escapes a lot of sellers—you have to attract the largest possible number of buyers just as soon as you can. A house shouldn't normally go on the market until it is totally ready, and at that moment you need to hit the market with an advertising blitz and create the nearest thing to a feeding frenzy.

Third, it must not be priced too high or too low.

Did I tell you that I'm a licensed auctioneer? Do you know what is the most important and difficult thing I have to do? Talk fast? No. My challenge is to draw the largest possible crowd. If on auction day I see a big crowd, I can enjoy myself; the rest of the day is showtime. So think like an auctioneer. "How can I get the most people here? How do I make them want to come inside? How do I make them comfortable? How do I make them feel secure? How do I make them feel excited?"

There is one important difference between an auction and a typical home sale: The auctioneer knows within seconds if his starting price is too high. The crowd gets quiet. Then the auctioneer lowers the asking price before anyone leaves. A homeowner doesn't have this benefit, so it is extremely important that he not overprice the property. If he does, not only will the crowd stay quiet, it will dwindle and he won't get a second chance to ask those buyers, "All right, what *will* you pay?"

## THE SELLER'S CHECKLIST
## I. PROTECTING YOUR INTERESTS

_____ Buy a notebook or ledger to record all pertinent data, and dig out every name, number, bill, and document that is relevant to the sale of your home. I am amazed at how frequently a seller gets all the way to the offer stage and then cannot find his tax bills, financing coupons, etc. If you were selling your car, you'd have filled the spare and found the jack and the extra keys you hadn't seen for two years.

_____ Talk to your insurance agent, especially if the house will be vacant at some point. Insurance is voided by some companies if a house is vacant for 30 days. Also ask about coverage for any rented furniture.

_____ No matter how confident you are of your insurance coverage, check your property for safety. Are you under six feet tall? Then is there a sharp corner on a heating duct or a nail in a basement joist that would rip open a six-foot person's scalp? Get the idea? Look for all the things that could happen to a 300-pound man, an 80-year-old grandmother, a child who is terrified of dogs, etc. Until I walked into my den and found my friends' 3-year-old throwing my darts, I hadn't even thought about the danger of those instruments.

_____ Get the name of a real estate attorney and ask for instructions on handling an earnest money check.

_____ Either be prepared to stay in frequent touch with an attorney or an experienced agent, or start studying the law today so that you have a better than average understanding of Washington real estate law. See the books mentioned in Chapter 1 and the Appendix—"Language".

_____ At the very least, you'll want to know some basic legal rights/obligations and financial schemes. You must understand your obligation to disclose any problems, and that you can be sued for "specific performance" if you try to back out of a contract. Just saying "sold, as is" does not nullify the requirement to disclose problems.

_____ Get several copies of the contracts you expect to use. If seller-financing will be involved, double-check with an attorney or agent to be sure that you have *all* the right documents.

_____ Read the fine print, front and back, on a purchase and sale agreement. Have a friend or spouse quiz you. Are you entitled to additional compensation for the oil in your tank? Can you take the curtain rods with you? Are you obligated to pay for a pest inspection? Know that fine print.

_____ If the house is to be vacated, look under "Sitting Services" in the Yellow Pages for "professional" house-sitters who are familiar with real estate situations. "Amateur" sitters often advertise in the classifieds.

_____ Make sure you get an attorney's advice on the differences between a lease-option and a lease-purchase before you commit yourself to either. The differences are quite complex and both will entail obligations that the average owner never suspects.

_____ Get advice on backup and contingency offers. These can be complex, but they are cards you want to keep in your deck.

_____ If you are trying to sell your rental property, bone up on "tenants' rights" (how come we never say "tenants' wrongs"?). Seattle's laws especially can be very tenant-favored, and tenants can be the most impossible roadblock of all.

_____ Watch out for the graduates of a git-rich seminar. Besides having unctuous personalities, they often give themselves away by writing incredibly small earnest money checks or promissory notes, and by making offers that ask sellers to "subordinate" their interest in a property, so that the buyer can use the property as collateral for a loan.

## II. GETTING YOUR FINANCES IN ORDER

_____ The seller who is her own agent is also her own broker, and the broker is the purse-string holder who tells the agent the limits on advertising. An expenditure of no more than 0.5%–1% of the selling price will usually suffice, if the price is realistic. Set this amount aside, get the prices of classified ads, and draw up an ad schedule. Vicious cycle: save money by not advertising → fewer people will come to the "auction" → house sold for less than top dollar → all money saved is lost in spades.

_____ Bread and butter, children and dirt, price and *terms*—these things just go together, so the seller needs to study and be able to explain various financing options, i.e. *terms,* and decide which ones are not only acceptable, but even beneficial, in an advertising campaign.

_____ Once you know what terms you can offer, begin to prepare a financing sheet for prospective buyers. Once you have established your price, show how much each option will cost the buyer in down payment, closing costs, and monthly payments. If you also get information and business cards from recommended lenders, it may just help a buyer feel that you have opened one more door and pointed the way.

_____ Contact your lender about prepayment penalties. If you obtained an FHA loan before August 2, 1985, you must give 30 days' written notice of your intent to pay off the old loan, or pay 30 days of interest.

_____ Verify that your present mortgage is or is not assumable. If it is FHA or VA, it is probably assumable, but you'll need some advice on your continuing liability and the methods and terms of assuming it. If you have a conventional loan, write to the lender with your loan number and see if they will permit it to be assumed (allow 30 days for an answer). If yes, get it in writing. If no, have your attorney see if they are just bluffing. Many an attorney has more than earned her fee on an assumption with just one glance at the documents and one letter to the lender. Also consult your attorney if you receive an offer that is "subject to the mortgage." Such an offer is asking you to keep the original loan in your name, which means you will remain "secondarily liable."

_____ Make sure you understand how buyers are qualified by the lenders for loans, especially if you are selling a condo or co-op. The homeowner's dues can easily be overlooked, yet they must be included in the formula for qualifying.

_____ If you will accept seller-financing, then you must review the process for obtaining a credit report on the buyer (Chapter 4, "Strategies for Buyers"), and you mustn't be shy about asking for a buyer's references, place of employment, and financial history. If this makes a buyer fidget, be gentle, but explain that the degree of your risk makes it necessary to ask the same questions a lender would ask. A typed form may make it easier for both you and the buyer. Keep in mind that many buyers who are seeking seller-financing already know that they probably wouldn't meet a lender's standards. See Chapter 11, "Qualifying for a Loan."

---

### 🏠 🏠 🏠
### FSBO A CONDO?

You're thinking of selling your own condo? Well, selling any shelter is sort of like plowing with a mule: It's difficult. But FSBOing a condo? That's more like plowing without the mule.

One of the most common problems occurs with the other owners in the building who have no intention of ever selling and who have given no thought to how their making it difficult to get in the building lowers the chances of your getting the best price. They object to any effort that makes it easy for buyers to visit, say, during an open house. Then they act suspicious of visitors and treat them poorly, just at the moment when a buyer is deciding if she wants to live in that building. Let everyone in your building know you will be selling and that you will appreciate their suggestions. Who knows? They may even know of a buyer.

---

## III. THE MENTAL PREPARATION

____ Sellers can get so wrapped up in financing, advertising, and even cleaning a house that they forget to put their own psychic closet in order. Selling can involve a great deal of tension. The seller who handles stress poorly may handle buyers just as badly. Give some thought now to how you're going to approach the task and the people you will encounter. Don't omit recreation, hobbies, and humor during this time; give some thought to scheduling these important breaks.

____ If you have children, they need to be included in the process. They can add to your problems or lighten the load. Explain that buyers rarely show up when it's convenient. Work out a plan for a blitzkrieg cleanup on short notice. If you have been thinking about a military academy for your teenager, this may be the time.

____ If you're selling rental property and can't afford to have it vacant, then make peace with your tenants. I can think of scores of tenants whose clutter, dogs, odors, and general lack of cooperation have made it impossible to sell a house.

On the other hand, many tenants keep a tidy house and smile through countless interruptions. They endure the invasion of privacy and the threat to their security (advise them to lock up valuables and to check their own renter's insurance). And what will you do for them? Give them 50% off the last month? 100%? Help them move? Let them know at the beginning that they will be rewarded for their cooperation.

_____ Review the summary on negotiating in Chapter 4 and read at least one of the books mentioned. This might also be a good time to pull out one of those pop-psych books such as *I'm OK, You're OK* to remind us of all the reasons and ways to be tolerant. You're likely to encounter more than one test of your patience, from the bargain-hunters who deliberately insult and degrade your castle (they've heard it makes you lose confidence in your price) to the 75 agents who want to know if they can be of assistance.

---

### 48 HOURS' NOTICE

Even ticked-off tenants must allow access within 48 hours of notice. But a great deal of real estate is conducted on "short notice" (as in "impulse buying"), so if tenants demand 48 hours, the chances of selling take a nosedive. Some insist on the full notice and then, at the appointed time, bolt the doors and go out a window, or stay home, cook fish, and make the buyer feel totally unwelcome (no exaggeration). If such a tenant is month-to-month, ask your attorney for advice on raising the rent. Substantially.

---

### ROLE-PLAYING

In my classes for sellers we try our hand at role-playing to demonstrate some of the stressful moments that occur with buyers and the range of attitudes and responses available to sellers.

Many people are uncomfortable with role-playing and feel silly, but it is an excellent way to prepare for some of these situations. One of the sellers below has a slim chance of negotiating successfully. Which one would you resemble?

**Buyer:** "Nice big kitchen—but what's that strong odor?"
**Seller #1:** "I don't know; I can't smell anything but your wife's perfume."
**Seller #2:** "Oh, I'm really sorry; my wife cooked fish last night. Do you folks like to cook a lot?"

\* \* \*

**Buyer:** "Say, who picked out these colors? This place looks like a fruit salad!"
**Seller #1:** "My mother selected those colors. I'll tell her you don't approve."
**Seller #2:** "Aren't those warm colors? If we repainted, would you want to select the colors?"

\* \* \*

I DON'T UNDERSTAND IT.
SEVEN YEARS AND NOT
ONE OFFER!

FOR SALE BY OGRE

_____ Responses to low offers: Keep in mind that you are negotiating a business arrangement. You can read all the books ever written on negotiation, but in a face-to-face encounter, when you're in your homeowner's armor ready to defend the honor of your unique castle, you may get angry with people you would ordinarily like to get to know. Consider copying the following idea and posting it on the bathroom mirror: "Reject offers, not people." Don't underestimate the discipline it takes to abide by those few words. See "Negotiating" in Chapter 4.

_____ Think about what your response to agents is going to be. If you haven't thought about this, you've never tried to sell a house before. The minute you run your first ad you're going to get calls. New agents don't know any other way to contact sellers, and experienced agents are confident they can demonstrate a marketing program superior to yours. After half a dozen calls, you'll think we must all have memorized the same speech. Sort of.

Some agents say they know a buyer who is looking for a home similar to yours, and some of them actually do. Will you pay a "half commission?" If you won't, the agent may lead her buyers elsewhere. On the other hand, you're a dolt if you pay a "full commission." Even if the agent or broker hasn't spent a minute or a dime on marketing your house, a few may ask you to pay for the listing side of the commission anyway. One agent told an owner that since she, the owner, did not have a listing agent he, the agent, would have to watch over both sides of the transaction, and therefore a full commission was appropriate. Hook, line, and sinker, and the rod tip, too.

_____ If you've successfully negotiated the purchase and sale agreement, congratulations, but your house is not sold yet. Leave your sign up at least until the buyers have their loan approval or until you've checked their credit and references. If anyone else calls about the house, have your spouse ready to put an ice cube down your back if you say it's sold. Say this instead: "At this point we have an offer, but we're still awaiting credit information and we'd be glad to accept a backup offer. We can show you the house this afternoon, or would sometime after dinner be better?"

_____ There are plenty of books out there on sales psychology and techniques, and we could have an endless debate on whether you could or should learn those techniques. Without practice you could be so awkward that they might hinder more than help. There is one excellent reason to read about these methods: You will then be aware when someone uses them on you. Sales psychology has gotten much more subtle and gracious. Polite is in, push is out. And the more intelligent the participants, the more likely polite will succeed.

_____ Decide on the minimum earnest money you expect. This can be awkward to communicate, so putting it on your fact sheet may remove this stumbling block. An earnest money of less than 5% of your price may not be a sufficiently strong hold on some buyers; however, Seattle-area tradition is generally in the range of 2%–3%. At least it was before our super-hot market started in the late eighties; then, 5%–10% in earnest money became common, as buyers in multiple-offer situations tried to convince sellers of their solvency.

_____ Keep an eye open for a trustworthy negotiator. Why? Negotiating can require an appearance of disinterestedness that a homeowner may not be able to sustain. When I was selling my own home in 1985 the buyer made a careless remark that made me quite angry. My "professional cool" evaporated, so I turned the negotiating over to my best friend, who managed to keep the deal together. "Pride of ownership" is an asset until—well, until it's time to let someone else do the talking.

## IV. THE RIGHT PRICE

_____ Review Chapter 6, on appraisals, especially if you have any notions about appraisals being consistent or accurate.

_____ Visit at least a dozen open houses in your neighborhood. A major gap in the seller's education lies in not seeing what buyers are seeing. Look at both the competition and your own home through the eyes of the buyers.

_____ Don't depend on your assessed value in determining your price. Many houses and condos sell below their assessed values, and a few sell for almost twice their assessment. Be prepared to explain to buyers the inconsistencies of assessed values and market values.

_____ Neither be naive nor callous in your relationship with an agent who offers to do a Competitive Market Analysis (CMA). The agent certainly hopes you will list with her if you can't sell it yourself. If you are sure that you will not list with any realty but you still ask for a CMA, you are stealing that agent's time. Better to steal her car. It's insured. Of course, if she offers to do the CMA no matter what you tell her, then by all means take advantage of the offer.

_____ Start right now to make an "attitude adjustment," if necessary, on how to price a home. In the first place, fight off all urges to base the price on what you need or want. Buyers are indifferent to any such "need" of yours.

The price must be appropriate for the market in your area. In Spokane I wouldn't add even two percent to what I thought I would get; I'd do my homework thoroughly and try to price it right on the money. "But shouldn't we have some room to negotiate?" you ask. Puh-lease, spare me the cliches. This is not Mexico or a Middle Eastern bazaar. This is Washington, the home of genteel purchasing.

If you overprice, the well-mannered buyer won't disagree with you. He'll wait for you to come to your senses, or go deal with someone who has, if he even sees your house to start with. You may have priced it above the figure where he stops looking.

In Seattle in 1990 we can't say what the best price is. We can only look at recent sales and make our best guess. The secret in a seller's market is to not accept the first offer on the first day, but to wait for other offers.

One of the most confusing things that may happen to a seller in a seller's market is that she may get multiple offers, all for thousands of dollars more than she asked (I said confusing, not bad). She will then say, "I must not have priced it high enough, huh?" It almost sounds greedy, doesn't it? How much should one ask? So much that we only get one offer? In other words, the question is nonsensical; our seller has the benefit of a genuine auction and yet she is second-guessing herself. Don't humans ever know when to be satisfied?

_____ If you are one of the unfortunate ones who insulated with urea formaldehyde, or bought a house containing it, you must disclose the presence of the insulation or risk a lawsuit. Have it tested (see "Laboratories—Testing" in the Yellow Pages), and then leave the lab results where buyers can see them. Even with the most encouraging lab results, you will still have to overcome the fears of a few buyers. Don't try too hard. Just tell them how long you've been in the house and try to look healthy.

## V. MAKING IT SHINE

*That broken pane's for the cat to get in on the porch;*
*if the buyers don't like it, screw 'em.*
— Unsuccessful Seller

_____ Review Chapter 8 on work orders. Every work order you put off until you get an offer is a hurdle a buyer has to jump over. First-time buyers don't jump very high.

_____ Walk across the street and take a good look at your house. Try to remember what attracted you when you first saw it. Now pretend that you are a buyer again and list the things that need attention or any assets that could use some highlighting.

_____ Envision the kind of people you think are most likely to move into your neighborhood. What colors are those people painting their houses? Few things give as sure a return on the dollar as paint. Speaking of colors, light (beige, camel, etc.) carpeting can do wonders for a home. Make sure all the rooms on one floor have the same carpeting, not mixed colors. Carpeting bought on sale will probably cost $14–$19 per yard, installed. A "Swedish-finished" floor, which is also a real attribute, costs $13–$15 per square yard.

_____ Look for opportunities to create interesting focal points, or privacy, with plants. Even a few flowers along the sidewalk can make quite a difference. Wind chimes, wind socks, pruned hedges—these can all say "active, caring people live here."

_____ Consider another cliche with no basis in fact: "Buyers make up their mind in the first 25 feet." Many people buy a house whose exterior turned them off. They went inside reluctantly. All the same, it can't hurt to make our buyers eager to see whether the inside is as nice as the walk from the car to the house.

_____ If the exterior gets any attention, make sure you give the area around the front door extra-special care. A buyer may be standing there, waiting for the door to open, noticing every crack in the siding, every scuff on the door, and every scratch on the lock made by the neighborhood burglar.

_____ If the house will be vacant anytime during the winter (approximately 10 months in Seattle), keep it warm. Not only do cold houses get musty, a cold buyer is not going to take any time to explore and develop a romance.

_____ If the house is vacant it still needs human touches. I have seen rented furniture make *the* difference, especially when the furniture was of a higher quality than the house itself. A couch, a coffee table, a dining room ensemble—not much—just enough to stir a fantasy of class.

_____ If the house is vacant but there have been pets, go back and set off flea bombs every two weeks. Fleas that haven't eaten in two weeks have been known to suck a buyer dry of all blood in 90 seconds. Horrible sight: a fleas-dried human!

_____ If the house is near any persistent sources of noise, there are three partial solutions: a board fence, weatherstripping, and/or music. Storm windows and stone walls are helpful but they are two of the least cost-effective measures known. Weatherstripping is the most cost-effective. The acoustics experts tell us that noise comes through openings and cracks, not so much through walls and doors. They must never have spent a night in a motel.

---

### A CONVINCING RESOURCE

Many of my tips on preparing a house for a sale are similar to those of one of the genuine experts in this endeavor, Barb Schwarz, a Bellevue broker. But mine are condensed and not nearly as convincing as when you hear Barb give a detailed explanation of how and why to do these things. Barb is now a very successful national speaker (formerly one of the most successful agents in the U.S.) who has made a 60-minute videotape on "staging™" your home. She takes you through a house room-by-room, looking at it through a buyer's eyes, and if you follow her methods her tape will pay for itself many times over (you may even be able to get your library to carry it).

Call or write: Barb Schwarz & Associates, Inc., 150 Bellevue Way S.E., Suite 106, Bellevue, WA 98004. (800) 352-7161, or (206) 454-7161.

_____ Take a tip from the Japanese homeowner: There can be great beauty in sparseness. Our materialistic insecurities make us clutter up our homes, which then look smaller than they are. It is also difficult for most buyers to imagine how a home would look with their own furniture and lifestyle. If your wall has 15 photographs, store 13 of them. The buyer needs to be able to imagine her pictures on that wall, not stare at pictures of unfamiliar families or scenes.

_____ Rent storage lockers and fill them with all those priceless items in your basement and closets. Move out every unnecessary piece of furniture that takes up room or brings down the quality of the house. Get rid of the knickknacks!

_____ Clean up the fireplace. Some sellers actually let buyers see that the fireplace is being used as a wastebasket. On the other hand, if you build a nice fire in the fireplace, the buyers know that you are just trying to impress them. Most of them gladly cooperate.

_____ *Assume* your house stinks. There's little chance that a friend, neighbor, or agent will tell any of us that our house stinks, even if we breed badgers and smoke ground-up fish bladders. So don't ask, just assume—especially if you smoke, or have a pet larger than a caterpillar. Air it out, bake lots of cookies, and always keep vanilla near the stove, ready to put a drop on a burner or on a lightbulb.

_____ Sell your pets to a laboratory. Just kidding. But look on them as twice the liability that you think they are. You don't notice the litter box, but buyers do. You don't fear your old dog, but some buyers will. And it's the buyer's peace of mind and comfort you must think of at this time, isn't it? A nice kennel, maybe, or your dearest and best friend? Visit the pet stores for heavy-duty deodorizers.

_____ Create light. Well, not literally, but get in the habit of opening drapes. Put in larger light bulbs. Cut bushes away from windows. And consider the use of white paint and mirrors, which make a room seem brighter and larger.

_____ Evaluate the items that catch buyers' eyes: wood floors, kitchen cabinets, countertops, and even doorknobs and shower fixtures. You can spend hundreds, even thousands, on oak cabinets and Swedish-finished floors, but your return on the dollar will always be unknown. Your return is also unknown on waxing a floor, changing the cabinet knobs, or installing a hand-held shower-massager, but the ratio of expense to risk is certainly more palatable.

_____ If a hardwood floor is covered wall-to-wall, make sure a corner of the carpet can be lifted so that a buyer can confirm the type of wood.

____ Train everyone in the house to keep the lid down on the toilet. The dog will just have to drink out of a bowl.

____ Put yourself in the frame of mind of someone newly in love, preparing for a visit from her lover: set the table with cloth napkins and your best silverware, put fresh flowers on the table, and do all of the other things that make us wonder why we didn't keep the house so inviting all along (wouldn't this be a great time to answer some personals ads in *Seattle Weekly*?). Of course it's assumed that you'll do the more mundane tasks, such as making the beds and washing the dishes.

____ Check the appearance of one last thing: yourself. Do many agents wear suits and ties just because it's the natural thing to do? Hardly. Sure, this is the casual Northwest, and of course you don't want to "intimidate" the buyers, but even the slouchiest of buyers has fleeting flights of fantasy about moving up in the world. We are selling upness, are we not?

If you want to be at least as successful as the professionals, then imitate the professionals. When a buyer visits, your behavior and appearance may influence him more than either you or he suspects.

## VI. COMMUNICATE IT

____ *You* know you are selling your house. Make sure everyone else does. You've already established an advertising budget. Now write out a detailed plan and spend the money. I know, you hope you can somehow sell without spending a dime. Brokers do too. We make a lot of newspaper publishers wealthy and they never say thanks. But there's really not much choice.

____ Think about how to provide easy access to the home. This is one of the major differences between listed and unlisted homes. Agents and their clients come and go throughout the day in listed homes. Do you have a neighbor who stays home and could open your house for a buyer? Pay for this service and give a lot of thought to how you can make it as safe as possible for both your house and your neighbor. This is a high-risk strategy; be very careful.

____ Evaluate any and all concerns of risk and security. Yes, it's possible a "buyer" is casing your home for a burglary. A burglar may also be confident that neighbors will think very little about someone walking around your house. Don't ever hold an open house by yourself; professional thieves often arrive as a couple and then split up to pocket jewelry, etc. Of course, if you've left anything like that out for grabs you're not too swift, are you?.

____ You're probably going to put your phone number on any yard sign. If no one is available to answer during the day, then you may as well have handed the neighborhood burglar a key to your home. Perhaps you can put your business number out there or use call-forwarding.

_____ Use an answering machine sparingly, and don't divulge a lot of information about the house. Buyers are listening closely for reasons why they *shouldn't* come see your house. Keep them curious; talk about "potential," or "flexibility," or "terms."

_____ Notice what kind of yard signs catch your eye and command your respect. Hand-scrawled signs placed in a window or stapled to a house tell the world that a rank amateur seller lives there. Remember: My consumer-students indicated their fear of dealing with another amateur.

_____ A yard sign placed at a right angle to the street, about five feet high, can be seen a block away at an intersection. Turn it parallel to the street and it practically disappears.

_____ Either buy or rent a professional-looking yard sign, or spend hours on a homemade one. Hardware stores and discount stores are selling large FSBO signs now, but most of them are pretty drab, and the colorful ones never seem to be in stock. Very decent homemade signs can be made quite easily with three-inch stick-on vinyl letters. Research says that the most eye-catching color combinations are black and gold, or red, white, and blue. An 18" × 24" piece of plywood is sufficient.

Other sources:
1. Realties. A number of offices have FSBO signs to loan. There is no obligation. Maybe a little.
2. FSBO-oriented companies. Some charge a flat fee instead of a commission. See "Real Estate Consultants" in the Yellow Pages. They may also rent signs.

_____ Make, rent, or borrow up to six professional-looking OPEN signs. Don't get your karma out of kilter by stealing a realty's OPEN signs. They cost close to $25 each and no, they're not covered by insurance, and yes, some of us brokers and agents will call your hand on it. We might loan a few to you, however, just out of appreciation for anyone who would ask.

_____ Educate and prepare yourself to handle your first open house. Attend 8–12 open houses and after each one write down what you liked and disliked, especially about the ways you were greeted and treated by the hosts or agents.

_____ Decide at the beginning that you will answer every visitor's questions with relentless honesty. It's just good business in the long run. Give Mark Twain credit for pointing out that no one is smart enough to remember which lie they told to which person. I once heard a wife tell a "white lie" that contradicted what the husband had already told the buyer. The buyer lost all confidence in dealing with them.

_____ Don't talk too much. Good modern sales skills are built around listening and asking questions. Psychologists have pointed out that you make a lasting impression on someone by asking them about themselves, not by talking about yourself.

_____ Let your house talk about itself. Let people have the joy of discovering the features of your house. You may simply leave a door ajar to encourage them to look. And if a feature needs explaining, tape an explanatory note to it. But guided tours? Not recommended. It's too easy to appear anxious and to communicate that anxiety.

_____ Inform buyers with taped-on notes if a fixture won't remain with the house. This is a "soft" way to communicate some bad news. But don't count on such a note being legal protection against a buyer's claim that the item was included in the price. Your attorney may advise you to write into any agreement which fixtures or plants or amenities you intend to remove. Again, check the fine print on the back of the standard agreements. (Barb Schwarz says that if you leave something lying about you don't intend to include in the sale, the buyers may want it all the more, so put it in storage. You might make an exception for the fireplace insert.)

_____ Tell people what they're looking at and which items will stay. Some sellers have cleverly put notes in the kitchen (or on the fact sheets) that said: "Refrigerator and microwave included with full-price offer." One broker told a funny/sad tale about how he had a "standard" little sign that read "Large master bedroom." He put it in the largest bedroom, which was actually quite modest. The buyers later said that that "large" bedroom was one of the reasons they bought the house. Hook, line, and sinker, again!

_____ Prepare yourself for the invasion of your cabinets and closets. I've seen two older women jump on buyers for opening their kitchen cabinets. They might as well have thrown ice water on them. They couldn't have chilled them any more. This is one reason why agents prefer that owners take a walk when buyers are present.

_____ Pay attention to buyers. You don't need to dog their footsteps, but if you are watching TV, reading, or writing letters, you are putting up a barrier that a shy or respectful person may not want to cross. Agents either stand or sit in a location that is conducive to conversation and away from traffic patterns. You do the same. And turn off the TV!

\_\_\_\_ Once you start to show your property, keep track of the names and numbers of the qualified buyers (not neighbors) who visit. There's an old cliché in real estate that if you haven't had an offer after 30 visitors, you're overpriced. Of course, in some markets it may be three buyers. Nevertheless, if you have overpriced you want to be able to call those buyers later and tell them you've reduced the price.

And you may just want to call and ask visitors if they thought your house was well-priced or if you can do something to improve its condition. Don't expect a lot of blunt honesty, but you might get a clue or two. You may even get lucky and learn of an objection that you can resolve to their satisfaction.

Be sure to keep the names and numbers of visitors until your transaction has closed. If your transaction "flips," you don't want to find yourself all the way back to square one.

It's not easy to get the phone number of every caller and visitor, but it's worth the effort. Here's one stratagem: Meet the buyer at the door, and as you hand him your sign-in book, say, "Hi, if you'll just sign our guest register, I'll get you a fact sheet and a cup of coffee." In other words, you'll reward him if he cooperates. Your guestbook should already have a signature with a phone number beside it. Most people will follow the example given. If there is no example, they will resist being the "pioneer."

\_\_\_\_ Review the books on negotiating and selling mentioned in earlier chapters. No one is a "born salesman." Every good salesperson learned his or her skills—some by reading, some by observing, and some by trial and error. The books nicely summarize what others have had to learn the hard way.

\_\_\_\_ Prepare fact sheets that are filled with facts, not with eloquent descriptions. You may include costs of heating, size of lot, age of roof, amount of insulation, and everything you would want to know if you were a buyer. Be accurate. Many a seller has wished she hadn't included a figure that was later disputed in a court case. If you are not absolutely sure, then omit it.

Buyers consistently want to see utility bills; it's a morbid compulsion similar to stopping at accidents and asking if anyone got hurt.

\_\_\_\_ Distribute fact sheets and invitations to open houses to your neighbors. I once heard a seller say that it was none of her neighbors' business. Wrong! Neighbors have friends and relatives who may be looking for a house.

____ Read the for-sale ads in the paper to see what phrases and descriptions catch your eye. You don't need to be a Steinbeck to write an effective ad. Just a plagiarist.

What is your home's single most attractive feature? What originally attracted *you* to this house? Is that what will attract the next owner? It has been estimated that three items in an ad will answer 80% of a buyer's curiosity: location, price, and size (number of beds/baths). Beyond that you're painting a verbal picture that costs up to a dollar a word.

____ Train yourself to ask every caller or visitor how they learned about your home. Otherwise you'll never know if your ads are catchy or placed in the right papers.

### HOW TO ACCEPT AN OFFER

We give so much thought to how to entice an offer, but so little to how to accept one. Isn't it obvious? If it's a good offer you just grab it and run, before the buyers change their minds. Right? But how would you feel if you were the buyer and someone did that? You might wonder if you had offered too much. You might even look for a way to get out of the deal.

Don't be too eager to accept. I have seen sellers take an hour to decide if they will accept a full-price offer. What was there to decide? Nothing. They just needed that time to grieve and accept the passing of an era in their lives. I also observed that this "struggle" made the buyers feel better too. They didn't feel that they had been taken advantage of, or had paid too much, when the sellers required some time to persuade themselves to let go of their home.

### WHAT CATCHES YOUR EYE?

"No Qualifying"      "UPDATED CHARMER"

"BANK REPO"

Hot!      *Immaculate!*      Downtown Bothell

SOUND & MOUNTAINS      "New In-city"      Walk to mall!

RENT BEATER

"Fruit trees"      FIXER

# TO LIST OR RESIST

The price for which we sell our homes is irrelevant, don't you agree? No? Well, perhaps you're in a bad mood. Will you feel better if I make you the hero of the following movie, *Gorillas Who No List*?

    You, Bobo, and Bebe put your treehouses on the market at the same time, and each of you ask $100,000. Bobo, the FSBO, sells his hut right away for $96,000, but has four work orders which cost $6,000; after the typical closing costs of 3% he nets $87,120. Bebe, another FSBO, sells her home for full price, but she has had to hire Tarzan to settle a territorial dispute so she only nets $84,000.

WHAT'LL IT BE?

Bobo and Bebe called you a chimp, or a chump, when you listed your house, but now you get to beat your chest. You sold your domicile for $99,500, and yes, you had to pay a commission and the same closing costs as the other two, and you did have one work order called, but your agent got the buyer to pay for it. So you netted $90,250. You can eat bananas all the way to the bank.

Is the above script totally make-believe? Not at all. Of course it's exaggerated to make a point, but I have actually seen sellers brag about how they didn't pay a commission and then admit that they took a low offer *and* had some expensive complexities. So they did pay a commission of sorts, and they got nothing in return.

Can we say, then, that as a rule people who list their houses actually net more than those who elect to FSBO? Absolutely not, even though a study done years ago "proved" that the average seller who listed would net about two percent more. Unfortunately the study was performed for the real estate industry, so that makes the results questionable. There is really no way to prove anything about all this.

My intention is merely to make the reader think, a verb given more lip service than energy. If you sell for "top dollar" without paying a commission, and have no costly problems, then obviously you will net the most money. If, however, you don't know how to negotiate a legitimate contract or avoid the costs of work orders, or if you don't have the time it takes to be your own agent, then you may lose more than you save by not paying a commission. Some of my friends have done very well handling their own transactions, but almost the same number have made mistakes that cost them from $6,000–$20,000, mistakes that an agent wouldn't have made or would have had to pay for in an out-of-court settlement. In the end, only you can weigh the pros and cons and decide if the risks and efforts offset the savings potential.

I have done both. I have sold my own property without listing it, and for the same and only reason that anyone else should: to save money (not to show off remodeling skills, marketing ability, and the like). Of course, I had a pretty good idea of how to handle the technicalities. On the other hand, during one tense session I had to let an agent-friend negotiate on my behalf because I lost my objectivity. I have also listed my own property, when I did not have the time to do the marketing and was confident that the agent would bring me an offer I would never have been able to get on my own. In fact, he sold some land of mine for five times what I had paid for it; I would have had a hard time looking the buyer in the eyes without questioning his sanity. I know I would have accepted a low offer, whereas my listing agent could convincingly tell the buyer he was getting a good deal at full price.

This commission thing is never a cut-and-dried issue. I recently saw one of

---

🏠 🏠 🏠
## WHAT DOES "AGENT" MEAN?

Technically, when the word agent is used in a contract it means the entire company. If you list your property with Jane Johnson at ABC Realty, all ABC Realty agents have just been "hired." Jane is just the one who will do the actual marketing work. If Bob Brown, another ABC Realty agent, produces a buyer, Bob still works for you, the seller. Reminder: The agent who lists and markets the property is the listing agent. The agent who works with the buyer is the selling agent. From 60% to 85% of the time, these two roles are played by two different agents. Of course, the listing agent can produce a buyer and do both jobs.

---

my neighbors about to accept an offer for $85,000 less than his home's market value. If he hadn't bumped into an agent, he probably would have taken the offer; even after paying the commission, he netted $75,000 more than he would have pocketed otherwise.

The goal is to sell with the highest possible price *and* net; they must go hand-in-hand. Can that be done without listing the property? Yes. How? By knowing the market, doing a thorough pricing effort, taking sufficient legal safeguards, preparing the home so that it shows well, following a high-energy marketing plan, and, finally, negotiating favorable terms on a contract.

Who can do all of that? Readers of this book. Forgive the immodesty, but if you're motivated enough to buy a book like this to educate yourself about the complexity of these efforts, then I'm fairly confident you have the good sense to be your own agent—or at least to do some of the agent's tasks and net some extra book-buying money.

On the other hand, every year my company lists the homes of many of our former students, who certainly have more than enough intelligence to do a great deal of their own marketing. Instead they elect to devote their time to their own professions rather than to imitating mine for a month or two.

## THE PROS AND CONS CAPSULE

The **advantages** of listing a property include:

**1.** More exposure and thus more people at one's "auction." Remember: The larger a crowd at an auction, generally the higher the sale prices.

**2.** Agent's expertise and objectivity, which usually translates into a home that shows better and appeals to the widest range of tastes.

**3.** Agent's availability to deal with buyers at all hours of the day and be there for that "impulse buyer."

**4.** Agent's experience with other properties, which makes her more aware of the most likely optimum price.

**5.** Agent's knowledge of work orders and financing, which results in numerous money-saving tips (or will, when the agent is knowledgeable).

**6.** Agent's detachment and experience, which results in a better negotiation with the buyer, both emotionally and technically, and produces a contract that won't be an emotional or financial drain later.

The **disadvantages** of listing a property include:

**1.** A conflict of interest if the agent and company are primarily devoted to an in-house sale (sold by either the listing agent or another agent in the same office), and especially in those instances where an agent wants to buy the property.

**2.** An atmosphere of tension, since the agent may take a more aggressive stance in the marketplace than the seller would. Just as an attorney may exacerbate the problems in a divorce by aggressively trying to protect one party, an agent can sometimes be more of an irritant than a salve.

**3.** A net after commission that is simply unacceptable. Yes, most commissions will "only" be from 5%–10% of the price, but if the commission is actually 50%–100% of the equity, then this seller should probably consider all of the alternatives.

**4.** A worse marketing job than the seller could have done herself. A really good agent can do wonders and is worth many tacos, but the seller who chooses poorly or gets unlucky may see incompetence unlike anything she could ever have imagined. One of my agents sold a listing two years ago for a seller who had not *once* seen or heard from her listing agent after the listing agreement was signed. Marketing? That listing agent used the lottery approach: Take as many listings as possible, by hook or by crook, and let them sell themselves. He and his kind make my entire profession look like a bunch of salted slugs, but what he's not doing is not illegal, usually, so it's up to consumers to check out an agent's record and reputation. Check out, then weed out.

## THE SELLER'S ALTERNATIVES

Just as the commission-and-net is not a cut-and-dried issue, neither is the question of whether you play on the FSBO team or the FSBA (For Sale By Agent) team. There are degrees. A seller can do her own marketing and then have an agent step in only to handle technical matters, or an unknown agent may walk up with an offer and ask for a "full" or a "reduced" commission, or an agent might even be hired by the hour for consultation. Let's go over the different types of listings, and then we can better explore some of these possibilities.

## TYPES OF LISTINGS

**1. Exclusive right to sell (ERTS).** This is the most common arrangement. The owner lists with one agent/company, although agents from other companies may have access to the property. If the listing company belongs to a multiple listing service (MLS), then with an ERTS listing it will have to cooperate with the other companies. The drawback of this type of listing is that if the seller finds his own buyer he still has to pay a commission. This makes sense to the industry for two reasons: (1) we don't want to invest a lot of time and money in a listing unless the odds are halfway decent that we'll get paid; (2) without the absolute right to a commission, many a stinky seller and buyer would get together behind an agent's back and strike an agreement, even if the agent's advertising and marketing had brought them together in the first place. In fact, most listing contracts include a "carryover" provision or "extender clause" that prevents this sort of maneuver for months after the contract with the seller expires. Most "ordinary" listing contracts are for 90 days (totally negotiable, of course), and the carryover clause often specifies that for another six months the seller may have to pay a commission if the buyer is someone who saw or learned of the property during the listing period.

**2. Exclusive agency (XA).** Again, the owner only lists with one agent/company, but the XA listing allows the seller to find his own buyer and not pay a commission. Until 1988, the MLS in the Puget Sound area would not accept this type of listing; it meant an increased likelihood of spending hours showing the property without getting paid. But pressure from the Federal Trade Commission forced acceptance of this option. When a property is listed under this arrangement, it must be marked in MLS publications with the XA abbreviation, so there *may* be a bit of a stigma and reluctance on the part of the agents at other companies to show the property. On the other hand, it allows the seller some of the best of both worlds: exposure to many more buyers, and the ability to sell his own listing.

---

**SEE TONNON**

For an expert's explanation of listings and the contracts used by companies and multiple listing services, read Alan Tonnon's *Washington Real Estate Law.* (See Appendix—"Language.")

---

**3. Open**. In this arrangement, the seller can sign a contract with dozens or hundreds of agents, promising only to pay a commission if one of them brings a "ready, willing and able" buyer. The amount of the commission can be different with each agent, and only the agent who brings an accepted offer has any claim. The drawback of this arrangement is that it does not provide the exposure of the MLS. On the other hand, it does encourage those agents signed to an open listing to readily bring their buyers. Some agents are very paranoid about showing a property if they don't have some written agreement with the seller, even though this could be signed when the offer is actually produced. This paranoia boils down to a fear of a behind-the-back move by the buyer and seller. With some justification, I've learned the hard way.

**4. Net**. The seller says, "I want to net this amount, Ms. Agent. Everything over that is yours." This arrangement addresses only the amount of the commission, whereas the three arrangements above are different legal arrangements with different structures and obligations. A net listing could theoretically be any one of the above three types of listing. It is unlikely, however, that any MLS will knowingly accept such an agreement, so it would most likely be used only in an open contract. In the hands of ethical and knowledgeable consumers and agents this can be a very viable and creative way to do business, but the requirements of ethical, knowledgeable behavior make most leaders of the real estate industry dubious that such standards would be consistently upheld. The fear is that the agent won't tell the seller if the property is worth a great deal more than the seller is asking, or won't bring offers for less than the asking price. This type of agreement, then, is usually discouraged. I once had an agent offer me a net listing on his own rental property—anything over $70,000 I could keep—but the property wasn't worth $70,000, so I lost his phone number. Isn't that just like an agent?

## SOME SAMPLE ALTERNATIVES

Companies and individual agents have varying degrees of flexibility and cupidity, so some companies are glad to play ball with new rules and some are

not. Some may even state or imply that the following arrangements are illegal or contrary to MLS rules. Get a second opinion. Or a second agent.

**1. Time-on-the-market rebate (ERTS or XA).** If a seller cooperates in preparing and pricing a property, she can argue that she has saved the agent money. If the property sells in its first day or two on the market, then obviously that listing agent has not expended the same effort as the agent who took an overpriced listing and marketed it for many weeks or months. Therefore, to encourage cleanliness and a reasonable starting price, a company may offer a rebate if the house sells in so many days or before any money has been spent on advertising.

Some agents mightily resist any such strategy. They feel that a commission is sort of like a bet on a horse; if it wins by a nose or ten lengths, they should win the same amount. They may argue that they deserve any windfall or "bonus" for having done a good job (when in reality the quick sale could be attributed to a hot market, not their efforts). They can argue their point of view; you can argue yours. There are many agents. There is always one who will see it your way.

**2. In-house sale rebate (ERTS or XA).** If the seller has agreed to pay a commission of six sacks of kibutnicks, she may argue that she should receive a rebate of one sack if the listing company sells its own listing, and maybe even two sacks if the selling agent and the listing agent are the same person. No agent or company is eager to do this, but some may cooperate simply because the world of business is competitive and we do whatever we have to do to get the business. The company's point of view is that it now has to do "both jobs," the marketing and then the processing of the sale. But obviously, an in-house sale is still a bit of a windfall for management (though usually not for the agents if there are two involved, unless their office pays an in-house bonus). From a capitalist-broker's point of view, all windfalls are richly deserved and make up for the years when we just make ends meet. But consumers are under no obligation to feel charitable toward any business.

**3. Time-commission reduction (ERTS or XA).** Some sellers ask if I will reduce my commission if it takes more than, say, 40 days to sell the property. This supposedly motivates me to market aggressively right from the start. But it does nothing to motivate the seller to price it right or keep it clean, so I would never enter into this arrangement unless there was practically no chance of it taking 40 days to sell. If we reversed this arrangement, i.e. increase the commission if it takes more than 40 days to sell the property, this could seemingly de-motivate the agent. But most agents prefer a $2,500 check for 10 days of marketing to a $2,800 check for 50 days of effort, so most agents would still try to sell the property quickly.

All the same, any seller in a hot market with a clean house in a highly desirable neighborhood who doesn't negotiate a bit on the commission is a bit of a pushover. My kind of pushover.

**4. Consumer participation.** This approach is as wide open as Las Vegas. The home can be listed or unlisted. You can have a commission, a flat fee or an hourly wage, and incorporate any of the options above. I'm simply talking about the seller participating in the marketing. I have had sellers hold their own open houses, buy their own advertising, show their homes, etc. The one thing I do not agree to do is to allow them to conduct the negotiation on their own, and under no circumstances do I share the contract writing.

Entire companies and even national franchises have sprung up offering discounted commissions or flat fees for different levels of good service. There is nothing magical about these ideas; many traditional companies have done such things for years, but they simply didn't make them a large or visible part of their business. The companies that offer these discounted programs are trying to build a better mousetrap, at least in competing with the traditional companies, but they must do a high-volume business in order to survive, which means that they must naturally offer fewer services. The option of variable service should always exist for the consumer, just as the consumer should always be aware of the advantages and disadvantages of the different levels of service.

## WHAT IS A REASONABLE COMMISSION?

The reader may have noticed that I avoid talking about the size or amount of commissions or fees. If I suggest any numbers I could be accused of everything from price-fixing to undercutting my competition to bestial practices, by either colleagues or consumers. We have to keep an open marketplace; free enterprise and competition are best in the long run. On the other hand, informed consumers are an essential part of the process and some readers, especially those from other states, don't have a clue as to what "typical" commissions are in Washington, and they can't just call up a neighbor and ask.

When I ask my students, "What do you think the typical commission on a house in the Puget Sound area is?" they generally answer, "Seven percent!" I then proceed to tell them never to believe that number is set by law. I have personally witnessed commissions from 4% to 10%, and know of others that have been higher or lower. In fact, we have an old tradition (which many agents now hate) of dropping or "sliding" the commission by 50% or so if the sale price is over $100,000. This originated long ago when few houses sold for more than $100,000. In many states, agents typically charge a commission of 6%, which sounds better, until you realize that they don't share our tradition of a sliding commission.

## SOME BUILT-IN LIMITATIONS

**1. The listing side.** In theory, a seller can negotiate a commission of any size, say 50 kibutnicks, but if other agents are making 400 kibutnicks on the average transaction, then why would a successful listing agent want to handle this transaction? And what level of competence will the seller get from an agent who agrees to such a fee?

**2. The selling side.** In our communications with other companies we inform each other of what the seller will pay if we produce a buyer. This is the "Selling Office Commission (SOC)," which most of the time is about half of the entire commission. (We avoid the charge of price-fixing by simply not advertising what the amount of the entire commission is.) Now, if a selling agent sees that she will make substantially less on a property, she may choose not to tell her buyers of its existence. The seller who thought he was clever by negotiating a reduced commission and saving a thousand kibutnicks, may actually lose several thousands by de-motivating those agents. But he may not. It's a risk that cannot be presciently calculated.

**3. The besides side.** Finally, it can be anywhere from foolish to dangerous

### THE FULL PRICE OFFER: ARE YOU OBLIGATED TO PAY?

The listing contract is usually created by a set of promises (the consideration): The agent promises to market the property, represent the seller's interests, and make every effort to produce a ready, willing, and able buyer. The seller promises to pay a commission if those things are done. Notice that I did not say that the seller had to accept an offer or actually close a transaction to be obligated to pay the commission. In other words, there is no law that says a seller must accept *any* offer, but by contract she may have to pay a commission if she receives an offer but decides instead to pull her house off the market. A consumer should fully understand the obligations of a listing contract or consult an attorney; the contracts are written by the industry, so naturally they are very protective of the companies' concerns. The seller may want to check with both her attorney and the agent/multiple listing service about writing in "no closing, no commission."

for an agent or broker to work for unusually low fees. I have had buyers who wanted just "a few hours" of my time and offered to pay a few hundred dollars for it. Since my errors-and-omissions insurance has a $1,200 deductible for any one transaction, and the minute I enter into any arrangement with these buyers I risk paying that amount, I made the decision long ago to send such buyers to an attorney. Somehow these "simple deals" often become very complicated and time-consuming. On the other hand, I have also provided information in literally a few seconds to buyers and sellers, that has saved them thousands of dollars—just one little piece of insider information—and then some of them felt I should be grateful when they gave me a bottle of wine or a free meal. Not only do I sometimes feel insulted, I may also make a point of never returning those people's calls in the future; they lose a resource because of their stinginess or naivete. If it takes me an hour to save a consumer $1,000, should I receive an hour's wage or a healthy percentage of the savings? There isn't any clear answer, is there? But there are two points of view: Consumers must not think that their point of view is the gospel. If they do, they'll be left wondering why their phone calls are never returned.

## TO EARN A COMMISSION

The following services may be offered by agents in your area. The higher the commission the more likely the consumer will feel entitled to all or most of these services, and the reverse may also be true: The lower the commission, the fewer services the agent may feel obligated to provide. Let's assume that the agent belongs to a multiple listing service; if he doesn't and if he is asking for a commission as large as the agent who does belong to one, then that seller should ask some hard questions about how the nonmember will bring as many buyers and as many equally high offers.

**1. The yard sign.** In some cases, a seller does not want or is unable to place a yard sign; for example, the seller doesn't want tenants to know that the property is for sale, or a neighborhood or project has rules against signs. Nevertheless, the yard sign is one of the most important marketing tools. The buyer who calls a company after seeing the sign has already seen the house and neighborhood, and if she is still interested we are "halfway home."

The agent who doesn't place a yard sign right away may be trying to sell the house herself and not split the commission. This is often at odds with the seller's interests, so the seller is within his rights to insist that that sign go up immediately.

**2. The multiple.** This is one of the few claims to genius that the industry can make: Competing companies cooperating in such a way as to offer a unique service to both buyers and sellers. Sheer brilliance! This system consistently brings more buyers to the seller's door, and thus the best possible price should evolve. Of course, the system breaks down frequently, especially when uninformed sellers allow it to. A company naturally wants to sell its listing within its own ranks, and in some cases this causes no harm, but the seller is paying for and is entitled to the advantages of the full exposure of the multiple listing and should insist on it.

---

### THAT E-WORD

The yard sign may say "an exclusive listing of..." See the information above about exclusive listings. The word misleads some consumers into thinking they must call the listing office, when in reality they can call any company. It's an unfortunate bit of marketing that doesn't do anything for my industry's credibility, but it's more of a disadvantage to the misled buyer than to the seller.

In a hot market where receiving numerous offers is the norm, the seller may have to "avoid" offers for a few days, until he is sure that other companies are aware of the listing and are showing the property. In a lukewarm market, the seller should ask to see a copy of the listing information in the listing catalog. This is one way to catch typos and mistakes that could lead to misunderstandings and even lawsuits. It also keeps the bad-apple agents from pocketing the listing.

**3. The open house.** This topic can start an argument among agents any day. Are open houses productive or a waste of time? It's a nice tradition that allows buyers to learn a lot about what's on the market, but whether it amounts to effective marketing, that's another question. Most agents tell you that a minority of houses are sold to someone who saw them at an open house, but there may still be something to say for the process. Each visitor *is* a potential buyer, and is also someone who can tell other buyers about the property. And half of the reason the tradition exists is to benefit the agents. They can meet many buyers and hopefully make appointments with them to show them properties later in the week. But the better the agent, the more likely she has all the buyers she wants and the less time she has to spend on open houses. She may give reasons why open houses don't work, or she may get a relatively new agent in the office to hold the house open.

---

### "MY AGENT NEVER SHOWED MY HOUSE!"

Almost every week I overhear or read of a seller who complained that her listing agent never once showed the house to any buyers. That agent has indeed made a mistake, but it wasn't necessarily in not showing the house. It was in not making it clear that showing the house is not her primary or even secondary goal, at least not in an area served by a multiple listing service. The listing agent's job is to market the property, i.e. to disseminate information to the public and to other agents. If 50 other agents bring their buyers, and if the listing agent is there taking the seller's side in negotiations, then the listing agent is doing exactly what she is paid to do.

---

**4. Broker's opens.** This is an open house in the middle of the week with the purpose of encouraging other agents to come view the property. Each neighborhood is usually "assigned" one particular day of the week. The listing agent may even provide food to entice these other agents. The cooler the market, or the worse the house, the better the food. When times are bad, we make a map so that we can get a full meal, soup at the first house and dessert at the last. Consumers are normally welcome to drop in. Wash your hands before you eat, and don't ask for a doggie bag. They're reserved for first-year agents.

**5. Fact sheets.** This is a minor service, but it can have a major impact, and it is one area where we see enormous differences in quality. Some agents handprint a skimpy fact sheet; some have one typeset, complete with a nice picture. A professional-looking piece of literature may signal an organized and safer transaction to some buyers. Proofread this sheet carefully for accuracy; a seller could be held responsible for errors in its contents, such as an incorrect square footage.

**6. Mail outs/invitations.** This service can take so much time that the more experienced and busier agents may not offer it as eagerly as a new agent might. It can range from mailed announcements to neighbors or other agents, all the way to hand-delivered invitations to neighbors for an open house. Neighbors love these, and often come out of curiosity—who knows, they may have a friend or relative who is looking for a house.

**7. Newspaper advertising.** It would be a broker's dream to sell every house without having to make the newspaper publisher wealthy. But how? Actually, the yard sign and the multiple listing service are believed to sell more houses than newspaper ads, but sellers want and expect ads, so most brokers struggle with some sort of compromise. If we have to promise newspaper ads to get the listing, then we usually bite the bullet, and pray that we'll be lucky and sell the property before we've sunk too much into them.

Too few companies and consumers try to work out some sort of creative compromise about advertising. A seller may agree to a "full commission" in order to be guaranteed advertising, without ever thinking that a discounted commission in which the seller pays for the advertising could be many hundreds of dollars cheaper. After all, the real estate company is going to make a profit on those ads if it can.

**8. Representation.** Although the agent is obligated to provide representation, it doesn't necessarily mean that the seller will get much of it or that it will be of very high quality. Specifically, it means that the agent should be available to answer calls from other agents and to inform and motivate them about the property. He should also be available to answer "sign calls" from consumers, and should know and tell the fine points of the property. Instead, some agents encourage low offers without authorization. Admittedly, many listings are overpriced, although we may not know this until they have been tested on the marketplace, but the agent who encourages low offers without authorization from the seller is blatantly violating the standards of the fiduciary duty, probably because he or she simply doesn't have sufficient spine to confront the seller about the price.

The listing agent must also be available and skilled in representing the seller's interests in the negotiations and the contract, and in following up with the selling agent to see that deadlines are met, financing is obtained, repairs are completed, etc.

## COMMON QUESTIONS

**1. Bonuses.** If the selling agent (not the listing agent) is offered a bonus (by the seller), with or without a condition, such as requiring a full-price offer, is this likely to be productive? This is probably a yes-no-maybe-sometimes strategy. Yes, it catches agents' eyes, but most aren't going to let it influence them to the extent that they'll show a house that they wouldn't otherwise show. And no, it won't be of much benefit if the house is overpriced, because few agents can or will persuade a buyer to pay "too much." I would reserve bonuses for houses with a complication—being a little off the beaten track or only accessible at certain times.

**2. Exceptions.** Can a seller write the name of a potential buyer (someone who saw the property before the listing was taken) on the listing contract and not pay a commission (or pay less of a commission) if that person buys the property? Yes. Until the Federal Trade Commission recently forced Washington multiples to accept listings with exceptions, the only way a seller could do this was to get the listing agent to agree to a release.

**3. Subagency.** Is the seller responsible for the actions of agents other than the listing agent? He may be. This is indeed one of life's inequities: A subagent may tell a lie or fail to disclose some problem and thereby leave the seller liable for a lawsuit. A number of real estate educators have been advocating a change for years in the policy of automatically extending subagency to all agents in a multiple listing service, but there has been little headway. A seller should consult with an attorney about the possibility of writing "subagency not offered" into a listing agreement. Another strategy might be to quiz the selling agent at the time of the offer; if he has strong ties or loyalties to the buyer then insist that he represent the buyer instead.

**4. Realty purchases.** Should a seller expect to get a good price for her property from one of those companies that promises to buy the house if they can't sell it? Why, of course, if she will simply leave out enough milk and cookies for Santa, and wish on a falling star, and never step on a crack, and never, ever break a mirror. Those companies are not interested in making money; they just like to do charitable things, so there is no reason on earth to suspect that they would ever make a low offer that would benefit them more than it would a seller. No reason.

**5. The lockbox.** The lockbox is a small weatherproof box containing keys to the house or condo. Agents have a master key or know a combination to open this lockbox. Is a lockbox really necessary, especially when it increases the chances of theft? The new "recording" lockbox in the Puget Sound area has made theft by that route relatively rare (although a seller who leaves money and jewels in the open is still as thick as an Omaha steak), and the box is an important tool for allowing and encouraging agents to show the property. I'll admit that in my busiest moments I have ignored properties that required me to go to the listing office to get the key. A shady listing agent could even urge the seller not to have a lockbox so that the likelihood of an in-house sale is increased; this could result in a lower offer to the seller and another violation of the agent's fiduciary duty.

---

### WHY AGENTS DON'T CALL

One of the most frequent complaints by consumers is that "my agent never called." I have been guilty of not calling as often as I should, all because I was embarrassed that I didn't have anything to tell the seller. When you've tried every marketing trick you know for two months and no offer has surfaced, you get tired of making excuses, so you start dreading the call and praying for the miracle. This isn't the seller's responsibility, but I hope she can find it in her heart to make a call occasionally herself and let the agent know that she just wanted to keep in touch. It helps to know that the seller isn't mad when we haven't scored, much less won the game. Thanks. I feel better. It's our fault. Humans are frail. So are agents. Only mothers are perfect.

---

### FINDING THE GOOD LISTING AGENT

Some of the qualities of a good listing agent are well known and universally sought—honesty, reliability, and competence. So we'll assume here you are already looking for those, and only want some specific guidelines or some tips on how to check out agents.

People have chosen their listing agents for any and all of the following reasons:

**1.** Listed a neighbor's property.

**2.** Came recommended by a friend or colleague.

**3.** Assisted the seller in her attempt to FSBO for a while.

**4.** Presented an impressive market analysis of properties in the area.

**5.** Regularly writes a local newsletter.

**6.** Presented evidence that the house would sell for more than any other agent seemed to believe.

Well, we were doing OK until number six. The first five were good examples of how you might find out something meaningful about the agent. Number six tells us more about the seller: She may be a greedy sucker. That's greedy and a sucker. No intelligent sellers ever fall for that old trick, do they? No, we must choose the listing agent because of his reliability and because of his marketing program. The agent with the best program will get the best price, not the one who makes the biggest promises. This should be obvious, but I recently listened to a CPA admit that even he chose the agent who made the biggest promise. Greed overruled logic. So what's new?

**References.** Ask for them and check them out. One of my students even went so far as to check the public records, where she found that a broker she was depending on had almost 100 lawsuits filed against him.

**Past work.** Ask for copies of fact sheets provided other sellers, and what steps were taken to sell unusual properties. It is often difficult for a consumer to catch technical errors in a fact sheet or in the listing catalog, but sometimes

---

**ASK THE PROS**

In Chapter 4, "Strategies for Buyers," we went over some ways to find good agents, including asking loan officers and real estate attorneys who are likely to know both the good and the bad agents. Be listening for any name that gets repeated.

the errors are so large that even a child could see them, so do look.

**Resumes.** Some agents are going to offer a resume without being asked. Others won't have anything prepared, and an interview may have to suffice. As one who interviews and hires people frequently, I find that resumes do tell me something about a person's values; for example, their ability to be neat when it counts. Anyone who fills out contracts had better be a t-crossing i-dotter. I'm also going to be looking for "confusion," or lack of direction. But, people do change and grow up, so past history isn't the whole story.

**Reputation.** Few consumers seem to be concerned with an agent's reputation among other agents, but then most never realize that if an agent does have a bad reputation in the industry, other agents may avoid showing the property. This can be checked out fairly easily by asking around, but don't be surprised if you feel a little bit sneaky. Only you know if you will be comfortable doing this. In any case, don't demand perfection; it comes at too high a price.

One of the most colorful cads I've ever known in the business told a seller that he, the agent, was the company broker. The seller didn't even bother to verify this, when in reality the agent had only been in the business about two months. He was smooth.

**Size of company.** The size of the company, whether we're talking about the individual office or a franchise, is probably the least important consideration and the most frequently overrated factor. If the company can provide the services and support that an agent requires, then the rest is up to the individual agent. The seller is primarily hiring a responsible human individual who will be reliable and attentive, not a parking lot full of Volvos or an exquisitely appointed foyer.

Occasionally I grumble about some of the smallest offices not having good phone coverage on weekends or evenings, and then I remember that some of the very largest companies are guilty of the same thing, so it's usually policy, not size, that determines a company's ability to provide good service. The full-page Sunday ads that some larger companies buy are very effective at impressing sellers (and lead to more listings), but as one who has worked for both large and small companies I must say I never saw those large ads produce any more, or even as much, in results as small, well-written, individual ads on weekdays. In the end, the most important thing will be the integrity and competence of the individual agent. Sellers should keep their priorities in order and never forget that they are always just one mistake away from a lawsuit.

**The walk-through.** If there is one way to find out if an agent will have good tips on selling and/or dealing with work orders, it is by touring the house with him. Ask lots of dumb questions, such as: Do you think this house will need to be rewired? How can we tell if the outlets are grounded? What floor plan improvements could be suggested to a buyer? etc.

**Full-time.** Do yourself and my industry a favor: Absolutely refuse to work with a part-time agent. Most agents find they need to be available from 60–80 hours a week; there's simply no telling when they will be needed. Part-timers may not be there when needed, and may not be aware of recent changes in financing and law, so they place everyone in jeopardy. Our work has become too complicated to accommodate amateurs, and that's all most part-timers can ever be. (I apologize to part-timers in small towns where it may be difficult or impossible to make ends meet with real estate commissions or any other single source of income.)

---

### A BACK-UP

An offer on a property can materialize at almost any hour, and agents do occasionally like to take a day off, go to a movie, etc., so we can't expect one to be available all 168 hours of the week, but someone from that company should be. It is a good idea to have the home numbers of at least one other agent and the broker. Oh hell, just get the entire company roster.

---

# MONDO CONDO

### BENEFITS VS. SACRIFICES
### DIGGING UP THE DETAILS

"**W**ell, I say condos are cells in a prison of volunteer inmates, and co-ops are cells in a prison run by old folks," said Danny Dimview.

"Oh, you're about as enlightened as a mushroom, and rooted in the same stuff," replied Carol Careerminded. "They're *options*, a way to build equity without having to spend all of your spare time maintaining the place. And how else could I feel so secure and afford to have my own pool?"

"Right, Alcatraz with pizazz," rejoined Danny.

"No, a home in a neighborhood of like-minded people, you shiitake!" answered Carol.

Obviously, this argument could rage on forever. It goes on in my own mind, because I have held both views at the same time, having lived in a Seattle condo for two mostly pleasant years. Pleasant, at least, until bedtime. A hallway and the building's parking garage, which had an automatic door built for a Boeing hangar, were right outside the bedroom window. And the building had *multitudes* of youthful renters who came and went all night long in search of their primeval needs: Brie, Perrier, and Bud. Renters are even genetically noisier than owners. That's in the Bible somewhere. "For they shall carouse until the wee hours, until thou dost foul thy mouth with admonitions and load thy chambers with ammunition." Tenants also like to leave their mark in other ways, such as by carving concise philosophies into the new elevator doors. That's helpful, in a way: The building's repair funds won't get so large as to attract people who want to launder money.

Condos also have bylaws and morelaws. And meetings. Every month owners may meet and make decisions, like how much to bill themselves for a new roof. What a country! Of course you don't *have* to attend the meetings of the "association." You can just wait and see how much you billed yourself. That way you don't have to listen to the infighting, or the tenants whining because they can't vote.

On the other hand, the positive comments at the beginning of this chapter about the amenities, the security, and having fewer maintenance concerns are often true. For those who cannot afford a house, buying a condo presents an opportunity to step onto the first rung of homeownership and build equity. Many condo neighbors coalesce into tight-knit groups that look out for each other, and since some 30,000,000 people now benefit from this type of habitat, we can assure any would-be purchaser that it is a part of city life that is here to stay and probably will increase in popularity.

Life in a condo can have its own unique set of benefits, just as it may have its own set of problems. The potential buyer has two distinct challenges: (1) to find out what a condo's problems are before the final signature, and (2) to find out if you have the right temperament for this lifestyle. If I seem to lean away from condos, don't mind me; it has something to do with this one night I spent in my BVDs chasing two renters with a canoe paddle.

---

### STRUCTURAL INSPECTIONS?

Many condo buyers are perplexed as to the need for a structural inspection. There's "so much less" for the inspector to look for. Or is there? In one inspection, 26 flaws were discovered in a Seattle condo building; the inspector highlighted the nine major problems, and the builder corrected all nine of them. In another probe the inspector pointed out that the roofing material had not been correctly applied. A copy of the report was then given to the board of directors, who could have taken a "we'll have to budget for that" position. Instead they approached the builder, who agreed to fix it at his expense (I would have asked the board to reimburse me for that inspection, you bet).

One of the most serious mistakes a buyer can make is to assume that all condos are alike. We have a building in Seattle that in its first four years has required $448,000 in repairs. I have seen a six-year-old building that had to have all new siding, and in one older building that was converted to electric heating, the wiring had been done incorrectly. After reviewing the above situations and interviewing Gabriella Girvalo, a Seattle agent who specializes in condos and who supplied many details for this chapter, I have come out foursquare for the inspection.

---

## THE CONDO

A condominium is technically a type of ownership (from the Latin "owning together"), and can be a townhouse, cabin, etc., but it has generally come to mean an entire apartment building built (or converted) by a developer who then sells said apartments (and perhaps keeps some for rentals). The term "condo" has also come to refer to each of the individual apartments. In order for the units to be sold they must have been recorded or registered under a master deed called "The Declaration." The declaration will contain a description of the individual apartments, provisions for bylaws, and the rights and liabilities of the individual owners. A survey map and a set of plans must also be on file.

CONDO LIFE HAS ITS SURPRISES

I TOLD THE COUPLE UPSTAIRS I COULD HEAR *THEIR* STEREO EVEN BETTER THAN MY OWN, SO NOW THEY WANT ME TO MAKE HALF THEIR PAYMENTS.

Unless 70% of the condo units are owner-occupied, it is either difficult or expensive to get bank financing (a 25% down payment usually eliminates most owner-occupancy questions). Lenders and agents often have lists of FHA or conventional "approved buildings." There is an even larger VA-approved list ("easier standards"), which lenders also accept for FHA financing if there is a 51% owner-occupancy. New condos can be especially tricky in this little financing challenge; for conventional or FHA financing they must have been built to FNMA or FHA specifications, which not all builders want to deal with. If these standards have been met, then a special financing arrangement probably exists for even the very first buyers in that building.

The complexities of buying new units, especially those still under construction, are so numerous as to make me wonder why anyone would ever do it. Well, the answer is sometimes obvious when you get a breathtaking view, or get to pick the appliances and carpeting, etc. Nevertheless, one should work with an experienced agent *and* attorney from day one. There are endless horror stories of buildings not being finished on time, or ever, and of builders who did not relinquish control on the project even when 51% of the units were owner-occupied. On the other hand, one reputable Seattle builder seems to make a point of living in his new projects for a while as a testament to their soundness. I wonder if he fixes leaking faucets?

The buyer purchases an "air lot." This is a legal term for a unit of real estate that may exist at, below, or above ground level, but which consists more of air than of studs and concrete. All of the unit owners become voting members of that building's association and thereby retain ownership and control of common areas (with each owner having an "undivided interest"), from hallways to parking lots. The association retains ownership of the walls and all that is contained therein, such as plumbing and wiring. So the individual owner only owns the "surfaces"—drywall, tile, wallpaper, carpeting, etc.—and all that is between the walls (appliances, tubs, toilets, and cabinets).

If a pipe bursts inside a wall, the owners' association is usually responsible for the damage to and inside the walls, but the damage inside the apartment has to be paid for by the individual owner's insurance, unless the association was negligent in some way, such as by ignoring a warning.

Some areas, such as patios, may be known as "limited common elements (or areas)," and may also be the responsibility of the association to maintain or repair, even though only one owner has the use of them. Only a careful reading of the condo's declaration outlines the extent of the individual's rights and responsibilities.

## THE CO-OP

The cooperative method of ownership often starts with a single-building owner who, little by little, transfers his interests to an entire group of residents. These residents buy shares of stock in a corporation, which owns the building, but their individual rights to inhabit and use the various units are guaranteed by a "proprietary lease," not by purchasing the individual apartments. For an explanation of this proprietary lease and other legal aspects of condos and co-ops, see Alan Tonnon's *Washington Real Estate Law.*

Until 1963 the condominium form of ownership was not legally recognized in Washington, and thus the co-op enjoyed quite a head start and period of popularity in the forties and fifties, especially for retired persons. However, the number of condos has grown for over 25 years (there are presently over 400 projects in downtown Seattle alone), and the number of co-ops has probably declined in that time, since some have been converted to condos. Approximately 40 cooperative associations remain in Seattle at this time. Since condos have begun to sell very rapidly, there has been some "carryover" in the appreciation and prices of co-ops, but it is too early to know the extent of this increase.

The differences between condos and co-ops are not "mere technicalities," but are so significant as to have created a measurable difference in the price per square foot. First of all, all the co-ops I know of in Seattle are older apartment buildings, usually converted into this arrangement. They are often very stylish, for example, "The Castles of Capitol Hill," built by Frederick Anhalt in the thirties and forties (ironically, some of the Anhalt buildings have also been converted into condos). But stylish or not, they are often "cheap." This is partially due to the fact that becoming a shareholder is often as difficult as joining an exclusive country club. Why?

Remember when Richard Nixon was once turned down for a co-op in New York City? Did it have anything to do with his moral turnips? No, it was the owners' fears of the disturbance and noise from newshounds. Co-op owners want *quiet* neighbors, preferably those who are estranged from their own children with no reconciliation in sight.

In Seattle I have watched co-op buyers wait several months for the owners to leisurely assemble and interview them. Then the owners have wanted to be sure that the new buyers did not like hard rock (as in music), that their pets did not weigh over 3.5 ounces or emit sounds over six decibels, and that they were not investors who intended to rent the unit.

Is it the eccentric nature or the advanced age of most co-op owners that explains this exclusive, keep-'em-out attitude? Not necessarily. They have a legitimate concern that the condo owner does not have: All co-op residents share the legal, financial, and tax liabilities for the whole building. If a *condo* owner doesn't pay her homeowner's dues or taxes, the association or county government, whichever is appropriate, can "attach" her individual unit. But if a co-op member can't pay his share of the taxes, it may become the entire corporation's problem. In other words, everyone may have to chip in. Thus, finding shareholders who are dependable and solvent, and who will not drive away other dependable types, is a realistic goal from the corporation's point of view. However, by their often lackadaisical approach to meeting with purchasers, and/or their inflexibility, they can make the selling process very difficult.

This, plus the general lack of bank financing (more on this later), may severely limit the units' values.

## HOMEOWNER'S DUES AND INSURANCE

First-time buyers may not be aware of the importance and complexities of homeowner's dues. These dues must be paid just as regularly as the mortgage payments, or else the association or other owners can take legal steps to collect them, even attaching a lien to the unit in the case of the condo. And one must never forget that for loan-qualifying purposes, the dues are figured right in as if they were part of the payment.

Although a portion of the dues goes for insurance on the building, this type of insurance does *not* cover the contents of the individual units. An individual "customized policy" is necessary. If the buyer is getting a loan, he will have no choice but to obtain such a policy. A potential tragedy for the buyer could occur if the seller sold by creative financing or allowed an assumption without requiring the buyer to furnish proof of insurance on the unit. This would require quite a combination of naiveté and penny-pinching on the part of the buyer, but it could happen.

---

### THE LEASE SCANDAL

A common scam of the past was for a builder to sell the units but retain ownership of the pool or clubhouse and then lease it to the owners. One Florida builder collected around $300,000 a year on a single pool. Such leasing arrangements are now rare. They are also unacceptable for VA and FHA financing.

---

There are some technical differences in how the elements of the condo's and co-op's dues may qualify for tax deductions, and in the purposes for which they are collected, but the methods and controls are basically the same. Each month an owner contributes his share to pay for upkeep of the grounds, a reserve fund for future repairs, insurance on the common areas, etc. When considering purchasing a co-op, if the dues seem unusually high keep in mind that the taxes are included (whereas they are paid separately in the case of a condo), but it may also partially be explained by the building's heating bill; with co-ops it is not uncommon for there to be just one central-wheezing plant. This will be the case with some of the older condos as well. A lender may require that any building with central heating carry a very large insurance policy, which the lender will ask to see, even in cases where the heating plant is not a concern.

So the homeowner's dues may naturally be somewhat higher in some of the older buildings, but one of the lesser-known problems for condo buyers is an artificially low assessment on a newer building. The builder may have estimated too low or even be holding back bills to keep the dues low until the units are sold. If the dues are noticeably less than those of other buildings in the area, some suspicion and investigation are in order.

## GOOD BUY OR OVERVALUED?

Are condos a good buy, and if so, then aren't the usually cheaper co-ops an even better deal? Let's answer the second question first: Are co-ops a bargain, keeping in mind that all bargains are relative? If the owner is happy with the location, size, atmosphere, and neighbors, and if the owner intends to live there a long time and either doesn't have sufficient income for a condo or prefers to invest the difference in some other manner, then yes, we might say that the co-op is a bargain. At this time in Seattle (1990), you can buy a one-bedroom downtown co-op (770 square feet) for as little as $35,000, whereas the low end for a comparable one-bedroom condo was more in the neighborhood of $55,000. The most expensive co-op noted was $99,500 (two bedrooms, 1,000 square feet). Two-bedroom condos started at $85,000, and the most expensive condo was $2,500,000 (one priced at $4,700,000, complete with pool and ballroom, was on the market last year). Finding a two-bedroom condo with secured parking for under $130,000 is becoming difficult.

Comparing four more-or-less typical co-ops with condos that are similar in size, I found that the per-square-foot costs averaged $57 and $85, respectively. However, the two-bedroom condo with secured parking starts at around $120 per square foot. To put this in perspective, the typical three-bedroom house in North Seattle (one to four miles away from downtown), depending on the style, with the land excluded, presently averages around $65–$85 per square foot of *finished* space. (So many sellers and agents incorrectly include the basement, garage, etc., that the actual average was closer to $45–$50, but that leaves us with even more of an apples-to-bananas comparison.) As you may have noted, if a condo comes anywhere close to resembling a house in amenities and size (bedroom count), it may be much more expensive than a house on a square-foot basis—but as I have said elsewhere, we don't appraise poetry by weighing it and we can't judge real estate solely on the basis of square-footage.

Thus far we have determined that the cost per square foot of a co-op is definitely lower than that of a condo or house, but we have to consider the whole picture. In the first place, since the co-op is not real estate in the eyes of the lender and is therefore ineligible for ordinary financing, it generally requires seller financing. This may seem like an advantage, until one considers that this often means a cash transaction or a relatively large down payment.

(A Seattle lender recently made the first co-op loan that we have heard of—a conventional "share loan." If these become commonplace it could mean a substantial increase in the popularity of this type of habitat. Why haven't lenders been eager to make loans on co-ops? If the buyer fell behind in his payments, what would the lender foreclose on? Shares in a corporation?)

When the economy is not booming there are few things harder to sell than a co-op. Co-ops don't generally provide the return due to appreciation that a condo or house will provide. And even if you can acquire the group's approval to rent the co-op unit, the tax advantages are likely to be less than from owning real estate, which can be depreciated. But as I stated earlier, if you intend the unit to be a long-term residence, or even the final residence, it can be cozy and cheap, and because of that procedure of being interviewed and approved by all of the other members, a very homogeneous group of neighbors may exist or evolve. There is one last factor to consider: "carryover" appreciation that occurs when condos become temporarily "rare."

As for the condo, the other species of close-knit living, the Seattle market has recently filled its sails after years of drifting in a calm. Although most of us don't expect to see prices appreciating at the same rate as for houses, we already see measurable increases (toward the end of 1989 houses in Seattle had appreciated over the previous year at the rate of 23%—another study said 42%—whereas condos appreciated 17%, bringing the average price to $95,000). This is heartening for the long-suffering owners, but frightening for the buyers, many of whom wish they had bought prior to 1990.

Why did condo prices stagnate for so long? Possibly because they were overvalued to start with, and because of overdevelopment. In 1979 over 10,000 condo units were built around Seattle, followed shortly thereafter by record interest rates and unemployment. Owners couldn't sell, and condos were labeled the worst possible investment, a label that has only recently begun to peel away. Also, when condos were still the new kid on the block and just beginning to develop a little popularity with retirees, singles, and career-focused types, the method of pricing was frequently based on a theory that they should cost 20%–25% less than the average house in that area. Looking back, one could argue they should have been 40%–50% less, especially when we compare them on a square-foot basis. It is entirely possible that condos started at too high a price and, in a good market when all properties were generally appreciating, the buyers simply weren't circumspect enough; they incorrectly assumed that condo values would rise. Ironically, we're seeing the same phenomenon now in houses: Buyers are paying top dollar and then some, believing—hoping—that appreciation will cure any mistakes on their part.

##  THE WASHINGTON CONDOMINIUM ACT

Effective July 1, 1990: To learn the details of the various ways in which the state has tried to protect the rights of condo purchasers, secure a copy of the Washington Condominium Act (Senate Bill 5208) by contacting the Attorney General's office or an agent or attorney who specializes in condos.

## AGENT ACCESS

One of my goals has always been to foster and balance self-reliance with advice or assistance from experts or resources. When it comes to the freestanding house the consumer can be very independent, but this can change drastically with condos. Many buildings are quite restrictive about the entry of strangers, as well as the use of for-sale signs or lockboxes. In some cases, the only way to know that a unit is for sale is to have an agent go through the listings. As the consumer reads through the steps below, she may conclude that finding an agent with condo experience is essential. I would have to agree in most cases. We know of one instance where it took four agents to finally track down the building's bylaws, obviously a formidable task for a consumer. Obviously formidable for three of the agents, too.

## TEN TIDBITS

In making an offer or analyzing the value of a condo, here are some of the questions that you will want answered. Although many of the same questions could be asked about co-ops, there are enough complexities and differences with co-ops that I recommend that a buyer seek out the rare attorney who has handled co-op sales. Don't try to be too self-reliant on this one.

**1. Standard forms.** The Purchase and Sale Agreement (Form #28) that we now use in the Puget Sound area for condos requires the seller to provide copies of the Declaration, Bylaws, and Rules. If after reading them the buyer disapproves, she has to state her disapproval before a deadline or else it will be assumed that she has none. The buyer's attorney may also recommend that she ask for copies of the budget/financial statement, any insurance policies, maintenance and/or management agreements, and minutes of the last year's meetings. As of July 1, 1990, all Washington sellers of a "used" condo must provide a "Resale Certificate." This certificate will require the seller to provide some of

### THE RESALE CERTIFICATE

This certificate requires that the seller furnish all of the following information or documents, in addition to the declaration, bylaws, and rules or regulations:

1. Any right-of-first-refusal information.

2. Amount of the homeowner's dues, and any outstanding assessments.

3. Any other fees owed.

4. Any anticipated building expenses exceeding 5% of the annual budget.

5. The amount of the reserves, and any allocations for future projects.

6. A balance sheet of the association, current to within 120 days.

7. The current operating budget of the association.

8. Any unsatisfied judgments or pending lawsuits.

9. Summary of the insurance coverage.

10. Any alterations to the unit or limited common elements that violate the declaration.

11. Number of units owned by the "declarant," and if control has passed to the association. Get your attorney to explain this needlessly confusing term, if he can. Say "builder," boys and girls.

12. Any violations of building or health codes.

13. Any pertinent leases (it may still be a good idea to inquire separately about the percentage of renters in the building).

NOTE: The purchaser has until five days after receipt of the certificate to cancel the sale. The certificate may have at least one major flaw: The information provided "is not guaranteed by the undersigned...." Unless the seller had reason to know that the information was inaccurate, the buyer is stuck. The seller can pass along bad or outdated information provided by the association, and is not liable for the association's failure to provide the information in a timely manner.

the above documents, plus other information about anticipated repairs, any pending lawsuits, etc. (The condo purchase and sale agreement should not be used for a co-op; see an attorney for the appropriate forms.)

**2. Another so-called standard form**. Some listing agents have their sellers fill out a "Form 17B—Property Information Form." This form has 57 questions that cover a wide range of concerns (it even asks if there are any landfills in the area). The purchaser can insist on seeing a copy of this, but the seller doesn't have to comply. The seller who doesn't comply will of course arouse concerns all the more. If the buyer is still interested in the property, then he might look over a blank Form 17B, select the questions that he considers the most important, and then insist on answers to just those questions.

---

### RIGHT OF FIRST REFUSAL AND LEASES

Many buildings have rules requiring a seller to offer the unit to other owners for so many weeks. This can cause an onerous delay. Some projects also require that a certain lease be used if the unit is rented. Be certain that these rules are not likely to interfere with your plans.

---

**3. Budget/financial statement.** This statement will, hopefully, answer all of your questions about recent expenditures on repairs, as well as the reserves for future repairs. The experts recommend that the reserves equal no less than 3%–5% of the total budget. In looking over the finances and insurance, determine if the building has earthquake insurance. It typically requires a separate, not-cheap policy, but I have recently become a believer, and now carry it on my own house even though it has a large deductible ($9,000).

**4. Management.** It never hurts to meet the manager. Then do a little snooping around to learn how pleased other owners in the building are with the management. I know of one building where the appearance of the common areas went from shabby to sparkling overnight with a change in managers. If you are a seller, the appearance of those areas is more important than you might have imagined; buyers won't wear a blindfold on their way to your immaculate unit.

The smaller projects may or may not have an on-site manager and/or a professional management firm assisting and advising the association, but any project with as many as 20 units that doesn't have both may be guilty of a "pennywise" policy.

**5. The minutes.** By law, every association has to meet once a year, but most meet much more often than that, even monthly in many cases. By reading the minutes of these meetings you can determine what the concerns and problems of the building have been over the last year. It may be necessary to read these in the manager's office. An interesting question to ask is what percentage of owners is required to constitute a quorum. Since as few as 25% can be a quorum, and proxies are allowed, a minority of the owners can control the entire building until a revolt takes place. Also, votes may be allocated according to the desirability and value of the unit, not on a one-vote-per-unit basis.

**6. Decor**. Many free spirits learn the hard way that their exuberance has to be contained within their own walls, and possibly even out of sight of the sidewalk. Political posters are banned in many buildings, i.e. must not be visible in a unit's windows, and a new buyer shouldn't even assume that Christmas decorations will be allowed in or on the windows and doors.

**7. Changes**. The new Washington Condominium Act has addressed and tried to ensure that buyers and owners have the right to make changes within their own units so long as the structural integrity of the building is not compromised. Even the right to buy and join two adjacent units by one owner has practically been guaranteed, but you should still check on any building policies or rules that may conflict. A couple in another state spent over $10,000 on legal fees in a fruitless attempt to install a washer-dryer in their unit.

---

### CABLE TV?

Never assume that cable television is installed or available to the building. Even if this isn't important to you, it could be important for resale.

---

**8. Secured parking/building**. This can be an important benefit, but it can also be a mistake to assume that the security is automatically good. One building actually leaves its main garage door wide open all day long, whereas another building has a truly secure, automatic door (secure at least until an owner's automatic door-opener is stolen), but any agile 14-year-old can climb over the back wall. The same goes for the units themselves; their windows and doors need to be secured just as much as those of a house. Cat burglars make a joke of ordinary measures, scaling balconies and popping skylights with hardly a pause. And who knows what those renters who are already in the building will do?

**9. The compass and view**. The advantage of buying on a cloudy day is that the seller can't brag about the view, but the disadvantage is that you may overlook the unit's solar orientation. I once had a north-facing apartment where the only sunshine I saw was reflected off windshields in the parking lot. That was the closest I've come to taking antidepressant drugs. Of course, I've seen a number of overheated south-facing units with faded furniture, too, but this is easier to control. Also check to see whether the view you are paying for can be blocked by future projects. Does this builder have any future projects planned? These questions can require some very challenging research at the Building Department for zoning and permit information, so hope for some honest, accurate answers from the seller and/or builder.

**10. Trash**. This distasteful subject needs to be confronted at some point. Where is it stored? How difficult is it to reach from the unit? Will the noise of clanging dumpsters reach the unit? If there are bins or boxes for recycling, this is one possible indication that management and owners take a little extra pride and care. The ideal time to check out this area is usually Sunday night; if it's ever going to be overflowing, this is the time.

---

Chapter 8 focuses on many structural-type concerns that relate to both houses and condos, and the last 10 questions of that chapter's checklist are condo-focused. Please combine that information with the material in this chapter for the highest degree of thoroughness. Those who want to participate in the governing of their building will find some information in the Appendix—"Condos."

# FIXERS
## OR, THE QUEST FOR THE GOLDEN GINGERBREAD

### HARLEQUIN REAL ESTATE

**F**our to six times a year I teach a class in *romance*, but the students think it is a class on finding and buying the elusive fixer-upper. The class is full of dreamers. They want to learn how to find their dream home for a song and make their fortunes with a $5,000 down payment, all rolled into one.

As a teacher, I have a genetic need to be as mean and discouraging as possible, to burst every penetrable bubble. The easiest way to do this is to say: "Students, look around you. Every person in this room has become your enemy, if they weren't already. They want *your* dream home. They will take it away from you if you let them. They can probably outbid you. They have more friends who will help them. If you have paid for the class, you can leave now. It's hopeless."

I do this for the best of reasons: to be kind. First of all, I want to awaken them to the realities of how much competition they will face as they try to accomplish something that is already relatively difficult, and second, I don't want any more competition myself. I've almost got the $5,000 saved.

If you're still not convinced, read on.

### WHY YOU SHOULD OR SHOULDN'T BUY A FIXER

**Should:** Allow me to list some reasons why you and I should ever pursue the fixer (vs. buying a nice, clean, trouble-free double-wide):

**1.** We may get more house for the dollar.

**2.** We may make some substantial money. We can even receive a compounded return on our "sweat equity." If our effort works out to be worth $20,000, and we now have a $100,000 house that appreciates at 6%, in seven years our effort will be worth a net of no less than $70,000 (a 19.6% annual return).

**3.** We may find ourselves enjoying a view or waterfront or even just a neighborhood we couldn't otherwise afford.

**4.** We salvage something that is more important than many communities realize. Newer homes are mere shelters; older homes are ties to history, full of spirits that enrich our lives. One day the old fellow who owned my home 40 years ago came to visit, and he related the history of the house even before he owned it; that has a value without price.

**5.** We help maintain the neighborhood. When we salvage and maintain individual houses, they generally become too valuable for the apartment-developer to demolish and replace.

**6.** We can have a very fulfilling experience as we independently design the days or months ahead, select materials and colors, and learn the pleasures of making old woods shine or a dumbwaiter or sliding door work again.

**7.** We may as well do it since there is no such thing as a trouble-free double-wide anyway. All homes require attention. We may as well get one that has some payback.

**Shouldn't:** Here is what I really believe: The above statements are all fly-paper, waiting to trap anyone attracted to all that sweet nonsense. Don't believe a word of it.

---

### THE FIXER ON THE BACK COVER

On the back cover of this book is one of the most touching fixers I have encountered. The "octagonal" was built around 75 years ago by its owner, complete with a winding staircase. It is still owned by a member of the family (who lives 200 yards away in a modern house). I have had excited callers tell me they wanted to buy that house, at least until I told them of its general location, which is 20 miles from the nearest town (I've promised the family not to reveal any more than that), in the middle of the....Yes, it has immense charm and history and it beckons to the romantic in all of us, but it would take a fortune to restore the "dentilated woodwork," etc. When we got through, we would have to live there, because there would be no buyer. In time, most of us who dream of doing these things would find that the silence and lack of challenge were smothering us. Perhaps not. Perhaps someone out there really could live in such an isolated spot. It would be nice to see it salvaged. The birds have already moved in. The birds can fly; we have to keep our feet on the ground.

**1.** You're going to get hurt. You. Not me. I'm not getting near another fixer. I'm so cautious now that the last time I was on a roof I carried an ice axe. And I used it. I've got so many splinters in me that I have to go to a pest exterminator every year for a checkup. I've stepped on so many nails that I've been embalmed with tetanus antitoxin.

**2.** You're going to lose your shirt. You'll start off undercapitalized and end up in foreclosure. The newspaper will even misspell your name. Your friends will ask, "That wasn't you, was it?"

**3.** Your marriage won't stop at the rocks; it'll end up on the lighthouse. Your spouse will move in with someone in a condo and demand support payments.

**4.** You'll pay too much to start with.

---

### 🏠 🏠 🏠
### DOES AVON SELL A COSMETIC FIXER?

BUT, BUT, BUT... "But I only want a cosmetic fixer," you whine. You nincompoop! *All* houses are cosmetic fixers. Do you think you're going to get a bargain just because a house smells like a veterinarian's waiting room, or the chimney has crashed through the porch? Get real! This is ordinary stuff! Mere indications that someone lives there. NO, NO, NO... *You* are not a fixer buyer; you are an ordinary, slightly tolerant wimp-buyer. Would a real fixer-buyer please step forward? Get this time-waster out of here. OK now, you, I've got a two-bed Cape Codder, owned by a little old lady who only lived in it on Sundays....

---

**5.** You'll totally underestimate how many decades you need to do the work, even if you have the skills, which everyone except you knows you don't.

**6.** You'll find that a homeless family has moved in while you were at the store, sold your tools, and proven that the toilet wasn't properly connected.

**7.** You'll have to endure 10,000 stupid comments from neighbors and friends who knew right from the start that you were going to fail. Like this one: "If you had listened to me in the first place, this wouldn't have happened."

You don't give up, do you? Keep reading.

## WHERE DO FIXERS COME FROM?

We can buy fixers from individuals, estates, or even government agencies, but how did any of these come to be in such bad shape? How could anything as valuable as a house ever be allowed to deteriorate, or even become worthless? The damage happens in several ways: everything from neglect to tasteless remodeling to outright vandalism.

The condition in which we find many homes can be explained by the personalities of their owners. Let's look at the four kinds of homeowners:

**1. The upkeepers.** A tiny group who consistently take steps to prevent problems (the kind of people who make the rest of us look lazy; a real pain to live next door to).

**2. The go-alongers.** The vast majority, who only react when a problem can no longer be denied.

**3. The overlookers.** The ugly minority, who insist that there really is no problem, and that Hitler did make the trains run on time.

**4. The can't-doers.** The elderly and all others who know they have a problem but have too little money, strength, skills, and occasionally too much pride to ask for help. Death often precedes a solution.

Come to think of it, we could describe our entire population the same way. Now, the first two categories account for few or none of the fixers in the world. It is primarily the Overlookers and Can't-doers, sometimes in combination with a bureaucracy or institution, that deliver opportunities, so let's look more closely at some of the people and problems we may encounter in buying a fixer.

**Overlooker #1: The slumlord.** The overlookers are made up of the lazy, naturally, but among them are also some very hardworking slumlords and eccentrics who simply put their efforts into other pursuits. Each human category presents a slightly different challenge. The slumlords cannot be trusted. Their entire motivation is greed. Therefore, honesty will suffer if they have to choose between the truth and a little more profit. Everything they tell us must be independently verified, and every agreement must be in writing.

**Overlooker #2: The eccentric.** As difficult to work with as slumlord personalities can be, slumlords are trained rats compared with full-fledged, self-contained eccentrics. They are nuts. Buyers who try to deal with them with a logical approach are nuts. The only possible way to acquire their property is to find out what they like to collect. They all like to collect something—coat hangers, extension cords, white belts, etc.—so contribute to their collection, and hope they leave you the property in their will. I like film canisters.

Are eccentrics really that difficult, that illogical? I remember talking to one who wanted $80,000 for a property that would bring $35,000 at best. He wouldn't budge and he wouldn't fix it. The city obtained a court order and soon the house was razed. The eccentric lost everything rather than compromise. He has lost at least three houses this way. If we ever fight another war, people this stubborn will come in handy; otherwise, they're the worst of neighbors.

**Can't-doers: The elderly and disabled.** If you have the opportunity to buy from an elderly person, be nice. If not generous, be somewhere between honest and fair. I have heard nauseating rationalizations from people who cheated an elderly or equally vulnerable person. Those buyers apparently don't believe in karma or the "great hoops of life." If you cheat, you'll be cheated. If you don't cheat, you'll probably still be cheated. Life's that way, but at least the virtuous have the right to complain.

Fixers can also be bought through estate sales and from banks or government agencies as "repos." These two categories come with their own set of problems:

**Estate sales.** Some estate attorneys are about as beneficial to a former client's estate as Dracula would be to a blood bank. They can treat potential buyers like road kill, and then justify every bit of their arrogance and bad manners as "protecting the client." They will rip your thoughtful, well-written contract to shreds and send back one that is illegible and indifferent to real estate law. The best way to deal with them is through your own attorney. Fight phlegm with phlegm.

**Repos.** Repossessed properties can be in good shape, but don't bet on it. A substantial percentage will be listing to starboard because they were vacant

---

### ♦ ♦ ♦
### "OH, LORD, MAKE IT FRIGHTENING!"

If you really want to pick up the rare bargains in fixers, then learn all you can about construction, because the best buys are often the ones that terrify the amateurs who think a problem is worse than it is. Several hundred lookers turned up their noses at a $45,000 fixer in the pricey Queen Anne neighborhood of Seattle, all because it had water in the basement. The problem cost the buyer $600 to fix. Five years later that house is worth somewhere around $145,000. Look for trouble, wallow in filth, and rejoice at foul odors!

for a while, or because their owners were deadbeats, or even because the displaced owner or tenant "got even" with someone.

One of the most serious limitations in buying fixers from bureaucracies or estates is the inability to conduct an inspection, formal or informal, prior to negotiating—not to mention the general lack of opportunity to do any kind of negotiating. If a buyer doesn't suspect that the plumbing or wiring has been vandalized or is totally decrepit for any number of reasons, then he may become the next link in a chain of foreclosures. Please see the words of observation on repos in Chapter 17.

---

🏠 🏠 🏠

#### MAJOR CAUTION

PLEASE SEE THE NOTE ON EVALUATING A HOUSE IF DRUGS HAVE BEEN MANUFACTURED OR SOLD THERE (CHAPTER 7). THESE HOUSES ARE OFTEN SO DANGEROUS AS TO BE WORTHLESS. TALK TO THE NEIGHBORS AND POLICE.

---

### WHY DO WE DO IT?
### THE THREE R'S

Here is a favorite question of mine in the classroom, one that stirs a little debate and reveals that most of the students don't have a very clear picture of the challenge ahead: "Fixers are bought for three reasons: the three R's. Reside, Rent, Resell. Which of these three motivations will be the easiest and the hardest to satisfy?"

**Reside.** It is a substantial challenge to find a fixer that will satisfy us as our residence. We want a size, style, and neighborhood that fall into our comfort zone. But since we are often more concerned with aesthetics than price, this fixer is not *the* most challenging kind of fixer purchase. This buyer may even be pleased with a 10% discount on the price.

**Rental.** We now have many more houses to pick from. We probably don't care as much about the neighborhood, the noise from an arterial, or the green paneling in the living room. If it doesn't require endless maintenance, and comes at a price that will provide an acceptable return on the dollar, that will satisfy many, if not all, landlords-to-be. I would conclude that this is the easiest of our challenging purchases.

**Resell.** Now we have a *real* challenge. To find a house that will appeal to many buyers when finished, at a price that will allow us to make some money, *and* to find it before anyone else does. Well, wake me when we get there. Not only does this purchase challenge us in the pursuit, it also requires the highest degree of skill in remodeling or rehabbing within a budget. If we go over our budget on our own home, we may be philosophical about that and delay or cut back some other expenditure. But to go over our budget on a resell is to pay tuition to the school of hard knocks. No refunds on tuition.

## HOW EXTENSIVE THE WORK?
## THE OTHER THREE R'S

Shall we restore, renovate, or remodel? In ordinary conversation we may use these words interchangeably without giving them much thought, but in our budgeting and scheduling we had darned well better know which we intend to do. They can be as different as cantaloupe and antelope. And many situations will combine some of each. Restoration is self-explanatory—it's for the purists with lots of time and/or money; renovation means "interpretive renovation," a compromise of convenience and history; remodeling can mean being practical or being totally gauche.

If you have followed any of the "This Old House" television series, you may have heard of cost overruns. Those of us who were the program's earliest fans saw a 100% budget overrun on the very first project. One would hope that the TV audience learned from this that overruns are to be expected for anything so complicated and ambitious. In the beginning shows, much of the emphasis was on rehabbing or restoring old materials, or replacing them with the most similar product available. This sort of thing is important for our historical continuity, and it allows us to perform a labor of love, but make no mistake about it—it can be expensive beyond belief.

A beginner may imagine stripping 50 years of paint from the woodwork, thinking that it only requires time. But *Geld ist Zeit*, and time is money, in any language spoken. Even at my customary self-payment rate of two dollars an hour, I have found it cheaper to buy all new materials. But of course this is not restoration.

In my last fixer, I compromised and used mostly new or recycled materials, but there was this one elaborate, carved oak mirror that got about 30 hours of my attention with dental tools. Such pieces could become important centerpieces for the new owner, and a link with history, if we sellers could only overcome the temptation to keep them ourselves.

If profit is your primary motive, then you will probably have to keep restorations or renovations to a minimum. In fact, a disemboweling, Shermanesque assault rather than a piecemeal remodel may be your best approach. Many is the time I wished I had simply gutted the place on the first day rather than salvaging parts here and there.

You may ask: "What if we'll be living there while we're doing the work?" I recommend a two-week vacation in downtown Beirut instead. Seriously? Seriously. If you don't have a separate floor, with separate "facilities," then you should at least attempt these guidelines:

**1.** If possible, do all major changes before moving in. Your motel bill will help keep you on schedule.

**2.** Try to schedule the work in the summer months. In winter, even if the work is indoors, some of us tend to work a shorter day, psychologically letting down as darkness approaches.

**3.** Plan on spending more money on help and time-saving materials to make up for all the typical estimating mistakes. Either that or spend the money on counseling.

---

### BREATHE THE DUST, BITE THE DUST

Asbestos and lead paint are commonly found in standing houses. Asbestos ceiling textures and lead paint were applied right up to about 1979. *Old House Journal* is one of several sources that point out how sanding or scraping a vinyl-asbestos floor or painted woodwork may have dangers that defy analysis. Read and ask questions before removing *any* ductwork, plaster, mortar, flooring, insulation, siding, or paint.

Recently a house in Georgia that was built in the late forties was found to have such a high percentage of asbestos in the plaster that it was condemned after some remodeling released the asbestos dust into the air. Today it sits boarded up. The insurance company refuses to pay. No one dares to tear it down.

---

### ESTIMATING HOW MUCH AND HOW LONG

Theories are the rules we would play by if we lived in a perfect world. They would be very valuable if we could simply get everyone to cooperate. Let's say we find a lovely old farmhouse in Bellingham, with a view of the bay, that will require two months of work and will eventually bring $175,000; we offer $110,000. But the seller receives three other offers, all of them over $160,000.

And even if we had been able to buy it for $110,000, we might have encountered delays due to building permits or dry rot or a thousand other problems that would have tripled our time estimate anyway.

In other words, we could have lost our shirt *and* our pants on this one. Obviously, it's important to have a substantial margin between the price we pay and the final value, just as it's vital to make an accurate estimate of repairs. But life doesn't cooperate. Other buyers, especially in the big city, where there may be three buyers for every property, make it extremely difficult to find a bargain. As I said earlier, I think you should give up now and save yourself a lot of heartache. The following instructions on estimating are for your amusement only, not to be taken seriously.

First of all, have you ever done any estimating? Of course you have. You've set out to drive to an appointment in a place you've never been before, and you've made an educated guess as to how long it will take. Your calculations included the distance, traffic at this time of day, and your particular style of driving. You've even included an extra 30 seconds for any problems. But the gas gauge says "delay," the coffee you spilled going out the door says "change your clothes," and the jammed interstate says "profuse apology."

Now really, did any of this come as a surprise? Hasn't it happened before? Then why did you practice denial this time? We remain eternally optimistic, don't we?

NOTA BENE: Well, this is what I am leading up to: I want you to believe me when I say that unrealistic optimism is as inevitable for beginners as slugs are in the lettuce, and therefore every beginner must triple every estimate.

Four times a year in my fixer classes we do an estimating exercise on enclosing a porch, and out of dozens of student teams not one has ever come close to the actual time that the project took me to do. In fact, their estimates are usually about the same as mine were, about one third of how long it took. Yes, I too admit to being the eternal optimist.

**Books.** All right, how do we do the written estimate? Well, if we were doing a project that included lots of "new work," we might turn to one of several books that are written for experienced remodelers. A book—such as W. P. Jackson's *Estimating Home Building Costs*—might tell us to figure two hours for each cubic yard of concrete for a new footing. However, it wouldn't mention the blackberries we have to dig out first. That's where we're back to guessing and tripling.

Perhaps the most helpful book is a Consumer's Union condensation of the R. S. Means series for contractors on estimating. This book, *Home Improvement Cost Guide*, contains 74 fairly typical remodeling projects and provides a breakdown of time and materials. It includes advice on how to modify the time according to one's degree of experience. Unfortunately, this consumer's group makes it difficult for consumers to acquire the book. It must be mail-ordered. (See the Appendix—"Inspecting" for details.)

**Professionals.** The phrase "free estimates" is as common as "going out of business," and is just about as useful for our purposes. In the first place, it just ain't harmonical to ask someone for an estimate if you intend to do the work yourself. Secondly, a contractor's estimate has the purpose of telling you what his charge will be, not how many hours it will take or what materials will be used. What we want and need is a breakdown of the time and a list of materials. Seattle has several specialists who charge by the hour to do estimates for amateurs. Look in the Yellow Pages under "Construction Estimates." This could be one of your best uses of money. In a smaller town, you're going to have to see if a contractor will agree to try this.

---

### TWO COMMON QUESTIONS

**1.** "Is it possible to hire professional help for an entire remodel and still sell at a profit?" It is usually quite difficult, unless one buys an expensive house to start with. Any time that a professional's charge amounts to more than 10% of the eventual price, we may be skating on a thin margin—unless, of course, we bought it at half of the eventual price, but few buyers are so lucky. To learn how someone has successfully used expensive professionals, buy Suzanne Brangham's book *Housewise.*

**2.** "Should we get a contractor's license so that we can buy materials at the contractor's price?" Probably not in the big city, where sales are common, and probably not unless you will be buying materials by the truckload. In the first place, as a former contractor, my discounts never matched the sales prices in a chain store; the only time the discount was worth anything was in a small town where they didn't have a Fred Meyer or a Pay 'n Pak, and where I needed a truckload of materials.

---

**Guesstimates.** Being a self-reliant cuss, I like to do my own estimates, although experience has shown that after 15 years I haven't improved one whit. But if you're foolish enough to do it my way, I'm foolish enough to teach it to you. It's called the Nickel-Dime-Nuts-n-Bolts method.

Nothing fancy. Nothing clever. I just sit down in the room where I'll do the project and start making an outline of everything that I can imagine will have to be done. I even talk out loud and walk through the motions. Over to one side of the outline I make a materials list. When we do this in the classroom, I think the students see the value of doing this exercise with someone else, because you fill in each other's gaps.

The advantages of doing this on-site are that you get measurements and perceive potential problems, including everything from storage to moving materials into the area. Beginners may need to be reminded to include around an hour a day for trips to the store and, on a medium-size project, to allow up to two days for setting up tools and cleaning and packing up at the end.

Finally, if I have the luxury of waiting several days, I come back another day and do the same thing all over again, without looking at my first estimate. Then I compare and make adjustments. If I'm lucky, I've found my notes from any similar projects and reviewed those. Now here is your opportunity to be better than your teacher: Triple your time estimate, and bet on it. I refuse. That's why as a contractor I won every project I ever bid, and that's why today I wish I had lost two-thirds of them. Memories.

How about the materials? This is *relatively* easy. Store personnel will be glad to tell you what quantities you will need, and some materials will even give advice right on the package. You just need measurements. But when a paint can says you can cover 400 square feet with one gallon, that's one of the four great

PRECISE COMMUNICATIONS CREATE SOUND CONTRACTS

lies in life. In general, you can figure on needing another 20% or so of *all* your materials. Anyway, estimating materials is a science compared with estimating the time.

Should you buy all of your materials right at the beginning? Only the most experienced contractors can do this and even come close. No, but "working backwards" is normal in remodeling: You need to already have or at least know the measurements of the dishwasher you intend to install if you are to know how big a compartment to build for it. Knowing this, I often watch the sales and classified ads, and buy windows or appliances or whatever I will need many months in advance. Of course, we don't always know or have the time to plan in advance.

Finally, don't imitate the show-offs who play the round-numbers game to impress or discourage others: "Oh, this will cost a good $20,000." If they like to rain on people's parades, they should stick to weather forecasting.

### WHATTA WE OFFER 'EM, GUV?

As I indicated before, it makes no difference what price we *should* pay for a fixer if the seller won't take it or if there are other people who will pay more. It also may not be too crucial what we pay if local prices are rising so quickly that a wait of a few months will wipe out minor mistakes (like paying $5,000 more than we intended).

In other words, the formula we are about to review is one that has limited value. It may be useless in a seller's market. It may even be useless in an ordinary market if our best offer offends the unrealistic or inflexible seller. And it may be unnecessary if luck is on our side. Nevertheless, it may help the beginner see where to start.

We have to work backwards: If we don't have a very good idea of what the property will be worth when finished, then we can't even start the process.

**Explanation to Price/Estimate Sheet** (see next page): Lines 1, 3, and 4 are self-explanatory. For closing costs (2 and 7) see Chapter 12, "From Offer to Closing." Our profit or wages (5) depend on our ambition, and perhaps even on whether we end up paying a commission to sell, but we shouldn't cut it too close. Look at the time estimated for the repairs and figure at least a reasonable hourly wage. Carrying charges (6) include all the costs that amateurs invariably forget (the first time), such as lost interest on all that money tied up in the down payment (may be offset by appreciation), or living expenses. Include eventual taxes on the profit, if any.

## PRICE/ESTIMATE SHEET

ADDRESS _____

WORST FEATURES _____

INCURABLE PROBLEMS _____

| WORK ORDERS, REPAIRS, OR CHANGES | ESTIMATED MATERIALS COST/TIME |
|---|---|
| 1. _____ | _____ |
| 2. _____ | _____ |
| 3. _____ | _____ |
| 4. _____ | _____ |
| 5. _____ | _____ |
| 6. _____ | _____ |
| TOTAL | _____ |

1. Eventual Value      $_____

MINUS

2. Selling Closing Costs      $_____

3. Materials Costs      $_____

4. Hired Labor      $_____

5. Our Profit or Wages      $_____

6. Carrying Charges      $_____

7. Buying Closing Costs      $_____

SUBTRACT TOTAL      $_____

8. Ideal Offer      $_____

## ACQUIRING SKILLS

Very few jobs surface in remodeling an old house that we couldn't learn to do in 20 to 30 years. Translated: A good remodeler never knows enough for the inevitable variety of challenges. However, those who acquire basic tool skills, read reference books, and don't lose their fingers will find few things that they can't do. But some will do it better than others.

I have come to a sad conclusion. Not everyone should be allowed to buy tools. Of course, tools don't kill people; people kill tools. Nevertheless, a license should be required, and all those who have ever used a chisel for a screwdriver, including my relatives, should be denied a license.

If you were applying for a job as a carpenter, you might be asked, "Rough or finish?" That is, are you best suited and experienced in the rough world of framing, or are you suited for the finish world of molding, hanging doors, trimming windows, and installing cabinets? The rough carpenter moves fast, likes loud tools, and thinks a chain saw is a precision tool. The finish carpenter hates noise, likes to work alone, washes his hands before and after eating, and dreams of joints so tight they can't be seen. Finish carpenters can do rough work but it's beneath them. They believe one is born to be a finish carpenter and that

WHEN YOU BUY A FIXER, ALL YOUR FRIENDS WILL HAVE HELPFUL TIPS.

rough carpenters have "framer's disease," which prevents them from ever rising above their position in life.

Which of these roles do you see yourself in? Tell me, what were your hobbies as a child? If you made model airplanes, did you put the decals on exactly where they belonged? If you sewed, did you care whether it was 8 stitches to the inch, or 12? If you have valued precision all your life, if you are inclined to notice that picture frames are askew, if you are compulsive about dotting an *i*, then you may have the makings of a finish carpenter.

What if you do not? Then your career in fixers may be very limited, unless you are one of those rare exceptions who can work out the challenges of paying for skilled labor and still manage to make money. When we begin, most of us need to be able to do just about any task that comes along. More than one fixer-buyer has found himself short on money and unable to produce great results himself.

Even if you have the proclivity and the gift, you will still need training and technical knowledge. All the talent in the world will not produce a tight miter joint the first time. So the question is, where does one acquire this training? A number of my students ask me if I know of some kind of apprentice program they can attend; by this they mean that they want me to teach them the tricks in exchange for taking me out to lunch. Even if I thought that was a good exchange I wouldn't want to do it. Remember, finish carpenters like to work alone. Amateurs drive us crazy. True, we don't remember that we were once beginners ourselves. So no, informal apprentice programs are not commonly available.

Start with shop classes. If you cannot attend any local vocational classes, then ask the owners of local hardware stores if they have ever thought about classroom demonstrations of various tools. At least one woodworking store in Seattle has had a very successful series on sharpening and using tools. Almost all of these stores carry videos that illustrate woodworking skills. A roofing store that wanted to advertise its "rooftop delivery" had one of its roofers give a priceless program on tips and shortcuts for nailing on a roof.

Help your friends every chance you get. And the more skilled they are, the quieter I recommend you stay. Watch. Keep questions to a minimum. One of my students actually dropped in one day with a portable TV, thinking we would watch a football game and apply ceramic tile at the same time. I went outside and set his car on fire so he would have something to do and not be a further hindrance.

Ask around to see if your community has a labor co-op. North Seattle has an excellent one, complete with a full-time coordinator who schedules some very ambitious projects, some of which also benefit some elderly homeowners who would be unable to get these improvements otherwise.

Finally, read. Subscribe to the magazines *Fine Homebuilding*, Rodale's *Practical Homeowner*, and *Old House Journal*. The first two are excellent, but *Old House* is especially unique and inspiring. Not only is it full of nowhere-else information on how to remove the unremovable, it will lift the spirits when the job has become downright tee-jus.

The various series of books on remodeling published by Sunset, Ortho, and Better Homes & Gardens are all quite helpful, and the Time-Life series is both good and hardbound, if that matters to you. Used bookstores often have the latter at half price. I have not found any one of the above series to have a distinct edge. When I can't find the answers in any book anywhere, I look in the Yellow Pages and ask two people in the appropriate field what they think.

For achieving the maximum price on any one house, be sure to read *Housewise* and Dan Lieberman's *Renovating Your Home for Maximum Profit*. (See the Appendix for details and other books.)

The answers are out there. So are the opportunities. So are the pitfalls. Good luck. I'll see you in the hardware store, or the emergency room.

## A LITTLE TEST

The following questions are not meant to leave you suicidal, but don't be surprised if a few gaps in your knowledge are exposed. The subjects include construction, strategies, and financing. Hopefully, you will see where you need to apply some effort. Don't dismiss the results; one of my students did, and absolutely butchered a perfectly sound house. The test said, "Hire help." He didn't. He said the test was "too hard." Tch, tch. So's life.

**1.** The easiest wall in which to "snake" electric wire is probably found in ☐ A. a 10-year-old house; ☐ B. a cinderblock house; ☐ C. a 70-year-old house.

**2.** A "cold joint" is found where ☐ A. two different kinds of pipe come together; ☐ B. two different pours of concrete come together; ☐ C. where a grounding wire is connected to the cold-water pipe.

**3.** If your attic contains "knob and tube," which of these materials would present a hazard? ☐ A. cellulose (treated paper) insulation; ☐ B. foil-faced insulation; ☐ C. fiberglass batts.

**4.** You need to run a pipe of a 1½-inch diameter through a floor joist; you have your choice of notching the joist at the top or bottom, or drilling a hole. Which one should you never do? ☐ A. notch top; ☐ B. drill hole; ☐ C. notch bottom.

**5.** You wish to add a wooden floor in a concrete basement. The floor should most likely be placed on ☐ A. mastic; ☐ B. rim joists; ☐ C. sleepers.

**6.** If an ordinary city property sells for $90,000, and the appraiser says the lot alone is worth $50,000, based on this information which financing complication is most likely? ☐ A. almost impossible to get title insurance; ☐ B. FHA will require extensive inspections; ☐ C. ordinary conventional loans will not be available.

**7.** Of the projects below, which one will an inexperienced but bright and self-reliant remodeler be most likely to make a mess of? ☐ A. putting in a new electric panel; ☐ B. sanding/finishing living room floors; ☐ C. putting on a new roof. (No, don't say, "All of them.")

**8.** Our remodeler tries her hand at estimating. Which area presents a particularly difficult challenge to estimate time requirements? ☐ A. repairing soffits and replacing gutters on one side of the house; ☐ B. painting the entire interior of kitchen and bathroom; ☐ C. tuckpointing the brick walls that support a porch.

**9.** A friend says she must buy 640 square feet of drywall, 50 studs, and 10 sheets of ½" CDX plywood. You tell her that just about anywhere in Washington she can expect her bill to be in the range of ☐ A. $80–$140; ☐ B. $210–$270; ☐ C. $340–$400; ☐ D. $470–$530.

**10.** You have found three fixers, all in good neighborhoods, all of whose owners want a $15,000 down payment and whose prices are appropriate for their potential selling price. You will then have $20,000 to put into remodeling. Which one should you buy if your purpose is to resell? ☐ A. an ugly five-bedroom house that needs all new plumbing, a roof, a furnace, and a new electrical panel; ☐ B. a 1,600-square-foot, three-bedroom house that needs two rooms carpeted, exterior painting, and a new kitchen; ☐ C. An 800-square-foot, two-bedroom house that you can "max out" with new kitchen, new bath, greenhouse windows, new furnace, new wiring, and even new front steps. Give this question some time and thought.

### ANSWERS

**1. A.** The older house (C) may have "firebreaks" in the walls that can make snaking the wire extremely difficult.

**2. B.** "Cold joint" is one of those terms we need to understand if we have water problems in a basement.

**3. B.** The aluminum foil face could lead to sparking across the old knob-and-tube wiring.

**4. C.** Notching the bottom is appropriate only if joist is cantilevered.

**5. C.** These are wooden strips placed on a floor.

**6. C.** A common rule is that if the lot is worth more than the house, ordinary conventional loans will not be available.

**7. B.** Finishing a floor requires *experience* and the excellent eye-hand coordination that finish carpenters possess; the other two require the ability to follow directions, with very basic tools. Don't argue with me on this; the Voice of Experience has spoken.

**8. A.** It is all too easy to underestimate the difficulty and complexity of overhead work. Put your hand over your head and see how long you can hold it there. Now try it with a hammer. The other two answers simply require extrapolating from a small job to a large job.

**9. B.**

**10. B.** Every dollar on this project went to something that showed, whereas the money spent on the large house (too large for most buyers) went to "invisible" expenditures, the things that buyers take for granted and feel little emotion about. Those expenditures would also eat up much of our $20,000 and leave us with less to put into visible improvements such as kitchen cabinets, carpeting, paint, and landscaping. The 1,600-square-foot house will have many buyers for its charms. With the little house, there is the likelihood of overimproving it, not getting our money back, and even running into problems with a low appraisal because other small houses haven't lured a buyer into paying so much. It will sell rapidly, but its size limits our profit potential too much.

## RATE THYSELF

A score of:

| | |
|---|---|
| **9–10** | Write your own book |
| **7–8** | Good foundation |
| **5–6** | OK, if you're humble and open |
| **3–4** | You need help; hit the books |
| **0–2** | Your typical lamb who still trusts wolves |

▟ ▟ ▟
## COMPLEMENTS TO YOUR SHELF

Neither this chapter nor even this entire book includes anywhere near all that the fixer-buyer needs to know. The chapters on finding properties, evaluating properties, work orders, financing, and preparing a home for the market must also be studied if one is to pursue this line of real estate. A fraction of the available and helpful books are listed in the Appendix.

# FORECLOSURES

**B**uying properties that are in the foreclosure process is one of the riskiest, most complicated, and potentially most rewarding challenges in real estate. It is possible to buy a property for half its "retail" value and double your money in just a few days, or you can lose a small fortune by acquiring a property that has so many structural problems or liens on it that it is virtually worthless. No responsible expert would say that you can count on making X dollars on the average foreclosed property. There is no such thing as an average foreclosure transaction. Each one is different and requires careful and specific research. It is not a game for dabblers. It is not a game at all. But it is, or can be, an extraordinary investment opportunity.

### THE HUMAN SIDE OF FORECLOSURES

I think we all see images of the Great Depression when we hear the word foreclosure—people being forced out into the snow, losing the farm, relentless bankers. During the 1930s over 30 percent of Washingtonians were late with their payments, and there are still many citizens who could tell us about the heartache of that time. If you think I'm going to tell you it's completely different today, you're chewing bark. True, it doesn't happen so often, but foreclosure remains a heart-wrenching reality.

Citizens are now better protected by laws, and grace periods have been established in which delinquent owners can make up back payments and stop foreclosure proceedings. No lender or seller can arbitrarily toss anyone into the snow. In fact, it can take quite a bit of time to evict people if they don't want to leave; many residents enjoy "rent-free" shelter for four to eight months after they've stopped making payments, and in some cases for several years.

All the same, foreclosure goes on, and it must. There will always be people who cannot keep up their payments, some because they are unfortunate, and some because they are undisciplined deadbeats. In any case, no lender or seller can afford the charity of simply allowing them to continue living on a property without making payments.

How about the investor who decides to focus on foreclosures? Since the foreclosure situation is here to stay, the best we can hope for is that good-hearted people will be the ones to invest in it. They can provide delinquent owners with more assistance than they are likely to receive from anyone else, although the owners often don't see it that way and often violently resist. I don't mean to imply that foreclosure investors are motivated by charity; that's silly. They do it for profit, but it can still be done fairly and with a conscience, so if you have decent friends who invest in foreclosures, don't give them any lip. Be glad it's them and not someone who would skin the cat for a lampshade.

If you're a conscientious person who is considering investing in foreclosures, remember that you aren't causing anyone to miss their payments, and your purchase of their property doesn't worsen their situation in any way. One way or the other, they will probably have to leave. On the other hand, if you become a success, don't ever forget to donate a big chunk of your time and money to those who have had less fortune. The homeless on our streets are a sign that something very basic has gone awry and desperately needs attention—not just from the government.

### FIRST, A CONDENSATION

Since the characters and terms can become very confusing, the reader should have a good grasp of the different roles and plots in a typical foreclosure scenario.

**Forecloser.** The person who is owed money for the property. Could be a lender or an individual noteholder (the former seller) who accepted seller-financing. To keep things simple, in the following examples we will call the forecloser "the lender."

**Trustee.** The individual who actually handles the foreclosure process if the original contract was a deed of trust (DOT). When a DOT is originally closed, the named trustee is typically a title company. However, when a payment is missed and a foreclosure is initiated, the title company passes its "crown" to an attorney who, as trustee, must send notice of the default, order a title report, and notify all parties with a legal interest in the action. If the original contract was a "real estate contract" (REC), an attorney handles the above steps, but he will not be called a trustee.

**Delinquent owner.** The person who is at risk of losing the property. This person could be a recent buyer, a longtime resident/owner of the property, or an investor/landlord. Most of us assume that a foreclosure occurs because the delinquent owner missed one or more payments. Generally that is the case, but it can also happen because he failed to live up to some other provision of the contract, such as keeping the taxes current, or maintaining or insuring the property.

**Contracts.** The original transaction could have taken place with any of three types of contracts: a two-party mortgage (old-fashioned and rare), a deed of trust (by far the most common), or a real estate contract (less common). Since DOT foreclosures are the most common, that is what we will usually be talking about.

## THE THREE OPPOR-TIME-ITIES

There are three different times when you, as an investor or homebuyer, may be able to purchase the property that is being foreclosed: pre-foreclosure (before the auction), at the auction, and post-foreclosure (after the auction but before the lender has disposed of the property). Now for the details.

**Pre-foreclosure.** The delinquent owner has missed one or more payments and the lender has formally initiated the necessary steps to foreclose. At this point you can approach the delinquent owner (who may or may not be the resident) and offer to buy his equity, make up the back payments, and prevent any further damage to his credit. You may be welcomed or you may be spat upon. The chances of your being the first caller are slim. You could also approach the lender (not likely) or the former seller (more likely), if she is the individual noteholder, and offer to buy her position, and then either continue the foreclosure or work out an arrangement.

There are generally two ways that we learn of these situations: by reading newspaper ads (long ads in the classifieds placed by the attorney or trustee, who gives the date and time of an upcoming auction on the foreclosed property) or by doing research at the courthouse (unlikely for most people). In the Seattle area there is a newsletter for "serious" foreclosure investors (see below and Appendix—"Foreclosures").

**The auction.** In general, a relatively informal auction is held at a public site, typically in a courthouse. If the foreclosed property was sold with a deed of trust (DOT) and the delinquent owner has not made up all late payments 11 days before the scheduled auction, then the trustee will proceed with the auction at the appointed time. Investors and those who have an interest in the property are invited to bid on it. The winner generally has no more than an hour to produce a cashier's check for the full amount.

**Post-foreclosure.** In those cases where no bids were received and the lender took back the property, it may be possible to approach the lender and work out a relatively normal financing arrangement. Since lenders do not make a habit of talking about what has transpired, you'll probably have to attend the auction to know if an opportunity exists.

### THE LANGUAGE

**REOs.** This is the industry term for repossessed properties: Real Estate Owned (by the bank). Some banks have a single REO officer, some have an entire department to market and sell their REOs, and some list the properties with different real estate agents. Banks don't always admit to the existence of their REO departments, so don't naively call them for information and expect to be looked upon as their savior. It can take time to penetrate the green curtain.

**Nonjudicial foreclosure.** A real estate contract (REC) and deed of trust (DOT) can be foreclosed without going to court, by following a few legal steps (generally handled by an attorney) and sticking to a required schedule (the process can take more time, but not less time, than the law allows; however, the delinquent owner could abandon the property sooner). If the seller wishes both to regain the property and get a personal judgment (a *deficiency judgment*) against the buyer (due to damages or loss in value), a judicial foreclosure will be required. This can take 18 to 24 months. Obviously, most sellers will choose the shorter method and just cut their losses.

**Deficiency judgment.** See above. Although this requires a court action that can take many months before clear title is available, in some cases a sheriff's "certificate of sale" may be acquired and the lender or seller may take possession of the property before the title is available or clear.

**Deed of trust (DOT).** Please see other references to this type of contract or "instrument," especially those in Chapter 2, "Language/Slanguage." In this situation, we have a three-party mortgage: the beneficiary (seller or lender), the grantor (buyer or borrower), and the trustee (a referee of sorts). Usually no less than seven months elapses between the time of the missed payment and the time the new owner can actually take possession. Although the delinquent owner can make up payments and attorneys' fees until 11 days before the auction, there is no redemption period once the auction (*trustee's sale*) is conducted. The typical cost of this proceeding is $800–$1200, and it usually occurs when a lender forecloses on a conventional loan.

There must be a minimum of 190 days between the time of the default (the missed payment) and the date when the property can be auctioned. However, the total time needed by the trustee for all of the required steps is only 120 days, so the trustee can wait 70 days to begin the procedure, or "pad" the calendar along the way, adding time here and there at different steps.

---

**🏠 🏠 🏠**
### THE DEED OF TRUST FORECLOSURE CALENDAR

John Smith sold a farm to Betty Badluck. For the first year John "carried the paper," but then Betty refinanced at PDQ Mortgage and cashed him out. Betty lost her job and now has missed a payment, and it will be up to the lender to initiate the foreclosure. The lender confers with Betty, who admits that the likelihood of getting a job and making up the back payment is very small. But, she has no other place to go, so she is unwilling to move out and deed the property back to the lender. So the lender must notify the trustee to begin the foreclosure procedure.

---

Here are the steps and times for the 120-day foreclosure process:

**Day 1** (or Day 70): The trustee records the "notice of default" and sends a copy to Betty by both first-class mail and registered or certified mail.

**Day 30**: The trustee records the "notice of sale" and sends a copy as above. Notice is also published in a community newspaper.

**Day 109** (or the 11th day prior to the auction): This is the last day that Betty can stop the sale by coming up with late payments and attorneys' fees.

**Day 120** (but at least 190 days from the day that the missed payment was due): The trustee holds the auction.

**Day 140** (20 days after the sale): The buyer at the auction is entitled to possession (and may have to initiate an eviction).

**Real estate contract (REC).** The "REC foreclosure action" takes only 90 days, but since the buyer can challenge the foreclosure for another 60 days, most title companies will hold off insuring the property until that time has elapsed. This temporarily prevents the seller from delivering title to the new buyer. No auction is held, unless the delinquent owner requests one. The delinquent owner can make up payments right until the day on which the "Declaration of Forfeiture" is recorded, but there is no redemption period. The attorney's fee and costs are in the range of $500–$750, an amount passed on to the new purchaser. These situations occur primarily with seller-financing (lenders don't commonly use RECs).

**Mortgage.** To clarify one bit of confusion: If you run across statistics that say that "88.3% of Spokane County's real estate transactions were closed with a mortgage," the statistician meant a DOT (which is technically a three-party mortgage), not the old-fashioned two-party mortgage, which virtually no one uses anymore. An old-style mortgage requires a judicial foreclosure. It has only one possible advantage (for the seller): Once the buyer is late with a payment, the seller can "accelerate" the note and the buyer cannot stop the foreclosure.

**Sheriff's sale.** This auction is reserved for that minority of foreclosures that are due to liens, judgments, and some old-style mortgages. A court action must precede a sheriff's sale. There will be a redemption period of 9 or 12 months.

**Deed in lieu of foreclosure.** The buyer deeds back the property to the beneficiary (seller or lender), if the beneficiary is willing. This may protect the buyer's credit.

**Vendor/vendee.** A vendor is the seller where an REC was used; the vendee is the buyer.

Once again, for a detailed and readable explanation of the many facets of foreclosures, see Alan Tonnon's *Washington Real Estate Law* (see Appendix— "Language.")

### MEET AN HONEST-TO-GOSH EXPERT

I am indebted to Doug Hallauer for sharing his expertise during an interview I conducted with him in early 1990. Doug started an investors' newsletter five years ago, at the age of 25. Since then he has achieved a net worth that has brought him halfway toward purchasing his dream yacht. His newsletters keep subscribers informed of foreclosures in three counties (King, Snohomish, and Pierce).

Doug's employees review up to 6,000 public documents a day to learn of foreclosure proceedings. The cost for the microfilm of the county records alone is $10,000 a year. I have only one caveat about Doug's advice in the following interview (edited for brevity): Doug depicts the learning process as fairly easy. He may be a bit unaware of how much aptitude he possesses. I recommend doubling the times he gives if you have to work at this venture the way I do. Details for ordering his newsletter are in the Appendix under "Foreclosures."

**JS:** *Can you tell us a little about the auction itself?*

**DH:** It's not a real formal or organized auction process— the auctions are every Friday, and they can be held in any public place. The majority of King County foreclosure auctions are at the King County Courthouse, all day long. Sometimes you may have anywhere between five and ten different trustees auctioning off properties at the same time. They read the description of the property, the description of the encumbrance, and they will say that the beneficiary is owed so much under the deed of trust, including the advances [e.g. insurance premiums] and attorneys' fees, and that'll be your minimum bid. Normally, if there are several people who are going to be bidding, the trustees will write down your name and address. You'll need a cashier's check—some of the trustees may give you an hour to come up with the exact amount, but some of them don't, so be sure and check with them about their policy before you attend and bid.

**JS:** *Are foreclosures an avenue for the beginning investor, or should someone start with a simple rental or two?*

**DH:** Well, it depends if you want to make money or not—I've seen a lot of money made in foreclosures. This is how I started out, and the only experience I had was from *Real Estate Practice in Washington* (now out of print). I did get my license, but it's inactive now. I bought my first property five years ago, $40,000 under market value. The purchase price was $100,000—it's worth about $250,000 now.

Absolutely it's a great place to start for the beginner, but you do need to get some fundamentals under your belt. If you're absolutely green you need a little bit of time—you do open yourself up for some liability.

**JS:** *If someone wanted to get into the foreclosure game today, what size grubstake would be the minimum?*

**DH:** A minimum? In this market I think a minimum would be about $10,000—that would restrict you to either before- or after-the-auction sales, because the public sales [auctions] are all cash. But you will need to get there before they list it. There *is* an exception: if you're buying at the trustee sale and you're bidding on second positions, which have smaller balances. If it's the second [mortgage] that's in foreclosure, you would buy the second and assume the underlying [first mortgage]. The trouble with smaller bids is that there's more competition, because more people can come up with $10,000. But a newsletter customer recently bought a house in Madison Park—cash outlay at the auction was only about $8,000 to buy a second. It was a little bit of a hassle to get the former owner out—it took about eight months. When they finally got him out, they mowed the lawn and sold it for $160,000. Total outlay, including the first mortgage, fees and all, was about $80,000.

Also, you can find properties and then get other people to put up the money. I have seen others put together a deal with no money, by assigning a property. But for buying at the auction [you often need] $60,000 to $80,000 cash for better neighborhoods.

**JS:** *Many of the so-called seminars make it sound like we can have an Arnold Schwarzenegger body and a successful investing career in "only 15 minutes a day." What sort of time do you find it takes?*

**DH:** That is a big fallacy. Of course there'll be people who will stumble into something. If you're willing to go a year before you buy a foreclosure, then you probably could put in just a few hours a week, but I would say if you want to be a little more realistic it's probably going to take 10 to 15 hours a week of looking at properties, making phone calls, contacting owners. That's for one county— more if you're going to try to cover other counties.

**JS:** *I ran into one of our old students who said he tried for 18 months to find something, then gave up. How many properties will we have to research and follow to the auction before making that first strike?*

**DH:** Probably 100 to 200 properties from the initial point of foreclosure. And then that gets narrowed down to...well, in any given week you may have three to four real good potentials that are still scheduled for auction, and then probably only one or two of those will actually go off at the auction. I don't think you can really survive by only buying at the auction in this market, because there are so many people moving in and they want housing, and people in trouble will sell to someone, whether it's an investor or just someone who wants housing. But I recommend all three strategies: buying from the owner, the auction, and from the lender. The optimum type to pursue in a post-auction purchase from the lender would be a house in a good neighborhood that needed enough work that the lender would be willing to let it go, but the lender would expect to net close to what he would net if he fixed it up and sold it on the open market. But you can buy these foreclosed properties for 20%–25% under market value.

It does take time—I spent six months before I bought my first property. You have to find a happy medium between buying at 50 cents on the dollar and just wanting a property. I think that the student who took 18 months didn't have a thorough enough knowledge of the foreclosure market.

**JS:** *Is this something that requires a gambler's personality—or is it something that can be relatively low in risk? If so, how?*

**DH:** To a certain degree, yes, it does require a willingness to gamble. If you're going to the auction and putting down cash, that could be a big chunk of your nest egg, and it also takes a little bit of a gambler's instinct. The thing is, smart investors will minimize that risk—and once that's done, the risk isn't any more than going out and buying in a retail situation—but you have to be thoroughly educated. And that's only half of it. You also have to be willing to put the time into the research and not take the shortcuts, because when you take shortcuts that's when the alligator comes and gets you. But you don't have to be a complete gambler, a Vegas person, not at all.

**JS:** *Should one rely heavily on an attorney or other expert, or strive to be almost totally self-reliant?*

**DH:** I firmly believe you should strive toward total self-reliance. If you aren't self-reliant, how are you going to know if an opportunity exists? True opportunities are only there for a brief period of time—probably less than a week—so you have to be able to act on that. If you don't feel comfortable about something, then absolutely, by all means use the experts—it'll make you sleep better at night; but keep in mind that you want to strive for self-sufficiency.

**JS:** *Does any area come to mind where someone can be too self-reliant? I'm thinking mostly about researching the title.*

**DH:** Yes, and you want to be a little bit careful here. There are a number of different ways to obtain title information, and one of the big things that make foreclosure investing exciting is the fact that there are problems with the title. Foreclosures also have cosmetic problems, maybe some structural problems at times. There tend to be more people out there who can handle structural and cosmetic deficiencies than problems with the title, and that's what really keeps a lot of people out of the foreclosure market. It's also what enables people to buy $160,000 homes for $80,000. Researching the title can be one of the areas where you might go wrong if you're too self-reliant, but there are a number of ways to get that title information. One is, of course, from the owner; another one is the trustee who's handling the foreclosure—he has a title report that's called the "trustee sale guarantee" [$5–$20 per copy]. Some of the trustees are not real cooperative, but the more active you get the more the trustees will work with you. If they see you at the auctions they know you're serious—because they get a lot of people kicking tires and wasting their time.

**JS:** *What if the trustee won't furnish a copy of the title report?*

**DH:** If they will not give you the information, I would try to negotiate with the owner. Before you close anything, obviously you're going to buy a policy, so you're covered there. But in the negotiating stages you do need to know what some of the encumbrances are so you can write something up based on the information the owner has. But always double-check it, because these owners are in distress and they're not always shooting straight with you. Another source of information is the title companies. And if you're buying just at the auctions, you're mainly concerned about the position of the particular loan that's in foreclosure and if there's anything ahead of you. The things that are behind you won't concern you.

**JS:** *Can you explain that, ahead and behind?*

**DH:** A first mortgage is ahead of a second. That means it was recorded before the second, and that's how they determine priority. [You can learn about the order of the mortgages from "property profiles," available free from title companies,] but those profiles will not give you the judgments and other liens, and if you're buying pre-foreclosure that's an important aspect. The other way you can do the research is by yourself at the recorder's office. They have forms down there that will walk you through a title search. There again it's very time-consuming. If you haven't done a whole lot of them you're going to miss a lot of things, so you're back to ordering a preliminary from the title company. The title companies now are getting a little wiser, and they are making you pay up front. There used to be a $50 to $60 cancellation fee, but now it costs between $100 and $200 to cancel the preliminary search for the title insurance.

**JS:** *Can you tell us about a few of your worst or most complicated situations and what you learned from them? It seems that you no longer try to purchase properties directly from the owner before the auction. Have you had less-than-great experiences in that effort? Have you ever been thrown off the porch?*

**DH:** Yeah, I have been thrown off the porch, cussed out, and that comes with the territory. You just have to let that bounce off, you can't take it personally. You're trying to help them out, and if you don't succeed they lose their house and they lose any equity that they have. I've seen people who have that kind of attitude go completely down the tubes and not have anything. Then there are a few slimy investors who make a bad name for those of us who are legitimate, just like in any other profession.

**JS:** *Have you had to do any evictions?*

**DH:** I personally haven't; I've been pretty fortunate. What I generally do is give the people some money if they leave the property in good condition and leave quickly. That's much cheaper in the long run than going through an unlawful detainer.

**JS:** *Are there any other problems that come to mind, areas where you would recommend that the beginner be especially wary and take protective steps?*

**DH:** Yes, you can get into some problems—there are always new things that can crop up. There are always lawsuits for one reason or another. The worst problems that come to mind are evicting people, or entering into agreements with the occupants and giving them leases with the option to buy the property back. I would be very wary of those, because I've seen more of those blow up than anything. If you end up in court, most of the time the people get their house back. My advice is definitely to see an attorney in those situations and definitely make sure in your agreement that the owners seek counsel. Make it mandatory that they seek counsel before they sign any of those documents. Every now and then you run into situations where people file for bankruptcy after the foreclosure and tie it up for a while. Usually it's just a stall tactic that will tie it up for a little longer. Those are your main problems. Other than those, it's just research on the title, knowing what kind of a position you're bidding on, and what type of an interest you're buying.

**JS:** *Can you recommend any books on buying foreclosures?*

**DH:** There's not one specific book. The majority of books are written for other states. Therefore it's real important to get a firm grasp on the fundamentals of Washington law. You need to go to the Revised Code and look at the details that surround and govern the foreclosure process, and the different types of instruments. Just get your hands on as many books and tapes as you can afford—they'll give a lot of creative ideas. But once you're armed with the fundamentals and know a little bit about the creative approaches, you really need to get out and get some hands-on experience. Start knocking on doors, attending sales, talking to investors, making bids. If you're not making bids, make "dry runs"—you'll learn a lot more than from any tapes or books that have been written.

## HOW ABOUT THOSE HUD HOMES?

The most conspicuous foreclosure sales are those conducted by the Department of Housing and Urban Development on FHA loans. HUD typically advertises these in the larger newspapers, and they conduct the sales by their own rules, using a silent auction instead of the trustee's low-key but verbal auction. Sealed bids are submitted according to the published rules. They do allow the delinquent owner to seek financing, and will point out which properties are in such bad shape as to defy financing.

Over the years HUD has improved their auction process tremendously, simplifying the rules, encouraging agents to bring their buyers, etc. All the same, beginners (either homebuyers or investors) are naive beyond belief to think that this is a low-risk or sure-profit venture. There is none of the give-and-take negotiating that can take place with an individual seller; instead, you give and the government takes. Period. You won't be able to make your offer subject to any inspection or any other concern. If you can't get financing you will most likely lose your earnest money.

You may be the only bidder, or one of 20. The price published in the newspaper or any other advertisement is a minimum starting point for bidding. Good properties will often bring bids 20%–30% or more over the minimum bid, so it is a turkey-shoot in the dark as to how much to offer. The only way that HUD will accept a low offer is if they receive no other bids.

No one I know who has followed these auctions has witnessed any "steals." In the first place, they are too well known, and it is too easy for many people to play the game. Thus, the chances of good opportunities are slim, regardless of what those out-of-town characters conducting seminars tell us. Bargains in real estate, as a rule, will be found only when they are either unpublicized or snapped up quickly, and neither of those criteria applies to HUD foreclosures.

## HOW ABOUT THE VA?

The foreclosures sold by the VA should offer more chances for a bargain because they are so poorly publicized. The VA does marketing about as well as Exxon cleans up beaches. Nevertheless, since the sales do not take place quickly, and since there are a number of people who do follow these sales, bargains are still uncommon.

However, since the VA can be difficult to work with, some people will get discouraged, and those with thick skins who hang in there may be rewarded for their patience. Of course, anyone with that much perseverance would do even better dealing with ordinary humans in ordinary situations.

To learn of VA foreclosures, either call them or visit them, and ask for a copy of their "catalog." In the past, they have been reluctant to maintain a mailing list. They're probably saving postage for the senators' franking privileges.

# INSIGHTS

If you really wa
way in 6 to 12 mo
to work on:

1. Fo
and tid
Don'

Investing is not something you le
me speak, boss? The successful in
I; she is simply someone who focu
eliminate major risks, and who then *makes decisions.*

I once had a student who estimated he had spent $70,000 on real estate seminars. He even hired me to ride around with him and look at potential investments. Those were expensive rides, but in all our time together he never bought anything. He knows 10 times more than the average investor, but when it comes to making a decision, apparently he feels that he doesn't know enough.

When he goes to expensive weekend courses taught by the "television gurus," he is surrounded by many people who share similar misconceptions or obstacles. For starters, he believes that the people teaching those courses know what they are talking about. Some do, some don't. Only a few deliver practical or detailed information, while some professional actors even urge illegal acts. I analyzed one seminar artist's two-hour "class," sentence by sentence; it consisted of 15% substance and 85% sales pitch.

Many real estate students also believe, or hope, that there is some easy way to make money, a shortcut that will allow them to make their fortunes without ever needing the basic self-discipline of saving a down payment. They apparently believe that if they pay enough money for talks or tapes, they will learn priceless secrets that are never shared in a much cheaper book or college course. I wonder how many seminars and sets of tapes these real estate groupies will pay for before they learn one secret: There are no secrets. Just hard work, basic knowledge, and risk-taking.

Expensive seminars are not totally without value. They can demonstrate creative approaches, as well as get people excited and motivated, and if that's what it takes to get you off your duff, then maybe they're worth it. But note one more thing: They are invariably taught by someone from out of town, i.e. someone who can leave on the next stage and not be around to answer to the hometown crowd. Remember: Skepticism is the beginning of wisdom.

## THE BASICALLY SOUND INVESTOR

...nt to become a real estate investor, you can be well on your ...nths if you follow a plan. Here is an outline of things you need

**...us.** Investing has to become important to you. Taverns, television, ...llywinks should become rare pastimes until you are well on your way. ...worry, you don't have to become obsessed. Not permanently.

**2. Growth.** Self-knowledge and confidence are very important, so recognize your shortcomings, think of ways to compensate for them, and work on change. But never stop believing that you have more than enough intelligence to succeed. Real changes don't come quickly to most humans, so most of us have to find classes, disciplines, slogans, and mentors to help us keep on track until we have reached our goal. Again, making decisions is one hurdle that some never clear; if this is your problem, confront it. Those who don't make decisions allow decisions to be made for them.

---

🏠 🏠 🏠

### DECISIONS MADE EASY

If I simply cannot decide which path to take, I flip a coin. I pay no attention to the coin's decision; I only notice my reaction to the decision. If I groan when I see which side came up, then I commit myself to the other path and never look back.

---

**3. Time.** I made my first investment 20 years ago after driving all over two states for three months. The only thing I learned was the going prices, but that seemed enough. When I encountered a bargain, I didn't hesitate. Don't follow my example. Allow a bit more time for learning real estate law and financing. If the people I encountered had not been as decent as my investment, they could have taken me to the cleaners. I was simply too naive. On the other hand, if a year from now you're no closer to making a move, then perhaps you do need an expensive seminar to get you adrenalinized.

**4. Knowledge.** As mentioned above, there are no secrets to investing. But there are a lot of details. An investor who has free evenings can become very knowledgeable about real estate law and financing in six months, perhaps even more learned in some ways than an agent, because the agent is often so busy applying knowledge that his spare time is used for resting. Remember, you don't have to be an expert to be a successful investor. On the other hand, you do want to know some experts to turn to for advice, from lenders to attorneys.

**5. Money.** While learning details and gaining confidence, you may also need time to build up your working capital. The chances of making a nothing-down purchase, especially your first time out, are so slim as to be laughable. And many nothing-down transactions are overleveraged or overpriced, so they're too risky for the beginner anyway. How much money? Go back and read the chapters on financing. Quit looking to be spoon-fed answers.

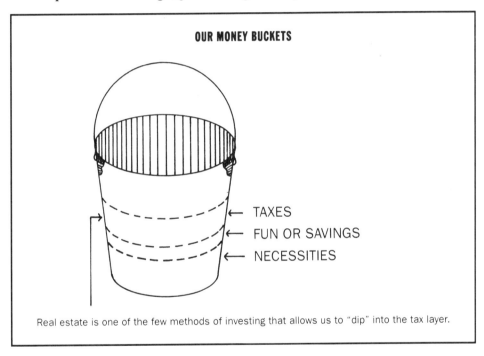

**OUR MONEY BUCKETS**

← TAXES
← FUN OR SAVINGS
← NECESSITIES

Real estate is one of the few methods of investing that allows us to "dip" into the tax layer.

**6. Commitment.** This sums up all of the above, and accounts for taking the big step when the opportunity arises. The first commitment is to talk to potential sellers, lots of them. (One young woman I know looks at 30 houses a week. She creates her own luck.) One day you will have to make that first big decision, and no one can or should do that for you. The only people I worry about making real estate investments are the elderly and those with a family. Young, single people should rarely hesitate to try new things and take chances. Life's too short to be a spectator. Each mistake makes us richer, if we can learn from those so-called mistakes.

*Boldness has genius, power, and magic in it.*—Goethe

## THE WRITTEN PLAN

A study demonstrating the value of written planning was made at a southwestern university some years ago. The planning habits of a number of executives were observed for some years. Those who recorded and tracked their goals on a daily basis ended up with salaries about 10 times as large as those who didn't. This study is often quoted in talks on time management and goal-setting, but even without this "proof," there is one advantage to written planning and goal-setting that should be evident: If you say that by a year from now you will have saved $10,000, you have to stop and think what you will do to accomplish that feat. You can then come up with daily and weekly measuring sticks that tell you if you are on course.

If you are not likely to plot your course, does this mean you'll work at the carwash the rest of your life? Not necessarily. Another study has demonstrated that entrepreneurs are often a full turn different from executive types, and may fly perfectly well just by the beat of their dance. Nevertheless, notemaking is unlikely to hurt.

Hold it! We have one last study. Interviews with a large group of successful entrepreneurs revealed one common trait: the ability to *feel* themselves achieving some goal, in detail and in color. If they wanted a luxury car, they could imagine themselves sliding onto the leather seats, inhaling the new-car smell, and driving out of the showroom. They then clearly imagined their elation as they achieved any one goal. Every night I visualize Linda Evans asking me over for a ham sandwich. With tomatoes. I'll keep you posted.

## THE VALUE OF TIME

I was only 22 when I climbed the mountain and consulted the oracle. "O, Wise One, I am young and not sure of how best to direct my energies. Should I devote my time to real estate or romance?"

The lonely old oracle grunted, "Get a lot while you're young."

Unfortunately, I misunderstood him and didn't make my first real estate investment for a number of years. I have always regretted not starting sooner, but I occasionally have investing students who are in their sixties, and I never tell them, "It's too late," especially since some of my students have made profits after just a few months of investing. But time is a precious friend when considering the advantages of compounded returns on our investments.

The advantage of time in longer compounded returns is obvious in one simple example: If Bob bought a bungalow for $80,000 with a 10% percent down payment, and it appreciated at an annual rate of 7%, and he sold it five years later without any closing costs for $112,200, he would reap $32,200, or four times his original investment (38.1% IRR).

If, however, Bob waited until the 10th year, he would sell the bungalow for $157,372, a profit of over $77,000, 2.4 times the five-year return, and almost 10 times his original investment (26.7% IRR).

But if Bob truly stuck to the long road and sold his investment after 20 years, the price would be $309,574 and the profit would be $229,575, or almost 29 times his original investment (18.5% IRR)!

It is obvious that Bob's money has grown in ever-increasing multiples, and his investment has returned more fruit than anything our friendly banker would have offered. If he had invested that money in an 8% CD, in 20 years Bob would have a total of $29,820 (15% tax bracket) or $24,520 (28% tax bracket). In other words, the ordinary real estate investment would return at least eight times more than the bank.

One does not have to be a genius to make a great deal of money in real estate—just persevering. On the other hand, if you have a touch of genius, you can make even larger amounts, or make large amounts quicker.

Let's examine some of the options that are available. First, take another look at Bob's example. Notice the "38.1% IRR" at the end of his five-year plan? IRR stands for "internal rate of return," which is investor talk for compounded return. In other words, if Bob wanted to buy an $8,000 CD (the amount of his down payment) that would match this real estate investment, he would have to find an S & L paying 38.1% each year, *for five years*. That's hard to find unless you personally know a senator.

But now look at the 20-year internal rate of return. It has dropped to 18.5%. Not bad, but why is our rate of return dropping? The explanation is more complicated than I know how to simplify, but suffice it to say that it has something to do with the relationship of the equity to the original investment. In other words, even though we're making an excellent return, that little old bungalow is still holding us back.

Let's add a touch of sophistication to our investing insight. Let's extend the concept of leverage, i.e. the ability to control a lot with a little. Let's sell the bungalow after five years, and take the $32,200 net, plus our original $8,000 down payment (total: $40,200), and use it as a 10% down payment for a $402,000 building that appreciates at the same 7% rate as the bungalow. After five years, the building is worth $563,825. The net is $161,825, and the IRR is 38.1%, the same as after five years with the bungalow.

If we now revise our 20-year plan to include the acquisition of four properties, selling and buying one every five years, instead of one bungalow, with all of the down payment and appreciation percentages remaining the same, at the end of 20 years our nest egg will be $5,102,307. That's five million dollars! Can this be?

We buy one little house, and 20 years later we're rich as Croesus? Why not? Well, you say, I left out closing costs. So what? Every saltworthy investor learns enough skills to offset closing costs. No, every year you and I read about multi-millionaires who started with a half-loaf of bread, and we want to believe they must have lied and cheated to have accomplished so much. That is the green-eyed monster of jealousy speaking. And fear. We are often so afraid that we shackle ourselves with all sorts of rationalizations when we should be learning the language of leverage and compounded returns. And we should start as early in life as we can to divert our interests from other, seemingly more interesting things.

## THE FIRST WALL

Of course, there is a major decision here that we must each face: Do we want to be successful? Of course we do! Are you sure? Read Friedman's *Overcoming the Fear of Success*, and see if you don't acquire some insight into why some people do so well, while most of us "lead lives of quiet desperation."

There is also a fear and grand rationalization about wealth turning us into monsters, and Lord knows we're such wonderful people just as we are that we wouldn't want that to happen. And if we had a lot of money, we'd have to hang

out with people who buy furs, eat veal, and wear colors that only a golfer would be buried in.

Well, let's take another look. First of all, money doesn't make you nice or mean. It just gives you more opportunities to practice your demeanor. In fact, if you're a decent and generous person, that's all the more reason for you to become wealthy. If we're going to have wealthy people in this world, then by all means they should be the noblest people we have. Wealthy philanthropists can create meaningful jobs, or a personal version of the Peace Corps, or whatever they feel the world needs more of.

## TYPES OF INVESTMENTS

This book is devoted to homes, and so is this chapter. I'll touch on some alternatives to managing single- or multi-family investments, but small-scale landlording will remain our primary focus.

If you're still trying to decide if you want to be an investor, and specifically a landlord, and some of your doubts focus on whether you would be making any kind of contribution to the world, just think back to a rotten landlord you have known. My favorite fishing buddy is a former landlord who was plain decent; I appreciate him so much I have let him pose with the whoppers I have caught. Unfortunately, there are few enterprises where just being fair is a significant service.

We read a lot about "socially responsible investing." If you buy stock, even in a toy company, you never know for sure how your money is being spent. But if you buy a rental, you control every aspect of it, with the exception of zoning and tax dollars, and that's about the best we can ever hope for.

**The first investment.** Most people's first real estate investment will be their own home. In fact, studies show that equity in a home is generally the major portion of the average American's net worth. This is both good and sad. Good that Americans at least do one thing right, and sad that we have no more knowledge or boldness than to make one good investment in a lifetime.

Is buying a home the first investment that you should make? Not necessarily. Of course, over the long haul it can mean the acquisition of a free and clear property, but in the early years you are primarily making the lenders a lot of money. I've had longtime renters consult me just after they have paid their taxes, and they are all hot to trot to buy a "tax advantage." After running the calculator for a few minutes, I've had to tell several people that with their present cheap rent they were actually better off staying put than buying a home. For the time being. But if taxes were a genuine concern and motivation, they should consider becoming a landlord. The majority have always found this distasteful.

What should be your first investment? Anything that has the least likely chance of creating legal complications. "Keep it simple" wouldn't be a bad theme at this time, but now is also a time when taking chances makes some sense. That is, if you don't have a fortune to lose, and if you're young and healthy, and if you know an experienced real estate attorney, and if you find a 10-unit building with a willing seller, I wouldn't have any objections. Of course, you could easily overleverage yourself and not have enough cash to deal with a leaking roof or a new fire escape, but my main concern would be getting into something so legally complicated that it would drag through the courts for years. It's easier to find cash and make repairs than it is to steer even the smallest ship through that nightmare known as the American justice system.

## RENTALS

You can start with your own home, if there's room, or if there's a basement that can be fixed up. Not only can you generate some extra income by renting out space, you can also gain some slight tax advantage. However, you may bump into zoning laws. In King County, a basement or attic apartment that has separate cooking facilities (known as a mother-in-law apartment) is illegal. Of course, thousands of them exist, but only at the mercy of neighbors who choose not to complain. In Spokane, which is large enough to have a similar concern about crowding or lowering property values or the quality of life, there is no such law. As the housing pressure mounts in King County, you may soon see some legal acceptance of mother-in-laws. In any case, check with your county zoning or building department before placing any ads.

**Single-family.** The goal is to buy a rental property with a relatively small down payment (5%–15%) at such a price and/or such an interest rate that the rent matches or exceeds your monthly payments. That can be very difficult to find. See the chapter on financing for down payment options.

Would we ever want to buy an alligator? A what? An alligator is a house that has a negative cash flow, something that may drown us and then devour us at its leisure. The answer is most likely yes in Seattle, as long as appreciation is still front-page news, but probably not in Spokane. There was a time when mediocre investors bought properties with negative cash flows for the "tax write-offs." Rarely did that make sense unless appreciation was offsetting the losses.

When I have asked my investing students how many of them would *not* buy a house that had a $300-a-month negative cash flow, most have raised their hands. Then I have added a qualifier: The house is appreciating at 15% each year. Let's see: In one year, a $150,000 house would gain $22,500 in value, while showing a tax-deductible loss of $3,600 in income, for a gross profit of at least

$19,400. Then the hands drop as the eyebrows and comprehension go up. That's one of my first themes in real estate: "Run the numbers; run *all* the numbers."

**Duplexes, etc.** Many first-time investors ask about the wisdom of buying a duplex or triplex, or even something larger, and living in one of the units. The advantages might include a smaller down payment and possibly easier qualifying (a vet can even buy a fourplex with nothing down, but must occupy one unit), but living so close to one's tenants can be a mistake. For over two years my real estate office was in my home, until I could afford a full-size commercial space; I learned firsthand why you don't want to be too close to your work. Anyway, it's a good idea never to live where your tenants can see if your car is in your driveway.

Are there any other possible disadvantages to a duplex versus a single-family rental? Yes. When it's time to sell them, there often aren't as many buyers, so they may not appreciate as much as single-family properties.

**Long-distance landlording.** Let's try to answer a common question: "If we're going to leave the state for a year, should we buy something now or wait until we get back?" More than one military career person has bought and kept houses in several states and retired with more income from tenants than from any pension, so it can be done. But it must be done with caution. The tenants have to be selected very carefully, the house should be "low maintenance," and you must either have a good agreement with the tenants on repairs and such or you must seek out a good management firm (which will probably want up to 10% of your gross right from the start).

## ANALYZING OR SETTING THE PRICE

The chapters on pricing and values are where the reader will find the full details needed for pricing a property, but investors have some of their own unique language and concerns. Let's start with one of the oldest, most dangerous, and most useful ideas: the *"one-percent rule."* Get out your scrap paper and calculator.

If we can buy a property for $80,000, and it rents for $800 a month (one percent of its price), then by the one-percent rule we should automatically take a second look. In fact, at 10% interest and with a 10% down payment, our principal and interest payments will be a mere $632. If all other costs (taxes, insurance, utilities, and maintenance) do not exceed $168, then we will have a positive cash flow. Tax benefits would presently amount to about another $50 per month.

Obviously, this simple guideline can help us quickly determine the relative value of income-producing properties, so what dangers could there be in relying on this for our decisions? Here are a few:

**1.** The one-percent property may not be appreciating as rapidly as other properties that have less immediate return. Other properties may also have more potential for improvements and raising the rent.

**2.** The property may need repairs that will eat up all profits for years to come.

**3.** The income may be relatively high because the seller has exceeded the legal occupancy rate or zoning.

**4.** The vacancy rate may be high, especially if the rent is relatively high for the neighborhood.

## BASIC TERMS

Investors who have ridden the merry-go-round more than once are likely to use some terms that require explaining, such as net operating income (NOI), cap rate, and gross rent multiplier (GRM). These are most often found in "business property investments" such as large complexes, but if you get an idea of what they mean, you'll know there's no magic in knowing or using these terms, and if you want to apply them to an analysis of even a simple duplex, you can.

**Gross Scheduled Income (GSI):** the rent, of course, but it may also include income from parking, vending machines, etc.

**Gross Residual Income (GRI):** the amount remaining after an estimated "vacancy factor" (a percentage) has been deducted from the GSI.

**Net Operating Income (NOI):** the amount remaining when the building's expenses have been deducted from the GRI. Typical expenses might include property taxes, insurance, utilities, maintenance, and management.

**Cap Rate:** short for capitalization rate. Often used in advertising to depict, roughly, the return on one's money, figured by dividing the *annual* net operating income by the price of the building. For example, if the NOI is $8,000, and the asking price is $88,000, then dividing 8,000 by 88,000 will result in .091, which would be quoted as a 9.1 cap rate. If we desire a cap rate of 10, i.e. a 10% return on our investment, then we would divide 8,000 by .10, and offer the seller the result, $80,000. So, as buyers, the higher the cap rate the better. But cap rates don't tell us anything about maintenance, vacancy rates, etc.

**Gross Rent Multiplier (GRM):** [also see GRM in Chapter 6, "Evaluating: Price"] the asking price divided by the annual GSI. Often stated in ads as (for

---

### 🏠 🏠 🏠
### GRM VS. THE ONE PERCENT RULE

If the monthly rent is one percent of the price, then the equivalent GRM will be 8.33. So if we have the per-unit cost and the monthly rent, we can instantly tell, by the one-percent rule, whether this property bodes well. Or if we learn from an ad or our own calculations that the GRM is less than 8.33, then we know the same thing. All things being equal, the lower the GRM the more interest we should show, and unless we can raise the rent or the building is appreciating rapidly, any GRMs over 8.33 should make us automatically cautious.

example) "6.9 times gross." Apparently, the price of the property in this instance is 6.9 times the annual income (GSI). If we only know the price and the number of units, we can figure out the income per unit, and then we may determine where that income stands in relation to other units in that area, or even apply the one-percent rule. For example, a fourplex with one bedroom in each unit is for sale for $83,300. The ad reads, "Only 6.2 times gross." We divide 83,300 by 4 for the per-unit cost of $20,825, and the price is divided by 6.2 for the annual GSI of $13,440, or $3,360/unit. If we divide 3,360 by 12 (months) we get $280. Now applying the one-percent rule, we can see that the monthly income of $280 is obviously more than one percent of the per-unit cost of $20,825, so we may want to take a good look at this opportunity. We can also compare the per-unit income with that of other one-bedroom units.

## THOUGHTS, TIPS, TRIVIA

**Real estate license.** Please don't get a real estate license to become an investor. Agents should serve the public, not themselves. All of us want to own good investments, but agents should walk the tightest wire so that they do not conflict with the needs of consumers. Unfortunately, many agents and brokers do not attempt to avoid this conflict of interest. If you do get your license, you must disclose to all parties that you have such a license, and both the reaction of sellers and the possibility of incurring liability may make you wish you didn't have it. I recommend taking the test but not maintaining an active license while your personal investing is a major activity.

**The newspaper.** Don't underestimate the importance of subscribing to several different types of newspapers. Some of the legal and business papers are drier than cornflakes in the desert, but when their points of view and information are combined with those of the local dailies, you start getting a better idea of where the community is going.

**Those columnists.** The Sunday *Seattle Times–P.I.* has several real estate columnists worth reading, but the newspaper owes the public a caveat: "This information may not be applicable in Washington." If a consumer followed all of their advice without getting a second opinion, I guarantee there would be some serious damage. Take all advice, including mine, "cum grano salis." And do read the columnists, especially for news from the other Washington, the dizzyland of the east; it looks as though Congress is (and always will be) tampering with the rules on financing, "passive loss," etc.

**Get rich slowly.** Instant wealth is all too similar to crash dieting: If good habits are not formed along the way, you are likely to find yourself right back where you started. So don't try to make your fortune on any one transaction, or even in the next six months. Just start learning basic disciplines and applying them daily.

**Swallow your frogs.** Fear is the number one problem for many investors (arrogance, for others). Glenn Ford once said, "If you don't do what you're afraid of, then fear's in charge." Another way to look at it is, "If you have to swallow a frog, don't look at it too long." For several years now I have tried to confront the devil of procrastination once a day and do something that I have been avoiding; each time, I feel an enormous sense of relief and accomplishment, even if it's just cleaning out the fireplace.

**Know your net worth.** The first thing I recommend to anyone who wants to become an investor is to learn exactly where you are now, so that a year from now you'll know how far you've come and how fast you're traveling. Otherwise, you're a blindfolded stroller. Along with this, I recommend (1) a consultation with a financial planner who knows real estate, and (2) the recording of all expenditures for at least two weeks so that you learn exactly what the "little" expenses in your life are.

**Dealing with tenants.** Being a good landlord is both an important service and a heck of a challenge. There are some excellent books on the subject, and in Seattle a local attorney teaches excellent classes on tenant law (see the Appendix). There are complex state laws, and Seattle has an additional set of laws. The first mistake you might make is to think that "common sense" will suffice. There are even right and wrong ways to place an ad for tenants: Do you want to put your phone number in the ad, or do you want to give the address and hold an open house? Do you ever take a deposit check on the weekend? How do you get a credit check? Would you use a tenant-screening service? Would you provide and maintain a washer and dryer? Do you ask present landlords for references? Do you know that you can't call a "nonrefundable fee" a "nonrefundable deposit?" There's a great deal to think about, so look over the references in the Appendix before you just jump into landlording.

**Shared equity.** I want to use this "trick play" approach to investing to illustrate something, not to advocate it or denigrate it. The shared equity scheme is where one person puts up all or most of the down payment in exchange for some portion of the appreciation and/or tax benefits. The other party lives on the property and makes the payments. There is no one way to do this. An attorney is essential for drawing up "buy-sell," or partnership agreements. Many people ask me what I think of this scheme. I appreciate the compliment of being regarded as an "expert," but they are asking the wrong person. My point is you don't succeed as an investor by just talking to "experts", you succeed by spending your time talking to potential sellers and partners until you eventually find someone who will work with you. And you don't develop a winning team with one trick play; you learn a lot of basic plays and then go out and meet the "opposition" and see what develops.

## EXCHANGING OR REPLACING

All investors have two major challenges: (1) to make money, and (2) to hold on to it. Uncle Sam is a major obstacle in the latter case. Therefore it's not enough just to make clever purchases; we have to be able to make clever sales as well. The details of the following schemes will require an attorney and/or a CPA, so only the highlights will be presented here.

When selling our own home, we escape all capital gains taxes on profits if we simply move into another house that costs as much as the "adjusted basis" of the one we have sold, within two years. Not one single day of grace is allowed, so the time is important. For a property to be considered our home, we must have lived in it three of the last five years, so we can use it as a rental for some of that time. One disadvantage of the home category is that if we have experienced any losses we cannot write them off on our taxes. If the losses are substantial we might be better off to declare the property a rental.

If we are over 55 we can sell and avoid paying taxes on as much as $125,000 of profit. The most common complications in this area occur when people over 55 marry and combine their estates. Some detailed advice and careful planning by a CPA or equivalent is essential.

Finally, there is the alternative called "exchanging." This has become increasingly common since Congress in all its wisdom eliminated the capital gains deduction. As of 1990, if you just sell, and the net profit combined with your income puts you in a higher tax bracket—well, that's burned beans for you. This amounts to a heavy tax penalty. However, if one makes just a little extra effort, this penalty can be delayed or avoided altogether.

The first thing an owner should do is find an attorney who is experienced in exchanging. The attorney is a must, in my opinion, and an experienced agent can be a real asset. The attorney, or "facilitator" (facilitators do not have to be attorneys), must hold the assets from the sale. You are not allowed to take possession of the funds.

Many people may be intimidated by this process or say, "I could never find anyone who would want to trade their property for mine." Good news: It's not usually that complicated, and you usually don't have to find a "trader." I had a client who was involved in one of these exchanges, and when she tried explaining it to her old-fashioned parents they tried to talk her into "keeping it simple" and just paying the taxes. Since the taxes could have amounted to over $20,000, the daughter was sufficiently motivated to ignore the parental pressure.

In a nutshell, with the simplest type of exchange, you sell your house but you have the transaction handled by a facilitator who controls the funds. Then you "designate" another property within 45 days, and you make sure that you buy and close on that property within 180 days of the first closing or by the time that your tax returns are due, whichever is earlier. You see, you just bought another property—you didn't really swap marbles with someone.

Now if you want to do this and have some cash in your pocket when it's all over, you may refinance either the property you're selling, before it has sold, or the one you've bought, after it closes. Your facilitator will explain the guidelines for this refinancing.

## AN EXERCISE: KNOW THESE TERMS

The following terms are commonly used in analyzing and discussing investments. They are defined elsewhere in this book and can be found in the Index.

| Assignment | Basis | Depreciation |
|---|---|---|
| Triple net | Improvement vs. repair | Improvement, as used in depreciation |
| REOs | | |

# ABBREVIATIONS

The following abbreviations and idioms are encountered on fact sheets or printouts of listings. In many cases they will be understood only when placed in context.

#02141 BR3 BA 2.5       BMK      $129,500

| Add 4225 LATONA NE | | | | Lt | Cty SEA | Mls= 110872 |
|---|---|---|---|---|---|---|
| Occ VACANT | | | Dist PHINNEY RDG | Prj | | Pts VACANT |
| Own MOUNTAIN | | | Oad 2820 GREENWOOD N | | | Oph 547-4567 |
| Soc 3.5/1.75 | | Bldr | | Off= 7116 527-5250 | | Key B |
| A 710 | | M 13 | G D1 | Pos CLOSING | Rep JUDY J.* | |
| | B | 1 2 | Terms C/O,CNV | | | Tax= 211442920667 |
| Entry | | X | R/O X | Flrs W/W,VINYL,HDWD | | Listdate 1/16/90 |
| Liv | | X | D/W X | Wdw Cv BLINDS | | 3/16/90 |
| Din | | X | G/D | Roof COMPOSITION | | Lndr GRT NW |
| Kitch | | X | PvdstY | Ext WOOD | | Ln= |
| Ex Fr | | X | Ufi N | Wtrhtr ELECTRIC | | Type CONV |
| Bdrms | | 3 | Sdwk Y | Heat GAS | | BalS 95000 |
| F/Bth | 1 | 1 | Gar A | Leased NONE | | Int % 9.75 ARM |
| 3/4 | | | Sep | View MOUNTAIN,CITY | | PmtS 915.00 T&I Y |
| 1/2 | | X | SewcnX | Bus YES | | TaxS 1311.00 Yr 89 |
| Util | X | | Wft | Wtrdist SEATTLE | | School Dist SEA |
| Fam | X | | Bchrt | Ho Dues NO | | Srhi |
| Rec | | | Pool | Ltsz 40X100 KCR | | Jrhi |
| Fpl | | 1 1 | Cblav Y | Apx Sf 1980 | | Elem |

COMPLETE REMODEL OF OWC BUNGALOW.BOX BEAMED CEILINGS IN LR & DR,GORGEOUS W/PEDESTAL SINK & CLAW FT TUB,BSMNT FIN W/FULL BATH-ALL SYSTEMS UPDATED,4TH BR OR FR OFF LR.NEW MASONRY FP HARDWOOD IN LR & DR.COLD SHOW.WORK COMPLETED ASAP.

Style 17    Gr 1    Ag 70    Bsm Y

| | | | |
|---|---|---|---|
| **A** | area of a city or map/grid system | **ComOwn %** | commonly owned space, as with condos |
| **A** | attached garage | **Comp** | composition roof |
| **AC** | air conditioning, or acre | **Cont** | contract (seller-financing considered); also, see "CTG" below |
| **Add** | address | | |
| **Ag** | age of structure | | |
| **AP** | appointment required | **Cpt** | carpet |
| **Apx SF** | approximate square footage | **CR** | call renter prior to viewing |
| **ARM** | adjustable rate mortgage | **Csh** | cash |
| **ASB** | asbestos | **CTG** | contingent offer has been made (buyer must sell his house) |
| **ASM** | assumption possible | | |
| **Asmp rate** | interest rate that can be assumed | | |
| | | **Cty** | city |
| **B** | basement | **D** | den |
| **B** | keybox is in place | **D** | detached garage |
| **BA** | bathroom(s) | **Din** | dining room |
| **Bal$** | balance on old mortgage | **Dist** | district of the city |
| **BB** | baseboard | **Dn** | down payment |
| **BBHW** | baseboard hot water (heat) | **DOT** | deed of trust (slang for seller-financing) |
| **Bchrt** | beach rights | | |
| **Bldr** | builder | **DR** | dining room |
| **Blend** | blended loan/interest rate possible | **Drps** | drapes |
| | | **DT** | see DOT |
| **Blt up** | built-up roof, as in flat, hot tar | **D/W** | dishwasher |
| | | **E** | eating space/nook |
| **BMK** | back on market (previous sale "flipped") | **EBB** | electric base board heat |
| | | **Elevn** | elevation condo is on |
| **BR** | bedroom(s) | **EM** | earnest money |
| **Brk** | brick | **ExFr** | extra finished room, e.g. a den |
| **Bsm** | basement | | |
| **BUP** | back-up (please) offers encouraged | **Ext** | exterior covering/siding |
| | | **FA** | forced air |
| **BU tar** | see Blt up | **Fam** | family room |
| **C** | carport, or common laundry | **FAO** | forced air oil heat |
| **CB** | circuit breakers | **F/bth** | full bath; has tub, may have shower, too |
| **Cblav** | cable television available | | |
| **CC** | closing costs | **F/C** | free and clear of old mortgages |
| **CC & R** | covenants, conditions, and restrictions | | |
| | | **Flrs** | floors (covered by, or made of) |
| **Cdr (or Ced)** | cedar | | |
| **CHG** | change in price or terms | **FNMA** | "Fannie Mae" (repossessed if FNMA is listed as "owner") |
| **Cl** | closing, when "possession" will be permitted | | |
| | | **Form 17** | a disclosure of defects form |
| **Cnv** | conventional loan/financing acceptable (preferred) | **Fpl** | fireplace |
| | | **FR** | family or rec room |
| **C/O** | cash-out desired (seller-financing not offered) | **FS wood** | free standing wood stove |
| | | **G** | grid on map (see "M") |
| **CO** | call owner before viewing home | **Gar** | garage |
| | | **G/D** | garbage disposal |
| **Cold show** | always ready to show/top condition | **Gr** | garage |
| | | **Hdcp** | handicapped modifications/access |
| **CommWft** | common waterfront rights | | |

| | |
|---|---|
| **HDW** | hardwood floors |
| **HO dues** | homeowner's dues, as with condos |
| **HT** | hot tar roof |
| **HWH** | hot water heater |
| **Incl** | taxes and insurance included in payment |
| **Int%** | interest rate on present mortgage |
| **Irreg** | irregular lot size |
| **K** | kilo, one thousand |
| **KCA** | King County Assessor's records (according to) |
| **KCR** | see "KCA" |
| **Key** | arrangements for seeing property (see "B" box) |
| **LA** | listing agent |
| **Leased** | appliances that seller may have to acquire |
| **ListDate** | first and last dates of listing contract |
| **Lino** | linoleum |
| **Liv** | living room |
| **Ln#** | loan number of present mortgage |
| **Lndr** | lender of present mortgage |
| **Lndr Appr** | lender's approval required to assume |
| **LO** | listing office has key |
| **LR3** | low rise 3 (type of zoning for "multiple family") |
| **Lt** | lot in a subdivision |
| **Ltsz** | lot size |
| **LVLR** | Levelor-type blinds |
| **M** | map page in a "Thomas Brothers" mapbook |
| **MF** | multi-family |
| **Mgr** | manager on premises |
| **MIL** | mother-in-law apartment |
| **Mls#** | multiple listing service computer number |
| **M/M** | Mr./Mrs. |
| **MT** | market time, time it took to sell |
| **Mtn** | mountain view |
| **N/A** | not applicable or not available |
| **ND** | none disclosed |
| **Neg** | negotiable |
| **NEW** | new listing, or newly built if after "Ag." |
| **Oad** | owner's address |

| | |
|---|---|
| **Occ** | occupant |
| **Off#** | listing office's code number |
| **Oph** | owner's phone number |
| **Own** | owner |
| **OWC** | old world charm (leaded glass, for example), or "owner will carry" (seller-financing possible) |
| **P** | partial basement |
| **Park** | allotted parking space |
| **Parq** | parquet floor |
| **PB4** | pending offer made before published in catalog |
| **PIC#** | picture number, the order in catalog |
| **Pmt$** | present payment |
| **Pos** | possession, when buyer will get the keys |
| **Poured** | poured (hot tar) roof |
| **Prj** | project, as in subdivision or condo |
| **Pts** | phone to show, call for permission |
| **PTS** | points owner willing to pay |
| **Pvdst** | paved street |
| **PVT** | private money, as in seller-financing |
| **R** | "roughed in," as in plumbing |
| **Rad** | radiators, or radiant heat |
| **REA** | real estate agent |
| **REC** | real estate contract (slang for seller-financing) |
| **Rec** | recreation room |
| **RED** | reduction in price |
| **Rep** | listing agent |
| **RMKS** | see remarks |
| **R/O** | range/oven |
| **S** | space, i.e. space available for expansion |
| **SB4** | sold before printed in catalog |
| **Sdg** | siding material |
| **Sdwk** | sidewalks |
| **Sep** | septic tank |
| **Sewcn** | sewer connection |
| **SF** | square feet or single family |
| **Sid** | see "Sdg." |
| **Slr** | seller |
| **Snd** | Sound view |
| **SO** | selling office |
| **Soc** | selling office's commission |
| **SR** | see remarks (usually pertains to key to home) |

| | | | |
|---|---|---|---|
| **ST Bond** | "state bond" financing available in area | **U** | underneath, as in parking |
| **Str #** | storage locker's number | **Ufi** | urea formaldehyde insulation |
| **Style** | coded reference, e.g. tri-level or rambler | **Unk** | unknown |
| **Sub Ten Rts** | subject to tenant's rights | **Unts** | units, number of |
| **SW Fin** | Swedish-finished wood floors | **Util** | utility room or area |
| **Swrcn** | sewer connection | **V** | view |
| **T & I** | are taxes and insurance included in payment? | **VA** | Veterans Administration |
| | | **VB** | vacant, keybox is in place |
| **Tax#** | tax assessor's number | **Vin** | vinyl flooring |
| **Tax$** | current annual taxes | **W/** | with |
| **Terms** | financing options | **WD** | wood exterior |
| **Terr** | territorial (trees, rooftops) view | **W/D** | washer/dryer |
| | | **Wdstv** | wood stove |
| **Tex brk** | "Texas brick," siding made of composition material | **Wdw Cv** | window coverings |
| | | **Wft** | waterfront or access |
| **T-1-11** | grooved, exterior plywood siding | **Wrap or Wrp** | type of financing; a "blend" of seller-financing and an assumption |
| **3/4** | bathroom with shower but no tub | **WtrHtr** | water heater |
| **Tnts rts** | tenant's rights, pertains to time of possession | **W/W** | wall-to-wall carpeting |
| | | **XA** | "exclusive agency" listing |
| **Tr cmp** | trash compactor | **Xch** | exchange/"trade" desired (as in tax-deferred exchange or sale) |
| **Type** | type of loan seller has now | | |

# RESOURCES

## ARCHITECTURE AND PRESERVATION

*A Field Guide to American Houses*
Virginia and Lee McAlester
Consumers Union, 1984
$19.95/525 pages

*A Guide to Architecture in Washington State*
Sally B. Woodbridge and Roger Montgomery
University of Washington Press, 1980
$12.95/500 pages

You may recognize many of the homes presented here, and enjoy learning their histories.

*Illustrated Dictionary of Historic Architecture*
Cyril M. Harris
Dover Publications, 1977
$14.95/581 pages

**"The Old House Journal"**
P.O. Box 50214
Boulder, CO 80321-0214
(800) 234-3797
Bi-monthly/$21

Precious details on restoring and salvaging.

**Kemp George**
9810 LeSaint Drive
Fairfield, OH 45014
(800) 343-4012

A slightly smaller catalog than below.

**The Renovator's Supply**
Millers Falls, MA 01349-1097
(413) 659-2211

A catalog of moldings, medallions (those plaster rings on the ceiling), tin ceilings, brass, and glass accessories for older homes. Catalog *supposedly* costs $3; just say Jim sent you.

**Foundation for Historic Preservation and Adaptive Reuse**
14705 27th Avenue NE
Seattle, WA, 98155
(206) 362-6247

Encourages and aids finding useful alternatives to destroying older buildings. Information on grants, education, and public speaking. Membership $15 and up.

**Historic Seattle Preservation and Development Authority**
207 ½ First S
Seattle, WA 98104
(206) 622-6952

Membership organization dedicated to protection of architectural heritage. Some publications, workshops, and tours. Join!

**National Trust for Historic Preservation**
1785 Massachusetts Ave NW
Washington, D.C. 20077-6412
Attn: Membership
$15 for single, $20 for family
(202) 673-4129

Includes a magazine and a newspaper with properties for sale. Very little on Washington because we're doing very little preservation. Still, a good resource.

**Historic Preservation Officer, Spokane:**
See entries under "Spokane," in "Washington State and Cities Resources."

## BUILDING AND REMODELING

*Even while they teach, men learn.*— Seneca

**All America's Real Estate Book**
Carolyn Janik and Ruth Rejnis
Viking Press, 1985
$29.95/851 pages

The cost may motivate you to turn to the library, but this well-written book is worth the trip and its check-off list for the buyer of a new home is the best I've found.

**Basic Remodeling Techniques**
David Edwards
Ortho Books, 1983
$6.95/96 pages

My choice for an inexpensive textbook when I teach introductory construction courses. Found in any bookstores and many hardware stores.

**Contractor's Guide to the Building Code**
Jack Hageman
Craftsman Book Co., 1982
$16.25/293 pages

Lots of technical data, but laypersons can use this too.

**The Helping Hands Guide to Hiring a Remodeling Contractor**
Leon Frechette (of Spokane)
CRS Inc., 1988
$14.00/124 pages

**"Fine Homebuilding"**
Taunton Press
63 South Main, Box 355
Newtown, CT 06470-9974
(800) 888-8286
$26/Six issues

Wonderful magazine for serious carpenters. Beautiful projects such as winding stairs and custom plasterwork.

**"Journal of Light Construction"**
Subscription Service
P.O. Box 686
Holmes, PA 19043-9969
(800) 345-8112
$22/Monthly

A little more for "hard-core" builders/remodelers; full of new and innovative building materials.

**"Practical Homeowner"**
P.O. Box 50421
Boulder, CO 80321-0421
(800) 525-0643
$13.97/Nine issues

Excellent magazine for every homeowner; lots on new items in heating, venting, and plumbing, plus good articles on financing, contractors, and more.

**Contractors Hotline**
(800) 647-0982

To check on a contractor's license or for information on working with a contractor.

**Home Owners Club**
1202 Harrison
Seattle, WA 98109
(206) 622-3500
$36/year (condo association, $50)

Members receive assistance in securing competent home services, with satisfaction guaranteed.

**"Well Home Program"**
Phinney Neighborhood Association
6532 Phinney N
Seattle, WA 98103
(206) 789-4993 or 783-2245

Short and evening classes for home owners on remodeling plus a storm window program.

## BUYER BROKERING AND AGENTS' OBLIGATIONS

*Agency Disclosure: The Complete Office Policy Guide*
John Reilly and Michael Somers
Real Estate Video Educational Institute, 1988
24007 Ventura Blvd, #110
Calabasas, CA 91302
(800) 582-7979
$43.90 (includes shipping) 218 pages

Every realty should own this.

*Agency Relationships*
John Reilly
Real Estate Education Co., 1987
$30.85/191 pages

Same value and address (to order) as above.

*Home Buyers: Lambs to The Slaughter*
Sloan Bashinsky
Menasha Ridge Press, 1984
$12.95/115 pages

Many tips for buyers. This book helped motivate consumers and industry alike to examine industry practices.

**"The Agency Educator"**
John Reilly
707 Richards St. PH-1
Honolulu, HI 96813
(808) 523-7021

A periodic newsletter.

**Real Estate Buyer's Agent Council, Inc.**
Barry Miller, Dir.
717 17th St., #1400
Denver, CO 80202
(303) 292-5454

Referrals for consumers as well as education for professionals.

**Single Agency Realty Association, Inc.**
P.O. Box 1791
Rockville, MD 20849-1791
(301) 353-1191

SARA promotes awareness of, and changes in, present system of "automatic sub-agency." Membership is $50. Excellent articles in newsletter but amateurish production weakens its credibility.

**Jim Stacey Realty**
2106 NE 65th
Seattle, WA 98115
(206) 524-4400

Free pamphlet on buyer brokering.

## CONDOS AND TIMESHARES

**Community Associations Institute**
Washington State Chapter
200 W. Mercer St., #511
Seattle, WA 98119-3958
(206) 282-5041

Newsletter, books, and seminars for those interested in participating in management or board functions. Can advise where to get information on condo ownership, laws, etc.

**Dept. of Licensing; Attn: Arnold Stoehr**
2424 Bristol Ct. SW
Olympia, WA 98504
(206) 753-4252

Excellent publication on technical aspects of time-shares with many tips for buyers. Free.

**International Resale Brokers Association**
Gail Baiman, (800) 237-5158
Wayne White, (407) 363-0807

Information on new time-share resale law.

## EDUCATION

*The McGraw-Hill Real Estate Handbook*
edited by Robert Irwin
McGraw-Hill, 1984
$59.95/624 pages

This serious book is for the professional who wants to know the history and background of real estate and financing, e.g. the background of the secondary market.

### Classes, in general:

1. For the layperson: many community colleges offer evening courses, some of which are approved for continuing education credit for agents, and, of course, I welcome everyone in the Seattle area to my classes through the University of Washington Experimental College. 543-4375, for a catalog.

2. For the agent, or would-be agent: In addition to the community colleges, look in the Yellow Pages under both "Real Estate Schools," and "Schools and Instruction—Business," or call the Department of Licensing, (206) 753-2250 (or 753-2262), and ask for a "clock hour book," a list of schools and courses. Also, ask for the "Candidate Guide" and "Law Relating to Licensing..."

As for a four-year college program, the only such thing is found in the business school at Washington State University, Pullman.

*"Knowledge is power."*—Francis Bacon.
*"Power is cheap."*—BPA

## ENVIRONMENT, HEALTH, AND ENERGY

*The Healthy Home*
Linda Mason Hunter
Rodale Press, 1989
$21.95/320 pages

An amazing book, jammed with details on asbestos, radon, formaledhyde, lighting, lead, security, noise, and water.

**"Savings on Utility Bills"**
James Dulley
*The Olympian*
6906 Royalgreen Dr.
Cincinnati, OH 45244

This is another column that answers energy/construction questions. Answers in *The Olympian* on Sunday.

**Washington Energy Extension Service**
Monday through Friday, 8am to 5pm
Energy Hotline: (800) 962-9731, or write: WEES, 914 E. Jefferson, #300, Seattle, WA 98122

Answers to practically any energy question (and related construction concerns). Questions may be answered in the Sunday *Seattle Times–Post Intelligencer.*

**Public Health Hazards Line**
In Seattle, 296-4692
Outside King County, (800) RECYCLE

If you move into a house where many cans or bottles of unknown substances were left, give this agency a call. Don't just dump. Anything in the drain comes back as rain.

**Public Information Numbers for Environmental Concerns:**
Asbestos Hotline ............... (800) 541-4406
Asbestos removal permits (800) 552-3565
    Seattle ......................... (206) 296-7436
Environmental Protection Agency:
    Asbestos ...................... (800) 272-3780
    Formaldehyde ............. (206) 442-1757
    Radon ......................... (800) 323-9727
State DSHS toxic substances
    ......................................... (206) 586-4501

**FranDon Lead Alert Kit**
Kerner Industries
275 Fairchild Avenue, Building 106
Chico, CA 95926
(800) 332-7723
$32.45

Lead poisoning: you may have seen Seattle's Don and Fran Wallace on TV ("20/20") or read about their accidental poisoning in *Reader's Digest.* They have developed a test for paint, solder, and dishes. I consider this a *must* for any home with children.

**Mail-order Radon Testing Kits**
Chem-Safe Inc., Pullman  (800) 537-7012
Cavalier Corp., Spokane  (509) 926-6217
Septech, Spokane .............(509) 467-6274
Westcoast Environmental
Services, Seattle................(206) 324-0920

**"On-Site Sewage Disposal Systems"**
Office of Environmental Health
Programs
Health Division, LD-11
Olympia, WA 98504

Rules and regulations of the State Board of Health.

# Financing

**The Mortgage Manual: Q & A for FHA, VA, and Conventional Loans**
Albert Santi
Mortgage Techniques, 1989 (4th ed)
$19.95/500 pages
(901) 755-8728

Mr. Santi also sells a "Reader Service Program," which keeps subscribers up to date on the *frequent* changes in loans. A bargain at $15.95. Another excellent tool for agents.

*The Ultimate Guide to Residential Real Estate Loans*
Andrew James McLean
John Wiley & Sons, 1989
$12.95/217 pages

Excellent book for borrowing and re-financing.

**"Realtors' Handbook: FmHA Single Family Housing"**
NAR, Real Estate Finance Division
777 14th St. NW
Washington D.C. 20005
(202) 383-1024

Free guide for agents in rural areas.

**Financial Planners Referral**
Registry of Financial Planning Practitioners
2 Concourse Pkwy, Suite 800
Atlanta, GA 30328
(404) 395-1605
Hotline: (800) 234-0697
          (800) 331-1706 for hearing impaired with TDD.

**Washington Association of Mortgage Brokers**
(800) 245-0451

Free mortgage hotline.

**State Bond Program**
State Housing Finance Commission
1111 Third Avenue, Suite 908
Seattle, WA 98104
(206) 464-7139

Low-interest loans for first-time buyers, with various limits on income, area, etc. These are mortgage revenue bonds not general obligation bonds. This group also administers the Mortgage Credit Certificate (MCC) program for tax credits.

# Fixers

*Housewise*
by Suzanne Brangham
Harper & Row, 1987
$8.95/291 pages

Not particularly strong on financing or repairs, but superb on motivation and example.

*The Old House Journal Compendium*
edited by Clem Labine and Carolyn Flaherty
Overlook Press, 1980
$27.95/390 pages

For everyone who loves old houses and needs all the help they can get, especially on fixing things no longer made or even recognized.

*Renovating Your Home for Maximum Profit*
Dan Lieberman and Paul Hoffman
Prima Publishing & Communication,
1989
$21.95/390 pages

Perhaps the best single book on what
one *should* do.

**Woodcraft**
5963 Corson S
Seattle, WA 98108
(206) 767-6394

Classes in use of power and hand tools,
and videotapes of same. Ask for
brochure of upcoming classes.

Also, see "Environment," "Inspecting,"
"Selling," and entries under "Seattle."

## FORECLOSURES

**"Investor's Edge"**
Box 698
Bellevue, WA 98009
(206) 827-4545

A weekly newsletter of properties being
repossessed, with auction dates, places,
etc. Subscribe to one, two, or three of
the following counties: King, Snohomish, Pierce. Cost ranges from $90 for a
trial subscription to $585 for the works
(48 issues).

**Unlimited Golden Opportunities Press**
P.O. Box 27218
Oakland, CA 94602
(415) 534-6472

Various books and tapes by John Beck, a
successful, down-to-earth California attorney. Hard to get information but not
cheap—$49 and up. The price won't
faze the serious.

## INSPECTING AND ESTIMATING

*The Complete Book of Home Inspection*
Norman Becker
McGraw-Hill Book Co., 1980
$8.95/172 pages

*The Complete House Inspection Book*
Don Fredriksson
Fawcett Columbine (Ballatine Books),
1988
$9.95/137 pages

*Estimating Home Building Costs*
W. P. Jackson
Craftsman Book Co., 1981
$14.00/320 pages

A useful book for those undertaking a
large project who know a lot about
construction. Not for small remodeling
projects.

*Home Improvement Cost Guide*
R .S. Means
Consumers Union Edition, 1985
$18.95/256 pages

Very valuable for the buyer who wants
an idea of what the 74 most popular projects would cost. To order by mail:
$21.95 to Consumer Reports Books,
9180 LeSaint Dr., Fairfield, OH 45014-
5452. (800) 272-0722.

*Red Flags Property Inspection Guide*
(with inspection forms)
James C. Prendergast
Professional Publishing Corp., 1987
122 Paul Drive
San Rafael, CA 94903
(800) 288-2006
$9.90 (forms are $6)

Good little book, with some quirks
(pages are not numbered). A good tool
for agents and brokers.

*What's It Worth: A Home Inspection
& Appraisal Manual*
Joseph V. Scaduto
TAB Books, 1989 (2nd ed.)
$16.95/271 pages

Lots of helpful pictures and easy to read.

## INVESTORS AND WELL-PREPARED BUYERS

*Landlord/Tenant Rights in Washington*
Sidney J. Strong, attorney
Self-Counsel Press
North Vancouver, B.C., 1989
$6.95/101 pages

A must for all landlords.

*Landlording*
Leigh Robinson
Group West, 1986
$17.95/350 pages

Thorough and funny, the perfect combination.

**Cain and Scott**
220 W Mercer, Suite 407
Seattle, WA 98119-9990
(206) 285-7100

Five different newsletters with useful information for all investors, but especially apartment buyers, from $20 to $250. One brochure describes all.

**"Property Dynamics Newsletter"**
Property Dynamics
1906 First St., Kirkland, WA 98033
(206) 827-8520
$60/Ten times a year

Demographic studies, vacancy rates, etc.

**Apartment Association of Seattle and King County**
210 Queen Anne N
Seattle, WA 98109
(206) 283-0816

For information on tenant screening, laws, and rental issues. May be able to offer assistance on mediation of tenant problems.

**Forecast Breakfast**
Institute of Real Estate Management
Nancy LeMay, (206) 462-0635

Every December this group arranges a breakfast for all parties interested in projections of the business climate for the Seattle area. Around $30.

**Seattle Tenants Union**
3902 S Ferdinand
Seattle, WA 98118
(206) 723-0500 or (800) 752-9993

**TRW Real Estate Information Services**
3237 16th W
Seattle, WA 98199
(206) 282-3359 or (800) 262-7432

Complete public information on properties, microfiche systems, etc., and custom reports for sellers.

**Classes on landlord-tenant law**
North Seattle YMCA
(206) 524-1400

Excellent information by Richard Cohan, an attorney who sells a Unique-to-Seattle lease.

**CompuServ**
(800) 848-8199

Demographic studies of zip code areas available to computer aficionados via modem. $25 to $40 to join, then $10 per report.

**Puget Sound Council of Governments**
Information Center
216 First Avenue S
Seattle, WA 98104
(206) 464-7532

Free periodic demographic reports for Puget Sound.

**"Real Estate Research Reports"**
Each of the cities/areas below publishes a compilation of statistics on vacancies, prices, employment, income, and such. Usually two issues a year ($45 to $70, or so), but can buy one. Can be found at each city's library, but cannot be checked out.
*Bellingham/Whatcom Co.:*
Dr Edwin Mayer,
Western Washington
University..........................(206) 676-3911
*Eastern Washington:*
Kristi Wilbert....................(509) 697-7050

*Seattle-Everett:*
James H. Hubert, ed ........(206) 587-2037
*Spokane:*
Ruthann Hashagen..........(509) 326-9222
*Tacoma:*
Dr Bruce Mann,
Univ. of Puget Sound .......(206) 756-3138

Also see "Foreclosures" and "Fixers."

## LANGUAGE AND LAW

### *All America's Real Estate Book*
Carolyn Janik and Ruth Rejnis
Viking Press, 1985
$29.95/851 pages

This may be the single best book on real
estate. See entry under "Building and
Remodeling" as well.

### *The Complete Guide to Washington Real Estate Practices*
Alan Tonnon
Washington Professional Publications
Bellevue, WA 1988 (3rd ed)
$19.95/645 pages

A highly-detailed dictionary of terms,
from abandonment to zoning.

### *How to Pass The Washington Real Estate Exam*
National Real Estate Institute, 1989
$23.95/300 pages

To order this or the two items below, call
(800) 221-9347.

### *Washington Real Estate Law*
Alan Tonnon
National Real Estate Institute, 1989
$34.95/521 pages

This is THE book for professionals or
lay folks.

### "Real Estate Selling Strategies"
National Real Estate Institute
$69/12 issues

A monthly 16-page newsletter, with
information on law, financing, and the
everyday problems of professionals in
real estate. See above.

### Land use information
(206) 943-3100 for consumers
(800) 562-6024 for Realtors.

Nick Adams is the Washington Association of Realtor's land use specialist,
knowledgeable about wetlands, septic
systems, moratoria, etc.

### Washington State Bar Association
500 Westin Bldg, 2001 Sixth
Seattle, WA 98121-2599
For referral service only: (800) 552-0787

The Washington State Bar Association
has a number of real estate pamphlets
and a referral service for King, Lewis,
Pierce, and Spokane counties. For single
copies of "Real Estate," "Landlord-
Tenant," "Signing Documents," or for a
brochure of all pamphlets, send a long,
SASE, for each pamphlet desired.

## SELLING AND PRICING

See entries under "Fixers" on what to do
to get the best price, and TRW under
"Investors" for a custom report for a
seller.

### *Appraising Residential Properties*
American Institute of Real Estate
Appraisers, 1988
P.O. Box 10956
Chicago, IL 60610-0956
$30/550 pages

A technical manual useful for agents.
Ask for the catalog of other publications.

### Refunds to sellers on FHA-Insured Mortgages
Contact: Distributive Shares Branch
P.O. Box 23699
Washington D.C. 20026-3699

### "How to Prepare Your Home for Sale, So It Sells"
BARB, Inc.
13620 NE 20th, Suite Q
Bellevue, WA 98005
(206) 644-BARB, (800) 392-7161

A 60-minute video tape by Barb Schwarz, one of the most successful agents in the industry. $59, plus shipping. Also, many seminars for professionals.

Also, see *What's It Worth*, under "Inspecting."

## TRAVEL, LEARN WASHINGTON, AND MOVING

*Best Choices in Eastern Washington*
edited by James Kelly
Cable & Gray, 1988
$12.95/416 pages
(800) 522-7753

*Exploring Washington's Smaller Cities*
Clifford Burke
Quartzite Books, 1987
$10.95/261 pages

Good tips on eleven cities, including Spokane, Bellingham, Port Angeles, Olympia, and Yakima.

*Ferryboat Field Guide to Puget Sound*
Robert Steelquist
American Geographic, 1989
$12.95/175 pages

*Positive Moves*
Carolyn Janik
Weidenfeld & Nicolson, 1988
$8.95

From technical to psychological, full of tips, such as the one on page 19 about ordering the 1,360 page relocation directory from the Employee Relocation Council ($20, (202) 857-0857).

*The Seattle Guide Book*
Archie Satterfield
Globe Pequot, 1989 (7th ed.)
$10.95/241 pages

Enormous amount of information.

**"Washington Atlas & Gazetteer"**
DeLorme Mapping
(207) 865-4171
$12.95/128 pages

Topographical maps of entire state. I love this book and use it constantly. (Available in local stores).

*Washington Handbook*
Dianne Lyons
Moon Publications, 1989
$11.95/350 pages

Excellent "all-inclusive" book with history, accomodations, entertainment, and addresses of Chambers of Commerce, etc.

**Ferry Schedules**
In Seattle:(206) 464-6400
Toll free: (800) 542-7052 or 0810

Schedules also available at Fred Meyer stores.

**Washington Public Shore Guide**
James W. Scott, project manager
University of Washington Press, 1986
$14.95/348 pages

Valuable summary on private and public uses of our shores.

**Gray Line Water Sightseeing**
500 Wall St., Suite 413
Seattle, WA 98121
(206) 441-1887

For visits to various islands.

## WASHINGTON STATE AND CITY RESOURCES

### SEATTLE

*The Greater Seattle Super Shopper*
Anne Damron
JASI, 1986 (6th ed.)
$7.95/198 pages

Invaluable for incurable scroungers. Useful for fixer buyers.

**Guide to day care and other child-oriented programs.**
Send $10.76 to ABC Directions, P.O. Box 46891, Seattle, WA 98126. Also, for a 256-page "Yellow Pages" of parenting services: *The Resourceful Parent*, by Patsy

Neher. MicroPublish, 1989. P.O. Box 781, Bellevue, WA 98009. $8.95. Bookstores or mail order ($10.93). (206) 392-4453.

### Seattle's "Whole City Catalog"

Office of Neighborhoods
684-0464

Any problem or need from City Hall?

### Attorney General, Fair Practices Division

This service offers some brochures and brief tapes on contracts, landlord-tenant questions, and buying a house. The tapes contain some mistakes (e.g. telling a buyer an inspection will cost $50 to $100 when the cost is usually $250 or more in Seattle), so double-check all information. 464-6684, in Seattle. After dialing this number, either listen to the recording, or if you want to hear a list of tapes in any of the following areas, press 1, then 3, then 035 for time-shares, or 037 for condos, or 039 for contracts, or 041 for landlord-tenants, or 049 for land, or 053 for real estate.

### Floating Homes Association

2329 Fairview E
Seattle, WA 98102
(206) 325-1132

Did you know Seattle has the largest floating home community east of the Orient? That's a big party.

### Gompers Program

Seattle Central Community College
(206) 587-5460

Classes in cabinet making, woodworking.

### King County Tax Assessor

For information on assessed value, legal descriptions, etc. The assessor's office also has a class every weekday morning (Admin Bldg, downtown Seattle) on how to research property values. (206) 296-7300, or (800) 325-6165, 8:30am–4:30pm, Monday through Friday. King County Tax Advisor: (206) 344-5202.

### All other County Assessors:

| | |
|---|---|
| Adams | (509) 659-0090 |
| Asotin | (509) 243-4116 |
| Benton | (509) 786-2046 |
| Chelan | (509) 663-8589 |
| Clallam | (206) 452-7831 |
| Clark | (206) 699-2391 |
| Columbia | (509) 382-2131 |
| Cowlitz | (206) 577-3010 |
| Douglas | (509) 745-8521 |
| Ferry | (509) 775-3161 |
| Franklin | (509) 545-3506 |
| Garfield | (509) 843-3631 |
| Grant | (509) 754-2011 |
| Grays Harbor | (206) 249-4121 |
| Island | (206) 679-7303 |
| Jefferson | (206) 385-3262 |
| Kitsap | (206) 876-7160 |
| Kittitas | (509) 962-6811 |
| Klickitat | (509) 773-3715 |
| Lewis | (206) 748-9121 |
| Lincoln | (509) 725-7011 |
| Mason | (206) 426-4852 |
| Okanogan | (509) 422-2510 |
| Pacific | (206) 875-6541 |
| Pend Oreille | (509) 447-4312 |
| Pierce | (206) 593-4034 |
| San Juan | (206) 378-2172 |
| Skagit | (206) 336-9370 |
| Skamania | (509) 427-5141 |
| Snohomish | (206) 259-0678 |
| Spokane | (509) 456-3696 |
| Stevens | (509) 684-6161 |
| Thurston | (206) 753-8257 |
| Wahkiakum | (206) 795-3791 |
| Walla Walla | (509) 525-6550 |
| Whatcom | (206) 676-6790 |
| Whitman | (509) 397-4622 |
| Yakima | (509) 575-4161 |

### Public Assistance

Possible assistance for low-income and/or senior citizens with property tax deferrals and discounts, credit counseling, utility discounts, and minor repairs:

| | |
|---|---|
| Fremont Public Assoc. | (206) 632-1285 |
| Seattle Urban League | (206) 461-3792 |
| Mayor's Office for Seniors | (206) 684-0500 |
| Senior Information and Assistance | (206) 448-3110 |

Senior Services (home repairs)
...........................................(206) 461-7802

**The Seattle Board of Realtists, Inc.**
1426 22nd Avenue
Seattle, WA 98122
(206) 328-8744 or 722-6770

Professional organization open to all
professionals, with some emphasis on
minority issues.

**Seattle Department of Construction**
(24 hour tape) .................(206) 684-8600
Permits..............................(206) 684-8850
Zoning..........(206) 684-8850 or 684-7899

**Seattle-King County Association of Realtors (SKCAR)**
2810 Eastlake E
Seattle, WA 98102
(206) 328-1980

**SPOKANE**

City Building
Department......................(509) 456-3240
Community/Econ
Development...............................456-4380
Environmental Programs..........456-4370
Historic Preservation ................456-4378
Planning and Zoning ................456-4375
County Assessor ..........................456-3696
County Health/Septic Systems
.....................................................456-6040
Sewer Information .....................456-3604

**Spokane Newcomer's Service**
(509) 624-1661

A great idea, but not very good at returning calls. Also, they don't mail out
any information, but once you're there,
they may be of help.

**Spokane Real Estate Groups**
Mortgage Lender's Association:
..........................................(509) 326-7720
Board of Realtors.............(509) 326-9222
Appraisers ........................(509) 747-0999

**Washington Association of Realtors**
P.O. Box 719
Olympia, WA 98507
(206) 943-3100, (800) 562-6024 for
members

**Washington Department of Licensing, Real Estate:**
Receptionist.....................(206) 586-4561
Administrator..............................753-6974
Educator......................................753-3194
Investigations ............................753-7506
Diciplinary .................................586-4602
Salespersons ..............................753-2250
See entry under "Education."

**Washington State "800" toll-free numbers:**
Attorney General (Seattle)
..........................................(800) 551-4636
Consumer Protection (Seattle)
..........................................(800) 551-4636
Emergency Management
(earthquakes) ...................(800) 562-6108
Ferry Information............(800) 542-0810
Information ......................(800) 321-2808
Insurance Claims.............(800) 562-6900
Low Interest Home Loans
..........................................(800) 432-3202
Recycling Hotline (Ecology)
..........................................(800) 732-9253
Vital Statistics
In-State.........................(800) 331-0680
Out-of State ................(800) 551-0562

NOTE: Attorney General (above) has
brochures for the asking on landlord-
tenant law, mobile homes, and cancellation rights. These are also available by
sending a SASE to "Troubleshooter,"
P.O. Box 70, Seattle, WA 98111.

**Puget Sound Housing Forum**
c/o J. Tayloe Washburn
1111 Third Avenue, Suite 3400
Seattle, WA 98101
(206) 447-8948

Provides an open forum for ideas related to the preservation and expansion of
housing in this five-county area.

## FOR HOME BUYERS ANYWHERE IN THE STATE

The following are phone numbers of various "magazine rack" publications advertising homes for sale. The publishers will mail a copy for any area of the state that they cover. Some also provide a rental guide.

"Harmon Homes"
(800) 678-5252

"Homes and Land"
(800) 277-7800

"Homes Digest"
(800) 874-8163

"Home Book"
(southern Washington/Clark Co.)
(206) 696-1664

"For Sale By Owner"
(Puget Sound)
(206) 882-0323

"Seavue Homes and Land Magazine"
(Olympic Peninsula)
1324-D O'Brien Road
Port Angeles, WA 98362

"Seamont Islander"
(islands and north Sound)
same address as Seavue above.

# INDEX

# G

# H

# I

# X

# Y

# Z

## About the Author

Jim Stacey bought his first 80 acres in 1968 for a thousand dollars and a handshake. Since then he has worked as an outdoor survival instructor, a licensed contractor, and a remodeling instructor while continuing to invest in real estate. He has been teaching real estate classes and advocating buyer brokering since 1984, and opened Jim Stacey Realty, *The Educators*, in 1985. When he isn't out searching for that elusive fishing cabin, Jim can be found playing basketball on Phinney Ridge, behind the house pictured on the back cover.

## DID YOU BORROW THIS BOOK?

Titles from Sasquatch Books are available at bookstores and other retail outlets through-out the Pacific Northwest. You may also order copies by mail or phone. To order by mail, fill out the order form below and return it to us with your payment. You can order by phone using VISA or MASTERCARD at: (206) 441-6202.

**WASHINGTON HOMES**
Buying, Selling, and Investing in Seattle and Statewide Real Estate
by Jim Stacey.................................................................... $14.95 × quantity _____ = _____

**NORTHWEST BEST PLACES 1990-1991**
Restaurants, Lodgings, and Touring in Oregon, Washington, and British Columbia
by David Brewster and Stephanie Irving................. $15.95 × quantity _____ = _____

**SEATTLE BEST PLACES** (4th edition)
Restaurants, Lodgings, Shopping, Nightlife, Arts, Sights, Outings, and Annual Events
by David Brewster and Kathryn Robinson .............. $10.95 × quantity _____ = _____

**SEATTLE CHEAP EATS** (3rd edition)
230 Terrific Bargain Eateries
by Kathryn Robinson ............................................... $7.95 × quantity _____ = _____

Subtotal $ _____

WA State residents add 8.1% sales tax................................................................ $ _____

Postage and handling ........................................................................................ $    1.50

**Total Order** =$ _____

☐ I have enclosed payment of $ _____ (payable to Sasquatch Books)
☐ Please charge this order to my credit card:

MasterCard# _____ Expiration Date _____

VISA# _____ Expiration Date _____

Signature _____

Name _____ Phone # _____

Address _____

City _____ State _____ Zip _____

SHIP TO:

Name _____

Address _____

City _____ State _____ Zip _____

Payment must accompany order. Please allow up to four weeks for delivery. Orders shipped via UPS unless otherwise specified.

☐ Please send me a complete Sasquatch Books catalog.

**SASQUATCH BOOKS**   1931 Second Avenue   Seattle, WA 98101   (206) 441-5555

# NOTES AND COMPUTATIONS